Room 5
(BOOK FAIR)

Webst

Of The English Language

New Revised Edition

Publishing Group

Imprint of Allied Publishing Group, Inc
Copyright © 2003 V. Nichols
Printed in the U.S.A.

a *(SYN.)* any, one.

abandon *(SYN.)* relinquish, resign, surrender, leave, give up, cease, forsake, waive, desert, quit, vacate, abjure, entirely, abdicate, leave undone, discard, evacuate, wicked, deserted, desolate, forsaken, rejected, cast off, profligate, marooned.

(ANT.) support, keep, fulfill, uphold, depend, stay, maintain, embrace, cherish, favor, adopt, join, unite, retain.

abandoned *(SYN.)* depraved, deserted.

(ANT.) befriended, cherished, chaste, moral, respectable, virtuous, righteous.

abase *(SYN.)* make humble, reduce, bring down, degrade, demote, mock, scorn, belittle, shame, despise, humiliate.

(ANT.) exalt, cherish, elevate, uplift, respect, dignify.

abash *(SYN.)* disconcert, bewilder, confuse, discompose, nonplus.

(ANT.) comfort, relax, hearten, nerve.

abashed *(SYN.)* ashamed, embarrassed, humiliated.

abate *(SYN.)* lessen, curtail, reduce, decrease, restrain, decline, stop, moderate, subside, slow, diminish, slacken.

(ANT.) grow, prolong, increase, extend, quicken, enhance, accelerate.

abbey *(SYN.)* nunnery, convent, cloisters, monastery.

abbot *(SYN.)* friar, monk.

abbreviate *(SYN.)* shorten,

lessen, abridge, condense, curtail, reduce, cut, compress, trim, restrict, clip.

(ANT.) lengthen, increase, expand, extend, enlarge.

abbreviation *(SYN.)* abridgment, reduction, condensation.

(ANT.) expansion, amplification, lengthening, dilation.

abdicate *(SYN.)* relinquish, renounce, vacate, waive, desert, abolish, quit, abandon, resign.

(ANT.) maintain, defend, stay, retain, uphold.

abdomen *(SYN.)* paunch, belly, stomach.

abduct *(SYN.)* take, kidnap.

aberrant *(SYN.)* capricious, devious, irregular, unnatural, abnormal, unusual.

(ANT.) methodical, regular, usual, fixed, ordinary.

aberration *(SYN.)* abnormality, irregularity, deviation, quirk, abortion, eccentricity.

(ANT.) norm, conformity, standard, normality.

abet *(SYN.)* support, connive, encourage, conspire, help, incite, aid, assist.

(ANT.) deter, check, hinder, frustrate, oppose, resist.

abettor *(SYN.)* accomplice, ally, confederate, associate, accessory.

(ANT.) opponent, rival, enemy.

abeyance *(SYN.)* inaction, cessation, pause, inactivity, rest, recess, dormancy, remission.

(ANT.) continuation.

abhor *(SYN.)* dislike, hate, loathe, execrate, avoid, scorn, detest, despise.

abhorrent *(SYN.)* loathsome, horrible, detestable, nauseating, hateful, despicable, disgusting, foul, offensive, terrible, revolting.

abide *(SYN.)* obey, accept, tolerate, endure, stay, reside.

ability *(SYN.)* aptness, capability, skill, dexterity, faculty, talent, aptitude, efficiency, capacity, effectiveness.

(ANT.) incapacity, incompetency, ineptitude, inability, disability.

abject *(SYN.)* sordid, infamous, wretched, mean, contempt.

abjure *(SYN.)* resign, relinquish, renounce, vacate, waive, desert, quit, leave, forsake, forewear, abdicate, surrender.

(ANT.) maintain, uphold, stay.

able *(SYN.)* qualified, competent, fit, capable, skilled, having power, efficient, clever, talented, adequate, skillful.

(ANT.) inadequate, trained, efficient, incapable, weak.

abnormal *(SYN.)* uncommon, unnatural, odd, irregular, eccentric, insane, unusual, weird, strange.

(ANT.) standard, natural, usual, normal, average.

aboard *(SYN.)* on board.

abode *(SYN.)* dwelling, habitat, hearth, home, residence, address, quarters, domicile.

abolish *(SYN.)* end, eradicate, annul, cancel, revoke, destroy, invalidate, overthrow, obliterate, abrogate, erase, eliminate.

(ANT.) promote, restore, contin-

ue, establish, sustain.

abominable *(SYN.)* foul, dreadful, hateful, revolting, vile, odious, loathsome, detestable, bad, horrible, terrible, awful, nasty, obnoxious, disgusting, unpleasant.

(ANT.) delightful, pleasant, agreeable, commendable, admirable, noble, fine.

abominate *(SYN.)* despise, detest, hate, dislike, abhor.

(ANT.) love, like, cherish, approve, admire.

abomination *(SYN.)* detestation, hatred, disgust, loathing, revulsion, antipathy, horror.

abort *(SYN.)* flop, fizzle, miscarry, abandon, cancel.

abortion *(SYN.)* fiasco, disaster, failure, defeat.

abortive *(SYN.)* unproductive, unsuccessful, failed, futile.

(ANT.) rewarding, effective, profitable, successful.

abound *(SYN.)* swarm, plentiful, filled, over-flow, teem.

(ANT.) scarce, lack.

about *(SYN.)* relating to, involving, concerning, near, around, upon, almost, approximately, of, close to, nearby, ready to, nearly.

above *(SYN.)* higher than, overhead, upon, over, superior to.

(ANT.) under, beneath, below.

aboveboard *(SYN.)* open, frank, honest, overt, plain, straightforward, trustworthy.

(ANT.) underhand, ambiguous, sneaky, wily.

abrasion *(SYN.)* rubbing, roughness, scratching, scraping, friction, chap, chafe, scrape.

abrasive *(SYN.)* hurtful, sharp, galling, annoying, grating, cutting, irritating, caustic.

(ANT.) pleasant, soothing, comforting, agreeable.

abreast *(SYN.)* beside, side by side, alongside.

abridge *(SYN.)* condense, cut, abbreviate, contract, shorten, reduce, summarize, curtail.

(ANT.) increase, lengthen, expand, extend.

abridgment *(SYN.)* digest, condensation, summary, abbreviation.

(ANT.) lengthening, expansion, enlargement.

abroad *(SYN.)* away, overseas, broadly, widely.

abrogate *(SYN.)* rescind, withdraw, revoke, annul, cancel, repeal.

abrupt *(SYN.)* sudden, unexpected, blunt, curt, craggy, precipitous, sharp, hasty, unannounced, harsh, precipitate, brusque, rude, rough, short, steep.

(ANT.) foreseen, smooth, warm, courteous, gradual, smooth, expected, anticipated.

abscess *(SYN.)* pustule, sore, inflammation, wound.

absence *(SYN.)* nonexistence, deficiency, shortcoming.

(ANT.) attendance, completeness, existence, presence.

absent *(SYN.)* out, away, truant, abroad, departed, inattentive, lacking, not present, off.

(ANT.) attending, attentive

absolute *(SYN.)* unconditional,

entire, actual, complete, thorough, total, perfect, essential, supreme, ultimate, unrestricted, positive, unqualified.

(ANT.) partial, conditional, dependent accountable, restricted, qualified, limited, imperfect, incomplete.

absolutely *(SYN.)* positively, really, doubtlessly.

(ANT.) doubtfully, uncertainly.

absolution *(SYN.)* pardon, forgiveness, acquittal, mercy, dispensation, amnesty.

absolutism *(SYN.)* autarchy, dictatorship, authoritarianism.

absolve *(SYN.)* exonerate, discharge, acquit, pardon, forgive, clear, excuse.

(ANT.) blame, convict, charge, accuse.

absorb *(SYN.)* consume, swallow up, engulf, assimilate, imbibe, engage, engross, take in, integrate, occupy.

(ANT.) discharge, dispense, emit, exude, leak, eliminate, bore, tire, weary, drain.

absorbent *(SYN.)* permeable, spongy, pervious, porous.

(ANT.) moisture proof, waterproof, impervious.

absorbing *(SYN.)* engaging, exciting, engrossing, entertaining, thrilling, intriguing, pleasing, fascinating.

(ANT.) dull, boring, tedious.

abstain *(SYN.)* forbear, forego, decline, resist, hold back, withhold, refrain.

(ANT.) pursue.

abstemious *(SYN.)* abstinent, sparing, cautious, temperate,

ascetic, self-disciplined, continent, sober.
(ANT.) uncontrolled, indulgent, abandoned, excessive.

abstinence *(SYN.)* fasting, self-denial, continence, forbearance, sobriety, refrain, abstention.
(ANT.) gluttony, greed, excess, self-indulgence, pursue.

abstract *(SYN.)* part, appropriate, steal, remove, draw from, separate, purloin, unconcrete, summarize, abridge.
(ANT.) return, concrete, unite, add, replace, specific, clear, particular, restore.

abstracted *(SYN.)* removed, stolen, abridged, taken away.
(ANT.) replaced, returned, alert, united, added.

abstraction *(SYN.)* idea, image, generalization, thought, opinion, impression, notion.
(ANT.) matter, object, substance.

abstruse *(SYN.)* arcane, obscure, complicated, abstract, refined, mandarin, esoteric, metaphysical.
(ANT.) uncomplicated, direct, obvious, simple.

absurd *(SYN.)* ridiculous, silly, unreasonable, foolish, irrational, nonsensical, impossible, inconsistent, preposterous, unbelievable.
(ANT.) rational, sensible, sound, meaningful, consistent, reasonable.

absurdity *(SYN.)* foolishness, nonsense, farce, drivel, joke, paradox, senselessness, folly.

abundance *(SYN.)* ampleness, profusion, large amount, copiousness, plenty.
(ANT.) insufficiency, absence, want, dearth, scarcity.

abundant *(SYN.)* ample, overflowing, plentiful, rich, teeming, large amount, profuse, abounding
(ANT.) insufficient, scant, not enough, scarce, deficient, rare, uncommon, absent.

abuse *(SYN.)* maltreatment, misuse, reproach, defamation, dishonor, mistreat, damage, ill-use, reviling, aspersion, desecration, invective, insult, outrage, profanation, perversion, upbraiding, disparagement, misemploy, misapply, hurt, harm, scold, berate.
(ANT.) plaudit, respect, appreciate, commendation, protect, praise, cherish.

abusive *(SYN.)* harmful, insulting, libelous, hurtful, slanderous, nasty, defamatory, injurious, scathing, derogatory.
(ANT.) supportive, helpful, laudatory, complimentary.

abut *(SYN.)* touch, border, meet, join, connect with.

abutment *(SYN.)* pier, buttress, bulwark, brace, support.

abysmal *(SYN.)* immeasurable, boundless, endless, stupendous, profound, unbelievable, infinite, consummate.

abyss *(SYN.)* depth, chasm, void, infinitude, limbo, unknowable.

academic *(SYN.)* learned, scholarly, theoretical, erudite, bookish, formal, pedantic.

(ANT.) ignorant, practical, simple, uneducated.

accede *(SYN.)* grant, agree, comply, consent, yield, endorse, accept, admit.

(ANT.) dissent, disagree, differ, oppose.

accelerate *(SYN.)* quicken, dispatch, facilitate, hurry, rush, speed up, forward, hasten, push, expedite.

(ANT.) hinder, retard, delay.

accent *(SYN.)* tone, emphasis, inflection, stress, consent.

accept *(SYN.)* take, approve, receive, allow, consent to, believe, adopt, admit.

(ANT.) ignore, reject, refuse.

acceptable *(SYN.)* passable, satisfactory, fair, adequate, standard, par, tolerable, unobjectionable.

(ANT.) poor, substandard, inadmissible.

access *(SYN.)* entrance, approach, course, gateway, door, avenue.

accessible *(SYN.)* nearby, attainable, achievable, affable, democratic, accommodating.

(ANT.) remote, unobtainable, unachievable, standoffish, forbidding, unfriendly.

accessory *(SYN.)* extra, addition, assistant, supplement, contributory, accomplice.

accident *(SYN.)* casualty, disaster, misfortune, mishap, chance, calamity, contingency, fortuity, misadventure, mischance, injury, event, catastrophe.

(ANT.) purpose, intention, calculation.

accidental *(SYN.)* unintended, chance, casual, fortuitous, contingent, unplanned, unexpected, unforeseen.

(ANT.) calculated, planned, willed, intended, intentional, on purpose, deliberate.

acclaim *(SYN.)* eminence, fame, glory, honor, reputation, credit, applaud, distinction, approve, notoriety.

(ANT.) infamy, obscurity, disapprove, reject, disrepute.

acclimated *(SYN.)* adapted, habituated, acclimatized, accommodated, seasoned, inured, weathered, reconciled.

accolade *(SYN.)* praise, honor, acclaim, recognition, applause, bouquet, testimonial, acclamation, salute.

accommodate *(SYN.)* help, assist, aid, provide for, serve, oblige, hold, house.

(ANT.) inconvenience.

accommodating *(SYN.)* obliging, helpful, willing, kind, cooperative, gracious, cordial, sympathetic, unselfish.

(ANT.) unfriendly, selfish, hostile, uncooperative.

accompany *(SYN.)* chaperon, consort with, escort, go with, associate with, attend, join.

(ANT.) abandon, quit, leave, desert, avoid, forsake.

accomplice *(SYN.)* accessory, ally, associate, assistant, sidekick, confederate.

(ANT.) opponent, rival, enemy, adversary.

accomplish *(SYN.)* attain, con-

summate, achieve, do, execute, carry out, fulfill, complete, effect, perform, finish.
(ANT.) *fail, frustrate, spoil, neglect, defeat.*

accomplished (SYN.) proficient, skilled, finished, well-trained, gifted, masterly, polished, able.
(ANT.) *unskilled, amateurish, crude.*

accomplishment (SYN.) deed, feat, statute, operation, performance, action, achievement, transaction.
(ANT.) *cessation, inhibition, intention, deliberation.*

accord (SYN.) concur, agree, award, harmony, conformity, agreement, give, tale, sum, statement, record, grant.
(ANT.) *difference, quarrel, disagreement.*

accordingly (SYN.) consequently, therefore, hence, so, thus.

accost (SYN.) approach, greet, speak to, address.
(ANT.) *avoid, shun.*

account (SYN.) description, chronicle, history, narration, reckoning, rate, computation, detail, narrative, relation, recital, consider, believe, deem, record, explanation, report, tale, story, anecdote, reason, statement, tale, ledger.
(ANT.) *confusion, misrepresentation, distortion.*

accountable (SYN.) chargeable, answerable, beholden, responsible, obliged, liable.

accredited (SYN.) qualified, licensed, deputized, certified, commissioned, vouched for, empowered.
(ANT.) *illicit, unofficial, unauthorized.*

accrue (SYN.) amass, collect, heap, increase, accumulate, gather, hoard.
(ANT.) *disperse, dissipate, waste, diminish.*

accrued (SYN.) accumulated, totaled, increased, added, enlarged, amassed, expanded.

accumulate (SYN.) gather, collect, heap, increase, accrue, assemble, compile, amass.
(ANT.) *spend, give away, diminish, dissipate.*

accumulation (SYN.) heap, collection, pile, store, hoard, stack, aggregation.

accurate (SYN.) perfect, just, truthful, unerring, meticulous, correct, all right.
(ANT.) *incorrect, mistaken.*

accusation (SYN.) charge, incrimination, indictment, arraignment.
(ANT.) *pardon, exoneration, absolve.*

accuse (SYN.) incriminate, indict, censure, denounce, charge, arraign, blame.
(ANT.) *release, vindicate, exonerate, acquit, absolve, clear.*

accustom (SYN.) addict, familiarize, condition.

accustomed (SYN.) familiar with, comfortable with.
(ANT.) *strange, unusual, rare, unfamiliar.*

acerbity (SYN.) bitterness, harshness, unkindness, sour-

ness, acidity, unfriendliness, acrimony, sharpness.
(ANT.) sweetness, gentleness, kindness, tenderness.

ache *(SYN.)* hurt, pain, throb.

achieve *(SYN.)* do, execute, gain, obtain, acquire, accomplish, perform, complete, accomplish, finish, fulfill, reach, attain, secure, procure.
(ANT.) fail, lose, fall short.

achievement *(SYN.)* feat, accomplishment, attainment, exploit, realization, performance, completion, deed.
(ANT.) botch, dud, mess, omission, defeat, failure.

acid *(SYN.)* tart, sour, bitter, mordant, biting, vinegary.
(ANT.) pleasant, friendly, bland, mild, sweet.

acknowledge *(SYN.)* allow, admit, agree to, concede, recognize, answer, grant, accept, receive.
(ANT.) reject, refuse, disavow, refute, deny.

acme *(SYN.)* summit, top, zenith, peak, crown.
(ANT.) bottom.

acquaint *(SYN.)* inform, teach, enlighten, notify, tell.

acquaintance *(SYN.)* fellowship, friendship, cognizance, knowledge, intimacy, familiarity, companionship, associate, colleague, companion.
(ANT.) inexperience, unfamiliarity, ignorance.

acquiesce *(SYN.)* submit, agree, concur, assent, comply, consent, succumb.
(ANT.) refuse, disagree, rebel,

argue.

acquire *(SYN.)* attain, earn, get, procure, assimilate, obtain, secure, gain, appropriate.
(ANT.) miss, surrender, lose, forego, forfeit.

acquirement *(SYN.)* training, skill, learning, achievement, attainment, education.

acquisition *(SYN.)* procurement, gift, purchase, proceeds, possession, grant.

acquisitive *(SYN.)* greedy, avid, hoarding, covetous.

acquit *(SYN.)* forgive, exonerate, absolve, cleanse, pardon, excuse, discharge.
(ANT.) doom, saddle, sentence, condemn.

acrid *(SYN.)* bitter, sharp, nasty, stinging, harsh.
(ANT.) pleasant, sweet.

acrimonious *(SYN.)* sharp, sarcastic, acerb, waspish, cutting, stinging, testy.
(ANT.) soft, kind, sweet, pleasant, soothing.

act *(SYN.)* deed, doing, feat, execution, accomplishment, performance, action, operation, transaction, law, decree, statute, edict, achievement.
(ANT.) inactivity, deliberation, intention, cessation.

acting *(SYN.)* officiating, substituting, surrogate, temporary, delegated.

action *(SYN.)* deed, achievement, feat, activity, exploit, movement, motion, play, behavior, battle, performance, exercise.
(ANT.) idleness, inertia, repose,

inactivity, rest.

activate *(SYN.)* mobilize, energize, start, propel, push.

(ANT.) paralyze, immobilize, stop, deaden.

active *(SYN.)* working, operative, alert, agile, nimble, supple, sprightly, busy, brisk, lively, quick, industrious, energetic, vigorous, industrious, occupied, vivacious, dynamic, engaged.

(ANT.) passive, inactive, idle, dormant, lazy, lethargic.

activism *(SYN.)* engagement, confrontation, agitation, commitment, aggression, fervor.

(ANT.) detachment, lethargy, disengagement, fence-sitting.

activist *(SYN.)* militant, doer, enthusiast.

activity *(SYN.)* action, liveliness, motion, vigor, agility, exercise, energy, quickness, enterprise, movement, briskness.

(ANT.) idleness, inactivity, dullness, sloth.

actor *(SYN.)* performer, entertainer.

actual *(SYN.)* true, genuine, certain, factual, authentic, concrete, real.

(ANT.) unreal, fake, bogus, nonexistent, false.

actuality *(SYN.)* reality, truth, deed, occurrence, fact, certainty.

(ANT.) theory, fiction, falsehood, supposition.

acute *(SYN.)* piercing, severe, sudden, keen, sharp, perceptive, discerning, shrewd,

astute, smart, intelligent.

(ANT.) bland, mild, dull, obtuse, insensitive.

adamant *(SYN.)* unyielding, firm, obstinate.

(ANT.) yielding.

adapt *(SYN.)* adjust, conform, accommodate, change, fit, alter, vary, modify.

(ANT.) misapply, disturb.

add *(SYN.)* attach, increase, total, append, sum, affix, augment, adjoin, supplement.

(ANT.) remove, reduce, deduct, subtract, detach, withdraw.

address *(SYN.)* greet, hail, accost, speak to, location, residence, abode, dwelling, speech, lecture, greeting, oration, presentation.

(ANT.) avoid, pass by.

adept *(SYN.)* expert, skillful, proficient.

(ANT.) unskillful.

adequate *(SYN.)* capable, commensurate, fitting, satisfactory, sufficient, enough, ample, suitable, plenty, fit.

(ANT.) lacking, scant, insufficient, inadequate.

adhere *(SYN.)* stick fast, grasp, hold, keep, retain, cling, stick to, keep, cleave.

(ANT.) surrender, abandon, release, separate, loosen.

adherent *(SYN.)* follower, supporter.

(ANT.) renegade, dropout defector.

adjacent *(SYN.)* next to, near, bordering, adjoining, touching, neighboring.

(ANT.) separate, distant, apart.

adjoin *(SYN.)* connect, be close to, affix, attach.

(ANT.) detach, remove,

adjoining *(SYN.)* near to, next, next to, close to, touching, bordering.

(ANT.) distant, remote, separate.

adjourn *(SYN.)* postpone, defer, delay, suspend, discontinue, put off.

(ANT.) begin, convene, assemble.

adjust *(SYN.)* repair, fix, change, set, regulate, settle, arrange, adapt, accommodate, modify, very, alter, fit.

administer *(SYN.)* supervise, oversee, direct, manage, rule, govern, control, conduct, provide, give, execute, preside, apply, contribute, help.

administration *(SYN.)* conduct, direction, management, supervision.

admirable *(SYN.)* worthy, fine, deserving, commendable, excellent.

admiration *(SYN.)* pleasure, wonder, esteem, approval.

(ANT.) disdain, disrespect, contempt.

admire *(SYN.)* approve, venerate, appreciate, respect, revere, esteem, like.

(ANT.) abhor, dislike, despise, loathe, detest, hate.

admissible *(SYN.)* fair, justifiable, tolerable, allowable, permissible.

(ANT.) unsuitable, unfair, inadmissible.

admission *(SYN.)* access, ad-

mittance, entrance, pass, ticket.

admit *(SYN.)* allow, assent, permit, acknowledge, welcome, concede, agree, confess, accept, grant.

(ANT.) deny, reject, dismiss, shun, obstruct.

admonish *(SYN.)* caution, advise against, warn, rebuke, reprove, censure.

(ANT.) glorify, praise.

admonition *(SYN.)* advice, warning, caution, remainder.

ado *(SYN.)* trouble, other, fuss, bustle, activity, excitement, commotion, action, hubbub, upset, confusion, turmoil.

(ANT.) tranquillity, quietude.

adolescent *(SYN.)* young, youthful, immature, teenage.

(ANT.) grown, mature, adult.

adoration *(SYN.)* veneration, reverence, glorification, worship homage.

adore *(SYN.)* revere, venerate, idolize, respect, love, cherish, esteem, honor.

(ANT.) loathe, hate, despise.

adorn *(SYN.)* trim, bedeck, decorate, ornament, beautify, embellish, glamorize, enhance, garnish, embellish.

(ANT.) mar, spoil, deform, deface, strip, bare.

adrift *(SYN.)* floating, afloat, drifting, aimless, unsettled.

(ANT.) purposeful, stable, secure, well-organized.

adroit *(SYN.)* adept, apt, dexterous, skillful, clever, expert.

(ANT.) awkward, clumsy, graceless, unskillful, oafish.

advance (SYN.) further, promote, bring forward, propound, proceed, aggrandize, elevate, improve, adduce, allege, propose, progress, move, advancement, upgrade.
(ANT.) retard, retreat, oppose, hinder, revert, withdraw, flee.

advantage (SYN.) edge, profit, superiority, benefit, mastery, leverage, favor, vantage, gain.
(ANT.) handicap, impediment, obstruction, disadvantage, detriment, hindrance, loss.

adventure (SYN.) undertaking, occurrence, enterprise, happening, event, project, occurrence, incident, exploit.

adventurous (SYN.) daring, enterprising, bold, chivalrous.
(ANT.) cautious, hesitating.

adversary (SYN.) foe, enemy, contestant, opponent, antagonist.
(ANT.) ally, friend.

adverse (SYN.) hostile, counteractive, unfavorable, opposed, disastrous, contrary, antagonistic, opposite, unlucky, unfriendly, unfortunate.
(ANT.) favorable, propitious, fortunate, friendly, beneficial.

adversity (SYN.) misfortune, trouble, calamity, distress, hardship, disaster.
(ANT.) benefit, happiness.

advertise (SYN.) promote, publicize, make known, announce, promulgate.

advice (SYN.) counsel, instruction, suggestion, warning, information, caution, exhortation, admonition, recommendation, plan, tip, guidance, opinion.

advisable (SYN.) wise, sensible, prudent, suitable, fit, proper, fitting.
(ANT.) ill-considered, imprudent, inadvisable.

advise (SYN.) recommend, suggest, counsel, caution, warn, admonish.

adviser (SYN.) coach, guide, mentor, counselor.

advocate (SYN.) defend, recommend, support, urge.
(ANT.) opponent, adversary, oppose.

aesthetic (SYN.) literary, artistic, sensitive, tasteful.
(ANT.) tasteless.

affable (SYN.) pleasant, courteous, sociable, friendly, amiable, gracious, approachable, communicative.
(ANT.) unfriendly, unsociable.

affair (SYN.) event, occasion, happening, party, occurrence, festivity, business, concern.

affect (SYN.) alter, modify, concern, regard, move, touch, feign, pretend, influence, sway, transform, impress.

affected (SYN.) pretended, fake, sham, false.

affection (SYN.) fondness, kindness, emotion, love, feeling, tenderness, attachment, disposition, endearment, liking, friendly, friendliness, warmth.
(ANT.) aversion, indifference, repulsion, hatred, repugnance, dislike, antipathy.

affectionate (SYN.) warm, loving, tender, fond, attached.

(ANT.) distant, unfeeling, cold.

affirm *(SYN.)* aver, declare, swear, maintain, endorse, certify, state, assert, ratify, pronounce, confirm, establish.

(ANT.) deny, dispute, oppose, contradict, demur, disclaim.

afflict *(SYN.)* trouble, disturb, bother, agitate, perturb.

(ANT.) soothe.

affliction *(SYN.)* distress, grief, misfortune, trouble.

(ANT.) relief, benefit, easement.

affluent *(SYN.)* wealthy, prosperous, rich, abundant, ample, plentiful, well-off, bountiful.

(ANT.) poor.

afford *(SYN.)* supply, yield, furnish.

affront *(SYN.)* offense, slur, slight, provocation, insult.

afraid *(SYN.)* fainthearted, frightened, scared, timid, fearful, apprehensive, cowardly, terrified.

(ANT.) assured, composed, courageous, bold, confident.

after *(SYN.)* following, subsequently, behind, next.

(ANT.) before.

again *(SYN.)* anew, repeatedly, afresh.

against *(SYN.)* versus, hostile to, opposed to, in disagreement.

(ANT.) pro, with, for, in favor of.

age *(SYN.)* antiquity, date, period, generation, time, senility, grow old, mature, dotage, ripen, mature, era, epoch.

(ANT.) youth, childhood.

aged *(SYN.)* ancient, elderly, old.

(ANT.) youthful, young.

agency *(SYN.)* office, operation.

agent *(SYN.)* performer, worker, actor, operator.

aggravate *(SYN.)* intensify, magnify, annoy, irritate, increase, heighten, nettle, make worse, irk, vex, provoke, embitter, worsen.

(ANT.) soften, soothe, appease, pacify, mitigate, ease, relieve.

aggregate *(SYN.)* collection, entirety, sum, accumulate, total, amount to, compile, conglomeration.

(ANT.) part, unit, ingredient, element.

aggression *(SYN.)* assault, attack, invasion, offense.

(ANT.) defense.

aggressive *(SYN.)* offensive, belligerent, hostile, attacking, militant, pugnacious.

(ANT.) timid, withdrawn, passive, peaceful, shy.

aghast *(SYN.)* surprised, astonished, astounded, awed, thunderstruck, bewildered.

agile *(SYN.)* nimble, graceful, lively, active, spry, alert, fast, quick, athletic.

(ANT.) inept, awkward, clumsy.

agility *(ANT.)* quickness, vigor, energy, activity, motion.

(ANT.) dullness, inertia, idleness, inactivity.

agitate *(SYN.)* disturb, excite, perturb, rouse, shake, arouse, disconcert, instigate, inflame, provoke, jar, incite, toss.

(ANT.) calm, placate, quiet, ease, soothe.

agitated *(SYN.)* jumpy, jittery,

nervous, restless, restive, upset, disturbed, ruffled.

agony *(SYN.)* anguish, misery, pain, suffering, torture, ache, distress, woe, torment, grief. *(ANT.) relief, ease, comfort.*

agree *(SYN.)* comply, coincide, conform, occur, assent, accede, tally, settle, harmonize, unite, yield, consent. *(ANT.) differ, disagree, protest, contradict, argue, refuse.*

agreeable *(SYN.)* amiable, charming, gratifying, pleasant, suitable, pleasurable, welcome, pleasing, acceptable, friendly, cooperative. *(ANT.) obnoxious, offensive, unpleasant, quarrelsome, contentious, touchy.*

agreement *(SYN.)* harmony, understanding, unison, contract, pact, stipulation, alliance, deal, bargain, treaty, contract, arrangement, settlement, accord, concord. *(ANT.) variance, dissension, discord, disagreement, difference, misunderstanding.*

agriculture *(SYN.)* farming, gardening, tillage, husbandry, cultivation, agronomy.

ahead *(SYN.)* before, leading, forward, winning, in advance. *(ANT.) behind.*

aid *(SYN.)* remedy, assist, helper, service, support, assistant, relief, help. *(ANT.) obstruct, hinder, obstacle, impede, hindrance.*

ail *(SYN.)* bother, trouble, perturb, disturb, suffer, feel sick.

ailing *(SYN.)* sick, ill.

(ANT.) hearty, hale, well.

ailment *(SYN.)* illness, disease, affliction, sickness.

aim *(SYN.)* direction, point, goal, object, target, direct, try, intend, intention, objective.

aimless *(SYN.)* directionless, adrift, purposeless.

air *(SYN.)* atmosphere, display, reveal, expose, publicize. *(ANT.) conceal, hide.*

airy *(SYN.)* breezy, light, gay, lighthearted, graceful, fanciful.

aisle *(SYN.)* corridor, passageway, lane, alley, opening, artery.

ajar *(SYN.)* gaping, open.

akin *(SYN.)* alike, related, connected, similar, affiliated, allied.

alarm *(SYN.)* dismay, fright, signal, warning, terror, apprehension, affright, fear, siren, arouse, startle, bell. *(ANT.) tranquillity, composure, security, quiet, calm, soothe, comfort.*

alarming *(SYN.)* appalling, daunting, shocking. *(ANT.) comforting, calming.*

alcoholic *(SYN.)* sot, drunkard, tippler, inebriate.

alert *(SYN.)* attentive, keen, clear-witted, ready, vigilant, watchful, observant. *(ANT.) sluggish, dulled, listless.*

alias *(SYN.)* anonym, assumed name.

alibi *(SYN.)* story, excuse.

alien *(SYN.)* adverse, foreigner, strange, remote, stranger, different, extraneous.

(ANT.) germane, kindred, relevant, familiar, accustomed.

alight *(SYN.)* debark, deplane, detrain, disembark.

(ANT.) embark, board.

alive *(SYN.)* existing, breathing, living, live, lively, vivacious, animated.

(ANT.) inactive, dead, moribund.

allay *(SYN.)* soothe, check, lessen, calm, lighten, relieve, soften, moderate, quite.

(ANT.) excite, intensify, worsen, arouse.

allege *(SYN.)* affirm, cite, claim, declare, maintain, assert.

(ANT.) deny, disprove, refute, contradict, gainsay.

allegiance *(SYN.)* faithfulness, duty, devotion, loyalty, fidelity, obligation.

(ANT.) treachery, disloyalty.

allegory *(SYN.)* fable, fiction, myth, saga, parable, legend.

(ANT.) history, fact.

alleviate *(SYN.)* diminish, soothe, solace, abate, assuage, allay, soften, mitigate, extenuate, relieve, let up, ease, slacken, relax, weaken.

(ANT.) increase, aggravate, augment, irritate.

alley *(SYN.)* footway, byway, path, passageway, aisle, corridor, opening, lane.

alliance *(SYN.)* combination, partnership, union, treaty, coalition, association, confederacy, marriage, pact, agreement, relation, interrelation, understanding, relationship.

(ANT.) separation, divorce,

schism.

allot *(SYN.)* divide, mete, assign, give, measure, distribute, allocate, share, grant, dispense, deal, apportion.

(ANT.) withhold, retain, keep, confiscate, refuse.

allow *(SYN.)* authorize, grant, acknowledge, admit, let, permit, sanction, consent, concede, mete, allocate.

(ANT.) protest, resist, refuse, forbid, object, prohibit.

allowance *(SYN.)* grant, fee, portion, ration, allotment.

allude *(SYN.)* intimate, refer, insinuate, hint, advert, suggest, imply, mention.

(ANT.) demonstrate, specify, state, declare.

allure *(SYN.)* attract, fascinate, tempt, charm, infatuate, captivate.

ally *(SYN.)* accomplice, associate, confederate, abettor, assistant, friend, partner.

(ANT.) rival, enemy, opponent, foe, adversary.

almighty *(SYN.)* omnipotent, powerful.

almost *(SYN.)* somewhat, nearly.

(ANT.) completely, absolutely.

alms *(SYN.)* dole, charity, donation, contribution.

aloft *(SYN.)* overhead.

alone *(SYN.)* desolate, unaided, only, isolated, lone, secluded, lonely, deserted, solitary, single, apart, solo, separate.

(ANT.) surrounded, attended, accompanied, together.

aloof *(SYN.)* uninterested, unin-

volved, apart, away, remote, unsociable, standoffish, separate, disdainful, distant.
(ANT.) warm, outgoing, friendly, cordial.

also *(SYN.)* in addition, likewise, too, besides, furthermore, moreover, further.

alter *(SYN.)* adjust, vary, deviate, modify, reserved, change.
(ANT.) maintain, preserve, keep.

alteration *(SYN.)* difference, adjustment, change, modification.
(ANT.) maintenance, preservation.

altercation *(SYN.)* controversy, dispute, argument, quarrel.

alternate *(SYN.)* rotate, switch, spell, interchange.
(ANT.) fix.

alternative *(SYN.)* substitute, selection, option, choice, replacement, possibility.

although *(SYN.)* though, even if, even though, despite, notwithstanding.

altitude *(SYN.)* elevation, height.
(ANT.) depth.

altogether *(SYN.)* totally, wholly, quite, entirely, thoroughly, completely.
(ANT.) partly.

altruism *(SYN.)* kindness, tenderness, generosity, charity, benevolence, liberality.
(ANT.) selfishness, unkindness, cruelty, inhumanity.

always *(SYN.)* evermore, forever, perpetually, ever, unceasingly, continually, constantly, eternally, everlastingly.

(ANT.) never, rarely, sometimes, occasionally.

amalgamate *(SYN.)* fuse, unify, unite, commingle, merge, blend, combine, consolidate.
(ANT.) decompose, disintegrate, separate.

amass *(SYN.)* collect, accumulate, heap up, gather, increase, compile, assemble, store up.
(ANT.) disperse, dissipate, spend.

amateur *(SYN.)* beginner, dilettante, learner, dabbler, neophyte, apprentice, novice, nonprofessional, tyro.
(ANT.) expert, master, adept, professional, authority.

amaze *(SYN.)* surprise, flabbergast, stun, dumbfound, astound, bewilder, aghast, thunderstruck, astonish.
(ANT.) bore, disinterest, tire.

ambiguous *(SYN.)* uncertain, vague, obscure, dubious, equivocal, unclear, deceptive.
(ANT.) plain, clear, explicit, obvious, unequivocal, unmistakable, certain.

ambition *(SYN.)* eagerness, goal, incentive, aspiration, yearning, longing, desire.
(ANT.) indifference, satisfaction, indolence, resignation.

ambitious *(SYN.)* aspiring, intent upon.
(ANT.) indifferent.

amble *(SYN.)* saunter, stroll.

ambush *(SYN.)* trap, hiding place.

amend *(SYN.)* change, mend, better, correct, improve.
(ANT.) worsen.

amends *(SYN.)* compensation, restitution, payment, reparation, remedy, redress.

amiable *(SYN.)* friendly, good-natured, gracious, pleasing, agreeable, outgoing, kind-hearted, kind, pleasant.

(ANT.) surly, hateful, churlish, disagreeable, ill-natured, ill-tempered, captious, touchy.

amid *(SYN.)* among, amidst, surrounded by.

amiss *(SYN.)* wrongly, improperly, astray, awry.

(ANT.) properly, rightly, right, correctly, correct.

ammunition *(SYN.)* shot, powder, shells, bullets.

among *(SYN.)* between, mingled, mixed amidst, amid, betwixt, surrounded by.

(ANT.) separate, apart.

amorous *(SYN.)* amatory, affectionate, loving.

amount *(SYN.)* sum, total, quantity, number, price, value, measure.

ample *(SYN.)* broad, large, profuse, spacious, copious, liberal, plentiful, full, bountiful, abundant, great, extensive, generous, wide, enough, sufficient, roomy.

(ANT.) limited, insufficient, meager, small, lacking, cramped, confined, inadequate.

amplification *(SYN.)* magnification, growth, waxing, accrual, enhancement, enlargement, heightening, increase.

(ANT.) decrease, diminishing, reduction, contraction.

amplify *(SYN.)* broaden, develop, expand, enlarge, extend.

(ANT.) confine, restrict, abridge, narrow.

amuse *(SYN.)* divert, please, delight, entertain, charm.

(ANT.) tire, bore.

amusement *(SYN.)* diversion, pastime, entertainment, pleasure, enjoyment, recreation.

(ANT.) tedium, boredom.

amusing *(SYN.)* pleasant, funny, pleasing, entertaining, comical.

(ANT.) tiring, tedious, boring.

analogous *(SYN.)* comparable, corresponding, like, similar, correspondent, alike, correlative, parallel, allied, akin.

(ANT.) different, opposed, incongruous, divergent.

analysis *(SYN.)* separation, investigation, examination.

analyze *(SYN.)* explain, investigate, examine, separate.

ancestral *(SYN.)* hereditary, inherited.

ancestry *(SYN.)* family, line, descent, lineage.

(ANT.) posterity.

anchor *(SYN.)* fix, attach, secure, fasten.

(ANT.) detach, free, loosen.

ancient *(SYN.)* aged, old-fashioned, archaic, elderly, antique, old, primitive.

(ANT.) new, recent, current, fresh.

anecdote *(SYN.)* account, narrative, story, tale.

anesthetic *(SYN.)* opiate, narcotic, sedative, painkiller, analgesic.

angel *(SYN.)* cherub, archangel,

seraph.

(ANT.) demon, devil.

angelic *(SYN.)* pure, lovely, heavenly, good, virtuous, innocent, godly, saintly.

(ANT.) devilish.

anger *(SYN.)* exasperation, fury, ire, passion, rage, resentment, temper, indignation, animosity, irritation, wrath, displeasure, infuriate, arouse, nettle, annoyance, exasperate.

(ANT.) forbearance, patience, peace, self-control.

angry *(SYN.)* provoked, wrathful, furious, enraged, incensed, maddened, indignant, irate, mad, inflamed.

(ANT.) happy, pleased, calm, satisfied, content, tranquil.

anguish *(SYN.)* suffering, torment, torture, distress, pain, heartache, grief, agony, misery.

(ANT.) solace, relief, joy, comfort, peace, ecstasy, pleasure.

animal *(SYN.)* beast, creature.

animated *(SYN.)* lively, spry, vivacious, active, vigorous, chipper, snappy.

(ANT.) inactive.

animosity *(SYN.)* grudge, hatred, rancor, spite, bitterness, enmity, opposition, dislike, hostility, antipathy.

(ANT.) good will, love, friendliness, kindliness.

annex *(SYN.)* join, attach, add, addition, wing, append.

annihilate *(SYN.)* destroy, demolish, end, wreck, abolish.

announce *(SYN.)* proclaim, give out, make known, notify, publish, report, herald, promulgate, advertise, broadcast, state, tell, declare, publicize.

(ANT.) conceal, withhold, suppress, bury, stifle.

announcement *(SYN.)* notification, report, declaration, bulletin, advertisement, broadcast, notice, message.

(ANT.) silence, hush, muteness, speechlessness.

annoy *(SYN.)* bother, irk, pester, tease, trouble, vex, disturb, inconvenience, molest, irritate, harry, harass.

(ANT.) console, gratify, soothe, accommodate, please, calm.

annually *(SYN.)* once a year.

anoint *(SYN.)* grease, oil.

answer *(SYN.)* reply, rejoinder, response, retort, rebuttal, respond.

(ANT.) summoning, argument, questioning, inquiry, query, ask, inquire.

antagonism *(SYN.)* opposition, conflict, enmity, hostility, animosity.

(ANT.) geniality, cordiality, friendliness.

antagonist *(SYN.)* adversary, rival, enemy, foe, opponent.

(ANT.) ally, friend.

antagonize *(SYN.)* against, provoke, counter, oppose, embitter.

(ANT.) soothe.

anthology *(SYN.)* garland, treasury, collection.

anticipate *(SYN.)* await, foresee, forecast, hope for, expect.

anticipated *(SYN.)* expected, foresight, hoped, preconceived.

(ANT.) dreaded, reared, worried, doubted.

antics *(SYN.)* horseplay, fun, merrymaking, pranks, capers, tricks, clowning.

antipathy *(SYN.)* hatred.

antiquated *(SYN.)* old, out-of-date, outdated, old-fashion.

antique *(SYN.)* rarity, curio, old, ancient, old-fashioned, archaic, out-of-date.

(ANT.) new, recent, fresh.

anxiety *(SYN.)* care, disquiet, fear, concern, solicitude, trouble, worry, apprehension, uneasiness, distress.

(ANT.) nonchalance, assurance, confidence, contentment, peacefulness, tranquillity.

anxious *(SYN.)* troubled, uneasy, perturbed, apprehensive, worried, concerned, desirous, bothered, agitated, eager, fearful.

(ANT.) tranquil, calm, peaceful.

anyway *(SYN.)* nevertheless, anyhow.

apartment *(SYN.)* suite, flat, dormitory.

apathy *(SYN.)* unconcern, indifference, lethargy.

(ANT.) interest, feeling.

aperture *(SYN.)* gap, pore, opening, cavity, chasm, abyss, hole, void.

(ANT.) connection, bridge, link.

apex *(SYN.)* acme, tip, summit, crown, top.

apologize *(SYN.)* ask forgiveness.

apology *(SYN.)* defense, excuse, confession, justification, alibi,

explanation, plea.

(ANT.) denial, complaint, dissimulation, accusation.

apostate *(SYN.)* nonconformist, unbeliever, dissenter, heretic, schismatic.

(ANT.) saint, believer.

appall *(SYN.)* shock, stun, dismay, frighten, terrify, horrify.

(ANT.) edify, please.

appalling *(SYN.)* fearful, frightful, ghastly, horrid, repulsive, terrible, dire, awful.

(ANT.) fascinating, beautiful, enchanting, enjoyable.

apparatus *(SYN.)* rig, equipment, furnishings, gear.

apparel *(SYN.)* clothes, attire, garb, clothing, garments, dress, robes.

apparent *(SYN.)* obvious, plain, self-evident, clear, manifest, transparent, unmistakable, unambiguous, ostensible, illusory, visible, seeming, evident, understandable.

(ANT.) uncertain, indistinct, dubious, hidden, mysterious.

apparition *(SYN.)* illusion, ghost, phantom, vision, fantasy, dream.

appeal *(SYN.)* plea, petition, request, entreaty, plead, beseech, beg, entreat, attract, solicitate.

(ANT.) repulse, repel.

appear *(SYN.)* look, arrive, emanate, emerge, arise, seem, turn up.

(ANT.) vanish, withdraw, exist, disappear, evaporate.

appearance *(SYN.)* advent, arrival, aspect, demeanor,

fashion, guise, apparition, manner, mien, look, presence.

(ANT.) disappearance, reality, departure, vanishing.

appease *(SYN.)* calm, compose, lull, quiet, relieve, assuage, pacify, satisfy, restraint, lesson, soothe, check, ease, alleviate, still, allay, tranquilize.

(ANT.) excite, arouse, incense, irritate, inflame.

append *(SYN.)* supplement, attach, add.

appendage *(SYN.)* addition, tail, supplement.

appetite *(SYN.)* zest, craving, desire, liking, longing, stomach, inclination, hunger, thirst, relish, passion.

(ANT.) satiety, disgust, distaste, repugnance.

appetizer *(SYN.)* hors d'oeuvre.

applaud *(SYN.)* cheer, clap, hail, approve, praise, acclaim.

(ANT.) disapprove, denounce, reject, criticize, condemn.

appliance *(SYN.)* machine, tool, instrument, device, utensil, implement.

applicable *(SYN.)* fitting, suitable, proper, fit, usable, appropriate, suited.

(ANT.) inappropriate.

apply *(SYN.)* affix, allot, appropriate, use, employ, petition, request, devote, avail, pertain, attach, ask, administer, assign, relate, utilize.

(ANT.) give away, demand, detach, neglect, ignore.

appoint *(SYN.)* name, choose, nominate, designate, elect, establish, assign, place.

(ANT.) discharge, fire, dismiss.

appointment *(SYN.)* rendezvous, meeting, designation, position, engagement, assignment.

(ANT.) discharge, dismissal.

appraise *(SYN.)* value, evaluate, place a value on.

appreciate *(SYN.)* enjoy, regard, value, prize, cherish, admire, go up, improve, rise, respect, esteem, appraise.

(ANT.) belittle, misunderstand, apprehend, degrade, scorn, depreciate, undervalue.

apprehend *(SYN.)* seize, capture, arrest, understand, dread, fear, grasp, perceive.

(ANT.) release, lose.

apprehension *(SYN.)* fear, misgiving, dread, uneasiness, worry, fearfulness, anticipation, capture, seizure.

(ANT.) confidence, composure, self-assuredness.

apprehensive *(SYN.)* worried, afraid, uneasy, bothered, anxious, concerned, perturbed, troubled, fearful.

(ANT.) relaxed.

apprentice *(SYN.)* amateur, recruit, novice, learner, beginner.

(ANT.) experienced, professional, master.

approach *(SYN.)* greet, inlet, come near, advance, access, passageway.

(ANT.) avoid, pass by, retreat.

appropriate *(SYN.)* apt, particular, proper, fitting, suitable, applicable, loot, pillage, purloin, rob, steal, embezzle,

assign, apportion, authorize.
(ANT.) improper, contrary, inappropriate, buy, repay, restore, return, unfit, inapt.

approval *(SYN.)* commendation, consent, praise, approbation, sanction, assent, endorsement, support.
(ANT.) reproach, censure, reprimand, disapprove.

approve *(SYN.)* like, praise, authorize, confirm, endorse, appreciate, think well of, ratify, commend, sanction.
(ANT.) criticize, nullify, disparage, disapprove, deny.

approximate *(SYN.)* near, approach, roughly, close.
(ANT.) correct.

apt *(SYN.)* suitable, proper, appropriate, fit, suited, disposed, liable, inclined, prone, clever, bright, alert, intelligent, receptive.
(ANT.) ill-becoming, unsuitable, unlikely, slow, dense.

aptness *(SYN.)* capability, dexterity, power, qualification, skill, ability, aptitude.
(ANT.) incompetency, unreadiness, incapacity.

aptitude *(SYN.)* knack, talent, gift, ability.

aqueduct *(SYN.)* gully, pipe, canal, waterway, channel.

arbitrary *(SYN.)* unrestricted, absolute, despotic, willful, unreasonable, unconditional, authoritative.
(ANT.) contingent, qualified, fair, reasonable, dependent, accountable.

arbitrate *(SYN.)* referee, settle, mediate, umpire, negotiate.

architecture *(SYN.)* structure, building, construction.

ardent *(SYN.)* fervent, fiery, glowing, intense, keen, impassioned, fervid, hot, passionate, earnest, eager, zealous, enthusiastic.
(ANT.) indifferent, nonchalant, apathetic.

ardor *(SYN.)* enthusiasm, rapture, spirit, zeal, fervent, eager, glowing, eagerness.
(ANT.) unconcern, apathy, disinterest, indifference.

arduous *(SYN.)* laborious, hard, difficult, burdensome, strenuous, strained.
(ANT.) easy.

area *(SYN.)* space, extent, region, size, zone, section, district, neighborhood, size.

argue *(SYN.)* plead, reason, wrangle, indicate, prove, dispute, denote, imply, object, discuss, debate, disagree.
(ANT.) reject, spurn, ignore, overlook, agree, concur.

argument *(SYN.)* debate, dispute, discussion, controversy.
(ANT.) harmony, accord, agreement.

arid *(SYN.)* waterless, dry, flat, dull, unimaginative, stuffy.
(ANT.) fertile, wet, colorful.

arise *(SYN.)* enter, institute, originate, start, open, commence, emerge, appear.
(ANT.) terminate, end, finish, complete, close.

aristocrat *(SYN.)* noble, gentleman, peer, lord, nobleman.
(ANT.) peasant, commoner.

armistice (SYN.) truce, pact, deal, understanding, peace, treaty, contract, alliance, agreement.

aroma (SYN.) smell, odor, fragrance, perfume, scent.

arouse (SYN.) stir, animate, move, pique, provoke, kindle, disturb, excite, foment, stimulate, awaken.

(ANT.) settle, soothe, calm.

arraign (SYN.) charge, censure, incriminate, indict, accuse.

(ANT.) acquit, release, vindicate, exonerate, absolve.

arraignment (SYN.) imputation, charge, accusation, incrimination.

(ANT.) pardon, exoneration, exculpation.

arrange (SYN.) classify, assort, organize, place, plan, prepare, devise, adjust, dispose, regulate, order, group, settle, adapt, catalog, systematize, prepare.

(ANT.) jumble, scatter, disorder, confuse, disturb, disarrange.

arrangement (SYN.) display, grouping, order, array.

array (SYN.) dress, adorn, attire, clothe, arrange, order, distribute, arrangement, display, exhibit.

(ANT.) disorder, disorganization, disarray.

arrest (SYN.) detain, hinder, restrain, seize, withhold, stop, check, obstruct, apprehend, interrupt, catch, capture.

(ANT.) free, release, discharge, liberate.

arrival (SYN.) advent, coming.

(ANT.) leaving, departure.

arrive (SYN.) come, emerge, reach, visit, land, appear.

(ANT.) exit, leave, depart, go.

arrogance (SYN.) pride, insolence.

(ANT.) humbleness, modesty, humility.

arrogant (SYN.) insolent, prideful, scornful, haughty, cavalier, proud.

(ANT.) modest, humble.

art (SYN.) cunning, tact, artifice, skill, aptitude, adroitness, painting, drawing, design, craft, dexterity, composition.

(ANT.) clumsiness, innocence, unskillfulness, honesty.

artery (SYN.) aqueduct, pipe, channel.

artful (SYN.) clever, sly, skillful, knowing, deceitful, tricky, crafty, cunning.

(ANT.) artless.

article (SYN.) story, composition, treatise, essay, thing, report, object.

artifice (SYN.) trick, clever, scheme, device.

artificial (SYN.) bogus, fake, affected, feigned, phony, sham, unreal, synthetic, assumed, counterfeit, unnatural, manmade, false, pretended.

(ANT.) genuine, natural true, real, authentic.

artisan (SYN.) worker, craftsman, mechanic.

artless (SYN.) innocent, open, frank, simple, honest, candid, natural, unskilled, ignorant, truthful, sincere.

(ANT.) artful.

ascend (SYN.) rise, scale, tower, mount, go up, climb.
(ANT.) fall, sink, descend.
ascertain (SYN.) solve, learn, answer.
ascribe (SYN.) attribute, assign.
ashamed (SYN.) shamefaced, humiliated, abashed, mortified, embarrassed.
(ANT.) proud.
ask (SYN.) invite, request, inquire, query, question, beg, solicit, demand, entreat, interrogate, charge, expect.
(ANT.) order, reply, insist, answer.
askance (SYN.) sideways.
askew (SYN.) disorderly, crooked, awry, twisted.
(ANT.) straight.
asleep (SYN.) inactive, sleeping, dormant.
(ANT.) alert, awake.
aspect (SYN.) appearance, look, view, outlook, attitude, viewpoint, phase, part, feature, side.
aspersion (SYN.) dishonor, insult, misuse, outrage, abuse, reproach, defamation.
(ANT.) plaudit, respect, commendation, approval.
asphyxiate (SYN.) suffocate, stifle, smother, choke, strangle, throttle.
aspiration (SYN.) craving, desire, hope, longing, objective, passion, ambition.
aspire (SYN.) seek, aim, wish for, strive, desire, yearn for.
assail (SYN.) assault, attack.
assassinate (SYN.) purge, kill, murder.

assault (SYN.) invade, strike, attack, assail, charge, bombard, onslaught.
(ANT.) protect, defend.
assemble (SYN.) collect, gather, meet, congregate, connect, manufacture.
(ANT.) disperse, scatter.
assent (SYN.) consent to, concede, agree, approval, accept, comply, permission.
(ANT.) deny, dissent, refusal, denial, refuse.
assert (SYN.) declare, maintain, state, claim, express, defend, press, support, aver, uphold, consent, accept, comply, affirm, allege, emphasize.
(ANT.) deny, refute, contradict, decline.
assertion (SYN.) statement, affirmation, declaration.
(ANT.) contradiction, denial.
assess (SYN.) calculate, compute, estimate, levy, reckon, tax, appraise.
asset (SYN.) property, wealth, capitol, resources, goods.
assign (SYN.) apportion, ascribe, attribute, cast, allot, choose, appropriate, name, elect, appoint, designate, specify.
(ANT.) release, relieve, unburden, discharge.
assignment (SYN.) task, job, responsibility, duty.
assimilate (SYN.) digest, absorb, blot up.
assist (SYN.) help, promote, serve, support, sustain, abet, aid, back.
(ANT.) prevent, impede, hinder, hamper.

assistance *(SYN.)* backing, help, patronage, relief, succor, support.

(ANT.) hostility, resistance, antagonism, counteraction.

assistant *(SYN.)* accomplice, ally, associate, confederate, abettor.

(ANT.) rival, enemy, adversary.

associate *(SYN.)* affiliate, ally, join, connect, unite, combine, link, mingle, partner, mix.

(ANT.) separate, disconnect, divide, disrupt, estrange.

association *(SYN.)* organization, club, union, society, fraternity, sorority, companionship, fellowship.

assorted *(SYN.)* varied, miscellaneous, classified, different, several, grouped, various.

(ANT.) alike, same.

assortment *(SYN.)* collection, variety, mixture, conglomeration.

assuage *(SYN.)* calm, quiet, lessen, relieve, ease, allay, moderate, alleviate, restrain.

assume *(SYN.)* arrogate, affect, suspect, believe, appropriate, take, pretend, usurp, simulate, understand, postulate, presume, suppose.

(ANT.) doff, demonstrate, prove, grant, concede.

assumption *(SYN.)* presumption, guess, theory, supposition, conjecture, postulate.

assurance *(SYN.)* confidence, conviction, self-reliance, surety, firmness, courage, promise, pledge, certainty, assertion, security, assuredness.

(ANT.) humility, shyness, suspicion, modesty.

assure *(SYN.)* promise, convince, warrant, guarantee, pledge.

(ANT.) equivocate, deny.

astonish *(SYN.)* astound, amaze, surprise, shock.

(ANT.) tire, bore.

astound *(SYN.)* shock, amaze, astonish, stun, surprise, floor.

asunder *(SYN.)* divided, separate, apart.

(ANT.) together.

asylum *(SYN.)* shelter, refuge, home, madhouse, institution.

athletic *(SYN.)* strong, active, ablebodied, gymnastic, muscular, well-built.

atone *(SYN.)* repay, make up.

atrocious *(SYN.)* horrible, savage, brutal, ruthless, dreadful, awful, horrifying, horrid, unspeakable, ghastly.

(ANT.) good, kind.

attach *(SYN.)* connect, adjoin, annex, join, append, stick, unite, adjoin, affix.

(ANT.) unfasten, untie, detach, separate, disengage.

attachment *(SYN.)* friendship, liking, regard, adherence, affection, devotion.

(ANT.) estrangement, opposition, alienation, aversion.

attack *(SYN.)* raid, assault, besiege, abuse, censure, offense, seige, onslaught, denunciation, aggression, bombardment, push, criticism, invade.

(ANT.) surrender, defense, opposition, aid, defend, protect, repel.

attain (SYN.) achieve, acquire, accomplish, gain, get, reach, win, complete, finish, secure, procure, fulfill, obtain, effect.
(ANT.) relinquish, discard, abandon, desert.

attainment (SYN.) exploit, feat, accomplishment, realization, performance.
(ANT.) omission, defeat, failure, neglect.

attempt (SYN.) essay, experiment, trial, try, undertaking, endeavor, effort.
(ANT.) laziness, neglect, inaction.

attend (SYN.) accompany, escort, watch, be serve, care for, follow, lackey, present, frequent, protect, guard.
(ANT.) desert, abandon, avoid.

attendant (SYN.) waiter, servant, valet.

attention (SYN.) consideration, heed, circumspection, notice, watchfulness, observance, application, reflection, study, care, alertness, mindfulness.
(ANT.) negligence, indifference, omission, disregard.

attentive (SYN.) careful, awake, alive, considerate, heedful, mindful, wary, assiduous, diligent, aware, alert.
(ANT.) indifferent, unaware, oblivious, apathetic.

attest (SYN.) testify, swear, vouch, certify.

attire (SYN.) apparel, dress, clothe.

attitude (SYN.) standpoint, viewpoint, stand, pose, aspect, position, disposition, opinion.

attorney (SYN.) lawyer.

attract (SYN.) enchant, interest, pull, fascinate, draw, tempt, infatuate, entice, lure, charm, captivate, allure.
(ANT.) deter, repel, repulse, alienate.

attractive (SYN.) enchanting, winning, engaging, pleasant, pleasing, seductive, magnetic, charming, inviting, alluring.
(ANT.) unattractive, obnoxious, repellent, repulsive, forbidding.

attribute (SYN.) give, apply, place, trait, characteristic, feature, nature, credit, assign, ascribe.

audacious (SYN.) daring, bold, arrogant, foolhardy, cavalier, haughty, insolent.
(ANT.) humble, shy.

audacity (SYN.) effrontery, fearlessness, temerity, boldness.
(ANT.) humility, meekness, circumspection, fearfulness.

audible (SYN.) distinct, bearable, plain, clear.
(ANT.) inaudible.

augment (SYN.) enlarge, increase, raise, expand, broaden, extend.

auspicious (SYN.) lucky, timely, favorable, promising, fortunate.
(ANT.) untimely, unfortunate.

austere (SYN.) stern, severe, harsh, strict.
(ANT.) lenient, soft.

authentic (SYN.) real, true, genuine, pure, accurate, reliable, legitimate, factual, actual, correct, verifiable, authoritative.

(ANT.) false, spurious, artificial, counterfeit, erroneous.

authenticate *(SYN.)* validate, warrant, guarantee, verify, certify.

authoritative *(SYN.)* certain, secure, commanding, sure, tried, influential, dependable.

(ANT.) uncertain, unreliable, dubious, fallible, questionable.

authority *(SYN.)* dominion, justification, power, permission, importance, supremacy.

(ANT.) incapacity, denial, prohibition, weakness, impotence.

authorize *(SYN.)* permit, sanction, legalize, approve, empower.

(ANT.) forbid, prohibit.

autograph *(SYN.)* endorse, sign, approve.

automatic *(SYN.)* self-acting, mechanical, spontaneous, uncontrolled, involuntary, self working.

(ANT.) hand-operated, intentional, deliberate, manual.

automobile *(SYN.)* auto, car.

auxiliary *(SYN.)* assisting, helping, aiding.

avail *(SYN.)* help, profit, use, value, benefit, advantage.

available *(SYN.)* obtainable, convenient, ready, handy, accessible, prepared.

(ANT.) unavailable, out of reach, inaccessible, unobtainable.

avarice *(SYN.)* lust, greed.

average *(SYN.)* moderate, ordinary, usual, passable, fair, intermediate, medium, median, mediocre, mean, middling.

(ANT.) outstanding, exceptional, extraordinary, unusual.

averse *(SYN.)* unwilling, opposed, against, involuntary.

(ANT.) willing.

aversion *(SYN.)* disgust, dislike, distaste, hatred, loathing, abhorrence, antipathy.

(ANT.) devotion, enthusiasm, affection, love.

avert *(SYN.)* avoid, prevent, prohibit.

(ANT.) invite.

avid *(SYN.)* greedy, eager.

avocation *(SYN.)* sideline, hobby.

avoid *(SYN.)* elude, forestall, evade, escape, dodge, avert, forbear, eschew, free, shun.

(ANT.) oppose, meet, confront, encounter, seek.

award *(SYN.)* reward, prize, medal, gift, trophy.

aware *(SYN.)* mindful, perceptive, apprised, realizing, conscious, observant, cognizant.

(ANT.) unaware, insensible, ignorant, oblivious.

away *(SYN.)* absent, departed, distracted, gone, not at home.

(ANT.) present, attentive, at home, attending.

awe *(SYN.)* surprise, respect, dread, astonishment, alarm.

awful *(SYN.)* frightful, horrible, dire, terrible, unpleasant, imposing, solemn, appalling, cruel, wicked, brutal, savage.

(ANT.) humble, lowly, pleasant, nice, commonplace.

awkward *(SYN.)* inept, unpolished, clumsy, gauche, rough, ungraceful, cumbersome.

(ANT.) adroit, graceful, polished, skillful.

awry *(SYN.)* askew, wrong, twisted, crooked, disorderly.

(ANT.) straight, right.

axiom *(SYN.)* fundamental, maxim, principle, theorem, adage, apothegm, byword, aphorism.

B

babble *(SYN.)* twaddle, nonsense, gibberish, prattle, balderdash, rubbish, chatter, baby talk, poppycock, jabber, maunder, piffle.

baby *(SYN.)* newborn, infant, neonate, babe, teeny, small, wee, little, undersized, midget, papoose, protect, cosset, pamper.

babyish *(SYN.)* infantile, childish, baby, whiny, unreasonable, immature, puerile, foolish, dependent.

(ANT.) mature, adult, sensible, reasonable, grown-up.

back *(SYN.)* help, assist, endorse, support, second, ratify, approve, posterior, rear.

(ANT.) anterior, front, face, undercut, veto, undermine, progress, accessible, near.

backbiting *(SYN.)* gossip, slander, abuse, malice, cattiness, aspersion, bad-mouthing.

(ANT.) compliments, praise, loyalty, friendliness, approval.

backbone *(SYN.)* vertebrae, spine, pillar, prop, skeleton, support, staff, mainstay, basis, mettle, courage, firmness,

determination.

(ANT.) timidity, weakness, cowardice, spinelessness.

backbreaking *(SYN.)* exhausting, fatiguing, tough, tiring, demanding, wearying, wearing, difficult.

(ANT.) light, relaxing, undemanding, slight.

backer *(SYN.)* underwriter, benefactor, investor, patron, sponsor.

backfire *(SYN.)* flop, boomerang, fail, disappoint.

(ANT.) succeed.

backing *(SYN.)* help, support, funds, money, assistance, grant, advocacy, endorsement.

(ANT.) criticism, detraction, faultfinding.

backlog *(SYN.)* inventory, reserve, hoard, amassment, accumulation.

backward *(SYN.)* dull, sluggish, stupid, loath, unwilling, regressive, slow, retarded.

(ANT.) progressive, precocious, civilized, advanced, forward.

bad *(SYN.)* unfavorable, wrong, evil, immoral, sinful, faulty, improper, wicked, corrupt, tainted, harmful, injurious, defective, poor, imperfect, inferior, substandard, contaminated, inappropriate, unsuited, rotten, unsuitable, sorry, upset, sick, suffering, unpleasant, spoiled, depraved.

(ANT.) good, honorable, reputable, moral, excellent.

badger *(SYN.)* tease, question, annoy, pester, bother, taunt, bait, provoke, torment, harass, hector.

baffle *(SYN.)* confound bewilder, perplex, puzzle, mystify, confuse.

(ANT.) inform, enlighten.

bag *(SYN.)* catch, snare, poke, sack.

bait *(SYN.)* enticement, captivate, ensnare, tease, torment, pester, worry, entrap, quee tion, entice, lure, trap, harass, tempt, badger.

balance *(SYN.)* poise, stability, composure, remains, residue, equilibrium, compare, equalize.

(ANT.) unsteadiness, instability.

bald *(SYN.)* bare, hairless, nude, open, uncovered, simple.

(ANT.) covered, hairy.

baleful *(SYN.)* evil, immoral, sinful, destructive, detrimental, noxious, wicked, bad, villainous, injurious.

(ANT.) good, moral, reputable, excellent, harmless.

balk *(SYN.)* unwilling, obstinate, stubborn, hesitate, check, stop.

(ANT.) willing.

ball *(SYN.)* cotillion, dance, globe, sphere, spheroid.

ballad *(SYN.)* poem, song, ditty.

ballot *(SYN.)* choice, vote, poll.

balmy *(SYN.)* soft, gentle, soothing, fragrant, mild.

(ANT.) tempestuous, stormy.

ban *(SYN.)* prohibit, outlaw, disallow, block, bar, exclude, obstruct, prohibition, forbid.

(ANT.) allow, permit.

banal *(SYN.)* corny, vapid, trite, overused, stale.

(ANT.) striking, original, fresh, stimulating, novel.

band *(SYN.)* company, association, crew, body, group, society, belt.

bandit *(SYN.)* thief, robber, outlaw, marauder.

bang *(SYN.)* hit, strike, slam.

banish *(SYN.)* drive away, eject, exile, oust, deport, dismiss, expel.

(ANT.) receive, accept, shelter, admit, harbor, embrace, welcome.

bank *(SYN.)* barrier, slope, storage, treasury, row, series, string, shore, embankment.

banner *(SYN.)* colors, standard, pennant, flag.

banquet *(SYN.)* feast, celebration, festival, dinner, regalement, affair, entertainment.

banter *(SYN.)* joke, tease, jest.

bar *(SYN.)* counter, impediment, saloon, exclude, obstacle, barricade, obstruct, hindrance, forbid, block, barrier, obstruction.

(ANT.) allow, permit, aid, encouragement.

barber *(SYN.)* coiffeur, hairdresser.

bare *(SYN.)* naked, nude, uncovered, undressed, unclothed, unfurnished, plain, barren, empty, disclose, reveal, expose, scarce.

(ANT.) dressed, garbed, conceal, covered, hide, disguise.

barefaced *(SYN.)* impudent, bold, insolent, brazen, shameless, audacious, rude, unabashed.

barely *(SYN.)* hardly, scarcely, just.

bargain *(SYN.)* agreement, arrangement, deal, contract, arrange, sale, agree.

baroque *(SYN.)* ornamented, elaborate, embellished, ornate, decorated.

barren *(SYN.)* unproductive, bare, unfruitful, infertile, blank, sterile.
(ANT.) productive, fruitful, fertile.

barricade *(SYN.)* fence, obstruction, fortification, barrier.
(ANT.) free, open, release.

barrier *(SYN.)* fence, wall, bar, railing, obstacle, hindrance, fortification, obstruction, restraint, limit, barricade.
(ANT.) assistance, encouragement.

barter *(SYN.)* exchange, deal, trade.

base *(SYN.)* bottom, rest, foundation, establish, found, immoral, evil, bad, wicked, depraved, selfish, worthless, cheap, debased, poor, support, stand, low, abject, lowly.
(ANT.) exalted, righteous, lofty, esteemed, noble, honored, refined, valuable.

bashful *(SYN.)* timorous, abashed, shy, coy, timid, diffident, modest, sheepish, embarrassed, humble, uneasy.
(ANT.) fearless, adventurous, aggressive, daring.

basic *(SYN.)* underlying, chief, essential, main, fundamental.
(ANT.) subsidiary, subordinate.

basis *(SYN.)* presumption, support, base, principle, underpinning, bottom, presupposition, foundation, postulate, ground, assumption, premise, essential.
(ANT.) implication, trimming, derivative, superstructure.

basket *(SYN.)* hamper, creel, bassinet.

bastion *(SYN.)* mainstay, support, staff, tower, stronghold.

bat *(SYN.)* strike, hit, clout, stick, club, knock, crack.

batch *(SYN.)* group, set, collection, lot, cluster, bunch, mass.

bath *(SYN.)* washing, shower, tub, wash, dip, soaping.

bathe *(SYN.)* launder, drench, swim, cover, medicate, immerse, wet, dip, soak, rinse, saturate.

baton *(SYN.)* mace, rod, staff, billy, crook, stick, fasces.

batten *(SYN.)* thrive, flourish, fatten, wax, expand, bloom, boom.
(ANT.) decrease, weaken, fail.

battle *(SYN.)* strife, fray, combat, struggle, contest, skirmish, conflict, fight, war, flight, warfare, action, campaign, strive against.
(ANT.) truce, concord, agreement, settlement, harmony, accept, concur, peace.

bauble *(SYN.)* plaything, toy, trinket.

bawd *(SYN.)* procuress, prostitute.

bawdy *(SYN.)* vulgar, smutty, filthy, dirty, obscene, pornographic.

bawl *(SYN.)* sob, shout, wail, cry loudly, bellow, weep, cry.

bawl out *(SYN.)* scold, upbraid, censure, reprove, reprimand.

bay *(SYN.)* inlet, bayou, harbor, lagoon, cove, sound, gulf.

bazaar *(SYN.)* fair, market, marketplace.

beach *(SYN.)* sands, seashore, seaside, strand, coast, shore.

beacon *(SYN.)* light, signal, watchtower, guide, flare, warning, alarm.

bead *(SYN.)* globule, drop, pill, blob.

beak *(SYN.)* nose, bill, proboscis.

beam *(SYN.)* gleam, ray, girder, cross member, pencil, shine, glisten, smile, glitter, gleam.

beaming *(SYN.)* joyful, bright, happy, radiant, grinning.
(ANT.) sullen, gloomy, threatening, scowling.

bear *(SYN.)* carry, support, take, uphold, suffer, convey, allow, stand, yield, endure, tolerate, produce, sustain, brook, transport, undergo, spawn, permit, suffer, abide, tolerate.
(ANT.) evade, shun, avoid, refuse, dodge.

bearable *(SYN.)* sufferable, supportable, manageable, tolerable.
(ANT.) terrible, painful, unbearable, awful, intolerable.

bearing *(SYN.)* course, direction, position, posture, behavior, manner, carriage, relation, reference, connection, application, deportment, air, way, conduct.

hearings *(SYN.)* orientation, whereabouts, location, direction, position, reading, course.

bear on *(SYN.)* affect, relate to.

bear out *(SYN.)* confirm, substantiate, justify, verify, prove.

bear up *(SYN.)* carry on, endure.

bear with *(SYN.)* tolerate, forbear.

beast *(SYN.)* monster, savage, brute, creature, animal.

beastly *(SYN.)* detestable, mean, low, hateful, loathsome, nasty, unpleasant, despicable, obnoxious, brutal, brutish, offensive.
(ANT.) considerate, sympathetic, refined, humane, fine, pleasant, great.

beat *(SYN.)* pulse, buffet, pound, defeat, palpitate, hit, thump, belabor, knock, overthrow, thrash, pummel, rout, smite, throb, punch, subdue, pulsate, dash, strike, overpower, vanquish, conquer, batter, conquer.
(ANT.) stroke, fail, defend, surrender, shield.

beaten *(SYN.)* disheartened, dejected, licked, discouraged, hopeless, downcast, enervated, down, depressed.
(ANT.) eager, hopeful, cheerful.

beatific *(SYN.)* uplifted, blissful, blessed, elated, happy, wonderful, joyful, divine.
(ANT.) awful, hellish, ill-fated, accursed.

beating *(SYN.)* caning, whipping, drubbing, flogging, lashing, scourging, walloping.

beau *(SYN.)* lover, suitor, swain, admirer.

beautiful *(SYN.)* pretty, fair, beauteous, lovely, charming, fine, comely, handsome, elegant, attractive.
(ANT.) repulsive, hideous, unsightly, foul, homely, plainness, unattractive, ugly, ugliness.

beauty *(SYN.)* handsomeness, fairness, charm, pulchritude, attractiveness, loveliness, comeliness, grace, allegiance.
(ANT.) ugliness, disfigurement, homeliness, plainness, deformity, eyesore.

becalm *(SYN.)* calm, quiet, smooth, still, hush, repose, settle.

because *(SYN.)* inasmuch as, as, since, for.

because of *(SYN.)* as a result of, as a consequence of.

beckon *(SYN.)* call, signal, summon, motion, gesture.

becloud *(SYN.)* obfuscate, confuse, befog, confound, obscure, muddle, screen.
(ANT.) illuminate, clarify, solve.

become *(SYN.)* change, grow, suit, be appropriate, befit.

becoming *(SYN.)* suitable, meet, befitting, appropriate, fitting, seemly, enhancing, attractive, pleasing, flattering, tasteful, smart, adorning, ornamental.
(ANT.) unsuitable, inappropriate, incongruent, ugly, unattractive, improper.

bed *(SYN.)* layer, cot, vein, berth, stratum, couch, accu-

mulation, bunk, deposit, cradle.

bedazzle *(SYN.)* glare, blind, dumbfound, flabbergast, stun, bewilder, furbish, festoon.

bedeck *(SYN.)* deck, adorn, beautify, smarten, festoon, garnish.

bedevil *(SYN.)* worry, fret, irk, torment, harass, pester, nettle, tease, vex, plague.
(ANT.) soothe, calm, delight, please.

bedlam *(SYN.)* tumult, uproar, madhouse, commotion, confusion, racket, rumpus, pandemonium.
(ANT.) calm, peace.

bedraggled *(SYN.)* shabby, sodden, messy, sloppy.
(ANT.) dry, neat, clean, well-groomed.

bedrock *(SYN.)* basis, foundation, roots, basics, essentials, fundamentals, bottom, bed, substratum, core.
(ANT.) top, dome, apex.

bedroom *(SYN.)* chamber, bedchamber.

beef *(SYN.)* brawn, strength, heft, gripe, sinew, fitness, huskiness, might.

beef up *(SYN.)* reinforce, vitalize, buttress, strengthen.
(ANT.) weaken, enervate, drain.

beefy *(SYN.)* solid, strong, muscular, heavy, stocky.

befall *(SYN.)* occur, come about, happen.

before *(SYN.)* prior, earlier, in advance, formerly.
(ANT.) behind, following, afterward, latterly, after.

befriend (SYN.) welcome, encourage, aid, stand by.
(ANT.) dislike, desert, avoid.

befuddle (SYN.) stupefy, addle, confuse, rattle, disorient.

beg (SYN.) solicit, ask, implore, supplicate, entreat, adjure, petition, beseech, pray, crave, request, entreat, implore.
(ANT.) grunt, cede, give, bestow, favor.

beget (SYN.) sire, engender, produce, create, propagate, originate, breed, generate, procreate, father.
(ANT.) murder, destroy, kill, abort, prevent, extinguish.

beggar (SYN.) scrub, tatterdemalion, pauper, wretch, ragamuffin, vagabond, starveling.

begin (SYN.) open, enter, arise, initiate, commence, start, inaugurate, originate, institute, create.
(ANT.) terminate, complete, finish, close, end, stop.

beginner (SYN.) nonprofessional, amateur, apprentice.
(ANT.) veteran, professional.

beginning (SYN.) outset, inception, origin, source, commencement, start, opening, emergence, inauguration.
(ANT.) termination, completion, end, close, consummation, closing, ending, finish.

begrime (SYN.) soil, dirty, smear, muddy, tarnish.
(ANT.) wash, clean, freshen, launder.

begrudge (SYN.) resent, envy, stint, withhold, grudge.

begrudging (SYN.) hesitant, reluctant, resentful, unwilling, forced, loath.
(ANT.) willing, eager, quick, spontaneous.

beguiling (SYN.) enchanting, interesting, delightful, intriguing, engaging, bewitching, attractive, enthralling, captivating.
(ANT.) boring, dull, unattractive, tedious.

behalf (SYN.) benefit, welfare, support, aid, part, interest.

behave (SYN.) deport, comport, manage, act, demean, bear, interact, operate, conduct.
(ANT.) rebel, misbehave.

behavior (SYN.) manners, carriage, disposition, action, deed, bearing, deportment, conduct, demeanor.
(ANT.) rebelliousness, misbehavior.

behest (SYN.) order, command, decree, mandate, bidding.

behind (SYN.) after, backward, at the back, in back of.
(ANT.) ahead, before.

behold (SYN.) look, see, view, observe, perceive, sight.
(ANT.) overlook, ignore.

being (SYN.) life, existing, existence, living, actuality, organism, individual.
(ANT.) death, expiration.

belabor (SYN.) repeat, reiterate, pound, explain, expatiate, din.

belated (SYN.) late, delayed, overdue, tardy.
(ANT.) well-timed, early.

belch (SYN.) emit, erupt, gush, disgorge, eructation, burp.

beleaguered (SYN.) bothered,

beset, annoyed, harassed, badgered, vexed, victimized.

belie (SYN.) distort, misrepresent, twist, disappoint.

belief (SYN.) trust, feeling, certitude, opinion, conviction, persuasion, credence, confidence, reliance, faith, view, creed, assurance.

(ANT.) heresy, denial, incredulity, distrust, skepticism, doubt.

believe (SYN.) hold, apprehend, fancy, support, accept, conceive, suppose, imagine, trust, credit.

(ANT.) doubt, reject, distrust, disbelieve, question.

believer (SYN.) adherent, follower, devotee, convert, zealot.

(ANT.) doubter, critic, skeptic.

belittle (SYN.) underrate, depreciate, minimize, decry, disparage, diminish, demean, slight, discredit, aggressive, militant, humiliate.

(ANT.) esteem, admire, flatter, overrate, commend.

belligerent (SYN.) aggressive, warlike, hostile, offensive, combative, militant.

(ANT.) easygoing, compromising, peaceful.

bellow (SYN.) thunder, roar, scream, shout, yell, howl.

bellwether (SYN.) leader, pilot, guide, ringleader, boss.

belly (SYN.) stomach, abdomen, paunch.

belonging (SYN.) community, loyalty, relationship, kinship, acceptance, rapport.

below (SYN.) under, less, beneath, underneath, lower.

(ANT.) aloft, overhead, above, over.

bemoan (SYN.) mourn, lament, grieve, sorrow, regret.

bend (SYN.) turn, curve, incline, submit, bow, lean, twist, yield, stoop, agree, suppress, oppress, mold, kneel, deflect, subdue, influence.

(ANT.) resist, straighten, break, stiffen.

beneath (SYN.) under, below.

(ANT.) above, over.

benediction (SYN.) thanks, blessing, prayer.

beneficial (SYN.) salutary, good, wholesome, advantageous, useful, helpful, serviceable, profitable.

(ANT.) harmful, destructive, injurious, detrimental.

benefit (SYN.) support, help, gain, avail, profit, account, favor, aid, good, advantage, serve, interest, behalf, service.

(ANT.) handicap, calamity, trouble, disadvantage, distress.

benevolence (SYN.) magnanimity, charity, tenderness, altruism, humanity, philanthropy, generosity, liberality, beneficence, good will, kindness.

(ANT.) malevolence, unkindness, cruelty, inhumanity.

benevolent (SYN.) kindhearted, tender, merciful, generous, altruistic, obliging, kind, good, well-wishing, philanthropy, liberal, unselfish, kindly, disposed, openhearted, humane, benign, friendly.

(ANT.) malevolent, greedy, wicked, harsh.

bent *(SYN.)* curved, crooked, resolved, determined, set, inclined, firm, decided.

(ANT.) straight.

berate *(SYN.)* scold.

beseech *(SYN.)* appeal, entreat, plead, ask, beg, implore.

beset *(SYN.)* surround, attack.

besides *(SYN.)* moreover, further, except for, in addition, also, as well, furthermore.

besiege *(SYN.)* assault, attack, siege, bombard, raid, charge.

bespeak *(SYN.)* engage, reserve, indicate, show, signify, express.

best *(SYN.)* choice, prime, select.

(ANT.) worst.

bestial *(SYN.)* brutal, beastly, savage, cruel.

bestow *(SYN.)* confer, place, put, award, give, present.

(ANT.) withdraw, withhold.

bet *(SYN.)* gamble, give, stake, wager, pledge, ante.

betray *(SYN.)* reveal, expose, mislead, trick, deceive, exhibit, show.

(ANT.) shelter, protect, safeguard.

betrothal *(SYN.)* marriage, engagement, contract.

better *(SYN.)* superior, preferable, improve.

(ANT.) worsen.

between *(SYN.)* among, betwixt.

beware *(SYN.)* take care, watch out, look sharp, be careful.

bewilder *(SYN.)* perplex, confuse, mystify, baffle, puzzle,

overwhelm.

(ANT.) clarify, enlighten.

beyond *(SYN.)* past, farther, exceeding.

bias *(SYN.)* slant, inclination, proneness, turn, bent, penchant, tendency, disposition, propensity, partiality, predisposition, leaning, proclivity, prejudice, bend, influence, slanting, predilection.

(ANT.) fairness, justice, evenhandedness, equity, impartiality.

bible *(SYN.)* guide, handbook, gospel, manual, sourcebook.

bibulous *(SYN.)* guzzling, intemperate, wine-bibbing, sottish, alcoholic.

(ANT.) sober, moderate.

bicker *(SYN.)* dispute, argue, wrangle, quarrel.

(ANT.) go along with, agree.

bid *(SYN.)* order, command, direct, wish, greet, say, offer, instruct, invite, purpose, tender, proposal.

bidding *(SYN.)* behest, request, decree, call, charge, beck, summons, solicitation, invitation, instruction, mandate.

big *(SYN.)* large, huge, bulky, immense, colossal, majestic, august, monstrous, hulking, gigantic, massive, great, enormous, tremendous, outgoing, important, considerable, generous, grand.

(ANT.) small, little, tiny, immature, petite.

big-hearted *(SYN.)* goodnatured, liberal, generous, unselfish, unstinting, charitablc, magnanimous.

(ANT.) cold, selfish, mean, uncharitable.

bigotry *(SYN.)* bias, blindness, intolerance, unfairness, prejudice, ignorance, mindlessness, passion, sectarianism.

(ANT.) acceptance, open-mindedness.

bile *(SYN.)* spleen, rancor, anger, bitterness, peevishness, ill-humor, nastiness, resentment, discontent, irascibility.

(ANT.) cheerfulness, affability, pleasantness.

bilge *(SYN.)* hogwash, drivel, gibberish, rubbish, bosh, foolishness, twaddle.

bilious *(SYN.)* petulant, crabby, ill-natured, cross, peevish, crotchety, cranky.

(ANT.) happy, agreeable, pleasant, good- natured.

bilk *(SYN.)* defraud, trick, cheat, hoodwink, deceive, fleece, rook, bamboozle.

bill *(SYN.)* charge, invoice, account, statement.

billet *(SYN.)* housing, quarters, berth, shelter, barrack, installation.

billow *(SYN.)* surge, swell, rise, rush, peaking, magnification, amplification, augmentation, increase, intensification.

(ANT.) lowering, decrease.

bind *(SYN.)* connect, restrain, band, fasten, oblige, obligate, engage, wrap, connect, weld, attach, tie, require, restrict.

(ANT.) unlace, loose, unfasten, untie, free.

binding *(SYN.)* compulsory, obligatory, mandatory, compelling, unalterable, imperative, indissoluble, unconditional, unchangeable.

(ANT.) adjustable, flexible, elastic, changeable.

binge *(SYN.)* fling, spree, carousal, toot.

birth *(SYN.)* origin, beginning, infancy, inception.

(ANT.) finish, decline, death, disappearance, end.

biscuit *(SYN.)* bun, roll, cake, muffin, bread, rusk.

bit *(SYN.)* fraction, portion, scrap, fragment, particle, drop, speck, harness, small amount, restraint, morsel, sum.

bite *(SYN.)* chew, nip, sting, pierce, snack, morsel.

biting *(SYN.)* cutting, sharp, acid, sneering, sarcastic.

(ANT.) soothing, kind, gentle, agreeable.

bitter *(SYN.)* distasteful, sour, acrid, pungent, piercing, vicious, severe, biting, distressful, stinging, distressing, ruthless, hated, hostile, grievous, harsh, painful, tart.

(ANT.) sweet, mellow, pleasant, delicious.

bizarre *(SYN.)* odd, peculiar, strange, uncommon, unusual.

(ANT.) usual, everyday, ordinary, inconspicuous.

black *(SYN.)* sooty, dark, ebony, inky, soiled, filthy, dirty, stained, somber, depressing, sad, dismal, gloomy.

(ANT.) white, clean, pristine, glowing, pure, cheerful, light-

skinned, sunny, bright.

blackball (SYN.) turn down, ban, blacklist, exclude, snub, reject, debar.

(ANT.) accept, include, invite, ask, bid.

blacken (SYN.) tar, ink, black, darken, besoot, smudge, begrime, discredit, defile, dull, dim, tarnish, ebonize, denounce, sully, libel, blemish, defame.

(ANT.) exalt, honor, whiten, brighten, shine, bleach.

blackmail (SYN.) bribe, payment, bribery, extortion, shakedown, coercion.

blackout (SYN.) faint, coma, unconsciousness, oblivion, amnesia, stupor.

bladder (SYN.) saccule, sac, vesicle, pouch, pod, cell, blister, container, cyst.

blade (SYN.) cutter, lancet, knife, sword.

blah (SYN.) lifeless, flat, jejune, lukewarm, stale, insipid, tasteless, pedestrian, tedious, dreary, uninteresting.

(ANT.) spirited, fascinating, vibrant, vigorous.

blame (SYN.) upbraid, criticize, fault, guilt, accuse, rebuke, charge, implicate, impeach, condemn, indict, responsibility, censure, denounce.

(ANT.) exonerate, credit, honor, absolve.

blameless (SYN.) moral, innocent, worthy, faultless.

(ANT.) blameworthy, culpable, guilty.

blanch (SYN.) whiten, bleach,

decolorize, peroxide, fade, wash out, dim, dull.

bland (SYN.) soft, smooth, gentle, agreeable, vapid, insipid, mild, polite.

(ANT.) harsh, outspoken, disagreeable.

blandish (SYN.) praise, compliment, overpraise, cajole, puff, adulate, salve, fawn, court, toady, butter up, please, jolly.

(ANT.) insult, criticize, belittle.

blank (SYN.) unmarked, expressionless, uninterested, area, void, vacant, empty.

(ANT.) marked, filled, alert, animated.

blanket (SYN.) quilt, coverlet, cover, comforter, robe, padding, carpet, wrapper, mantle, envelope, housing, coat, comprehensive, universal, across-the-board, omnibus.

(ANT.) limited, detailed, restricted, precise.

blare (SYN.) roar, blast, resound, jar, scream, swell, clang, peal, trumpet, hoot.

blasphemy (SYN.) profanation, impiousness, cursing, irreverence, sacrilege, abuse, ecration, swearing, contempt.

(ANT.) respect, piety, reverence, devotion.

blast (SYN.) burst, explosion, discharge.

blasted (SYN.) blighted, withered, ravaged, decomposed, spoiled, destroyed.

blastoff (SYN.) launching, expulsion, launch, shot, projection.

blatant (SYN.) shameless, noto-

blaze (SYN.) inferno, shine, flare, marking, fire, outburst, holocaust, notch, flame.

(ANT.) die, dwindle.

bleach (SYN.) pale, whiten, blanch, whitener.

(ANT.) darken, blacken.

bleak (SYN.) dreary, barren, cheerless, depressing, gloomy, windswept, bare, cold, dismal, desolate, raw, chilly.

(ANT.) lush, hopeful, promising, cheerful.

bleary (SYN.) hazy, groggy, blurry, fuzzy, misty, clouded, overcast, dim, blear.

(ANT.) clear, vivid, precise, clear-cut.

blemish (SYN.) injury, speck, flaw, marking, scar, disgrace, imperfection, stain, fault, blot.

(ANT.) purity, embellishment, adornment, perfection.

blend (SYN.) beat, intermingle, combine, fuse, unify, consolidate, unite, amalgamate, conjoin, mix, coalesce, intermix, join, merge, compound, combination, stir, mixture.

(ANT.) separate, decompose, analyze, disintegrate.

bless (SYN.) thank, celebrate, extol, glorify, adore, delight, praise, gladden, exalt.

(ANT.) denounce, blaspheme, slander, curse.

blessed (SYN.) sacred, holy, consecrated, dedicated, hallowed, sacrosanct, beatified, joyful, delighted, joyous, sainted, canonized, blissful.

(ANT.) miserable, sad, dispirited, cheerless.

blight (SYN.) decay, disease, spoil, sickness, wither, ruin, damage, harm, decaying, epidemic, affliction, destroy.

blind (SYN.) sightless, unmindful, rash, visionless, ignorant, unsighted, unconscious, discerning, heedless, oblivious, purblind, unknowing, screen, unaware, thoughtless, shade, unthinking, cover, curtain, without thought, headlong.

(ANT.) discerning, sensible, calculated, perceiving, perceptive, aware.

blink (SYN.) bat, glance, flicker, wink, twinkle.

bliss (SYN.) ecstasy, rapture, glee, elation, joy, blessedness, gladness, happiness, delight, felicity, blissfulness.

(ANT.) woe, sadness, sorrow, grief, unhappiness, torment, wretchedness, misery.

blissful (SYN.) happy, elated, rapturous, ecstatic, paradisiacal, joyous, enraptured.

blister (SYN.) bleb, swelling, welt, sore, blob, bubble, inflammation, boil, canker.

blithe (SYN.) breezy, merry, airy, lighthearted, light, gay, fanciful, graceful.

(ANT.) morose, grouchy, low-spirited, gloomy.

blitz (SYN.) strike, onslaught, thrust, raid, lunge, drive, incursion, assault, sally.

blizzard (SYN.) storm, snowstorm, snowfall, gale, tempest, blast, blow, swirl.

bloat (SYN.) distend, puff up, inflate, swell.

(ANT.) deflate.

blob (SYN.) bubble, blister, pellet, globule.

block (SYN.) clog, hinder, bar, impede, close, obstruct, barricade, blockade, obstruction, hindrance, obstacle, impediment, retard, check, stop.

(ANT.) forward, promote, aid, clear, advance, advantage, assist, further, open.

blockade (SYN.) barrier, fortification, obstruction, barricade.

bloom (SYN.) thrive, glow, flourish, blossom, flower.

(ANT.) wane, decay, dwindle, shrivel, wither.

blooming (SYN.) flush, green, vigorous, thriving, vital, abloom, healthy, fresh.

(ANT.) flagging, declining, whithering.

blooper (SYN.) muff, fluff, error, bungle, botch, blunder, fumble, howler, indiscretion.

blossom (SYN.) bloom, flower, flourish.

(ANT.) shrink, wither, dwindle, fade.

blot (SYN.) stain, inkblot, spot, inkstain, blemish, dishonor, disgrace, spatter, obliterate, soil, dry.

blot out (SYN.) wipe out, destroy, obliterate, abolish, annihilate, cancel, expunge, strike out, shade, darken, shadow, overshadow, obfuscate, cloud, eclipse.

blow (SYN.) hit, thump, slap, cuff, box, shock, move, drive, spread, breeze, puff, whistle, inflate, enlarge.

blue (SYN.) sapphire, azure, sad, unhappy, depressed, dejected, melancholy.

(ANT.) cheerful, optimistic, happy.

bluff (SYN.) steep, perpendicular, vertical, abrupt, precipitous, rough, open, frank, hearty, blunt, fool, mislead, pretend, deceive, fraud, lie, fake, deceit.

blunder (SYN.) error, flounder, mistake, stumble.

blunt (SYN.) solid, abrupt, rough, dull, pointless, plain, bluff, edgeless, unceremonious, obtuse, rude, outspoken, unsharpened, rounded, worn, crude, direct, impolite, short, curt, gruff.

(ANT.) tactful, polite, subtle, polished, suave, sharp, keen, pointed, diplomatic.

blur (SYN.) sully, dim, obscure, stain, dull, confuse, cloud, smear, stain, smudge.

(ANT.) clear, clarify.

blush (SYN.) redden.

board (SYN.) embark, committee, wood, mount, cabinet, food, get on, lumber.

boast (SYN.) vaunt, flaunt, brag, glory, exaggerate, bragging.

(ANT.) humble, apologize, minimize, deprecate.

body (SYN.) remains, bulk, mass, carcass, form, company, corpus, society, firmness, group, torso, substance, col-

lection, cadaver, trunk, group, throng, company, crowd.
(ANT.) spirit, intellect, soul.

bogus *(SYN.)* counterfeit, false, pretend, fake, phony.
(ANT.) genuine.

boil *(SYN.)* seethe, bubble, pimple, fume, cook, swelling, rage, foam, simmer, smolder.

boisterous *(SYN.)* rough, violent, rowdy, noisy, tumultuous.
(ANT.) serene.

bold *(SYN.)* daring, forward, pushy, striking, brave, dauntless, rude, prominent, adventurous, fearless, insolent, conspicuous, defiant, arrogant, cavalier, brazen, unafraid, intrepid, courageous, valiant, heroic, gallant, disrespectful, impudent, shameless.
(ANT.) modest, bashful, cowardly, timid, retiring, flinching, fearful, timorous, polite, courteous, deferential.

bolt *(SYN.)* break away, fastener, flee, take flight, lock.

bond *(SYN.)* fastener, rope, tie, cord, connection, attachment, link, promise.
(ANT.) sever, separate, untie, disconnect.

bondage *(SYN.)* slavery, thralldom, captivity, imprisonment, servitude, confinement, vassalage, enslavement.
(ANT.) liberation, emancipation, independence, freedom.

bonds *(SYN.)* chains, cuffs, fetters, shackles, irons, bracelets.

bone up *(SYN.)* learn, master, study, relearn.

bonus *(SYN.)* more, extra, premium, gift, reward, bounty.

bony *(SYN.)* lean, lank, thin, lanky, raw boned, fleshless, skinny, gangling, weight.
(ANT.) plump, fleshy, stout.

boom *(SYN.)* advance, grow, flourish, progress, gain, increase, roar, beam, rumble, reverberate, thunder, prosper, swell, thrive, pole, rush.
(ANT.) decline, fail, recession.

booming *(SYN.)* flourishing, blooming, thriving, vigorous, prospering, exuberant.
(ANT.) waning, dying, failing, declining,

boon *(SYN.)* gift, jolly, blessing, pleasant, godsend, windfall.

boorish *(SYN.)* coarse, churlish, uncivil, ill-mannered, ill-bred, uncivilized, crude, uncouth.
(ANT.) polite, genteel cultivated, well- mannered.

boost *(SYN.)* push, lift, help, hoist, shove.
(ANT.) depress, lower, belittle, submerge, disparage, decrease, decline, reduction, downturn.

booster *(SYN.)* supporter, fan, rooter, plugger, follower.

boot *(SYN.)* shoe, kick.

booth *(SYN.)* enclosure, cubicle, stand, compartment, box.

booze *(SYN.)* spirits, drink, liquor, alcohol.

border *(SYN.)* fringe, rim, verge, boundary, edge, termination, brink, limit, brim, outskirts, frontier, margin.
(ANT.) interior, center, mainland, core, middle.

borderline *(SYN.)* unclassifiable, indeterminate, halfway, obscure, inexact, indefinite, unclear.
(ANT.) precise, absolute, definite.

bore *(SYN.)* tire, weary, hole, perforate, pierce, drill.
(ANT.) arouse, captivate, excite, interest.

boredom *(SYN.)* ennui, doldrums, weariness, dullness, tedium.
(ANT.) stimulation, motive, activity, stimulus, excitement.

boring *(SYN.)* monotonous, dull, dead, flat, tedious, wearisome, trite, prosaic, humdrum.

born *(SYN.)* hatched, produced.

borrow *(SYN.)* copy, adopt, simulate, mirror, assume, usurp, plagiarize, take.
(ANT.) allow, advance, invent, originate, credit, lend.

bossy *(SYN.)* overbearing, arrogant, domineering, lordly, tyrannical, highhanded, arbitrary, oppress.
(ANT.) flexible, easy-going, cooperative.

botch *(SYN.)* blunder, bungle, fumble, goof, muff, mishandle, mismanage.
(ANT.) perform, realize.

bother *(SYN.)* haunt, molest, trouble, annoy, upset, fleeting, transient, harass, inconvenience, momentary, disturb, passing, pester, tease, irritate, worry, vex.
(ANT.) prolonged, extended, long, protracted, lengthy,

comfort, solace.

bothersome *(SYN.)* irritating, vexatious, worrisome, annoying, distressing, troublesome, disturbing.

bottle *(SYN.)* container, flask, vessel, decanter, vial, ewer, jar.

bottleneck *(SYN.)* obstacle, obstruction, barrier, block, blockage, detour.

bottom *(SYN.)* basis, fundament, base, groundwork, foot, depths, lowest part, underside, foundation, seat, buttocks, rear, behind.
(ANT.) top, peak, apex, summit, topside.

bough *(SYN.)* branch, arm, limb.

bounce *(SYN.)* recoil, ricochet, rebound.

bound *(SYN.)* spring, vault, hop, leap, start, surrounded, jump, limit, jerk, boundary, bounce, skip, tied, shackled, trussed, fettered, certain, sure, destined, compelled, required.
(ANT.) unfettered, free.

boundary *(SYN.)* bound, limit, border, margin, outline, circumference, perimeter, division, frontier, edge.

boundless *(SYN.)* limitless, endless, inexhaustible, unlimited, eternal, infinite.
(ANT.) restricted, narrow, limited.

bounteous *(SYN.)* plentiful, generous, liberal, abundant.
(ANT.) scarce.

bountiful *(SYN.)* bounteous, fertile, plentiful, generous, abundant.

(ANT.) sparing, infertile, scarce.

bounty *(SYN.)* generosity, gift, award, bonus, reward, prize, premium.

bourgeois *(SYN.)* common, ordinary, commonplace, middle-class, conventional.

(ANT.) upper-class, unconventional, loose, aristocratic.

bout *(SYN.)* round, contest, conflict, test, struggle, match, spell, fight.

bow *(SYN.)* bend, yield, kneel, submit, stoop.

bowels *(SYN.)* entrails, intestines, innards, guts, stomach.

box *(SYN.)* hit, fight, crate, case, container.

boy *(SYN.)* male, youngster, lad, kid, fellow, buddy, youth.

(ANT.) girl, man.

boycott *(SYN.)* picket, strike, ban, revolt, blackball.

boy friend *(SYN.)* date, young man, sweetheart, courtier, beau.

brace *(SYN.)* strengthen, tie, prop, support, tighten, stay, strut, bind, truss, crutch.

bracelet *(SYN.)* armband, bangle, circlet.

bracing *(SYN.)* stimulating, refreshing, restorative, fortifying, invigorating.

bracket *(SYN.)* join, couple, enclose, relate, brace, support.

brag *(SYN.)* boast, flaunt, vaunt, bluster, swagger.

(ANT.) demean, debase, denigrate, degrade, depreciate, deprecate.

braid *(SYN.)* weave, twine, wreath, plait.

brain *(SYN.)* sense, intelligence, intellect, common sense, understanding, reason.

(ANT.) stupid, stupidity.

brake *(SYN.)* decelerate, stop, curb.

(ANT.) accelerate.

branch *(SYN.)* shoot, limb, bough, tributary, offshoot, part, division, expand, department, divide, spread, subdivision.

brand *(SYN.)* make, trademark, label, kind, burn, trade name, mark, stamp, blaze.

brave *(SYN.)* bold, daring, gallant, valorous, adventurous, heroic, magnanimous, chivalrous, audacious, valiant, courageous, fearless, intrepid, unafraid.

(ANT.) weak, cringing, timid, cowardly, fearful, craven.

brawl *(SYN.)* racket, quarrel, fracas, riot, fight, melee, fray, disturbance, dispute, disagreement.

brawn *(SYN.)* strength, muscle.

(ANT.) weakness.

brazen *(SYN.)* immodest, forward, shameless, bold, brassy, impudent, insolent, rude.

(ANT.) retiring, self-effacing, modest, shy.

breach *(SYN.)* rupture, fracture, rift, break, crack, gap, opening, breaking, quarrel, violation.

(ANT.) observation.

break *(SYN.)* demolish, pound, rack, smash, burst, rupture, disobey, violate, crack,

infringe, crush, squeeze, transgress, fracture, shatter, wreck, crash, atomize, disintegrate, collapse, splinter, crack, gap, breach, opening, rupture.
(ANT.) restore, heal, join, renovate, mend, repair.

breed (SYN.) engender, bear, propagate, father, beget, rear, conceive, train, generate, raise, procreate, nurture, create, mother, produce, originate, generate, raise, nurture.
(ANT.) murder, abort, kill.

breeze (SYN.) air, wind, zephyr, breath.
(ANT.) culm.

brevity (SYN.) briefness, conciseness.
(ANT.) length.

brew (SYN.) plot, plan, cook, ferment, prepare, scheme.

bribe (SYN.) buy off.

bridle (SYN.) control, hold, restrain, check, harness, curb, restraint, halter.
(ANT.) release, free, loose.

brief (SYN.) curt, short, fleeting, passing, compendious, terse, laconic, succinct, momentary, transient, temporary, concise, compact, condensed.
(ANT.) long, extended, prolonged, lengthy, protracted, comprehensive, extensive, exhaustive.

brigand (SYN.) bandit, robber, thief.

bright (SYN.) luminous, gleaming, clever, witty, brilliant, lucid, vivid, clear, smart, intelligent, lustrous, clever,

shining, shiny, sparkling, shimmering, radiant, cheerful, lively, gay, happy, lighthearted, keen, promising, favorable, encouraging.
(ANT.) sullen, dull, murky, dark, gloomy, dim, lusterless, boring, colorless, stupid, backward, slow.

brilliant (SYN.) bright, clear, smart, intelligent, sparkling, shining, alert, vivid, splendid, radiant, glittering, talented, ingenious, gifted.
(ANT.) mediocre, dull, lusterless.

brim (SYN.) border, margin, lip, rim, edge.
(ANT.) middle, center.

bring (SYN.) fetch, take, carry, raise, introduce, propose.
(ANT.) remove, withdraw.

brink (SYN.) limit, verge, rim, margin, edge.

brisk (SYN.) fresh, breezy, cool, lively, spry, refreshing, spirited, jolly, energetic, quick, active, animated, nimble, agile, sharp, keen, stimulating, invigorating.
(ANT.) musty, faded, stagnant, decayed, hackneyed, slow, lethargic, sluggish, still, dull, oppressive.

briskness (SYN.) energy, exercise, motion, rapidity, agility, action, quickness, activity, vigor, liveliness, movement.
(ANT.) inertia, idleness, sloth, dullness, inactivity.

bristle (SYN.) flare up, anger, rage, seethe, get mad.

brittle (SYN.) crumbling, frail,

breakable, delicate, splintery, crisp, fragile, weak.

(ANT.) *tough, enduring, unbreakable, thick, strong, sturdy, flexible, supple.*

broach (SYN.) set afoot, introduce, inaugurate, start, mention, launch, advance.

broad (SYN.) large, wide, tolerant, expanded, vast, liberal, sweeping, roomy, expansive, extended, general, extensive, full.

(ANT.) *restricted, confined, narrow, constricted, slim, tight, limited, negligible.*

broadcast (SYN.) distribute, announce, publish, scatter, circulate, spread, send, transmit, relay.

broaden (SYN.) spread, widen, amplify, enlarge, extend, increase, add to, expand, stretch, deepen, magnify.

(ANT.) *tighted, narrow, constrict, straiten.*

broad-minded (SYN.) unprejudiced, tolerant, liberal, unbigoted.

(ANT.) *prejudiced, petty, narrow-minded.*

brochure (SYN.) booklet, pamphlet, leaflet, mailing, circular, tract, flier.

broil (SYN.) cook, burn, heat, roast, bake, scorch, fire, grill, singe, sear, toast.

broken (SYN.) flattened, rent, shattered, wrecked, destroyed, reduced, smashed, crushed, fractured, ruptured, interrupted, burst, separated.

(ANT.) *whole, integral, united,* repaired.

bromide (SYN.) banality, platitude, stereotype, commonplace, slogan.

brood (SYN.) study, consider, ponder, reflect, contemplate, meditate, young, litter, offspring, think, deliberate.

brook (SYN.) rivulet, run, branch, stream, creek.

brother (SYN.) comrade, man, kinsman, sibling.

(ANT.) *sister.*

brotherhood (SYN.) kinship, kindness, fraternity, fellowship, clan, society, brotherliness, bond, association, relationship, solidarity.

(ANT.) *strife, discord, acrimony, opposition.*

brow (SYN.) forehead, eyebrow.

browbeat (SYN.) bully, domineer, bulldoze, intimidate, henpeck, oppress, grind.

browse (SYN.) look, skim, scan, graze, read, feed.

bruise (SYN.) hurt, injure, wound, damage, abrasion, injury, contusion, harm.

brunt (SYN.) force, impact, shock, strain, oppression, severity.

brush (SYN.) rub, wipe, clean, bushes, remove, broom, whisk, paintbrush, hairbrush, underbrush, thicket.

brusque (SYN.) sudden, curt, hasty, blunt, rough, steep, precipitate, rugged, craggy, gruff, surly, abrupt, short, bluff.

(ANT.) *smooth, anticipated, courteous, expected, gradual, personable.*

brutal *(SYN.)* brute, cruel, inhuman, rude, barbarous, gross, sensual, ferocious, brutish, coarse, bestial, carnal, remorseless, ruthless, savage, mean, pitiless, barbaric.

(ANT.) kind, courteous, humane, civilized, gentle, kindhearted, mild.

brute *(SYN.)* monster, barbarian, beast, animal, wild, savage.

buckle *(SYN.)* hook, fastening, fastener, bend, wrinkle, clip, clasp, distort, catch, strap, fasten, collapse, yield, warp.

bud *(SYN.)* develop, sprout.

buddy *(SYN.)* companion, comrade, friend, partner, pal.

budge *(SYN.)* stir, move.

budget *(SYN.)* schedule, ration.

buff *(SYN.)* shine, polish, burnish, rub, wax.

buffoon *(SYN.)* jester, fool, clown, jokester, zany, comedian, chump, boor, dolt.

bug *(SYN.)* fault, hitch, defect, catch, snag, failing, rub, flaw, snarl, weakness, annoy, pester, hector, vex, nag, nettle.

bugbear *(SYN.)* bogy, specter, demon, devil, fiend.

build *(SYN.)* found, rear, establish, constructed, raise, set up, erect, assemble.

(ANT.) raze, destroy, overthrow, demolish, undermine.

buildup *(SYN.)* gain, enlargement, increase, praise, commendation, promotion, jump, expansion, uptrend, testimonial, plug, puff, blurb, endorsement, compliment.

(ANT.) reduction, decrease, decline.

bulge *(SYN.)* lump, protuberance, bump, swelling, protrusion, extend, protrude.

(ANT.) hollow, shrink, contract, depression.

bulk *(SYN.)* lump, magnitude, volume, mass, most, majority.

bulky *(SYN.)* great, big, huge, large, enormous, massive, immense, monstrous, clumsy, cumbersome, unwieldy.

(ANT.) tiny, little, small, petite, handy, delicate.

bulletin *(SYN.)* news, flash, message, statement, newsletter.

bullheaded *(SYN.)* dogged, stubborn, mulish, rigid.

(ANT.) flexible, submissive, compliant

bully *(SYN.)* pester, tease, intimidate, harass, domineer.

bulwark *(SYN.)* wall, bastion, abutment, bank, dam, rampart, shoulder, parapet, backing, maintainer, embankment, safeguard, reinforcement, sustainer.

bum *(SYN.)* idler, loafer, drifter, hobo, wretch, beggar, vagrant.

bumbling *(SYN.)* bungling, inept, blundering, clumsy, incompetent, awkward, maladroit, ungainly.

(ANT.) facile, handy, dexterous, proficient.

bump *(SYN.)* shake, push, hit, shove, prod, collide, knock, bang.

bumpy *(SYN.)* uneven, jolting, rough, jarring, rocky, coarse.

(ANT.) flat, smooth, flush, polished, level.

bunch *(SYN.)* batch, bundle, cluster, company, collection.

bundle *(SYN.)* package, mass, collection, batch, parcel, packet, box.

bungle *(SYN.)* tumble, botch, foul up, boggle, mess up, blunder.

bunk *(SYN.)* berth, rubbish, nonsense, couch, bed, cot.

buoyant *(SYN.)* light, jolly, spirited, effervescent, blithe, lively, resilient, vivacious, afloat, floating, cheery.

(ANT.) hopeless, dejected, sullen, depressed, despondent, pessimistic, downcast, glum.

burden *(SYN.)* oppress, afflict, trouble, encumber, tax, weight, load, worry, contents, trial, lade.

(ANT.) lighten, alleviate, ease, mitigate, console, disburden.

burdensome *(SYN.)* arduous, cumbersome, bothersome, oppressive, irksome, trying, hard, difficult.

bureau *(SYN.)* office, division, department, unit, commission, board, chest, dresser.

bureaucrat *(SYN.)* clerk, official, functionary, servant, politician.

burglar *(SYN.)* thief, robber.

burial *(SYN.)* interment, funeral.

burly *(SYN.)* husky, beefy, heavy-set, brawny, strapping.

(ANT.) skinny, scrawny.

burn *(SYN.)* scorch, blaze, scald, sear, char, incinerate, fire, flare, combust, flame, consume.

(ANT.) quench, extinguish.

burnish *(SYN.)* polish, shine, buff, wax, rub.

burrow *(SYN.)* tunnel, search, seek, dig, excavate, hunt, den, hole.

burst *(SYN.)* exploded, broken, erupt.

bury *(SYN.)* hide, inhume, conceal, immure, cover, entomb, secrete.

(ANT.) reveal, display, open, raise, disinter.

business *(SYN.)* employment, profession, trade, work, art, engagement, vocation, occupation, company, concern, firm, partnership, corporation.

(ANT.) hobby, avocation, pastime.

bustle *(SYN.)* noise, flurry, action, trouble, fuss, stir, excitement.

(ANT.) calmness, composure, serenity, peacefulness.

busy *(SYN.)* careful, industrious, active, patient, assiduous, diligent, perseverant, hardworking, occupied, engaged, employed.

(ANT.) unconcerned, indifferent, apathetic, lethargic, careless, inactive, unemployed, lazy, indolent.

busybody *(SYN.)* gossip, tattletale, pry, meddler, snoop.

but *(SYN.)* nevertheless, yet, however, though, although, still.

button *(SYN.)* clasp, close, fasten, hook.

buttress (SYN.) support, brace, stay, frame, prop, reinforcement, bulwark, backing, encourage, sustain, reassure, boost, bolster.

buxom (SYN.) well-developed, chesty, ample, fleshy, full-figured.

buy (SYN.) procure, get, purchase, acquire, obtain.
(ANT.) vend, sell.

buzz (SYN.) whir, hum, thrum, drone, burr.

by (SYN.) near, through, beside, with, from, at, close to.

bygone (SYN.) bypast, former, earlier, past, older, erstwhile, onetime, forgotten.
(ANT.) immediate, present, current, modern.

bypass (SYN.) deviate from, go around, detour around.

by-product (SYN.) offshoot, spin-off, effect, extra, outgrowth.

bystander (SYN.) passerby, onlooker, watcher, viewer, observer.

byway (SYN.) passage, detour, path.

byword (SYN.) adage, proverb, commonplace, axiom, shibboleth, apothegm, motto, slogan.

C

cab (SYN.) coach, taxi, car, hack, taxicab, carriage.

cabin (SYN.) cottage, shack, shanty, hut, dwelling, house.

cabinet (SYN.) ministry, council, committee, case, cupboard.

cable (SYN.) wire, cord, rope, telegraph.

cache (SYN.) bury, hide, cover, store.

cad (SYN.) knave, rascal, scoundrel, rogue.

cafe (SYN.) coffeehouse

cagey (SYN.) cunning, wary, clever, tricky, cautious, shrewd, evasive.
(ANT.) innocent, straightfoward, guileless, naive.

calamity (SYN.) ruin, disaster, casualty, distress, hardship, trouble, misfortune, bad luck.
(ANT.) blessing, fortune, welfare.

calculate (SYN.) count, compute, figure, estimate, consider, tally, determine, measure, subtract, add, divide, multiply, judge.
(ANT.) guess, miscalculate, assume, conjecture.

calculating (SYN.) crafty, shrewd, scheming, cunning.
(ANT.) simple, guileless, direct, ingenuous.

calculation (SYN.) figuring, reckoning, computation, estimation.
(ANT.) guess, assumption

calendar (SYN.) timetable, schedule, diary.

call (SYN.) designate, name, yell, cry, ask, shout, speak, cry out, call out, exclaim, command, term, label, phone, ring up, collect, waken, awaken, ring, wake, arouse, rouse, outcry, need.

callous (SYN.) insensitive, impenitent, obdurate, unfeeling, indurate, hard, insensible, heartless.

(ANT.) soft, compassionate, tender.

calm *(SYN.)* appease, lull, quiet, soothe, composed, tranquilize, dispassionate, still, imperturbable, peaceful, pacify, alloy, assuage, unruffled, mild, tranquil.

(ANT.) tempestuous, disturbed, emotional, turmoil, incite, inflame, excite, upset, disturb, arouse.

campaign *(SYN.)* movement, cause, crusade.

can *(SYN.)* tin, container.

canal *(SYN.)* gully, duct, waterway.

cancel *(SYN.)* eliminate, obliterate, erase, delete, nullify, repeal, revoke, cross out, expunge, void, recall, set aside, abolish, rescind.

(ANT.) perpetuate, confirm, ratify, enforce, enact.

candid *(SYN.)* free, blunt, frank, plain, open, sincere, honest.

(ANT.) sly, contrived, scheming.

candidate *(SYN.)* applicant, aspirant, nominee.

canine *(SYN.)* pooch, dog, puppy.

canny *(SYN.)* artful, skillful, shrewd, clever, cautious, cunning.

cant *(SYN.)* dissimulation, patois, jargon, shoptalk, deceit, argot.

(ANT.) honesty, frankness, truth.

cantankerous *(SYN.)* crabby, grouchy, irritable, surly, ill-natured, grumpy, irascible.

canyon *(SYN.)* gulch, gully, arroyo, ravine, gorge.

cap *(SYN.)* top, cover, crown, lid.

capability *(SYN.)* aptness, ability, capacity, aptitude, dexterity, power, efficiency, qualification.

(ANT.) incapacity, disability, incompetency.

capable *(SYN.)* clever, qualified, able, efficient, competent, skilled, fit, skillful, accomplished, fitted.

(ANT.) unfitted, incapable, incompetent, inept, inadequate.

capacity *(SYN.)* capability, power, ability, talent, content, skill, volume, size.

(ANT.) inability, stupidity, incapacity, impotence.

cape *(SYN.)* pelisse, cloak, mantle, neck, point, headland, peninsula.

caper *(SYN.)* romp, frisk, cavort, frolic, gambol.

capital *(SYN.)* leading, chief, important, property, wealth, money, city, cash, assets, principal, resources, primary, first, funds.

(ANT.) unimportant, trivial, secondary.

capricious *(SYN.)* undependable, erratic, inconstant, fickle, changeable, irregular, inconsistent.

caption *(SYN.)* heading, title, headline.

captivate *(SYN.)* fascinate, charm, delight.

captive *(SYN.)* convict, prisoner, hostage.

captivity *(SYN.)* detention, imprisonment, custody, confinement, bondage, slavery.

(ANT.) liberty, freedom.

capture *(SYN.)* catch, grip, apprehend, clutch, arrest, snare, seize, nab, seizure, catching, grasp, take prisoner, recovery.

(ANT.) set free, lose, liberate, throw, free, release.

car *(SYN.)* auto, automobile, motorcar, vehicle.

carcass *(SYN.)* remains, frame, corpse, form, bulk, mass, corpus, association, body, cadaver.

(ANT.) mind, spirit, intellect, soul.

cardinal *(SYN.)* chief, primary, important, prime, major, essential.

(ANT.) subordinate, secondary, auxiliary.

care *(SYN.)* concern, anxiety, worry, caution, solicitude, charge, ward, attention, regard, supervision, consider, consideration, keeping, protection, attend, watch, supervise, guardianship.

(ANT.) neglect, disregard, indifference, unconcern, negligence.

career *(SYN.)* occupation, profession, job, calling, vocation, trade.

carefree *(SYN.)* lighthearted, happy, unconcerned, breezy, jolly.

careful *(SYN.)* prudent, thoughtful, attentive, cautious, painstaking, scrupulous, heedful, circumspect, vigilant, guarded, discreet, watchful, wary, concerned, meticulous.

(ANT.) nice, careful, heedless, messy, careless, accurate, sloppy, meticulous.

careless *(SYN.)* imprudent, heedless, unconcerned, inattentive, lax, indiscreet, desultory, reckless.

(ANT.) careful, nice, cautious, painstaking, prudent, accurate.

caress *(SYN.)* hug, fondle, embrace, pet, pat, stroke, kiss, cuddle.

(ANT.) vex, buffet, annoy, tease.

carnage *(SYN.)* massacre, liquidation, slaughter, genocide, butchery, extermination.

carnal *(SYN.)* base, corporeal, animal, lustful, worldly, sensual, bodily, gross, fleshy, voluptuous.

(ANT.) intellectual, spiritual, exalted, temperate.

carnival *(SYN.)* fete, fair, jamboree, festival.

carol *(SYN.)* hymn, song, ballad.

carp *(SYN.)* pick, praise, complain.

carpet *(SYN.)* mat, rug.

carping *(SYN.)* discerning, exact, captions, accurate, important.

(ANT.) superficial, cursory, approving, encouraging, unimportant, insignificant.

carriage *(SYN.)* bearing, conduct, action, deed, behavior, disposition, deportment.

carry *(SYN.)* convey, transport, support, bring, sustain, bear, hold, move, transfer, take.
(ANT.) drop, abandon.

carve *(SYN.)* hew, shape, cut, whittle, chisel, sculpt.

case *(SYN.)* state, covering, receptacle, condition, instance, example, happening, illustration, sample, suit, action, claim, lawsuit, crate, container, carton, box.

cash *(SYN.)* currency, money.

casket *(SYN.)* coffin, box, crate.

cast *(SYN.)* fling, toss, throw, pitch, form, company, shape, sort, mold, hurl, sling, shed, direct, impart, turn, actors, players, type, variety.

caste *(SYN.)* class, grade, order, category, status, elegance, set, rank, station, social standing, denomination, excellence, genre.

castle *(SYN.)* mansion, palace, chateau.

casual *(SYN.)* chance, unexpected, informal, accidental, incidental, offhand, unplanned, relaxed, fortuitous, spontaneous.
(ANT.) planned, expected, calculated, formal, deliberate, dressy, premeditated, pretentious.

casualty *(SYN.)* calamity, fortuity, mishap, loss, injured, dead, wounded, accident, victim.
(ANT.) design, purpose, intention, calculation.

catalog *(SYN.)* classify, group, list, inventory, directory, index.

catastrophe *(SYN.)* mishap, calamity, disaster, adversity, accident.
(ANT.) fortune, boon, triumph, blessing, advantage, welfare.

catch *(SYN.)* hook, snare, entrap, ensnare, capture, grip, apprehend, grasp, take, grab, nab, arrest, contract, snare, seize, apprehension, bolt, pin, clasp, trap.
(ANT.) lose, free, liberate, throw, release.

catching *(SYN.)* contagious, pestilential, communicable, infectious, virulent.
(ANT.) noncommunicable, healthful.

category *(SYN.)* class, caste, kind, order, genre, rank, classification, sort, type, set, excellence.

cater *(SYN.)* coddle, oblige, serve, humor, baby, mollycoddle, pamper, spoil, indulge, provide.

cause *(SYN.)* effect, incite, create, induce, inducement, occasion, incentive, prompt, principle, determinant, reason, origin, motive.

caustic *(SYN.)* bitter, disagreeable, distasteful, acrid, sour, spiteful, pungent, tart, painful, cruel, insulting, peevish, mean, ruthless.
(ANT.) mellow, sweet, delicious, pleasant.

caution *(SYN.)* heed, vigilance, care, prudence, counsel, warning, wariness, advice, warn, injunction.

(ANT.) carelessness, heedlessness, incaution, abandon, recklessness.

cautious *(SYN.)* heedful, scrupulous, attentive, prudent, thoughtful, discreet, guarded, circumspect, vigilant, wary, careful.

(ANT.) improvident, headstrong, foolish, forgetful, indifferent.

cavalcade *(SYN.)* column, procession, parade.

cavalier *(SYN.)* contemptuous, insolent, haughty, arrogant.

cave *(SYN.)* grotto, hole, shelter, lair, den, cavern.

cave in *(SYN.)* fall in, collapse.

cavity *(SYN.)* pit, hole, crater.

cavort *(SYN.)* caper, leap, frolic, hop, prance.

cease *(SYN.)* desist, stop, abandon, discontinue, relinquish, end, terminate, leave, surrender, resign.

(ANT.) occupy, continue, persist, begin, endure, stay.

cede *(SYN.)* surrender, relinquish, yield.

celebrate *(SYN.)* honor, glorify, commemorate, keep, solemnize, extol, observe, commend, praise.

(ANT.) decry, overlook, profane, disregard, disgrace.

celebrated *(SYN.)* eminent, glorious, distinguished, noted, illustrious, famed, well-known, popular, renowned, famous.

(ANT.) obscure, hidden, anonymous, infamous, unknown.

celebrity *(SYN.)* somebody, personage, heroine, hero, dignitary.

celestial *(SYN.)* godlike, holy, supernatural, divine, paradisiacal, transcendent, superhuman.

(ANT.) diabolical, profane, mundane, wicked.

cement *(SYN.)* solidify, weld, fasten, secure.

cemetery *(SYN.)* graveyard.

censure *(SYN.)* denounce, reproach, upbraid, blame, disapproval, reprehend, condemn, criticism, disapprove, reprove.

(ANT.) commend, approval, forgive, approve, praise, applaud, condone.

center *(SYN.)* heart, core, midpoint, middle, nucleus, inside.

(ANT.) rim, boundary, edge, border, periphery, outskirts.

central *(SYN.)* chief, necessary, main, halfway, dominant, mid, middle, inner, focal, leading, fundamental, principal.

(ANT.) side, secondary, incidental, auxiliary.

ceremonious *(SYN.)* correct, exact, precise, stiff, outward, external.

(ANT.) material, unconventional, easy, heartfelt.

ceremony *(SYN.)* observance, rite, parade, pomp, ritual, protocol.

(ANT.) informality, casualness.

certain *(SYN.)* definite, assured, fixed, inevitable, sure, undeniable, positive, confident, particular, insecure, unquestionable.

(ANT.) *probable, uncertain, doubtful, questionable.*

certainly (SYN.) absolutely, surely, definitely.

(ANT.) *dubiously, doubtfully, questionably.*

certainty (SYN.) confidence, courage, security, assuredness, firmness, assertion, statement.

(ANT.) *humility, bashfulness, modest, shyness.*

certificate (SYN.) affidavit, document.

certify (SYN.) validate, affirm, verify, confirm, authenticate.

certitude (SYN.) confidence, belief, conviction, feeling, faith, trust.

(ANT.) *doubt, incredulity, denial, heresy.*

cessation (SYN.) ending, finish, stoppage, termination, conclusion, end.

chafe (SYN.) heat, rub, warm, annoy, disturb.

chagrin (SYN.) irritation, mortification, embarrassment, annoyance, vexation, worry, bother, shame, annoy, irk, humiliation, irritate, vex, frustrate, humiliate, embarrass, mortify, exasperate.

challenge (SYN.) question, dare, call, summon, threat, invite, threaten, demand.

chamber (SYN.) cell, salon, room.

chance (SYN.) befall, accident, betide, disaster, opportunity, calamity, occur, possibility, prospect, happen, luck, fate.

(ANT.) *design, purpose,* inevitability, calculation, certainty, intention.

change (SYN.) modification, alternation, alteration, mutation, variety, exchange, shift, alter, transfigure, veer, vary, variation, substitution, substitute.

(ANT.) *uniformity, monotony, settle, remain, endure, retain, preserve, endurance, stability.*

changeable (SYN.) fitful, fickle, inconstant, unstable, shifting.

(ANT.) *stable, uniform, constant, unchanging.*

channel (SYN.) strait, corridor, waterway, artery, duct, canal, way, trough, groove, passageway.

chant (SYN.) singing, incantation, hymn, sing, carol, psalm, song.

chaos (SYN.) confusion, jumble, turmoil, anarchy, disorder, muddle.

(ANT.) *organization, order, tranquillity, tidiness, system.*

chaotic (SYN.) confused, disorganized, disordered, messy.

(ANT.) *neat, ordered, systematic, organized.*

chap (SYN.) break, fellow, person, crack, split, man, rough, individual, boy.

chaperon (SYN.) associate with, escort, convoy, accompany, consort with.

(ANT.) *avoid, desert, leave, abandon, quit.*

chapter (SYN.) part, section, division.

char (SYN.) scorch, singe, burn.

character (SYN.) description,

class, kind, repute, mark, individuality, disposition, traits, personality, reputation, symbol, features, quality, eccentric, nature.

characteristic *(SYN.)* exclusive, distinctive, special, mark, feature, property, typical, unique, attribute, distinguishing, trait, quality.

charge *(SYN.)* arraignment, indictment, accusation, sell for, attack, assail, assault, indict, blame, allegation, custody, imputation.

(ANT.) pardon, flee, exculpation, excuse, absolve, exoneration.

charitable *(SYN.)* benevolent, generous, liberal, altruistic, kind, obliging, considerate, unselfish.

(ANT.) petty, mean, harsh, wicked, greedy, stingy, malevolent.

charity *(SYN.)* benevolence, kindness, magnanimity, altruism.

(ANT.) malevolence, cruelty, selfishness.

charm *(SYN.)* allure, spell, enchantment, attractiveness, magic, witchery, amulet, talisman, lure, enchant, bewitch, fascinate.

charming *(SYN.)* attractive, enchanting, fascinating, alluring, appealing, agreeable.

(ANT.) revolting, repugnant, repulsive.

chart *(SYN.)* design, plan, cabal, plot, sketch, stratagem, map, diagram, conspiracy, graph.

charter *(SYN.)* lease, hire, rent, alliance.

chase *(SYN.)* hunt, run after, pursue, trail, follow, persist.

(ANT.) escape, flee, abandon, elude, evade.

chasm *(SYN.)* ravine, abyss, canyon, gorge.

chaste *(SYN.)* clear, immaculate, innocent, sincere, bare, clean, modest, pure, decent, virtuous, virginal, sheer, absolute, spotless.

(ANT.) polluted, tainted, foul, impure, sinful, worldly, sullied, defiled.

chastise *(SYN.)* punish, castigate, correct.

(ANT.) release, acquit, free, exonerate.

chat *(SYN.)* argue, jabber, blab, plead, consult, converse, lecture, discuss, talk, conversation, tattle.

cheap *(SYN.)* poor, common, inexpensive, shabby, low-priced, beggary, low-cost, shoddy, mean, inferior.

(ANT.) honorable, dear, noble, expensive, costly, well made, elegant, dignified.

cheat *(SYN.)* deceive, fool, bilk, outwit, victimize, dupe, gull, hoodwink, swindler, cheater, trickster, fraud, defraud, charlatan, crook, chiseler, con artist, hoax, swindle.

check *(SYN.)* dissect, interrogate, analyze, contemplate, inquire, question, scrutinize, arrest, stop, halt, block, curb, control, investigate, review,

examine, test, counterfoil, stub, barrier, watch.
(ANT.) overlook, disregard, advance, foster, continue, promote, omit, neglect.

cheer (SYN.) console, gladden, comfort, encourage, applause, encouragement, joy, glee, gaiety, mirth, soothe, sympathize, approval, solace.
(ANT.) depress, sadden, discourage, derision, dishearten, discouragement, antagonize.

cheerful (SYN.) glad, jolly, joyful, gay, happy, cherry, merry, joyous, lighthearted.
(ANT.) mournful, sad, glum, depressed, gloomy, sullen.

cherish (SYN.) prize, treasure, appreciate, nurse, value, comfort, hold dear, foster, nurture, sustain.
(ANT.) disregard, neglect, deprecate, scorn, reject, undervalue, abandon.

chic (SYN.) fashionable, modish, smart, stylish, trendy.

chide (SYN.) admonish, rebuke, scold, reprimand, criticize, reprove.
(ANT.) extol, praise, commend.

chief (SYN.) chieftain, head, commander, captain, leader, principal, master, boss, leading, ruler.
(ANT.) servant, subordinate, secondary, follower, incidental, accidental, auxiliary, attendant.

childish (SYN.) immature, childlike, infantile, babyish.
(ANT.) mature, adult, seasoned, grownup.

chill (SYN.) coolness, cold, cool, coldness, brisk, frosty.
(ANT.) hot, warm, heat, heated, warmth.

chilly (SYN.) cold, frigid, freezing, arctic, cool, icy, passionless, wintry, unfeeling.
(ANT.) fiery, heated, passionate, ardent.

chivalrous (SYN.) noble, brave, polite, valorous, gallant, gentlemanly, courteous.
(ANT.) crude, rude, impolite, uncivil.

chivalry (SYN.) courtesy, nobility, gallantry, knighthood.

choice (SYN.) delicate, elegant, fine, dainty, exquisite, pure, refined, subtle, splendid, handsome, option, selection, beautiful, minute, pretty, pick, select, uncommon, rare, precious, valuable, thin, small.
(ANT.) coarse, rough, thick, blunt, large.

choke (SYN.) throttle, gag, strange.

choose (SYN.) elect, determine, pick, select, cull, opt.
(ANT.) reject, refuse.

chop (SYN.) hew, cut, fell, mince.

chore (SYN.) routine, task, job, duty, work.

chronic (SYN.) persistent, constant, lingering, continuing, perennial, unending, sustained, permanent.
(ANT.) fleeting, acute, temporary.

chronicle (SYN.) detail, history, narrative, account, description, narration, recital.

(ANT.) misrepresentation, confusion, distortion.

chuckle *(SYN.)* titter, laugh, giggle.

cinema *(SYN.)* effigy, film, etching, appearance, drawing, engraving, illustration, likeness, image, panorama, painting, picture, photograph.

circle *(SYN.)* disk, ring, set, group. class, club, surround, encircle, enclose, round.

circuit *(SYN.)* circle, course, journey, revolution, tour.

circuitous *(SYN.)* distorted, devious, indirect, roundabout swerving, crooked, tortuous.

(ANT.) straightforward, straight, direct, honest

circular *(SYN.)* chubby, complete, curved, bulbous, cylindrical, round, ringlike, globular, entire, rotund.

(ANT.) straight.

circumference *(SYN.)* border, perimeter, periphery, edge.

circumspection *(SYN.)* care, worry, anxiety, concern, caution, attention, vigilance.

(ANT.) neglect, negligence, indifference.

circumstance *(SYN.)* fact, event, incident, condition, happening, position, occurrence, situation.

circumstances *(SYN.)* facts, conditions, factors, situation, background, grounds, means, capital, assets, rank, class.

cite *(SYN.)* affirm, assign, allege, advance, quote, mention, declare, claim, maintain.

(ANT.) refute, gainsay, deny,

contradict.

citizen *(SYN.)* native, inhabitant, national, denizen, subject, dweller, resident.

city *(SYN.)* metropolis, municipality, town.

civil *(SYN.)* courteous, cultivated, accomplished, public, municipal, respectful, genteel, polite, considerate, gracious.

(ANT.) uncouth, uncivil, impertinent, impolite, boorish.

civilization *(SYN.)* cultivation, culture, education, breeding, enlightenment, society, refinement.

(ANT.) ignorance, vulgarity.

civilize *(SYN.)* refine, tame, polish, cultivate, instruct, teach.

claim *(SYN.)* aver, declare, allege, assert, affirm, express, state, demand, maintain, defend, uphold.

(ANT.) refute, deny, contradict.

clamor *(SYN.)* cry, din, babel, noise, racket, outcry, row, sound tumult, shout, uproar.

(ANT.) hush, serenity, silence, tranquillity, stillness, quiet.

clan *(SYN.)* fellowship, kindness, solidarity, family, association, fraternity

(ANT.) discord, strife, opposition, acrimony.

clandestine *(SYN.)* covert, hidden, latent, private, concealed, secret, unknown.

(ANT.) exposed, known, conspicuous, obvious

clarify *(SYN.)* educate, explain, expound, decipher, illustrate, clear, resolve, define, interpret, unfold.

(ANT.) darken, obscure, baffle, confuse.

clash *(SYN.)* clank, crash, clang, conflict, disagreement, opposition, collision, struggle, mismatch, contrast, disagree, collide, interfere.

(ANT.) accord, agreement, harmony, blend, harmonize, match, agree.

clasp *(SYN.)* grip, hold, grasp, adhere, clutch, keep, have, maintain, possess, occupy, retain, support, confine, embrace, fastening, check, detain, curb, receive.

(ANT.) relinquish, vacate, surrender, abandon.

class *(SYN.)* category, denomination, caste, kind, genre, grade, rank, order, elegance, classification, division, sort, family, species, set, excellence.

classic *(SYN.)* masterpiece.

classification *(SYN.)* order, category, class, arrangement, grouping, organization.

clause *(SYN.)* condition, paragraph, limitation, article.

claw *(SYN.)* hook, talon, nail, scratch.

clean *(SYN.)* mop, tidy, neat, dustless, clear, unsoiled, immaculate, unstained, untainted, pure, dust, vacuum, scour, decontaminate, wipe, sterilize, cleanse, scrub, purify, wash, sweep.

(ANT.) stain, soil, pollute, soiled, impure, dirty.

cleanse *(SYN.)* mop, purify, wash, sweep.

(ANT.) stain, soil, dirty, pollute.

clear *(SYN.)* fair, sunny, cloudless, transparent, apparent, limpid, distinct, intelligible, evident, unmistakable, understandable, uncloudy, light, bright, certain, manifest, lucid, obvious, unobstructed.

(ANT.) obscure, unclear, muddled, confused, dark, cloudy, blocked, obstructed, questionable, dubious, foul, overcast.

clearly *(SYN.)* plainly, obviously, evidently, definitely, surely, certainly.

(ANT.) questionably, dubiously.

clemency *(SYN.)* forgiveness, charity, compassion, grace, mercy, leniency, pity.

(ANT.) punishment, vengeance, retribution.

clever *(SYN.)* apt, dexterous, quick, adroit, quick-witted, talented, bright, skillful, witty, ingenious, smart, intelligent, shrewd, gifted, expert, sharp.

(ANT.) unskilled, slow, stupid, backward, maladroit, bungling, dull, clumsy.

cleverness *(SYN.)* intellect, intelligence, comprehension, mind, perspicacity, sagacity, fun.

(ANT.) sobriety, stupidity, solemnity, commonplace, platitude.

client *(SYN.)* patron, customer.

cliff *(SYN.)* scar, bluff, crag, precipice, escarpment.

climax *(SYN.)* apex, culmination, peak, summit, consummation, height, acme, zenith.

(ANT.) depth, base, anticlimax, floor.

climb *(SYN.)* mount, scale, ascend.

(ANT.) descend.

clip *(SYN.)* snip, crop, cut, mow, clasp.

cloak *(SYN.)* conceal, cover, disguise, clothe, cape, guard, envelop, hide, mask, protect, shield.

(ANT.) divulge, expose, reveal, bare, unveil.

clod *(SYN.)* wad, hunk, gobbet, lump, chunk, clot, gob, dunce, dolt, oaf, fool.

clog *(SYN.)* crowd, congest, cram, overfill, stuff.

cloister *(SYN.)* monastery, priory, hermitage, abbey, convent.

close *(SYN.)* adjacent, adjoining, immediate, unventilated, stuffy, abutting, neighboring, dear, oppressive, mean, nearby, near, devoted.

(ANT.) afar, faraway, removed, distant.

close *(SYN.)* seal, shut, clog, stop, obstruct, cease, conclude, complete, end, terminate, occlude, finish.

(ANT.) unlock, begin, open, unbar, inaugurate, commence, start.

closet *(SYN.)* cabinet, locker, wardrobe, cupboard.

cloth *(SYN.)* fabric, goods, material, textile.

clothe *(SYN.)* garb, dress, apparel.

(ANT.) strip, undress.

clothes *(SYN.)* array, attire, apparel, clothing, dress, garb, garments, raiment, drapery, vestments.

(ANT.) nudity, nakedness.

clothing *(SYN.)* attire, clothes, apparel, array, dress, drapery, garments, garb, vestments.

(ANT.) nudity, nakedness.

cloud *(SYN.)* fog, mist, haze, mass, collection, obscure, dim, shadow.

cloudy *(SYN.)* dim, dark, indistinct, murky, mysterious, indefinite, vague, sunless, clouded, obscure, overcast, shadowy.

(ANT.) sunny, clear, distinct, limpid, lucid, clarified, cloudless, clearheaded, brilliant, bright.

clue *(SYN.)* sign, hint.

clumsy *(SYN.)* bungling, inept, rough, unpolished, bumbling, awkward, ungraceful, gauche, ungainly, unskillful.

(ANT.) polished, skillful, neat, graceful, dexterous, adroit.

cluster *(SYN.)* batch, clutch, group, bunch, gather, pack, assemble, crowd.

clutch *(SYN.)* grip, grab, seize, hold.

coalition *(SYN.)* combination, association, alliance, confederacy, entente, league, treaty.

(ANT.) separation, divorce.

coarse *(SYN.)* unpolished, vulgar, refined, rough, smooth, impure, rude, crude, gruff, gross, cultivated, delicate, cultured.

(ANT.) delicate, smooth, refined, polished, genteel, cultivated, suave, fine, cultured.

coast *(SYN.)* seaboard, seashore, beach, shore, drift,

glide, ride.

coax *(SYN.)* urge, persuade, wheedle, cajole.

(ANT.) force, bully, coerce.

code *(SYN.)* crypt, cryptogram, cipher.

coerce *(SYN.)* constrain, compel, enforce, force, drive, oblige, impel.

(ANT.) prevent, persuade, convince, induce.

coercion *(SYN.)* emphasis, intensity, energy, dint, potency, power, vigor, strength, compulsion, force, constraint, violence.

(ANT.) impotence, frailty, feebleness, persuasion.

cognizance *(SYN.)* apprehension, erudition, acquaintance, information, learning, knowledge, lore, science, scholarship, understanding.

(ANT.) illiteracy, misunderstanding, ignorance.

cognizant *(SYN.)* conscious, aware, apprised informed, mindful, observant, perceptive.

(ANT.) unaware, ignorant, oblivious, insensible.

coherent *(SYN.)* logical, intelligible, sensible, rational, commonsensical, reasonable.

coiffeur *(SYN.)* hairdresser.

coiffure *(SYN.)* haircut, hairdo.

coincide *(SYN.)* acquiesce, agree, accede, assent, consent, comply, correspond, concur, match, tally, harmonize, conform.

(ANT.) differ, disagree, protest, contradict.

coincidence *(SYN.)* accident, chance.

(ANT.) plot, plan, prearrangement, scheme.

coincident *(SYN.)* identical, equal, equivalent, distinguishable, same.

(ANT.) distinct, contrary, disparate, opposed.

coincidental *(SYN.)* unpredicted, unexpected, chance, unforeseen, accidental, fortuitous.

cold *(SYN.)* cool, freezing, chilly, frigid, icy, frozen, wintry, arctic, unfriendly, indifferent, phlegmatic, stoical, passionless, chill, unemotional, heartless, unfeeling.

(ANT.) hot, torrid, fiery, burning, ardent, friendly, temperate, warm, passionate.

collapse *(SYN.)* descend, decrease, diminish, fail, downfall, failure, decline, fall, drop, sink, subside, topple.

(ANT.) soar, steady, limb, mount, arise.

colleague *(SYN.)* companion, attendant, comrade, associate, crony, mate, friend, partner.

(ANT.) enemy, stranger, adversary.

collect *(SYN.)* assemble, amass, concentrate, pile, accumulate, congregate, obtain, heap, gather, solicit, secure, procure, raise, get, mass, hoard, consolidate.

(ANT.) divide, dole, assort, dispel, distribute, disperse.

collected *(SYN.)* cool, calm, composed, peaceful, imper-

turbable, placid, sedate, quiet.
(ANT.) excited, violent, aroused, agitated.

collection *(SYN.)* amount, conglomeration, sum, entirety, aggregation, hoard, accumulation, pile, store, aggregate, total, whole.
(ANT.) part, unit, particular, element, ingredient.

collide *(SYN.)* hit, smash, crash, strike.

collision *(SYN.)* conflict, combat, duel, battle, encounter, crash, smash, fight, contention, struggle, discord.
(ANT.) concord, amity, harmony, consonance.

collusion *(SYN.)* combination, cabal, intrigue, conspiracy, plot, treason, treachery.

colossal *(SYN.)* enormous, elephantine, gargantuan, huge, immense, gigantic, prodigious.
(ANT.) little, minute, small, miniature, diminutive, microscopic, tiny.

combat *(SYN.)* conflict, duel, battle, collision, encounter, fight, contest, oppose, war, contention, struggle, discord.
(ANT.) consonance, harmony, concord, yield, surrender, succumb, amity.

combination *(SYN.)* association, confederacy, alliance, entente, league, compounding, mixture, blend, composite, federation, mixing, compound, blending, union.
(ANT.) separation, division, schism, divorce.

combine *(SYN.)* adjoin, associate, accompany, conjoin, connect, link, mix, blend, couple, unite, join.
(ANT.) detach, disjoin, divide, separate, disconnect.

come *(SYN.)* near, approach, reach, arrive, advance.
(ANT.) depart, leave, go.

comely *(SYN.)* charming, elegant, beauteous, beautiful, fine, lovely, pretty, handsome lovely.
(ANT.) hideous, repulsive, foul, unsightly.

comfort *(SYN.)* contentment, ease, enjoyment, relieve, consolation, relief, cheer, console, calm, satisfaction, soothe, encourage, succor, luxury, solace.
(ANT.) depress, torture, discomfort, upset, misery, disturb, agitate, affliction, discompose, uncertainty, suffering.

comfortable *(SYN.)* pleasing, agreeable, convenient, cozy, welcome, acceptable, relaxed, restful, gratifying, easy, contented, rested, satisfying, pleasurable.
(ANT.) miserable, distressing, tense, strained, troubling, edgy, uncomfortable.

comical *(SYN.)* droll, funny, humorous, amusing, ludicrous, witty, ridiculous, odd.
(ANT.) sober, solemn, sad, serious, melancholy.

command *(SYN.)* class, method, plan regularity, rank, arrangement, series, sequence, point, aim, conduct, manage, guide, bid, system, succession, bidding, direct, order, demand, direction, rule, dictate, decree.

(ANT.) consent, obey, misdirect, distract, deceive, misguide, license, confusion.

commanding *(SYN.)* imposing, masterful, assertive, authoritative, positive.

commence *(SYN.)* open, start.
(ANT.) stop, end, terminate.

commend *(SYN.)* laud, praise, applaud, recommend.
(ANT.) censure, blame, criticize.

commendable *(SYN.)* deserving, praiseworthy.
(ANT.) bad, deplorable, lamentable.

commensurate *(SYN.)* keep, celebrate, observe, honor, commend, extol, glorify, laud, praise, honor.
(ANT.) decry, disgrace, disregard, overlook, profane, dishonor.

comment *(SYN.)* assertion, declaration, annotation, explanation, review, commentary, report, remark, observation, utterance, criticism, statement.

commerce *(SYN.)* business, engagement, employment, art, trade, marketing, enterprise, occupation.
(ANT.) hobby, pastime, avocation.

commission *(SYN.)* board, committee, command, permit, order, permission, delegate, authorize, deputize, entrust.

commit *(SYN.)* perpetrate, per-

form, obligate, do, commend, consign, relegate, bind, delegate, empower, pledge, entrust, authorize, trust.
(ANT.) neglect, mistrust, release, free, fail, loose.

commitment *(SYN.)* promise, responsibility, pledge, duty.

commodious *(SYN.)* appropriate, accessible, adapted, favorable, handy, fitting, timely.
(ANT.) inconvenient, troublesome, awkward.

commodity *(SYN.)* article, merchandise, wares, goods.

common *(SYN.)* ordinary, popular, familiar, mean, low, general, vulgar, communal, mutual, shared, natural, frequent, prevalent, joint, conventional, plain, usual, universal.
(ANT.) odd, exceptional, scarce, noble, extraordinary, different, separate, rare, unusual, distinctive, refined.

commonplace *(SYN.)* common, usual, frequent, ordinary, everyday.
(ANT.) distinctive, unusual, original.

commonsense *(SYN.)* perceptible, alive, apprehensible, aware, cognizant, conscious, comprehending, perceptible.
(ANT.) unaware, impalpable, imperceptible.

commotion *(SYN.)* confusion, chaos, disarray, ferment, disorder, stir, tumult, agitation.
(ANT.) tranquillity, peace, certainty, order.

communicable *(SYN.)* infectious, virulent, catching, transferable, contagious.

(ANT.) hygienic, noncommunicable, healthful.

communicate *(SYN.)* convey, impart, inform, confer, disclose, reveal, relate, tell, advertise, publish, transmit, publicize, divulge.

(ANT.) withhold, hide, conceal.

communicative *(SYN.)* un reserved, open, frank, free, straightforward, unrestrained.

(ANT.) secretive.

communion *(SYN.)* fellowship, participation, association, sacrament, union.

(ANT.) nonparticipation, alienation.

community *(SYN.)* public, society, city, town, village.

compact *(SYN.)* contracted, firm, narrow, snug, close, con-stricted, packed, vanity, treaty, agreement, tense, taught, tight, parsimonious, compressed, stingy.

(ANT.) slack, open, loose, relaxed, unconfined, unfretted, sprawling, lax.

companion *(SYN.)* attendant, comrade, consort, friend, colleague, partner, crony, mate, associate.

(ANT.) stranger, enemy, adversary.

companionship *(SYN.)* familiarity, cognizance, acquaintance, fellowship, knowledge, intimacy.

(ANT.) unfamiliarity, inexperience, ignorance.

company *(SYN.)* crew, group, band, party, throng, house,

assemblage, troop, fellowship, association, business, concern, partnership, corporation, companionship, firm.

(ANT.) seclusion, individual, solitude, dispersion.

comparable *(SYN.)* allied, analogous, alike, akin, like, correspondent, correlative, parallel.

(ANT.) opposed, incongruous, dissimilar, unalike, different, divergent

compare *(SYN.)* discriminate, match, differentiate, contrast, oppose.

comparison *(SYN.)* likening, contrasting, judgment.

compartment *(SYN.)* division, section.

compassion *(SYN.)* mercy, sympathy, pity, commiseration, condolence.

(ANT.) ruthlessness, hardness, brutality, inhumanity, cruelty.

compassionate *(SYN.)* sympathizing, benign, forbearing, good, tender, affable, humane, indulgent, kind, sympathetic.

(ANT.) inhuman, merciless, unkind, coldhearted, unsympathetic, cruel.

compatible *(SYN.)* consistent, agreeing, conforming, accordant, congruous, harmonious, cooperative, agreeable, constant, correspondent.

(ANT.) discrepant, paradoxical, disagreeable, contradictory.

compel *(SYN.)* drive, enforce, coerce, constrain, force, oblige, impel.

(ANT.) induce, coax, prevent, wheedle, persuade, cajole,

convince.

compensate *(SYN.)* remunerate, repay, reimburse, recompense.

compensation *(SYN.)* fee, earnings, pay, payment, recompense, allowance, remuneration, remittance, settlement, stipend, repayment, salary, wages.

(ANT.) present, gratuity, gift.

compete *(SYN.)* rival, contest, oppose, vie.

(ANT.) reconcile, accord.

competence *(SYN.)* skill, ability, capability.

competent *(SYN.)* efficient, clever, capable, able, apt, proficient, skillful, qualified.

(ANT.) inept, incapable, unfitted, awkward, incompetent, inadequate.

competition *(SYN.)* contest, match, rivalry, tournament.

competitor *(SYN.)* rival, contestant, opponent.

(ANT.) ally, friend, colleague.

complain *(SYN.)* lament, murmur, protest, grouch, grumble, regret, moan, remonstrate, whine, repine.

(ANT.) rejoice, praise, applaud, approve.

complaint *(SYN.)* protest, objection, grievance.

complement *(SYN.)* supplement, complete.

(ANT.) clash, conflict.

complete *(SYN.)* consummate, entire, ended, full, thorough, finished, full, whole, concluded, over, done, terminate, unbroken, total, undivided.

(ANT.) unfinished, imperfect,

incomplete, start, partial, begin, commence, lacking.

completion *(SYN.)* achievement, attainment, end, conclusion, close, finish, windup, accomplishment, realization.

(ANT.) omission, neglect, failure, defeat.

complex *(SYN.)* sophisticated, compound, intricate, involved, perplexing, elaborate, complicated.

(ANT.) basic, simple, rudimentary, uncompounded, uncomplicated, plain.

complexion *(SYN.)* paint, pigment hue, color, dye, stain, tincture, tinge, tint, shade.

(ANT.) paleness, transparency, achromatism.

compliant *(SYN.)* meek, modest, lowly, plain, submissive, simple, unostentatious, unassuming, unpretentious.

(ANT.) proud, vain, arrogant, haughty, boastful.

complicated *(SYN.)* intricate, involved, complex, compound, perplexing.

(ANT.) simple, uncompounded.

compliment *(SYN.)* eulogy, flattery, praise, admiration, honor, adulation, flatter, commendation, tribute.

(ANT.) taunt, affront, aspersion, insult, disparage, criticism.

complimentary *(SYN.)* gratis, free.

comply *(SYN.)* assent, consent, accede, acquiesce, coincide, conform, concur, tally.

(ANT.) differ, dissent, protest, disagree.

component (SYN.) division, fragment, allotment, moiety, apportionment, scrap, portion, section, share, segment, ingredient, organ.

(ANT.) whole, entirety.

comport (SYN.) carry, conduct, behave, act, deport, interact, operate, manage.

compose (SYN.) forge, fashion, mold, make, construct, create, produce, shape, form, constitute, arrange, organize, write, invent, devise, frame.

(ANT.) misshape, dismantle, disfigure, destroy.

composed (SYN.) calm, cool, imperturbable, placid, quiet, unmoved, sedate, peaceful, collected, tranquil.

(ANT.) aroused, nervous, agitated, perturbed, excited.

composer (SYN.) author, inventor, creator, maker, originator.

composition (SYN.) paper, theme, work, essay, compound, mixture, mix.

composure (SYN.) calmness, poise, control, self-control, self-possession.

(ANT.) anger, rage, turbulence, agitation.

compound (SYN.) blend, confound, jumble, consort, aggregate, complicated, combination, combined, mixture, complex, join.

(ANT.) segregate, separate, divide, simple, sort.

comprehend (SYN.) apprehend, discern, learn, perceive, see, grasp, understand.

(ANT.) mistake, misunderstand, ignore.

comprehension (SYN.) insight, perception, understanding, awareness, discernment.

(ANT.) misconception, insensibility.

comprehensive (SYN.) wide, inclusive, complete, broad, full.

(ANT.) fragmentary, partial, limited, incomplete.

compress (SYN.) press, compact, squeeze, pack, crowd.

(ANT.) spread, stretch, expand.

comprise (SYN.) contain, hold, embrace.

(ANT.) emit, encourage, yield, discharge.

compulsion (SYN.) might, energy, potency, strength, vigor.

(ANT.) persuasion, impotence, frailty.

compulsory (SYN.) required, obligatory, necessary, unavoidable.

(ANT.) elective, optional, free, unrestricted.

computation (SYN.) reckoning, record.

(ANT.) misrepresentation.

compute (SYN.) count, calculate, determine, figure.

(ANT.) conjecture, guess, miscalculate.

comrade (SYN.) attendant, companion, colleague, associate, friend.

(ANT.) stranger, enemy, adversary.

con (SYN.) cheat, bamboozle, trick, swindle.

conceal (SYN.) disguise, cover, hide, mask, screen, secrete, veil, withhold.

(ANT.) reveal, show, disclose,
expose.

concede *(SYN.)* permit, suffer,
tolerate, grant, give, admit,
acknowledge, allow, yield.

(ANT.) forbid, contradict,
protest, refuse, deny, negate,
resist.

conceit *(SYN.)* pride, vanity,
complacency, conception,
idea, egotism, self-esteem,
caprice, fancy, whim.

(ANT.) humility, meekness,
humbleness, modesty.

conceited *(SYN.)* proud, arrogant, vain, smug, egotistical.

(ANT.) humble, modest, self-
effacing.

conceive *(SYN.)* design, create,
imagine, understand, devise,
concoct, perceive, frame,
grasp, invent.

(ANT.) imitate, reproduce, copy.

concentrate *(SYN.)* localize,
focus, condense, ponder, meditate, center, scrutinize.

(ANT.) scatter, diffuse, dissipate, disperse.

concentrated *(SYN.)* compressed, thick, dense.

(ANT.) sparse, quick, dispersed.

concept *(SYN.)* fancy, conception, image, notion, idea, sentiment, thought.

(ANT.) thing, matter, substance,
entity.

conception *(SYN.)* consideration, deliberation, fancy, idea,
notion, regard, thought, view.

concern *(SYN.)* matter, anxiety,
affair, disturb, care, business,
solicitude, interest, affect,

involve, touch, trouble, interest, worry.

(ANT.) unconcern, negligence,
disinterest, tire, bore, calm,
soothe, indifference.

concerning *(SYN.)* regarding,
about, respecting.

concerted *(SYN.)* united, joint,
combined.

(ANT.) individual, unorganized,
separate.

concession *(SYN.)* admission,
yielding, granting.

(ANT.) insistence, demand.

concise *(SYN.)* pity, neat, brief,
compact, succinct, terse.

(ANT.) wordy, lengthy, verbose,
prolix.

conclude *(SYN.)* close, decide,
achieve, complete, end, finish,
terminate, arrange, determine,
settle, perfect, perform.

(ANT.) start, begin, commence.

concluding *(SYN.)* extreme,
final, last, terminal, utmost.

(ANT.) first, foremost, opening,
initial.

conclusion *(SYN.)* end, finale,
termination, deduction, close,
settlement, decision, finish,
resolution, determination,
completion, issue, judgment.

(ANT.) commencement, inception, opening, beginning.

conclusive *(SYN.)* decisive,
eventual, final, terminal, ultimate.

(ANT.) original, first, inaugural.

concord *(SYN.)* agreement, unison, understanding, accordance, stipulation.

(ANT.) disagreement, discord,
dissension.

concrete (SYN.) solid, firm, precise, definite, specific.
(ANT.) undetermined, vague, general.

concur (SYN.) agree, assent, consent, accede.
(ANT.) dissent, protest, differ.

condemn (SYN.) denounce, reproach, blame, upbraid, convict, rebuke, doom, judge, censure, reprehend, punish, reprobate, sentence.
(ANT.) condone, extol, forgive, absolve, praise, applaud, approve, pardon, excuse.

condense (SYN.) shorten, reduce, abridge, abbreviate, concentrate, digest, compress, diminish.
(ANT.) enlarge, increase, swell, expand.

condition (SYN.) circumstance, state, situation, case, plight, requirement, position, necessity, stipulation, predicament, provision, term.

conditional (SYN.) dependent, relying.
(ANT.) casual, original, absolute.

condolence (SYN.) commiseration, concord, harmony, pity, sympathy, warmth.
(ANT.) harshness, indifference, unconcern.

conduct (SYN.) control, deportment, supervise, manage, behavior, deed, actions, act, behave, manners.

confederate (SYN.) ally, abettor, assistant.
(ANT.) enemy, rival, opponent, adversary.

confer (SYN.) gossip, grant, speak, tattle, blab, chat, deliberate, consult, award, give, bestow, talk, mutter.
(ANT.) retrieve, withdraw.

confess (SYN.) avow, acknowledge, admit, concede, grant, divulge, reveal.
(ANT.) disown, renounce, deny, conceal.

confession (SYN.) defense, justification, excuse, apology.
(ANT.) dissimulation, denial, complaint.

confidence (SYN.) firmness, self-reliance, assurance, faith, trust, pledge, declaration, self-confidence, reliance, self-assurance, courage, statement.
(ANT.) distrust, shyness, mistrust, bashfulness, diffidence, doubt, modesty, suspicion.

confident (SYN.) certain, sure, dauntless, self-assured.
(ANT.) uncertain, timid, shy.

confine (SYN.) enclose, restrict, hinder, fence, limit, bound.
(ANT.) release, expose, free, expand, open.

confirm (SYN.) acknowledge, establish, settle, substantiate, approve, fix, verify, assure, validate, ratify, corroborate, strengthen.
(ANT.) disclaim, deny, disavow.

confirmation (SYN.) demonstration, experiment, test, trail, verification.
(ANT.) fallacy, invalidity.

confirmed (SYN.) regular, established, habitual, chronic.
(ANT.) occasional, infrequent.

conflict (SYN.) duel, combat,

fight, collision, discord, interference, inconsistency, contention, struggle, opposition, oppose, controversy, contend, engagement, variance.
(ANT.) consonance, harmony, amity.

confiscate *(SYN.)* capture, catch, gain, purloin, steal, take, clutch, grip, seize, get, obtain, bear.

conflagration *(SYN.)* flame, glow, heat, warmth, fervor, passion, vigor.
(ANT.) apathy, cold, quiescence.

conform *(SYN.)* adapt, comply, yield, submit, obey, adjust, agree, fit, suit.
(ANT.) misapply, misfit, rebel, vary, disagree, disturb.

conformity *(SYN.)* congruence, accord, agreement, correspondence.

confound *(SYN.)* confuse, baffle, perplex, puzzle, bewilder.

confront *(SYN.)* confront, defy, hinder, resist, thwart, withstand, bar.
(ANT.) submit, agree, support, succumb.

confuse *(SYN.)* confound, perplex, mystify, dumbfound, baffle, puzzle, jumble, mislead, mistake, bewilder.
(ANT.) explain, instruct, edify, illumine, enlighten, illuminate, solve.

confused *(SYN.)* deranged, indistinct, disordered, muddled, bewildered, disconcerted, disorganized, perplexed.
(ANT.) organized, plain, clear, obvious.

confusion *(SYN.)* commotion, disarray, agitation, disorder, chaos, ferment, stir, perplexity, tumult, bewilderment, disarrangement, uncertainty, muss, mess, turmoil.
(ANT.) order, tranquillity, enlightenment, comprehension, understanding, tidiness, organization, peace.

congregate *(SYN.)* gather, foregather, meet, convene.
(ANT.) scatter, dispel, disperse, dissipate.

congruous *(SYN.)* agreeing, conforming, constant, correspondent.
(ANT.) incongruous, inconsistent, discrepant.

conjecture *(SYN.)* law, supposition, theory.
(ANT.) proof, fact, certainty.

conjunction *(SYN.)* combination, junction, connection, link.
(ANT.) separation, disconnection, separation, diversion.

connect *(SYN.)* adjoin, link, combine, relate, join, attach, unite, associate, affix.
(ANT.) detach, separate, disjoin, untie, dissociation, disconnect, unfasten.

connection *(SYN.)* conjunction, alliance, link, affinity, bond, tie, association, relationship, union.
(ANT.) isolation, dissociation, separation, disassociation, disunion.

conquer *(SYN.)* master, beat, humble, defeat, overcome, rout, win, succeed, achieve, gain, overpower, quell, subdue, crush, vanquish.

(ANT.) cede, yield, retreat, surrender.

conquest (SYN.) triumph, victory, achievement.

(ANT.) surrender, failure, defeat.

conscientious (SYN.) upright, straight, honest, incorruptible, scrupulous.

(ANT.) careless, irresponsible, slovenly.

conscious (SYN.) cognizant, informed, perceptive, aware, intentional, sensible, awake, purposeful, deliberate.

(ANT.) unaware, insensible, asleep, comatose, ignorant.

consecrate (SYN.) exalt, extol, hallow, honor.

(ANT.) mock, degrade, debase, abuse.

consecrated (SYN.) holy, divine, devout, spiritual.

(ANT.) evil, worldly, secular.

consent (SYN.) permission, leave, agree, let, assent, agreement, license, permit.

(ANT.) refusal, opposition, denial, dissent, prohibition.

consequence (SYN.) outcome, issue, result, effect, significance, importance.

(ANT.) impetus, cause.

consequential (SYN.) significant, important, weighty.

(ANT.) trivial, unimportant, minor, insignificant.

consequently (SYN.) hence, thence, therefore.

conservative (SYN.) conventional, reactionary, cautious, moderate, careful.

(ANT.) radical, liberal, rash, foolhardy, reckless.

conserve (SYN.) save, retain, reserve, guard, keep, support, sustain.

(ANT.) dismiss, neglect, waste, reject, discard.

consider (SYN.) heed, ponder, contemplate, examine, study, weigh, reflect, think about, regard, deliberate, respect.

(ANT.) ignore, overlook, disdain, disregard, neglect.

considerable (SYN.) much, noteworthy, worthwhile, significant, important.

considerate (SYN.) careful, considerate, heedful, prudent, kind, thoughtful, polite, introspective, reflective.

(ANT.) thoughtless, heedless, inconsiderate, selfish, mean.

consideration (SYN.) kindness, care, heed, politeness, empathy, notice, watchfulness, kindliness, thoughtfulness, courtesy, concern, sympathy, thought, attention, reflection, fee, pay, study.

(ANT.) omission, oversight, negligence.

consistent (SYN.) conforming, accordant, compatible, agreeing, faithful, constant, harmonious, expected, regular, congruous, correspondent.

(ANT.) paradoxical, discrepant, contrary, antagonistic, opposed, eccentric, inconsistent, incongruous.

consolation (SYN.) enjoyment, sympathy, relief, ease, contentment, comfort, solace.

(ANT.) discomfort, suffering, discouragement, torture, burden, misery.

console *(SYN.)* solace, comfort, sympathize with, assuage, soothe.

(ANT.) worry, annoy, upset, disturb, distress.

consolidate *(SYN.)* blend, combine, conjoin, fuse, mix, merge, unite.

(ANT.) decompose, separate, analyze, disintegrate.

consort *(SYN.)* companion, comrade, friend.

(ANT.) stranger, enemy, adversary.

conspicuous *(SYN.)* distinguished, clear, manifest, salient, noticeable, striking, obvious, prominent, visible.

(ANT.) hidden, obscure, neutral, common, inconspicuous.

conspiracy *(SYN.)* machination, combination, treason, intrigue, cabal, treachery, plot, collusion.

conspire *(SYN.)* plan, intrigue, plot, scheme.

constancy *(SYN.)* devotion, faithfulness, accuracy, precision, exactness.

(ANT.) faithlessness, treachery, perfidy.

constant *(SYN.)* continual, invariable, abiding, permanent, faithful, invariant, true, ceaseless, enduring, unchanging, steadfast, unchangeable, loyal, stable, immutable, staunch, steady, fixed.

(ANT.) fickle, irregular, wavering, infrequent, occasional,

mutable.

constantly *(SYN.)* eternally, ever, evermore, forever.

(ANT.) rarely, sometimes, never, occasionally.

consternation *(SYN.)* apprehension, dismay, alarm, fear, fright, dread, horror, terror.

(ANT.) bravery, courage, boldness, assurance.

constitute *(SYN.)* compose, found, form, establish, organize, create, appoint, delegate, authorize, commission.

constitution *(SYN.)* law, code, physique, health, vitality.

constrain *(SYN.)* necessity, indigence, want, poverty.

(ANT.) luxury, freedom, uncertainty.

construct *(SYN.)* build, form, erect, make, fabricate, raise, frame.

(ANT.) raze, demolish, destroy.

construction *(SYN.)* raising, building, fabricating.

constructive *(SYN.)* useful, helpful, valuable.

(ANT.) ruinous, destructive.

construe *(SYN.)* explain, interpret, solve, render, translate.

(ANT.) distort, confuse, misconstrue.

consult *(SYN.)* discuss, chatter, discourse, gossip, confer, report, rumor, deliberate, speech, talk.

(ANT.) writing, correspondence, silence.

consume *(SYN.)* engulf, absorb, use, expend, exhaust, devour, devastate, destroy, engross.

(ANT.) emit, expel, exude, dis-

charge.

consumer (SYN.) user, buyer, purchaser.

consummate (SYN.) close, conclude, do, finish, perfect, terminate.

consummation (SYN.) climax, apex, culmination, peak.

(ANT.) depth, base, floor.

contact (SYN.) meeting, touching.

contagious (SYN.) infectious, virulent, communicable, catching.

(ANT.) noncommunicable, healthful, hygienic.

contain (SYN.) embody, hold, embrace, include, accommodate, repress, restrain.

(ANT.) emit, encourage, yield, discharge.

contaminate (SYN.) corrupt, sully, taint, defile, soil, pollute, dirty, infect, poison.

(ANT.) purify.

contemplate (SYN.) imagine, recollect, consider, study, reflect upon, observe, deliberate, muse, ponder, plan, intend, view, regard, think about, reflect, think, mean.

(ANT.) forget, guess, conjecture.

contemplative (SYN.) simultaneous, meditative, thoughtful, contemporaneous, studious.

(ANT.) inattentive, indifferent, thoughtless.

contemporary (SYN.) modern, present, simultaneous, fashionable, coexisting, contemporaneous, up-to-date.

(ANT.) old, antecedent, past, ancient, succeeding, bygone.

contempt (SYN.) detestation, malice, contumely, disdain, derision, scorn.

(ANT.) respect, reverence, admiration, esteem, awe.

contemptible (SYN.) base, mean, vile, vulgar, nasty, low, detestable, selfish, miserable, offensive.

(ANT.) generous, honorable, noble, exalted, admirable.

contemptuous (SYN.) disdainful, sneering, scornful, insolent.

(ANT.) modest, humble.

contend (SYN.) dispute, combat, contest, assert, claim, argue, maintain.

content (SYN.) pleased, happy, contented, satisfied.

(ANT.) restless, dissatisfied, discontented.

contented (SYN.) delighted, fortunate, gay, happy, joyous, lucky, merry.

(ANT.) gloomy, blue, depressed.

contention (SYN.) combat, duel, struggle, discord, battle, variance.

(ANT.) concord, harmony, amity, consonance.

contentment (SYN.) delight, happiness, pleasure, satisfaction.

(ANT.) misery, sorrow, grief, sadness, despair.

contest (SYN.) dispute, debate, competition, tournament, oppose, quarrel, squabble.

(ANT.) allow, concede, agree.

continence (SYN.) forbearance, temperance.

(ANT.) self-indulgence, excess,

intoxication.

contingency *(SYN.)* likelihood, possibility, occasion, circumstance.

contingent *(SYN.)* depending, subject.

(ANT.) independent, original, casual.

continual *(SYN.)* constant, unceasing, everlasting, unremitting, endless, continuous, uninterrupted, regular, connected, consecutive ceaseless.

(ANT.) periodic, rare, irregular, occasional, interrupted.

continue *(SYN.)* proceed, extend, endure, persist, resume, renew, recommence, last, remain, prolong, pursue.

(ANT.) check, cease, discontinue, stop, suspend.

continuous *(SYN.)* continuing, uninterrupted, ceaseless, unceasing, incessant, constant.

(ANT.) intermittent, irregular, sporadic.

contract *(SYN.)* condense, diminish, reduce, bargain, restrict, agreement, compact, pact, shrink, get, treaty, shorten.

(ANT.) lengthen, extend, swell, expand, elongate.

contraction *(SYN.)* reduction, shortening.

(ANT.) enlargement, expansion, extension.

contradict *(SYN.)* gainsay, counter, oppose, confute, dispute.

(ANT.) verify, confirm, agree, support.

contradictory *(SYN.)* inconsis-

tent, conflicting, incompatible, paradoxical, unsteady.

(ANT.) congruous, consistent, correspondent.

contrary *(SYN.)* disagreeable, perverse, hostile, stubborn, opposite, opposing, opposed, disagreeing, disastrous, conflicting, headstrong, unlucky.

(ANT.) lucky, agreeable, propitious, favorable, like, obliging, similar, complementary, tractable, fortunate.

contrast *(SYN.)* differentiate, distinction, disagreement, distinguish, differ, discriminate, difference, oppose.

(ANT.) agreement, similarity, likeness.

contribute *(SYN.)* grant, give, donate, bestow, provide, offer.

(ANT.) deny, withhold.

contribution *(SYN.)* grant, gift, offering, donation.

contrition *(SYN.)* grief, regret, self-reproach.

(ANT.) self-satisfaction, complacency.

contrive *(SYN.)* devise, intend, plan, make, invent, plot, hatch, form, project, arrange, manage, maneuver, scheme, sketch.

control *(SYN.)* govern, regulate, rule, command, dominate, direct, manage, check, repress, curb, management, mastery, direction, restraint, superintend, restrain.

(ANT.) ignore, forsake, follow, submit, abandon.

controversy *(SYN.)* disagreement, dispute, debate.

(ANT.) agreement, harmony, accord, concord, decision.

convenience *(SYN.)* accessibility, aid, benefit, help, service, availability.

(ANT.) inconvenience.

convenient *(SYN.)* adapted, appropriate, fitting, favorable, handy, suitable, accessible, nearby, ready, available, advantageous, timely.

(ANT.) inconvenient, troublesome, awkward.

convention *(SYN.)* meeting, conference, assembly, practice, custom, rule.

conventional *(SYN.)* common, regular, usual, everyday, habitual, routine, accustomed.

(ANT.) exotic, unusual, bizarre, extraordinary.

conversant *(SYN.)* aware, intimate, familiar, versed, close, friendly, sociable.

(ANT.) affected, distant, cold, reserved.

conversation *(SYN.)* colloquy, dialogue, chat, parley, discussion, talk.

converse *(SYN.)* jabber, talk, argue, comment, harangue, plead, rant, spout, discuss, chat, speak, reason.

conversion *(SYN.)* alteration, change, mutation, modification, metamorphosis.

convert *(SYN.)* change, alter, turn, transform, shift, modify, exchange, win over, vary, veer.

(ANT.) establish, stabilize, settle, retain.

convey *(SYN.)* carry, bear, communicate, transport, transmit, support, sustain.

(ANT.) drop, abandon.

conveyance *(SYN.)* van, car, train, truck, plane.

convict *(SYN.)* felon, offender, criminal.

conviction *(SYN.)* opinion, position, view, faith, belief, confidence, feeling, reliance, trust.

(ANT.) doubt, heresy, incredulity, denial.

convince *(SYN.)* persuade, assure, exhort, induce, influence.

(ANT.) deter, compel, restrain, dissuade.

convivial *(SYN.)* jolly, social, jovial, gregarious.

(ANT.) solemn, stern, unsociable.

convoy *(SYN.)* with, attend, chaperone.

(ANT.) avoid, desert, quit, leave.

cool *(SYN.)* frosty, chilly, icy, cold, wintry, quiet, composed, collected, distant, unfriendly.

(ANT.) hot, warm, heated, overwrought, excited, hysterical, friendly, outgoing.

cooperate *(SYN.)* unite, combine, help, contribute, support.

coordinate *(SYN.)* attune, harmonize, adapt, match, balance.

copious *(SYN.)* ample, abundant, bountiful, overflowing, plentiful, profuse, rich.

(ANT.) scant, scarce, insufficient, meager, deficient.

copy *(SYN.)* facsimile, exemplar, imitation, duplicate, reproduction, likeness, print, carbon, transcript.

(ANT.) prototype, original.

cordial (SYN.) polite, friendly, affable, genial, earnest, gracious, warm, ardent, warmhearted, hearty, sincere.

(ANT.) unfriendly, cool, aloof, hostile, ill-tempered, reserved.

core (SYN.) midpoint, heart, kernel, center, middle.

(ANT.) outskirts, border, surface, outside, boundary, rim.

corporation (SYN.) business, organization, crew, group, troop, society, company, conglomerate, firm.

(ANT.) individual, dispersion, seclusion.

corpse (SYN.) cadaver, carcass, remains, body, form.

(ANT.) spirit, soul, mind, intellect.

corpulent (SYN.) obese, portly, chubby, stout.

(ANT.) slim, thin, slender, lean, gaunt.

correct (SYN.) true, set right, faultless, impeccable, proper, accurate, precise, mend, right, rebuke, punish, amend, rectify, better, emend, caution, discipline, exact, strict.

(ANT.) condone, aggravate, false, inaccurate, wrong, untrue, faulty.

correction (SYN.) order, improvement, regulation, instruction, amendment, remedy, rectification, repair, training, punishment.

(ANT.) confusion, turbulence.

correlative (SYN.) allied, correspondent, similar, parallel.

(ANT.) different, opposed, divergent.

correspond (SYN.) compare, coincide, match, agree, suit, fit, write.

(ANT.) differ, diverge, vary.

correspondent (SYN.) allied, alike, comparable, like, parallel, similar.

(ANT.) different, opposed, divergent, dissimilar.

corridor (SYN.) hallway, hall, foyer, passage, lobby, passageway.

corrode (SYN.) erode.

corrupt (SYN.) untrustworthy, treacherous, unscrupulous, wicked, evil, low, contaminated, perverted, bribe, depraved, corrupted, degrade, venal, tainted, dishonest, impure.

(ANT.) upright, honest, pure, sanctify, edify, purify, sanctified, scrupulous.

corrupted (SYN.) crooked, dishonest, impure, spoiled, unsound.

cost (SYN.) price, value, damage, charge, loss, sacrifice, penalty.

costly (SYN.) dear, expensive.

(ANT.) cheap, inexpensive.

costume (SYN.) dress, clothes, apparel, clothing, garb.

couch (SYN.) davenport, sofa, loveseat.

council (SYN.) caution, instruction, committee, cabinet, board, suggestion.

counsel (SYN.) guidance, attorney, lawyer, counselor, hint,

imply, opinion, advice, offer, advise.

(ANT.) declare, dictate, insist.

count *(SYN.)* consider, number, enumerate, total, figure, compute, tally, estimate.

(ANT.) conjecture, guess, miscalculate.

countenance *(SYN.)* visage, face, aspect, support, appearance, approval, encouragement, favor.

(ANT.) forbid, prohibit.

counteract *(SYN.)* thwart, neutralize, offset, counterbalance, defeat.

counterfeit *(SYN.)* false, fraudulent, pretended, pretend, sham, imitate, forgery, artificial, bogus, fake, spurious, imitation, unreal.

(ANT.) authentic, natural, real, genuine, true.

country *(SYN.)* state, nation, forest, farmland.

(ANT.) city.

couple *(SYN.)* team, pair, accompany, associate, attach, combine, connect, brace, join, link, unite.

(ANT.) detach, separate, disjoin, disconnect.

courage *(SYN.)* fearlessness, boldness, chivalry, fortitude, mettle, spirit, daring, bravery, prowess, intrepidity, valor, resolution.

(ANT.) fear, timidity, cowardice.

courageous *(SYN.)* bold, dauntless, brave, daring, intrepid, valorous, plucky, fearless, heroic, valiant.

(ANT.) fearful, weak, timid.

course *(SYN.)* passage, advance, path, road, progress, way, direction, bearing, route, street, track, trail, way.

courteous *(SYN.)* civil, respectful, polite, genteel, well-mannered, gracious, refined.

(ANT.) discourteous, rude, uncivil, impolite, boorish.

courtesy *(SYN.)* graciousness, politeness, respect.

(ANT.) discourtesy, rudeness.

covenant *(SYN.)* agreement, concord, harmony, unison, compact, stipulation.

(ANT.) variance, discord, dissension, difference.

cover *(SYN.)* clothe, conceal, disguise, curtain, guard, envelop, mask, cloak, shield, hide, screen, protect, embrace, top, lid, covering, stopper, protection, refuge, spread, overlay, include, veil.

(ANT.) bare, expose, reveal.

covert *(SYN.)* potential, undeveloped, concealed, dormant.

(ANT.) explicit, visible, manifest.

covetous *(SYN.)* greedy, acquisitive, avaricious.

(ANT.) generous.

coy *(SYN.)* embarrassed, sheepish, shy, timid.

(ANT.) fearless, outgoing, bold, adventurous, daring.

crack *(SYN.)* snap, break, split.

craft *(SYN.)* talent, skill, expertness, ability, cunning, guile, deceit, trade, profession, occupation.

crafty *(SYN.)* covert, clever, cunning, skillful, foxy, tricky,

sly, underhand, shrewd.
(ANT.) frank, sincere, gullible, open, guileless, ingenuous.

craggy *(SYN.)* rough, rugged, irregular, uneven.
(ANT.) level, sleek, smooth, fine, polished.

crank *(SYN.)* cross, irritable, bad-tempered, testy.
(ANT.) cheerful, happy.

crash *(SYN.)* smash, shatter, dash.

crave *(SYN.)* want, desire, hunger.
(ANT.) relinquish, renounce.

craving *(SYN.)* relish, appetite, desire, liking, longing, passion.
(ANT.) renunciation, distaste, disgust.

crazy *(SYN.)* delirious, deranged, idiotic, mad, insane, imbecilic, demented, maniacal.
(ANT.) sane, sensible, sound, rational, reasonable.

creak *(SYN.)* squeak.

create *(SYN.)* fashion, form, generate, engender, formulate, make, originate, produce, cause, ordain, invent, beget, design, construct, constitute.
(ANT.) disband, abolish, terminate, destroy, demolish.

creative *(SYN.)* imaginative, ingenious, resourceful, clever, inventive, innovative.
(ANT.) unromantic, dull, literal.

credence *(SYN.)* confidence, faith, feeling, opinion, trust.
(ANT.) doubt, denial.

credit *(SYN.)* believe, accept, belief, trust, faith, merit, honor, apprehend, fancy, hold,

support.
(ANT.) doubt, question, distrust.

creditable *(SYN.)* worthy.
(ANT.) dishonorable, shameful.

credulous *(SYN.)* trusting, naive, believing, gullible.
(ANT.) suspicious.

creed *(SYN.)* belief, precept, credo, faith, teaching.
(ANT.) practice, deed, conduct, performance.

creek *(SYN.)* brook, spring, stream.

crime *(SYN.)* offense, insult, aggression, wrong.
(ANT.) right, innocence, morality.

criminal *(SYN.)* unlawful, crook, gangster, outlaw, illegal, convict, delinquent, offender, malefactor, felonious, felon, transgressor.

cripple *(SYN.)* hurt, maim, injure.

crisis *(SYN.)* conjuncture, emergency, pass, pinch, acme, climax, contingency, juncture, exigency.
(ANT.) calm, normality, stability, equilibrium.

crisp *(SYN.)* crumbling, delicate, frail, brittle.
(ANT.) calm, stability.

criterion *(SYN.)* measure, law, rule, principle, gauge, proof.
(ANT.) fancy guess, chance, supposition.

critic *(SYN.)* reviewer, judge, commentator, censor.

critical *(SYN.)* exact, fastidious, caviling, faultfinding, accurate, condemning, reproachful, risky, dangerous, momen-

criticize (SYN.) examine, analyze, inspect, blame, censure, appraise, evaluate, scrutinize.
(ANT.) neglect, overlook, approve.

critique (SYN.) criticism, inspection, review.

crony (SYN.) colleague, companion, chum, buddy, comrade, friend.
(ANT.) stranger, enemy, adversary.

crooked (SYN.) twisted, corrupt, hooked, curved, criminal, dishonest, bent, impaired.
(ANT.) improved, raised, honest, upright, enhanced.

crop (SYN.) fruit, produce, harvest, cut, mow, reaping, result, yield.

cross (SYN.) mix, mingle, traverse, interbreed, annoyed, irritable, cranky, testy, angry, mean.
(ANT.) cheerful.

crouch (SYN.) duck, stoop.

crow (SYN.) boast, brag.

crowd (SYN.) masses, flock, host, squeeze, mob, multitude, populace, throng, swarm.

crown (SYN.) coronet, apex, crest, circlet, pinnacle, tiara, skull, head, top, zenith.
(ANT.) base, bottom, foundation, foot.

crude (SYN.) rude, graceless, unpolished, green, harsh, rough, coarse, ill-prepared, unfinished, raw, boorish, unrefined, uncouth.
(ANT.) finished, refined, polished, cultured, genteel, cultivated.

cruel (SYN.) ferocious, mean, heartless, unmerciful, malignant, savage, brutal, pitiless, inhuman, ruthless, merciless, barbarous.
(ANT.) humane, forbearing, kind, compassionate, gentle.

cruelty (SYN.) harshness, meanness, savagery, brutality.
(ANT.) compassion, kindness.

crumb (SYN.) jot, grain, mite, particle, shred.
(ANT.) mass, bulk, quantity.

crunch (SYN.) champ, gnaw, nibble.

crush (SYN.) smash, break, crash.

cry (SYN.) yowl, yell, roar, shout, scream, wail, weep, bawl, sob.

cryptic (SYN.) puzzling, mysterious, enigmatic, hidden, secret, vague, obscure, occult, unclear.

cull (SYN.) elect, choose, select.
(ANT.) reject, refuse.

culprit (SYN.) delinquent, felon, offender.

cultivate (SYN.) plant, seed, farm, till, refine, educate, teach.

cultivation (SYN.) farming, horticulture, agriculture.

culture (SYN.) humanism, upbringing, cultivation, breeding, education, learning, civilization, refinement.
(ANT.) illiteracy, vulgarity, ignorance.

cultured (SYN.) sophisticated, worldly.
(ANT.) crude, simple, uncouth, ingenuous.

cumbersome (SYN.) bulky, clumsy, awkward, unmanageable.
(ANT.) handy.

cunning (SYN.) clever, wily, crafty, foxy, skillful, tricky, ingenious, foxiness, ability, skill, wiliness, devious, shrewdness, cleverness.
(ANT.) honest, naive, openness, straightforward, direct.

curb (SYN.) check, restraint, hinder, hold, limit, control, stop.
(ANT.) aid, loosen, incite, encourage.

cure (SYN.) help, treatment, heal, medicine, relief, remedy.

curiosity (SYN.) marvel, rarity, phenomenon, admiration, amazement, bewilderment, wonder.
(ANT.) apathy, indifference, expectation.

curious (SYN.) interrogative, interested, peculiar, queer, nosy, peeping, prying, inquisitive, unusual.
(ANT.) unconcerned, incurious, ordinary, indifferent, uninterested.

current (SYN.) up-to-date, contemporary, present, new, tide, stream.
(ANT.) antiquated, old, bygone, ancient, past.

curse (SYN.) oath, denounce, swear, condemn.
(ANT.) blessing, advantage.

cursory (SYN.) frivolous, shallow, slight.
(ANT.) complete, deep, profound, thorough.

curt (SYN.) hasty, short, abrupt, brusque, brief, blunt, rude, harsh.
(ANT.) friendly, smooth, gradual, polite, courteous.

curtail (SYN.) condense, contract, reduce, limit, abbreviate.
(ANT.) lengthen, extend.

curtain (SYN.) blind, drapery, drape, shade.

curve (SYN.) crook, deflect, bend, incline, turn, twist.
(ANT.) resist, stiffen, straighten.

cushion (SYN.) pillow, pad, check, absorb.

custodian (SYN.) guard, keeper, guardian, watchman.

custody (SYN.) guardianship, care.
(ANT.) neglect, disregard, indifference.

custom (SYN.) fashion, rule, routine, practice, usage.

customary (SYN.) common, usual, regular, everyday, general.
(ANT.) exceptional, irregular, rare, unusual, abnormal.

customer (SYN.) client, buyer.

cut (SYN.) slash, gash, prick, slit, sever, cleave, mow, incision, chop, lop, slice.

cut back (SYN.) decrease, reduce.

cut in (SYN.) butt in, interfere.

cut off (SYN.) cease, terminate.

cylindrical (SYN.) circular, rotund, spherical, round.

D

dab *(SYN.)* coat, pat, smear.

dabble *(SYN.)* splatter, toy, splash, fiddle, putter.

dabbler *(SYN.)* amateur, dilettante, tinkerer, trifler.
(ANT.) master, expert, scholar, specialist, authority.

daft *(SYN.)* crazy, foolish, insane.

dagger *(SYN.)* knife, dirk, blade.

daily *(SYN.)* every day, diurnal, regularly.

dainty *(SYN.)* slender, pleasing, delicate, frail, pleasant, pretty, petite, graceful, fine, elegant.
(ANT.) uncouth, vulgar, coarse, tough.

dally *(SYN.)* dawdle, linger, lag, delay, loiter.
(ANT.) rush, hurry, dash, get going, bustle.

dam *(SYN.)* dike, levee, barrier, slow, stop, obstruct, block.
(ANT.) free, release, loose, unleash.

damage *(SYN.)* spoil, deface, impair, mar, hurt, impairment, destruction, injure, harm.
(ANT.) repair, benefit, mend, rebuild, improve, ameliorate.

dame *(SYN.)* woman, lady.

damn *(SYN.)* denounce, descry, curse, reprove, blame.
(ANT.) bless, honor, glorify, praise, accept, applaud, consecrate.

damnable *(SYN.)* blameworthy, evil, detestable, execrable, outrageous, bad, horrible.
(ANT.) good, commendable, worthy, praise-worthy.

damp *(SYN.)* humid, dank, moisture, wetness, humidity.
(ANT.) arid, dry.

dampen *(SYN.)* wet, depressed, moisten, dull, suppress, sprinkle, discouraged, retard, slow, inhibit, deaden, muffle.
(ANT.) dehumidify, increase, encourage.

dance *(SYN.)* bounce, flit, skip, sway, prance, bob, glide, caper, cavort, frisk.

dandle *(SYN.)* jounce, joggle, bounce, jiggle, nestle, cuddle, caress.

dandy *(SYN.)* coxcomb, fop, swell, great, fine, wonderful, excellent.
(ANT.) rotten, terrible, awful, miserable, slob.

danger *(SYN.)* jeopardy, risk, threat, hazard, uncertainty, peril.
(ANT.) safety, immunity, security, defense.

dangerous *(SYN.)* risky, insecure, threatening, critical, perilous, unsafe, uncertain, hazardous.
(ANT.) trustworthy, secure, protected, safe.

dangle *(SYN.)* droop, swing, flap, hang, sag.

dank *(SYN.)* moist, muggy, wet.
(ANT.) dry.

dapper *(SYN.)* spruce, trim, natty, dashing, neat.
(ANT.) untidy, sloppy, shabby, messy, unkempt.

dappled *(SYN.)* spotted, flecked, brindled, variegated, piebald, pied.

(ANT.) uniform, solid, unvaried.

dare (SYN.) brave, call, question, defy, risk, challenge.

daredevil (SYN.) lunatic, thrillseeker, madcap, adventurer.

daring (SYN.) foolhardy, chivalrous, rash, fearless, courageous, intrepid, valiant, courage, bravery, brave, precipitate, bold.

(ANT.) timid, cowardice, timidity, cautious.

dark (SYN.) somber, obscure, gloomy, black, unilluminated, dim, evil, hidden, secret, swarthy, murky, opaque, dismal, mournful, sable, sullen, shadowy, sinister, dusky, mystic, shadowy, unlit, sunless, shaded, wicked, occult.

(ANT.) lucid, happy, cheerful, illuminated, pleasant.

darling (SYN.) dear, adored, sweetheart, cherished.

(ANT.) uncherished, unlovable, rejected, forlorn.

darn (SYN.) repair, mend.

dart (SYN.) scurry, arrow, barb, hurry, dash, throw, missile, run, hasten, scamper, toss, rush, cast.

dash (SYN.) pound, thump, beat, smite, buffet, thrash, smash, break, scurry, run, dart, rush, scamper, hint, pinch, hit, strike.

(ANT.) stroke, hearten, encourage, defend.

dashing (SYN.) swashbuckling, dapper, flamboyant, handsome.

(ANT.) dull, colorless, shabby, lifeless.

dastardly (SYN.) craven, cowardly, mean, rotten, villainous, dishonorable.

(ANT.) heroic, brave, highminded, courageous.

data (SYN.) information, statistics, proof, facts, evidence.

date (SYN.) interview, appointment, commitment, engagement, meeting, rendezvous, regale, entertain.

dated (SYN.) out-of-date, oldfashioned, outmoded.

(ANT.) latest, now, current, fashionable, hot.

daub (SYN.) coat, grease, soil, scribble, cover, stain, smear, scrawl.

daunt (SYN.) discourage, dishearten, intimidate, frighten, deter.

(ANT.) enspirit, encourage.

dauntless (SYN.) fearless, brave, bold, courageous, intrepid, valiant.

(ANT.) fearful, timid, cowardly.

dawn (SYN.) sunrise, start, outset, daybreak, origin, commencement.

(ANT.) dusk, sunset, nightfall, end, conclusion, finish.

daydream (SYN.) woolgather, muse.

daze (SYN.) perplex, stun, puzzle, bewilder, upset, confuse, ruffle, confusion, stupor, bewilderment.

dazzle (SYN.) surprise, stun, astonish, impress, bewilder, stupefy.

dead (SYN.) departed, lifeless, deceased, insensible, inanimate, dull, defunct, gone, unconscious, inoperative, inactive, inert, spiritless.

(ANT.) animate, functioning, active, living, alive, stirring.

deaden *(SYN.)* anesthetize, numb, paralyze.

deadlock *(SYN.)* standstill, impasse, stalemate.

deadly *(SYN.)* lethal, mortal, fatal, deathly, baleful.

deaf *(SYN.)* stone-deaf, unhearing, unheeding, unaware, unheedful, stubborn, oblivious, inattentive.

(ANT.) aware, conscious.

deafening *(SYN.)* vociferous, noisy, stentorian, resounding, loud.

(ANT.) soft, inaudible, subdued.

deal *(SYN.)* act, treat, attend, cope, barter, trade, bargain, apportion, give, distribute, deliver.

dear *(SYN.)* valued, esteemed, expensive, beloved, costly, darling, high-priced, loved, precious.

(ANT.) hateful, reasonable, inexpensive, cheap, unwanted.

dearth *(SYN.)* shortage, lack, scarcity.

death *(SYN.)* decease, extinction, demise, passing.

(ANT.) life.

debase *(SYN.)* lower, degrade, alloy, adulterate, defile, humiliate, depress, abase, pervert, corrupt.

(ANT.) restore, improve, vitalize, enhance.

debate *(SYN.)* wrangle, discuss, plead, argue, discussion, contend, argument, controversy, dispute.

(ANT.) agreement, reject, accord, ignore, spurn.

debonair *(SYN.)* urbane, sophisticated, refined, dapper, well-bred.

debris *(SYN.)* rubbish, litter, junk, wreckage, refuse, detritus, ruins, trash, residue.

debt *(SYN.)* amount due, liability, obligation.

decay *(SYN.)* decrease, spoil, ebb, decline, waste, disintegrate, wane, dwindle, molder, deteriorate, perish, wither, rot, collapse, putrefy, die, decompose.

(ANT.) progress, rise, increase, grow, flourish.

deceased *(SYN.)* lifeless, departed, dead, insensible, defunct.

(ANT.) living, alive.

deceit *(SYN.)* duplicity, cheat, fraud, chicanery, trick, cunning, deception, guile, beguilement, deceitfulness, dishonesty, wiliness.

(ANT.) truthfulness, openness, forthrightness, honesty, candor.

deceitful *(SYN.)* false, fraudulent, insincere, dishonest, deceptive.

(ANT.) sincere, honest.

deceive *(SYN.)* cheat, defraud, hoodwink, mislead, swindle.

decency *(SYN.)* decorum, dignity, property, respectability.

decent *(SYN.)* befitting, fit, suitable, becoming, respectable, adequate, seemly, fitting, comely, appropriate, proper, tolerable, decorous.

(ANT.) vulgar, gross, improper, unsuitable, indecorous, reprehensible, indecent, coarse.

deception (SYN.) trick, cheat, sham, deceit, trickery, craftiness, treachery, beguilement, cunning.

(ANT.) openness, frankness, candor, probity, truthfulness, honesty.

deceptive (SYN.) specious, fallacious, deceitful, false, delusive, unreliable, illusive, tricky, dishonest, deceiving, misleading, delusory.

(ANT.) honest, real, genuine, true, truthful, authentic.

decide (SYN.) resolve, determine, terminate, conclude, close, settle, adjudicate, choose, end.

(ANT.) waver, hesitate, vacillate, doubt, suspend.

decipher (SYN.) render, unravel, construe, solve, decode, translate, elucidate, determine.

(ANT.) misconstrue, distort, misinterpret, confuse.

decision (SYN.) resolution, determination, settlement.

decisive (SYN.) determined, firm, decided, unhesitating, resolute.

declaration (SYN.) pronouncement, notice, affirmation, statement, announcement, assertion.

declare (SYN.) assert, promulate, affirm, tell, broadcast, express, proclaim, aver, say,

pronounce, profess, announce.

(ANT.) deny, withhold, conceal, suppress.

decline (SYN.) descend, decay, dwindle, refuse, incline, wane, sink, depreciate, deny, diminish, weaken.

(ANT.) accept, ascend, ameliorate, increase.

decompose (SYN.) rot, disintegrate, molder, decay, crumble.

decorate (SYN.) trim, paint, deck, enrich, color, beautify, enhance, furbish, furnish, adorn, ornament.

(ANT.) uncover, mar, deface, defame, debase.

decoration (SYN.) ornamentation, embellishment, adornment, furnishing, award, citation, medal.

decoy (SYN.) lure, bait.

decrease (SYN.) lessen, wane, deduct, diminish, curtail, deduct, remove, lessening, decline.

(ANT.) expansion, increase, enlarge, expand, grow.

decree (SYN.) act, order, edict, statute, declaration, announce.

decrepit (SYN.) feeble, puny, weakened, infirm, enfeebled, languid, rickety, weak, run-down, tumble-down, dilapidated, faint.

(ANT.) strong, forceful, vigorous, energetic, lusty.

decry (SYN.) lower, belittle, derogate, minimize, undervalue.

(ANT.) praise, commend, magnify, aggrandize.

dedicate (SYN.) sanctify, consecrate, hallow, devote, assign.

dedicated *(SYN.)* disposed, true, affectionate, fond.

(ANT.) indisposed, detached, untrammeled, disinclined.

deduct *(SYN.)* lessen, shorten, abate, remove, eliminate, curtail, subtract.

(ANT.) grow, enlarge, add, increase, amplify, expand.

deed *(SYN.)* feat, transaction, action, performance, act, operation, achievement, document, certificate, title, accomplishment.

(ANT.) intention, cessation, inactivity, deliberation.

deem *(SYN.)* hold, determine, believe, regard, reckon, judge, consider, account, expound, view.

deep *(SYN.)* bottomless, low, unplumbed, acute, obscure, involved, absorbed.

(ANT.) shallow.

deface *(SYN.)* spoil, impair, damage, mar, hurt, scratch, mutilate, disfigure, harm.

(ANT.) mend, benefit, repair, enhance.

defamation *(SYN.)* invective, reproach, upbraiding, abuse, insult, outrage, reviling, desecration.

(ANT.) respect, approval, laudation, commendation.

default *(SYN.)* loss, omission, lack, failure, dereliction.

(ANT.) victory, achievement, sufficiency, success.

defeat *(SYN.)* quell, vanquish, beat, overcome, overthrow, subdue, frustrate, spoil, conquest.

(ANT.) submit, retreat, cede, yield, surrender, lose.

defect *(SYN.)* shortcoming, fault, omission, blemish, imperfection, forsake, leave, weakness, failure.

(ANT.) perfection, flawlessness, support, join, completeness.

defective *(SYN.)* faulty, imperfect, inoperative, flawed, inoperable.

(ANT.) flawless, perfect, faultless.

defend *(SYN.)* screen, espouse, justify, protect, vindicate, fortify, assert, guard, safeguard, shield.

(ANT.) oppose, assault, submit, attack, deny.

defense *(SYN.)* resistance, protection, bulwark, fort, barricade, trench, rampart, fortress.

defer *(SYN.)* postpone, delay.

(ANT.) speed, hurry, expedite.

deference *(SYN.)* fame, worship, adoration, reverence, admiration, respect, fame, dignity, homage.

(ANT.) dishonor, derision, reproach, contempt

defiant *(SYN.)* rebellious, antagonistic, obstinate.

(ANT.) yielding, submissive.

deficient *(SYN.)* lacking, short, incomplete, defective, scanty, insufficient, inadequate.

(ANT.) enough, ample, sufficient, adequate.

defile *(SYN.)* pollute, march, corrupt, dirty, file, debase, contaminate.

(ANT.) purify.

define *(SYN.)* describe, fix, establish, label, designate, set, name, explain.

definite *(SYN.)* fixed, prescribed, certain, specific, exact, determined, distinct, explicit, correct.

(ANT.) indefinite, confused, undetermined, equivocal.

definitely *(SYN.)* certainly, assuredly, absolutely, positively, surely.

definition *(SYN.)* sense, interpretation, meaning, explanation.

deft *(SYN.)* handy, adroit, clever, adept, dexterous, skillful, skilled.

(ANT.) inept, clumsy, maladroit, awkward.

defunct *(SYN.)* lifeless, dead, departed, expired, extinct, spiritless, inanimate.

(ANT.) living, alive, stirring.

defy *(SYN.)* hinder, oppose, withstand, attack, resist, confront, challenge, flout, dare, thwart.

(ANT.) yield, allow, relent, surrender, submit, accede.

degenerate *(SYN.)* dwindle, decline, weaken, deteriorate, decrease.

(ANT.) ascend, ameliorate, increase, appreciate.

degrade *(SYN.)* crush, reduce, subdue, abash, humble, lower, shame, demote, downgrade, abase, mortify.

(ANT.) praise, elevate, honor.

degree *(SYN.)* grade, amount, step, measure, rank, honor, extent.

deign *(SYN.)* condescend, stoop.

dejected *(SYN.)* depressed, downcast, sad, disheartened, blue, discouraged.

(ANT.) cheerful, happy, optimistic.

delectable *(SYN.)* tasty, delicious, savory, delightful, sweet, luscious.

(ANT.) unsavory, distasteful, unpalatable, acrid.

delegate *(SYN.)* emissary, envoy, ambassador, representative, commission, deputize, authorize.

delete *(SYN.)* erase, cancel, remove.

(ANT.) add.

deleterious *(SYN.)* evil, unwholesome, base, sinful, bad, wicked, immoral, destructive, injurious, hurtful, damaging, detrimental.

(ANT.) moral, excellent, reputable, healthful, healthy, helpful, constructive, good.

deliberate *(SYN.)* studied, willful, intended, contemplated, premeditated, planned, methodical, designed.

(ANT.) fortuitous, hasty, accidental.

delicate *(SYN.)* frail, critical, slender, dainty, pleasing, fastidious, exquisite, precarious, demanding, sensitive, savory, fragile, weak.

(ANT.) tough, strong, coarse, clumsy, hearty, hale, vulgar, rude.

delicious *(SYN.)* tasty, luscious, delectable, sweet, savory.

(ANT.) unsavory, distasteful, unpalatable, unpleasant, acrid.

delight (SYN.) joy, bliss, gladness, pleasure, ecstasy, happiness, rapture.

(ANT.) revolt, sorrow, annoyance, displeasure, disgust, displease, revulsion, misery.

delightful (SYN.) pleasing, pleasant, charming, refreshing, pleasurable.

(ANT.) nasty, disagreeable, unpleasant.

delirious (SYN.) raving, mad, giddy, frantic, hysterical, violent.

deliver (SYN.) impart, publish, rescue, commit, communicate, free, address, offer, save, give, liberate,

(ANT.) restrict, confine, capture, withhold.

deluge (SYN.) overflow, flood.

delusion (SYN.) mirage, fantasy, phantasm, vision, dream, illusion, phantom, hallucination.

(ANT.) substance, actuality.

delve (SYN.) dig, look, search, scoop, explore, hunt.

demand (SYN.) claim, inquire, ask, need, require, obligation, requirement, necessitate.

(ANT.) tender, give, present, waive, relinquish, offer.

demean (SYN.) comport, bear, operate, commit, carry, act, manage, deport.

demeanor (SYN.) manner, way, conduct, actions, behavior.

demented (SYN.) insane, crazy, mad, mental, psychotic,

lunatic.

demolish (SYN.) ruin, devastate, ravage, annihilate, wreck, destroy, raze, exterminate, obliterate.

(ANT.) erect, make, save, construct, preserve, establish.

demolition (SYN.) wrecking, destruction.

(ANT.) erection, construction.

demon (SYN.) fiend, monster, devil, ogre, spirit.

demonstrate (SYN.) evince, show, prove, display, illustrate, describe, explain, manifest, exhibit.

(ANT.) hide, conceal.

demonstration (SYN.) exhibit, show, presentation, exhibition, display, rally.

demur (SYN.) waver, falter, delay, stutter, doubt, vacillate, hesitate, scruple.

(ANT.) proceed, decide, resolve, continue.

demure (SYN.) meek, shy, modest, diffident, retiring, bashful, coy.

den (SYN.) cave, lair, cavern.

denial (SYN.) disallowance, proscription, refusal, prohibition.

denounce (SYN.) condemn, blame, reprove, reprehend, censure, reproach, upbraid, reprobate.

(ANT.) condone, approve, forgive, commend, praise.

dense (SYN.) crowded, slow, close, obtuse, compact, dull, stupid, compressed, thick, concentrated, packed, solid.

(ANT.) sparse, quick, dispersed,

clever, dissipated, empty, smart, bright.

dent *(SYN.)* notch, impress, pit, nick.

deny *(SYN.)* refuse, withhold, dispute, disavow, forbid, refute, contradict, abjure, confute, gainsay.
(ANT.) confirm, affirm, admit, confess, permit, allow, concede, assert.

depart *(SYN.)* quit, forsake, withdraw, renounce, desert, relinquish, perish, decease.
(ANT.) tarry, remain, come, abide, stay, arrive.

departure *(SYN.)* valediction, farewell.

depend *(SYN.)* trust, rely, confide.

dependable *(SYN.)* secure, trustworthy, certain, safe, trusty, reliable, tried.
(ANT.) unreliable, fallible, dubious, uncertain.

dependent *(SYN.)* relying, contingent, subordinate, conditional.
(ANT.) original, casual, absolute, independent.

depict *(SYN.)* explain, recount, describe, portray, characterize, relate, narrate.

deplore *(SYN.)* repine, lament, bemoan, wail, bewail, weep, grieve, regret.

deport *(SYN.)* exile, eject, oust, banish, expel, dismiss, ostracize, dispel, exclude.
(ANT.) receive, admit, shelter, accept, harbor.

deportment *(SYN.)* deed, behavior, manner, action, carriage, disposition, bearing, demeanor.

deposit *(SYN.)* place, put, bank, save, store, sediment, dregs, addition, entry.
(ANT.) withdraw, withdrawal.

depreciate *(SYN.)* dwindle, decrease, decay, belittle, disparage, weaken, minimize, descend, deteriorate.
(ANT.) ascend, ameliorate, praise, increase, applaud, appreciate.

depress *(SYN.)* deject, dishearten, sadden, dampen, devaluate, devalue, lessen, lower, cheapen, reduce, dispirit, discourage, sink.
(ANT.) exalt, cheer, exhilarate.

depression *(SYN.)* hopelessness, despondency, pessimism, dip, cavity, pothole, hole, despair, gloom, melancholy, sadness, sorrow, recession, decline, desperation, discouragement.
(ANT.) eminence, elation, optimism, happiness, confidence, elevation, hope.

deprive *(SYN.)* bereave, deny, strip.
(ANT.) provision, supply, provide.

derelict *(SYN.)* decrepit, shabby, dilapidated, neglected, forsaken, deserted, remiss, abandoned, lax.

dereliction *(SYN.)* want, lack, failure, miscarriage, loss, default, deficiency, omission, fiasco.
(ANT.) sufficiency, success, achievement, victory.

derision *(SYN.)* irony, satire, banter, raillery, sneering, gibe, ridicule.

derivation *(SYN.)* source, birth, inception, start, beginning, spring, commencement, foundation, origin.

(ANT.) issue, end, outcome, harvest, product.

derive *(SYN.)* obtain, acquire, get, receive.

descend *(SYN.)* wane, lower, move, slope, incline, decline, slant, sink.

(ANT.) increase, appreciate, ameliorate, ascend.

descendant *(SYN.)* child, issue, progeny, offspring.

describe *(SYN.)* portray, picture, recount, depict, relate, characterize, represent, narrate.

description *(SYN.)* history, record, recital, account, computation, chronicle, reckoning, narration, detail, narrative.

(ANT.) misrepresentation, confusion, caricature.

desecration *(SYN.)* profanation, insult, defamation, reviling, abuse, maltreatment, aspersion, perversion, dishonor.

(ANT.) respect, commendation, approval, laudation.

desert *(SYN.)* forsake, wilderness, resign, abjure, abandon, wasteland, waste, leave, surrender, abdicate, quit, barren, uninhabited.

(ANT.) uphold, defend, stay, maintain, accompany, support.

deserter *(SYN.)* runaway, rene-

gade, fugitive, defector.

deserts *(SYN.)* right, compensation, due, reward, requital, condign.

deserve *(SYN.)* earn, warrant, merit.

design *(SYN.)* drawing, purpose, outline, devise, intend, draw, contrive, draft, cunning, plan, artfulness, delineation, scheming, sketch, intent, invent, objective, mean, contrivance, plotting, intention, create.

(ANT.) candor, accident, result, chance.

designate *(SYN.)* manifest, indicate, show, specify, denote, reveal, name, appoint, select, assign, disclose, signify, imply, nominate, intimate.

(ANT.) divert, mislead, conceal, falsify, distract.

desirable *(SYN.)* coveted, wanted.

desire *(SYN.)* longing, craving, yearning, appetite, lust, long for, crave, covet, want, request, ask, need, wish, aspiration, urge.

(ANT.) hate, aversion, loathing, abomination, detest, loathe, abhor, distaste.

desist *(SYN.)* cork, stop, cease, hinder, terminate, abstain, halt, interrupt, seal, arrest, plug, bar.

(ANT.) promote, begin, speed, proceed, start.

desolate *(SYN.)* forlorn, waste, bare, lonely, abandoned, wild, deserted, uninhabited, empty, sad, miserable, wretched, unhappy, bleak, forsaken.

(ANT.) crowded, teeming, populous, happy, cheerful, fertile, attended.

despair *(SYN.)* discouragement, pessimism, depression, hopelessness, despondency, gloom, desperation.

(ANT.) elation, optimism, hope, joy, confidence.

desperado *(SYN.)* criminal, crook, thug, gangster, hoodlum.

desperate *(SYN.)* reckless, determined, despairing, wild, daring, hopeless, despondent, audacious.

(ANT.) optimistic, composed, hopeful, collected, calm, assured.

despicable *(SYN.)* vulgar, offensive, base, vile, contemptible, selfish, low, mean, worthless, nasty.

(ANT.) noble, admirable, generous, worthy, dignified.

despise *(SYN.)* hate, scorn, detest, loathe, disdain, abhor, condemn, dislike, abominate.

(ANT.) honor, love, approve, like, admire.

despite *(SYN.)* notwithstanding.

despoil *(SYN.)* plunder, rob, loot.

despondent *(SYN.)* sad, dismal, depressed, somber, ejected, melancholy, sorrowful.

(ANT.) joyous, cheerful, merry, happy.

despot *(SYN.)* tyrant, ruler, oppressor, dictator.

despotic *(SYN.)* authoritative, unconditional, absolute, entire, unrestricted.

(ANT.) dependent, conditional, qualified, accountable.

destiny *(SYN.)* fate, portion, outcome, consequence, result, fortune, doom, lot.

destitute *(SYN.)* poor, penurious, needy, impecunious, impoverished, indigent.

(ANT.) opulent, wealthy, affluent, rich.

destroy *(SYN.)* raze, devastate, ruin, end, demolish, wreck, extinguish, annihilate, exterminate, obliterate, waste, slay, kill, eradicate.

(ANT.) make, construct, start, create, save, establish.

destroyed *(SYN.)* rent, smashed, interrupted, flattened, wrecked, broken, ruptured, crushed.

(ANT.) whole, repaired, integral, united.

destruction *(SYN.)* ruin, devastation, extinction, demolition.

(ANT.) beginning, creation.

destructive *(SYN.)* deadly, baneful, noxious, deleterious, injurious, pernicious, fatal, detrimental.

(ANT.) salutary, beneficial, creative.

detach *(SYN.)* deduct, remove, subtract, curtail, divide, shorten, decrease, disengage, reduce, separate, diminish.

(ANT.) hitch, grow, enlarge, increase, connect, amplify, attack, expand.

detail *(SYN.)* elaborate, commission, part, itemize, portion, division, fragment, assign, circumstance, segment.

detain (SYN.) impede, delay, hold back, retard, arrest, restrain, stay.
(ANT.) quicken, hasten, expedite, forward, precipitate.

detect (SYN.) discover, reveal, find, ascertain, determine, learn, originate, devise.
(ANT.) hide, screen, cover, mask.

determinant (SYN.) reason, incentive, source, agent, principle, inducement.
(ANT.) result, effect, consequence, end.

determine (SYN.) decide, settle, end, conclude, ascertain, induce, fix, verify, resolve, establish, necessitate.

detest (SYN.) loathe, hate, despise.
(ANT.) savor, appreciate, like, love.

detriment (SYN.) injury, harm, disadvantage, damage.
(ANT.) benefit.

detrimental (SYN.) hurtful, damaging, harmful.
(ANT.) salutary, advantageous, profitable, beneficial.

develop (SYN.) evolve, unfold, enlarge, amplify, expand, create, grow, advance, reveal, unfold, mature, elaborate.
(ANT.) wither, contract, degenerate, stunt, deteriorate, compress.

development (SYN.) growth, expansion, progress, unraveling, elaboration, evolution, maturing, unfolding.
(ANT.) compression, abbrevia-

tion, curtailment.

deviate (SYN.) deflect, stray, divert, diverge, wander, sidetrack, digress.
(ANT.) preserve, follow, remain, continue, persist.

device (SYN.) tool, utensil, means, channel, machine, agent, vehicle, gadget, apparatus, tools, instrument, contrivance.
(ANT.) preventive, impediment, hindrance, obstruction.

devilish (SYN.) diabolical, fiendish, diabolic, satanic, demonic.

devious (SYN.) tortuous, winding, distorted, circuitous, tricky, crooked, roundabout, cunning, erratic, indirect.
(ANT.) straight, direct, straightforward, honest.

devise (SYN.) create, concoct, invent, originate.

devote (SYN.) assign, dedicate, give, apply.
(ANT.) withhold, relinquish, ignore, withdraw.

devoted (SYN.) attached, dedicated, prone, wedded, addicted, ardent, earnest, loyal, disposed, inclined, fond, affectionate, faithful.
(ANT.) untrammeled, disinclined, detached, indisposed.

devotion (SYN.) piety, zeal, ardor, loyalty, dedication, religiousness, consecration, affection, love, devoutness, fidelity, attachment.
(ANT.) unfaithfulness, aversion, alienation, indifference.

devour (SYN.) consume, gulp,

gorge, waste, eat, ruin, swallow, destroy.

devout *(SYN.)* sacred, religious, spiritual, holy, theological, pietistic, pious, sanctimonious, reverent.

(ANT.) profane, skeptical, atheistic, secular, impious.

dexterity *(SYN.)* talent, capability, qualification, aptness, skill, ability.

(ANT.) unreadiness, incapacity, disability, incompetence.

dexterous *(SYN.)* clever, adroit, handy, deft, facile, skillful, skilled, proficient.

(ANT.) awkward, clumsy.

dialect *(SYN.)* slang, jargon, cant, speech, idiom, tongue, diction, vernacular.

(ANT.) nonsense, drivel, babble, gibberish.

dialogue *(SYN.)* interview, chat, discussion, conference, exchange, talk, conversation.

diary *(SYN.)* memo, account, journal, words.

dicker *(SYN.)* haggle, bargain, negotiate.

dictate *(SYN.)* deliver, speak, record, command, order, direct.

dictator *(SYN.)* oppressor, tyrant, despot, persecutor, overlord, autocrat.

die *(SYN.)* fade, wane, cease, depart, wither, decay, decline, sink, expire, perish, decease, go, diminish, fail, languish, decrease.

(ANT.) live, begin, grow, survive, flourish.

difference *(SYN.)* inequality, variety, disparity, discord, distinction, dissension, dissimilarity, disagreement, contrast, separation.

(ANT.) harmony, similarity, identity, agreement, likeness, compatibility, kinship, resemblance.

different *(SYN.)* unlike, various, distinct, miscellaneous, divergent, sundry, contrary, differing, diverse, variant, incongruous, divers, unlike, changed, dissimilar, opposite.

(ANT.) similar, congruous, same, alike, identical.

differentiate *(SYN.)* separate, discriminate, distinguish, perceive, recognize, discern.

(ANT.) confuse, omit, mingle, confound, overlook.

difficult *(SYN.)* involved, demanding, arduous, trying, complicated, hard, laborious, perplexing, hard, intricate.

(ANT.) simple, easy, facile, effortless.

difficulty *(SYN.)* trouble, hardship, predicament, trouble.

(ANT.) ease.

diffuse *(SYN.)* spread, sparse, scattered, scanty, dispersed, thin, rare.

(ANT.) concentrated.

dig *(SYN.)* burrow, excavate, appreciate, understand.

digest *(SYN.)* consume, eat, reflect on, study, shorten, consider, summarize, abridge, abstract, abridgment, synopsis.

dignified *(SYN.)* serious, solemn, noble, stately, elegant.

dignify *(SYN.)* honor, elevate.
(ANT.) shame, degrade, humiliate.

dignity *(SYN.)* stateliness, distinction, bearing.

digress *(SYN.)* divert, wander, bend, stray, deflect, sidetrack, crook.
(ANT.) preserve, continue, remain, follow, persist.

dilate *(SYN.)* increase, widen, amplify, enlarge, augment, expand.
(ANT.) shrink, contract, restrict, abridge.

dilemma *(SYN.)* strait, condition, scrape, difficulty, plight.
(ANT.) ease, calmness, satisfaction, comfort.

diligent *(SYN.)* patient, busy, hard-working, active, perseverant, assiduous, industrious, careful.
(ANT.) unconcerned, indifferent, apathetic, lethargic, careless.

dim *(SYN.)* pale, shadowy, faint, faded, unclear, vague, darken, dull, indistinct.
(ANT.) brighten, brilliant, bright, illuminate, glaring.

dimension *(SYN.)* size, importance, measure, extent.

diminish *(SYN.)* suppress, lower, decrease, shrink, wane, abate, reduce, lessen, assuage.
(ANT.) enlarge, revive, amplify, increase.

diminutive *(SYN.)* small, wee, tiny, little, minute.
(ANT.) large, big, great, gigantic, huge.

din *(SYN.)* tumult, clamor, sound, babble, outcry, row, noise, racket.
(ANT.) quiet, stillness, hush.

dine *(SYN.)* lunch, eat, sup, feed.

dingy *(SYN.)* dull, dark, dismal, dirty, drab, murky, gray.
(ANT.) cheerful, bright.

dip *(SYN.)* immerse, plunge, submerge, wet, swim.

diplomacy *(SYN.)* knack, dexterity, skill, address, poise, tact, finesse.
(ANT.) vulgarity, blunder, awkwardness, incompetence.

diplomatic *(SYN.)* politic, adroit, tactful, discreet, judicious, gracious, polite, discriminating.
(ANT.) rude, churlish, gruff, boorish, impolite, coarse.

dire *(SYN.)* horrible, terrible, appalling, fearful, harrowing, grievous, ghastly, awful, horrid, terrifying, dreadful, frightful, horrifying, monstrous, horrendous, repulsive.
(ANT.) lovely, enchanting, fascinating, beautiful, enjoyable.

direct *(SYN.)* rule, manage, bid, order, level, command, conduct, regulate, point, indicate, show, aim, control, sight, guide, instruct, train, govern.
(ANT.) swerving, untruthful, misguide, distract, indirect, crooked, deceive.

direction *(SYN.)* way, order, course, instruction, tendency, management, route, trend, guidance, administration, supervision, inclination.

directly *(SYN.)* immediately, straight.

dirt *(SYN.)* pollution, soil, filthiness, filth.

(ANT.) cleanliness, cleanness.

dirty *(SYN.)* muddy, base, pitiful, filthy, shabby, foul, soiled, nasty, mean, grimy, low, obscene, untidy, indecent, unclean, messy, squalid, contemptible, sloppy.

(ANT.) pure, neat, wholesome, clean, presentable.

disability *(SYN.)* inability, weakness, handicap, incapacity, injury, unfitness, incompetence, impotence.

(ANT.) power, ability, strength, capability.

disable *(SYN.)* weaken, incapacitate, cripple.

(ANT.) strengthen.

disabled *(SYN.)* deformed, limping, weak, crippled, maimed, defective, unsatisfactory, unconvincing, feeble.

(ANT.) vigorous, athletic, sound, agile, robust.

disadvantage *(SYN.)* drawback, hindrance, handicap, inconvenience, obstacle.

(ANT.) advantage, benefit, convenience.

disagree *(SYN.)* quarrel, dispute, differ, conflict.

(ANT.) agree.

disagreement *(SYN.)* nonconformity, variance, difference, objection, challenge, remonstrance, dissent.

(ANT.) assent, acceptance, compliance, agreement.

disappear *(SYN.)* end, fade out, vanish.

(ANT.) emerge, appear.

disappoint *(SYN.)* fail, displease, mislead, dissatisfy.

(ANT.) please, satisfy, gratify.

disappointment *(SYN.)* dissatisfaction, defeat, discouragement, failure.

(ANT.) pleasure, satisfaction, gratification.

disapprove *(SYN.)* object to, disfavor, oppose.

(ANT.) approve.

disaster *(SYN.)* casualty, mishap, misfortune, catastrophe, accident, adversity, calamity.

(ANT.) fortune, advantage, welfare.

disavow *(SYN.)* reject, revoke, disclaim, retract, disown.

(ANT.) recognize, acknowledge.

disband *(SYN.)* scatter, split, dismiss, separate.

disbelief *(SYN.)* doubt, incredulity, skepticism.

(ANT.) certainty, credulity.

discard *(SYN.)* scrap, reject.

discern *(SYN.)* distinguish, see, descry, separate, differentiate, perceive, discriminate, detect, observe, recognize.

(ANT.) omit, confuse, overlook, mingle, confound.

discernment *(SYN.)* perception, sharpness, intelligence, perspicacity, acuity, keenness.

(ANT.) dullness, stupidity.

discharge *(SYN.)* remove, relieve, dismiss, banish, unburden, shoot, fire, explosion, eject, detonation, liberation, release, unload, discard, send.

(ANT.) *retain, employ, enlist, hire, accept, recall, detain.*

disciple (SYN.) learner, follower, student, adherent, supporter, scholar, pupil, devotee.

(ANT.) *guide, leader.*

discipline (SYN.) training, order, instruction, drill, restraint, regulation, practice, correction, control, self-control, train, teach, exercise.

(ANT.) *carelessness, sloppiness, confusion, negligence, messiness, chaos, turbulence.*

disclaim (SYN.) retract, reject, deny, renounce, disavow, revoke.

(ANT.) *recognize, acknowledge.*

disclose (SYN.) show, divulge, betray, uncover, discover, reveal, expose.

(ANT.) *hide, cloak, mask, cover, obscure, conceal.*

discomfit (SYN.) malaise, concern, confuse, baffle, perplex, disconcert.

discomfort (SYN.) malaise, concern, anxiety, uneasiness.

disconcerted (SYN.) disturbed, agitated, upset.

disconnect (SYN.) divide, separate, unhook, disengage.

(ANT.) *connect, bind, attach, unify, engage.*

disconsolate (SYN.) depressed, downcast, sorrowful, dejected, dismal, sad, unhappy, wretched, somber, cheerless, morose, miserable, mournful.

(ANT.) *delightful, merry, glad, cheerful, happy.*

discontent (SYN.) displeased, disgruntled, unhappy, dissat-isfied, vexed.

discontinue (SYN.) postpone, delay, adjourn, stay, stop, defer, suspend, end, cease, interrupt.

(ANT.) *prolong, persist, continue, start, begin, proceed, maintain.*

discord (SYN.) disagreement, conflict.

(ANT.) *concord, accord, agreement.*

discourage (SYN.) hamper, obstruct, restrain, block, dishearten, retard, check, dispirit, thwart, depress, hinder, stop.

(ANT.) *expedite, inspire, encourage, promote, inspirit, assist, further.*

discourteous (SYN.) gruff, rude, vulgar, blunt, impolite, saucy, uncivil, boorish, rough.

(ANT.) *stately, courtly, civil, dignified, genteel.*

discover (SYN.) find out, invent, expose, ascertain, devise, reveal, learn, determine, detect.

(ANT.) *hide, screen, cover, conceal, lose.*

discredit (SYN.) disbelieve, dishonor, doubt, disgrace, shame.

discreet (SYN.) politic, discriminating, judicious, adroit, prudent, cautious, wise, tactful, careful, diplomatic.

(ANT.) *incautious, rude, coarse, boorish, tactless, imprudent, indiscreet, careless, gruff.*

discrepant (SYN.) incompatible, wavering, contrary, irreconcilable, unsteady, illogical, contradictory.

(ANT.) correspondent, compatible, consistent.

discriminating *(SYN.)* exact, particular, critical, accurate, discerning.

(ANT.) unimportant, shallow, insignificant, superficial.

discrimination *(SYN.)* perspicacity, discernment, racism, wisdom, bias, sagacity, prejudice, intelligence, understanding.

(ANT.) thoughtlessness, senselessness, arbitrariness.

discuss *(SYN.)* gossip, plead, discourse, blab, lecture, talk, chat, spout, mutter, deliberate, consider, reason, comment.

discussion *(SYN.)* speech, chatter, lecture, conference, talk, dialogue, conversation, rumor.

(ANT.) silence, correspondence, writing.

disdain *(SYN.)* derision, hatred, contempt, scorn, contumely, reject, haughtiness, detestation.

(ANT.) respect, esteem, reverence, admire, prize, honor, admiration, awe, regard.

disdainful *(SYN.)* haughty, scornful, arrogant, contemptuous.

(ANT.) awed, admiring, regardful.

disease *(SYN.)* malady, disorder, ailment, illness, affliction, infirmity, complaint, sickness.

(ANT.) soundness, health, vigor.

disentangle *(SYN.)* unwind, untie, clear, unravel, unknot, unsnarl, untangle.

disfigured *(SYN.)* deformed,

marred, defaced, scarred.

disgrace *(SYN.)* odium, chagrin, shame, mortification, embarrassment, humiliate, scandal, dishonor.

(ANT.) renown, glory, respect, praise, dignity, honor.

disgraceful *(SYN.)* ignominious, shameful, discreditable, disreputable, scandalous, dishonorable.

(ANT.) renowned, esteemed, respectable, honorable.

disguise *(SYN.)* excuse, simulation, pretension, hide, camouflage, make-up, mask, conceal, screen, affectation.

(ANT.) show, reality, actuality, display, reveal, sincerity, fact.

disgust *(SYN.)* offend, repulse, nauseate, revolt, sicken.

(ANT.) admiration, liking.

disgusting *(SYN.)* repulsive, nauseating, revolting, nauseous, repugnant

dishearten *(SYN.)* depress, sadden, discourage.

disheveled *(SYN.)* misused, sloppy, rumpled, untidy.

dishonest *(SYN.)* crooked, impure, unsound, false, contaminated, corrupt, putrid, thievish, vitiated, tainted.

(ANT.) upright, honest, straightforward.

dishonor *(SYN.)* disrepute, scandal, indignity, chagrin, mortification, shame, obloquy, defamation, humiliation, disgrace.

(ANT.) renown, glory, praise, honor, dignity.

disinclined *(SYN.)* unwilling,

reluctant, loath.

disingenuous *(SYN.)* tricky, deceitful, scheming, dishonest, underhanded, cunning, artful, crafty, insidious.

disintegrate *(SYN.)* decompose, dwindle, spoil, decay, wane, ebb, decline, rot.

(ANT.) increase, flourish, rise, grow.

disinterested *(SYN.)* unbiased, open-minded, neutral, impartial, unprejudiced.

dislike *(SYN.)* aversion, dread, reluctance, abhorrence, disinclination, hatred, repugnance.

(ANT.) devotion, affection, enthusiasm, attachment.

disloyal *(SYN.)* false, treasonable, apostate, unfaithful, recreant, treacherous, untrue, perfidious, traitorous.

(ANT.) true, devoted, constant, loyal.

dismal *(SYN.)* dark, lonesome, somber, bleak, dull, sad, doleful, sorrowful, cheerless, depressing, dreary, funeral, gloomy, melancholy.

(ANT.) lively, gay, happy, lighthearted, charming, cheerful.

dismantle *(SYN.)* take apart, wreck, disassemble.

dismay *(SYN.)* disturb, bother, dishearten, horror, alarm, bewilder, frighten, scare, discourage, confuse.

(ANT.) encourage, hearten.

dismiss *(SYN.)* remove, discharge, discard, release, liberate, exile, banish, eject, oust.

(ANT.) retain, detain, engage, hire, accept, recall.

disobedient *(SYN.)* refractory, forward, unruly, insubordinate, defiant, rebellious.

(ANT.) submissive, compliant, obedient.

disobey *(SYN.)* invade, break, violate, infringe, defile.

disorder *(SYN.)* tumult, chaos, jumble, confusion, muddle, turmoil, anarchy.

(ANT.) organization, neatness, system, order.

disorganization *(SYN.)* jumble, confusion, muddle, anarchy.

(ANT.) system, order.

disorganized *(SYN.)* muddled, confused, indistinct, bewildered, mixed.

(ANT.) organized, lucid, clear, plain.

disown *(SYN.)* deny, renounce, reject, repudiate, forsake, disinherit.

disparaging *(SYN.)* belittling, deprecatory, discrediting, deprecating.

disparage *(SYN.)* undervalue, depreciate, lower, belittle, derogate, minimize, decry, discredit.

(ANT.) exalting, praise, aggrandize, magnify, commend.

disparagement *(SYN.)* lowering, decrying, undervaluing, belittling, minimizing.

(ANT.) praise, exalting, aggrandizement, magnification.

dispassionate *(SYN.)* calm, cool, composed, controlled, unemotional, imperturbable.

dispatch *(SYN.)* throw, impel, transmit, emit, cast, finish, report, message, send, speed,

achieve, conclude, communication, promptness, discharge.
(ANT.) reluctance, get, retain, bring, slowness, hold.

dispel *(SYN.)* disseminate, scatter, disperse, separate, diffuse.
(ANT.) collect, accumulate, gather.

dispense *(SYN.)* deal, give, allot, assign, apportion, mete, distribute, grant, allocate, measure.
(ANT.) refuse, withhold, confiscate, retain, keep.

disperse *(SYN.)* dissipate, scatter, disseminate, diffuse, separate, dispel.
(ANT.) collect, amass, gather, assemble, accumulate.

dispirited *(SYN.)* unhappy, dejected, disheartened, sad, depressed, melancholy.
(ANT.) cheerful, happy, optimistic.

displace *(SYN.)* remove, transport, lodge, shift, move.
(ANT.) retain, stay, remain.

display *(SYN.)* parade, exhibit, show, expose, reveal, demonstrate, showing, uncover, flaunt.
(ANT.) hide, cover, conceal.

displeasure *(SYN.)* dislike, disapproval, dissatisfaction, distaste, discontentment.

disposal *(SYN.)* elimination, adjustment, removal, release, arrangement, administration, settlement.

dispose *(SYN.)* settle, adjust, arrange.

disposition *(SYN.)* behavior, character, deed, deportment,

action, manner, bearing, temperament, nature, demeanor, personality, carriage.

dispossess *(SYN.)* eject, expel, evict, oust, dislodge.

disprove *(SYN.)* refute, deny, invalidate, controvert.

dispute *(SYN.)* squabble, debate, argument, controversy, contention, disagreement, bicker, contest, argue, contend, quarrel, contradict, discuss, deny, oppose, altercate.
(ANT.) harmony, concord, agreement, allow, concur, agree, concede, decision.

disregard *(SYN.)* slight, omit, ignore, inattention, oversight, skip, neglect, overlook.
(ANT.) regard, include.

disrepair *(SYN.)* ruin, decay, dilapidation, destruction.

disreputable *(SYN.)* dishonored, notorious, dishonorable, disgraced.

disrespectful *(SYN.)* fresh, impertinent, rude, impolite, impudent.
(ANT.) polite, respectful, courteous.

dissect *(SYN.)* examine, cut, analyze.

disseminate *(SYN.)* publish, circulate, spread, publish, broadcast.

dissent *(SYN.)* objection, challenge, disagreement, protest, difference, nonconformity, variance, noncompliance.
(ANT.) assent, acceptance, compliance, agreement.

dissertation *(SYN.)* thesis, treatise, disquisition.

dissimilar *(SYN.)* diverse, unlike, various, distinct, contrary, sundry, different, miscellaneous.

(ANT.) same, alike, similar, congruous.

dissimulation *(SYN.)* pretense, deceit, sanctimony, hypocrisy, cant.

(ANT.) honesty, candor, openness, frankness, truth.

dissipate *(SYN.)* misuse, squander, dwindle, consume, waste, lavish, diminish.

(ANT.) save, conserve, preserve, accumulate, economize.

dissolve *(SYN.)* liquefy, end, cease, melt, fade, disappear.

distant *(SYN.)* stiff, cold, removed, far, afar, unfriendly, remote, faraway, separated, aloof, reserved.

(ANT.) nigh, friendly, close, cordial, near.

distasteful *(SYN.)* disagreeable, unpleasant, objectionable.

distend *(SYN.)* swell, widen, magnify, expand, enlarge.

distinct *(SYN.)* plain, evident, lucid, visible, apparent, different, separate, individual, obvious, manifest, clear.

(ANT.) vague, indistinct, uncertain, obscure, ambiguous.

distinction *(SYN.)* importance, peculiarity, trait, honor, fame, characteristic, repute, quality, renown, prominence, attribute, property.

(ANT.) substance, essence, being.

distinctive *(SYN.)* odd, exceptional, rare, individual, eccentric, special, strange.

(ANT.) ordinary, general, common, normal.

distinguish *(SYN.)* recognize, differentiate, divide, classify, descry, discern, separate, perceive, detect.

(ANT.) mingle, conjoin, blend, found, omit, confuse.

distinguished *(SYN.)* eminent, illustrious, renowned, celebrated, elevated, important, famous, prominent.

(ANT.) ordinary, common, unknown, undistinguished, obscure, unimportant.

distort *(SYN.)* contort, falsify, twist, misrepresent.

distract *(SYN.)* occupy, bewilder, disturb, divert, confuse.

(ANT.) focus, concentrate.

distracted *(SYN.)* abstracted, preoccupied, absent.

(ANT.) attentive, attending, watchful, present.

distraction *(SYN.)* entertainment, confusion, amusement, diversion.

distress *(SYN.)* torment, misery, trouble, worry, pain, agony, torture, anguish, anxiety, disaster, wretchedness, peril, danger, suffering.

(ANT.) joy, solace, comfort, relief.

distribute *(SYN.)* deal, sort, allot, mete, classify, share, issue, dole, apportion, allocate, dispense, group.

district *(SYN.)* domain, place, territory, country, region, division, neighborhood, section, area, land.

distrust *(SYN.)* scruple, unbelief, suspect, mistrust, hesitation, suspense, uncertainty, doubt, suspicion, ambiguity.
(ANT.) faith, conviction, trust, belief, determination.

disturb *(SYN.)* perturb, vex, confuse, worry, agitate, derange, unsettle, perplex, rouse, bother, trouble, annoy, interrupt, discompose.
(ANT.) quiet, order, calm, settle, pacify, soothe.

disturbance *(SYN.)* disorder, commotion, confusion, riot, fight, brawl.
(ANT.) calm, tranquillity, serenity.

disturbed *(SYN.)* neurotic, psychopathic, psychoneurotic, psychotic.
(ANT.) normal.

diverge *(SYN.)* fork, separate.
(ANT.) converge, join, merge.

diverse *(SYN.)* unlike, various, different, several.

diversify *(SYN.)* change, modify, alter.

diversion *(SYN.)* entertainment, sport, distraction, amusement, recreation.

divert *(SYN.)* detract, amuse, confuse, distract, deflect, entertain, tickle.
(ANT.) tire, bore, weary.

divide *(SYN.)* share, split, detach, cleave, apportion, sunder, part, distribute, allocate, disunite, estrange, separate, allot, sever.
(ANT.) merge, unite, convene, join, gather, combine.

divine *(SYN.)* holy, supernatural, godlike, transcendent, celestial, heavenly.
(ANT.) mundane, wicked, blasphemous, profane, diabolical.

division *(SYN.)* partition, separation, sharing, section, segment, part, portion.
(ANT.) union, agreement.

divorce *(SYN.)* disjoin, disconnect, separate, divide.

divulge *(SYN.)* discover, release, expose, show, betray, reveal, admit, disclose, uncover.
(ANT.) hide, conceal, cloak, cover.

dizzy *(SYN.)* staggering, unsteady, giddy, confused.
(ANT.) rational, clear-headed, unconfused.

do *(SYN.)* effect, conduct, perform, work, suffice, accomplish, finish, transact, serve, discharge, execute, complete, carry on, make, settle, conclude, fulfill, consummate, produce, observe, practice.

docile *(SYN.)* pliant, tame, complaint, teachable, obedient, submissive, yielding.
(ANT.) unruly, obstinate, mulish.

dock *(SYN.)* moor, clip, anchor, tie.

doctor *(SYN.)* heal, treat, medic, remedy, cure.

doctrine *(SYN.)* tenet, precept, belief, dogma, teaching, principle, creed.
(ANT.) deed, practice, conduct, perform.

doctrinaire *(SYN.)* formal, dogmatic, overbearing, authoritarian, formal, arrogant, magisterial.

(ANT.) skeptical, indecisive, fluctuating.

document *(SYN.)* report, minute, memorial, vestige, account, note, trace.

dodge *(SYN.)* equivocate, recoil, elude, evade, avoid, duck.

dogma *(SYN.)* tenet, doctrine, belief, teaching, creed.

(ANT.) deed, practice, conduct, performance.

dogmatic *(SYN.)* formal, domineering, authoritarian, doctrinaire, opinionated, dictatorial, positive, arrogant, authoritative, overbearing, doctrinal, magisterial.

(ANT.) skeptical, indecisive, fluctuating.

doing *(SYN.)* feat, performance, act, deed, action, accomplishment, transaction.

(ANT.) intention, inactivity, cessation, inhibition.

dole *(SYN.)* deal, spread, allot, relief, divide, apportion, alms, welfare, distribute, dispense.

doleful *(SYN.)* dark, depressed, sad, dismal, dejected, bleak, dull, blue, sorrowful, unhappy, morose, lonesome, mournful, somber.

(ANT.) lively, cheerful, joyous.

dolt *(SYN.)* blockhead, dunce.

domain *(SYN.)* place, division, region, territory, empire, country, charge, kingdom, realm, quarter, dominion, bailiwick, jurisdiction, land.

domestic *(SYN.)* family, tame, native, servant, homemade, household, internal.

(ANT.) alien, foreign, outside.

domesticate *(SYN.)* train, tame, housebreak, teach.

domicile *(SYN.)* dwelling, residence, home, abode.

dominate *(SYN.)* control, manage, rule, influence, command, govern, tyrannize, direct, regulate.

(ANT.) follow, ignore, abandon, submit, forsake.

domination *(SYN.)* mastery, sway, ascendancy, transcendence.

don *(SYN.)* wear, slip on.

donation *(SYN.)* gift, bequest, present, benefaction, grant, contribution, offering, largess, boon.

(ANT.) earnings, purchase, deprivation, loss.

done *(SYN.)* complete, concluded, finished, over, terminated.

doom *(SYN.)* fortune, issue, result, destruction, destiny, consequence, fate, outcome, destine, ruin, death, lot.

doomed *(SYN.)* fated, predestined, destined, foreordained.

dormant *(SYN.)* unemployed, inert, lazy, unoccupied, idle, indolent.

(ANT.) working, employed, occupied, active, industrious.

dose *(SYN.)* quantity, amount, portion.

dote *(SYN.)* indulge, treasure, coddle, pamper, spoil.

(ANT.) ignore.

double *(SYN.)* copy, fold, duplicate.

doubt *(SYN.)* distrust, incredulity, suspicion, hesitation, uncertainty, question, scruple, ambiguity, skepticism, suspect, mistrust, unbelief, suspense.

(ANT.) *conviction, belief, determination, trust, certainty.*

doubtful (SYN.) uncertain, unsettled, dubious, questionable, unsure, undetermined.

doubtless (SYN.) certainly, undoubtedly, assuredly, positively, unquestionably.

dour (SYN.) gloomy, sulky, crabbed, morose, fretful.

(ANT.) *joyous, pleasant, amiable, merry.*

douse (SYN.) immerse, quench, dip, dunk, extinguish.

dowdy (SYN.) messy, unkempt, untidy, sloppy, shabby frowzy.

downcast (SYN.) sad, disheartened, unhappy, down-hearted, dejected, dispirited, discourage, depressed, glum.

downfall (SYN.) destruction, comedown.

downgrade (SYN.) reduce, lower, diminish, decrease, depreciate.

(ANT.) *improve, upgrade, appreciate.*

downhearted (SYN.) glum, discouraged, depressed, gloomy, downcast, sad, dejected.

(ANT.) *enthusiastic, cheerful, happy.*

downpour (SYN.) cloudburst, deluge, flood.

downright (SYN.) totally, positively, completely, definitely.

dowry (SYN.) endowment, gift, settlement, talent, ability.

drab (SYN.) flat, dull, lifeless, unattractive.

draft (SYN.) air, induction, wind, enrollment, drawing, outline.

drag (SYN.) heave, pull, tug, crawl, draw, tarry, tow, haul, delay.

drain (SYN.) empty, deprive, dry, filter, spend, tap, exhaust, waste, sap, use.

(ANT.) *fulfill, fill.*

drama (SYN.) show, play, production, piece.

dramatist (SYN.) playwright.

drape (SYN.) flow, cover, hang.

drastic (SYN.) severe, rough, violent, tough, intense.

draw (SYN.) tug, obtain, trace, lure, drag, attract, persuade, induce, haul, write, remove, extend, stretch, take out, allure, pull, prolong, extract, draft, delineate, unsheathe, lure, depict, entice, sketch.

(ANT.) *shorten, contract, propel, alienate, drive.*

drawback (SYN.) snag, hitch, disadvantage, deficiency, difficulty, check, obstacle, hindrance, impediment.

(ANT.) *gain, benefit, windfall, advantage.*

drawing (SYN.) likeness, print, view, engraving, portrait, sketch, illustration, picture, scene.

drawn (SYN.) tired, haggard, taut, strained, harrowed, weary, tense, sapped, spent.

(ANT.) *rested, relaxed, energetic, fresh.*

draw out (SYN.) protract, extend, persist, prolong,

lengthen, sustain, continue.
(ANT.) *reduce, curtail, shorten, abridge.*

draw up (SYN.) draft, write out, prepare, compose, indite, formulate, wait, stay.

dread (SYN.) awe, horror, fear, terror, apprehension.
(ANT.) *courage, boldness, assurance, confidence.*

dreadful (SYN.) dire, inspiring, ghastly, appalling, horrid, terrible, awful, frightful, horrible, bad, hideous, awesome, outrageous, repulsive.
(ANT.) *fascinating, beautiful, enjoyable, enchanting, lovely.*

dream (SYN.) fantasy, wish, hope, vision, daydream, reverie, imagine, fantasize, fancy, invent, muse.

dream up (SYN.) cook up, create, concoct, contrive, originate, imagine, devise.

dreary (SYN.) dull, sad, bleak, lonesome, gloomy, chilling, somber, depressing, dismal, cheerless, dark.
(ANT.) *lively, hopeful, gay, cheerful, bright, joyous.*

dregs (SYN.) riffraff, scum, outcasts, dross, leftovers, flotsam.

drench (SYN.) wet, bathe, flood, soak, saturate.

dress (SYN.) garb, frock, gown, clothing, costume, apparel, attire, wardrobe, garments, vesture, clothes, wear, don, robe, raiment.
(ANT.) *undress, strip, divest, disrobe.*

dresser (SYN.) fop, dandy.

dressing (SYN.) bandage, seasoning, medicine, sauce.

dressy (SYN.) flashy, swank, showy, dapper.
(ANT.) *dowdy, drab, frumpy, shabby, tacky.*

dribble (SYN.) fall, drip, leak, slaver, slobber.

drift (SYN.) roam, tendency, meander, sail, float, direction, intention, stray.

drifter (SYN.) hobo, tramp, vagabond.

drill (SYN.) employment, lesson, task, use, activity, operation, training.
(ANT.) *relaxation, indolence, rest, idleness, repose.*

drink (SYN.) gulp, swallow, imbibe, beverage, refreshment, potion.

drip (SYN.) dribble, drop, trickle.

drive (SYN.) impel, coerce, oblige, force, push, direct, constrain, journey, urge, enforce, trip, handle, ride, propel, control, run, compel.

drivel (SYN.) slaver, drool, spit, spittle, dribble, slobber, saliva, nonsense, twaddle, rubbish, babble, gibberish.

driver (SYN.) motorist, operator, teamster, trucker, motorman, pilot, coachman.

droll (SYN.) laughable, funny, amusing, witty, comical.
(ANT.) *sober, sad, solemn, melancholy.*

drone (SYN.) buzz, hum, loafer, idler, nonworker.

drool (SYN.) drivel, slaver, dribble, spit, gibber, jabber, twaddle, trickle, salivate.

droop *(SYN.)* dangle, weaken, hang, sink, fail, settle, sag, weary, languish, despond.

(ANT.) stand, tower, extend, rise, straighten.

drop *(SYN.)* droop, dribble, topple, collapse, downward, drip, trickle, tumble, gob, droplet, reduction, slump, slip, fall, dismiss, decline.

(ANT.) ascend, mount, steady, arise, soar.

drop out *(SYN.)* back out, withdraw, stop, forsake, abandon, leave, quit.

droppings *(SYN.)* faces, dung, waste, manure, excrement, ordure, guano.

dross *(SYN.)* dregs, impurity, leftovers, residue, debris, leavings, remains.

drove *(SYN.)* flock, herd.

drown *(SYN.)* sink, inundate, submerge, immerse.

drowse *(SYN.)* nap, doze, catnap, snooze, sleep, slumber, rest, drop off, repose.

drowsy *(SYN.)* dozing, torpid, soothing, dreamy, sleepy, comatose, sluggish, lulling, calming, restful, lethargic.

(ANT.) alert, awake, sharp, keen, acute.

drub *(SYN.)* wallop, thrash, beat, thump, cane, flog, rout, outclass, overcome, pummel, defeat, outplay.

drubbing *(SYN.)* walloping, flogging, beating, pounding, pommeling, thrashing, rout, licking, clobbering.

drudge *(SYN.)* work, labor,

hack, slave, toil, grub, grind, toiler, flunky, menial, servant.

drudgery *(SYN.)* toil, travail, effort, task, work, endeavor, labor.

(ANT.) recreation, indolence, leisure.

drug *(SYN.)* remedy, medicine, stupefy, anesthetize, numb, benumb.

drugged *(SYN.)* numb, doped, numbed, stupefied, dazed, groggy, benumbed.

druggist *(SYN.)* apothecary, chemist, pharmacologist.

drunk *(SYN.)* tight, intoxicated, soused, drunken, inebriated, alcoholic, besotted, sot, toper, boozer, wino, rummy, dipsomaniac, lush, tipsy.

drunkard *(SYN.)* sot, drunk, alcoholic, lush.

dry *(SYN.)* thirsty, dehydrated, vapid, plain, arid, uninteresting, drained, parched, barren, waterless, dull, tedious, boring, desiccated, tiresome.

(ANT.) fresh, wet, soaked, fascinating, lively, moist, interesting.

dub *(SYN.)* nickname, name, christen, call, style, term, confer, bestow, denominate, characterize, tag, label.

dubious *(SYN.)* unsure, uncertain, undecided, hesitant, spurious, unreliable, puzzling, questionable, ambiguous.

(ANT.) decided, fixed, irrefutable, definite, genuine, sound, authentic, trustworthy.

duck *(SYN.)* douse, dip, submerse, submerge, immerse,

plunge, wet, souse, drench, engulf, avoid, shun, lower, bob, hedge, shy, evade, swerve, quail.

(ANT.) raise, confront, face, elevate, cope with, undertake, assume, face up to.

duct *(SYN.)* pipe, tube, passage, vein, canal, funnel, gutter, main, trough, artery.

due *(SYN.)* payable, unpaid, owing, owed, imminent, expected.

duel *(SYN.)* competition, contest, engagement, rivalry, combat, strife, encounter, battle, conflict, dispute, strive.

dues *(SYN.)* assessment, fees, cost, levy, admission, fare, toll, demand, contribution.

duffer *(SYN.)* bungler, slouch, blunderer, novice, incompetent, fumbler, lummox.

(ANT.) master, expert, pro.

dull *(SYN.)* commonplace, slow, sad, dreary, boring, stupid, uninteresting, blunt, tedious, dulled, dumb, tiring, monotonous, obtuse, tiresome, dense, unimaginative, unfeeling, lifeless, dismal.

(ANT.) clear, animated, interesting, lively.

dullard *(SYN.)* dolt, dunce, moron, clod, blockhead, numskull.

dumb *(SYN.)* dull, witless, ignorant, mute, speechless, brainless, dense, stupid.

(ANT.) discerning, bright, alert, clever, intelligent.

dumbfound *(SYN.)* stagger, stun, nonplus, stupefy, over-whelm, amaze, confuse, bewilder, surprise, astonish.

dumfounded *(SYN.)* shocked, astonished, flabbergasted, astounded, stunned.

dump *(SYN.)* heap, fling down, drop, empty, unload, clear out, dispose of, tipple, discharge, overturn, dismiss, abandon.

(ANT.) store, fill, load, hoard, pack.

dunce *(SYN.)* deadhead, nitwit, booby, idiot, ignoramus, num skull, noddy, fool.

dungeon *(SYN.)* jail, prison, keep, cell.

dunk *(SYN.)* plunge, douse, submerge, dip.

(ANT.) uplift, elevate, recover.

dupe *(SYN.)* sucker, victim, gull, pushover, fool, cheat, deceive, defraud.

duplicate *(SYN.)* replica, replicate, facsimile, copy, reproduce, clone, double, twin.

(ANT.) prototype.

duplicity *(SYN.)* dissimulation, deception, hypocrisy, deceitfulness, insincerity, guile.

(ANT.) openness, artlessness, candor, genuineness.

durability *(SYN.)* might, strength, force, sturdiness, intensity, potency, vigor.

(ANT.) weakness, frailty, feebleness.

durable *(SYN.)* constant, firm, fixed, unchangeable, enduring, abiding, lasting.

(ANT.) unstable, temporary, perishable, transitory.

duration *(SYN.)* time, term, period, while, stage, era, epoch, interim.

duress *(SYN.)* force, demand, compulsion, emergency, pressure.

dusky *(SYN.)* sable, black, dark, darkish, swarthy, tawny, gloomy, overcast, misty, opaque, shadowy.
(ANT.) light, fair, white, pale, shining, clear, bright.

dusty *(SYN.)* sooty, unclean, dirty, musty, grubby, unswept, crumbly, friable, chalky, messy, grimy.
(ANT.) polished, immaculate, clean, shiny.

dutiful *(SYN.)* docile, faithful, obedient.
(ANT.) disobedient, willful, unruly, headstrong.

duty *(SYN.)* bond, responsibility, accountability, faithfulness, function, obligation, conscience, assignment, part, engagement.
(ANT.) freedom, choice.

dwarf *(SYN.)* midget, runt, reduce, minimize, tiny.
(ANT.) mammoth, colossus, monster, giant.

dwell *(SYN.)* inhabit, roost, settle, abide, live, reside.

dwelling *(SYN.)* seat, quarters, abode, home, hearth, residence, house, domicile.

dwell on *(SYN.)* insist, linger over, harp on, emphasize.
(ANT.) skip, neglect, skim over, disregard.

dwindle *(SYN.)* wane, decrease, diminish, fade, subside, ebb, shrivel, lessen.
(ANT.) enlarge, wax, increase,

grow, gain.

dying *(SYN.)* failing, expiring, waning, passing, final, declining, receding, dwindling, vanishing, disappearing,
(ANT.) thriving, growing, booming, flourishing.

dynamic *(SYN.)* active, forceful, kinetic, energetic, motive, mighty, vigorous.
(ANT.) sleepy, stable, inert, fixed, dead, still, uninspiring, ineffectual, listless.

E

eager *(SYN.)* avid, hot, anxious, fervent, enthusiastic, impatient, ardent, impassioned, yearning.
(ANT.) unconcerned, apathetic, impassioned, dull, uninterested, indifferent.

early *(SYN.)* betimes, opportune, first, advanced, soon, shortly.
(ANT.) retarded, late, tardy, belated, overdue.

earmark *(SYN.)* peculiarity, characteristic, brand, sign, stamp.

earn *(SYN.)* attain, win, get, achieve, obtain, gain, deserve, collect, net, acquire, merit.
(ANT.) waste, consume, forfeit.

earnest *(SYN.)* sincere, decided, determined, serious, eager.
(ANT.) indifferent, frivolous, insincere.

earnings *(SYN.)* wages, pay, salary, income.

earth *(SYN.)* globe, dirt, land, world, turf, soil, sod, ground.

earthly *(SYN.)* mundane, everyday, worldly.
(ANT.) heavenly.

earthy *(SYN.)* coarse, earthen, crude, unrefined, vulgar.
(ANT.) elegant polished, refined.

ease *(SYN.)* lighten, alleviate, pacify, soothe, allay, comfort, contentedness, assuage, reduce, rest, facilitate, relaxation, calm, mitigate, contentment, relax.
(ANT.) worry, disturb, confound, aggravate, difficulty, trouble, intensify, distress.

easily *(SYN.)* readily, effortlessly, smoothly, naturally.
(ANT.) hardly, arduously, painfully, laboriously.

easiness *(SYN.)* repose, comfort, satisfaction, contentment, liberty, leisure, simplicity.
(ANT.) unrest, torment, arduousness, difficulty, discomfort.

easy *(SYN.)* light, simple, facile, gentle, effortless, unhurried, comfortable, cozy, relaxed, plain, uncomplicated, restful.
(ANT.) hard, demanding, awkward, strict, difficult, formal.

eat *(SYN.)* consume, swallow, dine, corrode, chew, lunch, devour.

eavesdrop *(SYN.)* spy, listen, snoop, overhear.

eavesdropper *(SYN.)* monitor, listener, snoop, spy.

ebb *(SYN.)* diminish, recede, decline, decrease, retreat, lessen.
(ANT.) wax, grow, thrive, increase, swell.

ebullient *(SYN.)* vivacious, buoyant, exuberant.
(ANT.) lethargic, sad, gloomy, depressed.

eccentric *(SYN.)* odd, irregular, unusual, abnormal, peculiar.
(ANT.) ordinary, conventional, normal.

eccentricity *(SYN.)* kink, idiosyncrasy, whim, freak, caprice, foible, quirk, oddness, aberration.
(ANT.) normality, conventionality, ordinariness.

ecclesiastical *(SYN.)* religious, churchly, clerical.

echelon *(SYN.)* rank, level, grade, place, status.

echo *(SYN.)* response, imitation, suggestion, trace, reaction, imitate, repeat.

eclectic *(SYN.)* selective, diverse, broad, liberal, comprehensive.
(ANT.) limited, narrow, rigid, confined.

eclipse *(SYN.)* conceal, screen, hide, cover, obscure, overcast.

economical *(SYN.)* saving, thrifty, careful, frugal, provident, sparing.
(ANT.) wasteful, extravagant, lavish, improvident, prodigal.

economize *(SYN.)* pinch, scrimp, save.

economy *(SYN.)* saving, thrift.

ecstasy *(SYN.)* frenzy, gladness, delight, madness, joy, glee, exaltation, pleasure, trance, rapture.
(ANT.) misery, melancholy, sadness.

ecstatic *(SYN.)* overjoyed, thrilled, delighted, happy, elated.

edge *(SYN.)* margin, brim, verge, brink, border, keenness, extremity, rim, boundary, trim.

(ANT.) dullness, center, bluntness.

edgy *(SYN.)* tense, touchy, nervous, irritable.

edict *(SYN.)* declaration, order, ruling, decree, pronouncement, command, law, proclamation.

edifice *(SYN.)* construction, building, establishment.

edit *(SYN.)* check, revise, correct, amend.

educate *(SYN.)* instruct, teach, school, train.

education *(SYN.)* training, development, knowledge, learning, cultivation, schooling, instruction, study.

eerie *(SYN.)* weird, fearful, ghastly, spooky, strange.

efface *(SYN.)* obliterate, erase.

effect *(SYN.)* produce, consequence, evoke, cause, make, complete, outcome, result, determine.

effective *(SYN.)* efficient, practical, productive.

(ANT.) useless, wasteful, ineffective.

efficiency *(SYN.)* efficacy, capability, effectiveness, competency.

(ANT.) wastefulness, inability.

efficient *(SYN.)* efficacious, skillful, capable, adept, competent, useful, effectual, effective, apt, proficient.

(ANT.) inefficient, unskilled,

ineffectual, incompetent.

effort *(SYN.)* labor, endeavor, pains, essay, trial, exertion, struggle, strain, try, attempt.

effortless *(SYN.)* simple, easy.

egg *(SYN.)* stir, ovum, incite, urge, embryo, provoke.

egoism *(SYN.)* self-interest, conceit, pride, selfishness, egotism.

(ANT.) modesty, generosity, selflessness.

eject *(SYN.)* expel, remove, oust, eliminate.

(ANT.) include.

elaborate *(SYN.)* detail, develop, decorative, ornate.

(ANT.) simplify, simple, unadorned.

elapse *(SYN.)* expire.

elastic *(SYN.)* yielding, flexible, adaptable, pliable.

elated *(SYN.)* delighted, rejoicing, overjoyed, jubilant.

(ANT.) sad, unhappy.

elder *(SYN.)* senior.

(ANT.) younger.

elderly *(SYN.)* aged, old.

(ANT.) young, youthful.

elect *(SYN.)* appoint, choose.

electrify *(SYN.)* shock, charge, stir, upset, generate, agitate.

elegant *(SYN.)* tasteful, refined, cultivated, polished, fine.

(ANT.) crude, coarse, unpolished, tasteless.

elementary *(SYN.)* simple, primary, basic, fundamental.

(ANT.) involved, complex, sophisticated, complicated.

elevate *(SYN.)* raise, lift.

(ANT.) lower, drop.

elf *(SYN.)* devil, fairy, imp.

elicit (SYN.) summon.

eligible (SYN.) fit, suitable, qualified.

eliminate (SYN.) expel, eject, remove, dislodge, extirpate, erase.
(ANT.) admit, involve.

elite (SYN.) nobility, upper-class, aristocracy, gentry.
(ANT.) mob, proletariat.

elongate (SYN.) extend, prolong, lengthen.

elope (SYN.) escape, flee.

eloquent (SYN.) expressive, fluent, articulate, meaningful.
(ANT.) inarticulate.

else (SYN.) different, another, other.

elude (SYN.) escape, miss, avoid, dodge.
(ANT.) add, include.

emaciated (SYN.) wasted, thin, starved, withered, shriveled, gaunt, shrunken, drawn.

emancipate (SYN.) liberate, free, deliver, save.
(ANT.) restrain.

embankment (SYN.) shore, dam, bank, fortification, buttress.

embargo (SYN.) prohibition, restriction, restraint.

embark (SYN.) board, depart.

embarrass (SYN.) discomfit, rattle, distress, hamper, fluster, entangle, abash, mortify, perplex, confuse, shame.
(ANT.) relieve, encourage, help

embassy (SYN.) ministry, legation, consulate.

embed (SYN.) root, inset, enclose, plant.

embellish (SYN.) adorn, deco-

rate, ornament.

embezzle (SYN.) pilfer, misuse, rob, misappropriate, steal, take.

embitter (SYN.) provoke, arouse, anger, inflame.

emblem (SYN.) token, mark, symbol, badge.

embody (SYN.) comprise, cover, embrace, include.

embrace (SYN.) espouse, accept, receive, comprehend, contain, welcome, comprise, clasp, include, adopt, hug.
(ANT.) spurn, reject, bar, exclude, repudiate.

embroider (SYN.) decorate, adorn, stitch, trim, overstate, embellish, ornament, exaggerate, magnify.

emerge (SYN.) surface, show, appear.

emergency (SYN.) strait, pass, crisis, urgency, predicament.

eminent (SYN.) renowned, glorious, distinguished, noted, celebrated, elevated, glorious, important, prominent.
(ANT.) ordinary, commonplace, unknown, undistinguished, common.

emissary (SYN.) envoy, minister, delegate, agent, spy.

emit (SYN.) expel, breathe, shoot, hurl, ooze, vent, belch, discharge.

emotion (SYN.) passion, turmoil, perturbation, affection, sentiment, feeling, trepidation, agitation.
(ANT.) dispassion, indifference, tranquillity, calm, restraint.

emotional (SYN.) ardent, pas-

sionate, zealous, impetuous, overwrought, enthusiastic.
(ANT.) tranquil, calm, placid.

emphasis (SYN.) accent, stress, insistence.

emphatic (SYN.) positive, definite, forceful, energetic.
(ANT.) lax, quiet, unforceful.

employ (SYN.) avail, use, devote, apply, utilize, engage, sign, hire, retain, contract.
(ANT.) reject, discard.

employee (SYN.) laborer, worker, servant.
(ANT.) boss, employer.

employer (SYN.) owner, boss, proprietor, manager, superintendent, supervisor.
(ANT.) employee, worker.

employment (SYN.) occupation, work, business, position, job, engagement.
(ANT.) leisure, idleness, slothfulness.

empower (SYN.) enable, sanction, permit, warrant.

empty (SYN.) void, devoid, unfilled, barren, unoccupied, unfurnished, vacant, blank, evacuate, unload, hollow.
(ANT.) supplied, full, occupied.

emulate (SYN.) follow, imitate, copy.

enable (SYN.) authorize, empower, sanction, qualify.

enact (SYN.) legislate, portray, pass, stage, represent.

enchant (SYN.) charm, titillate, fascinate, bewitch, delight, thrill, captivate.
(ANT.) tire, bore.

encircle (SYN.) comprise, include, bound, encompass.

enclose (SYN.) envelop, confine, bound, surround, encompass, encircle.
(ANT.) open, exclude, distend, expose, develop.

encompass (SYN.) include, surround, encircle.

encore (SYN.) repetition, repeat, again.

encounter (SYN.) battle, meet, oppose, run into, face, collide.

encourage (SYN.) incite, favor, cheer, impel, countenance, inspirit, exhilarate, animate, hearten, embolden, support.
(ANT.) deter, dispirit, deject, dissuade.

encroach (SYN.) interfere, trespass, intrude, infringe.

encumber (SYN.) hamper, load, burden.

end (SYN.) completion, object, close, aim, result, conclusion, finish, extremity, intent, halt, stop, limit, purpose, cessation, expiration, termination.
(ANT.) opening, start, introduction, beginning, inception.

endanger (SYN.) imperil, hazard, risk.
(ANT.) secure.

endear (SYN.) allure, charm.

endeavor (SYN.) strive, struggle, exertion, attempt, try, labor.

endless (SYN.) constant, nonstop, continuous, incessant, everlasting.

endorse (SYN.) approve, accept, sign, confirm, pass.

endow (SYN.) provide, furnish, bestow, give, contribute.
(ANT.) divest.

endure *(SYN.)* experience, undergo, sustain, last, bear, continue, remain, undergo, persist, brook, tolerate, suffer.
(ANT.) wane, die, perish, succumb, fail.

enemy *(SYN.)* foe, antagonist, rival, opponent, competitor, adversary, opposition.
(ANT.) colleague, ally, friend, accomplice.

energy *(SYN.)* strength, vim, force, power, stamina, vigor.
(ANT.) feebleness, lethargy.

enervate *(SYN.)* enfeeble, weaken, debilitate, exhaust, devitalize.
(ANT.) invigorate.

enfold *(SYN.)* clasp, surround, wrap, embrace, hug.

enforce *(SYN.)* make, drive, compel, execute, force.

engage *(SYN.)* absorb, occupy, employ, hold, involve, hire, agree, engross, retain, promise, commit, entangle.
(ANT.) fire, disengage, discharge, dismiss.

engaged *(SYN.)* affianced, betrothed, busy, occupied.

engaging *(SYN.)* fascinating, appealing, enticing, interesting, tempting, lovely, beguiling, charming, enchanting, delightful, exquisite.
(ANT.) ordinary, boring.

engender *(SYN.)* develop, breed, cause, generate, produce.

engineer *(SYN.)* direct, conduct, guide, lead, manage.

engrave *(SYN.)* print, cut, inscribe, carve, sketch.

engross *(SYN.)* engage, enthrall, fascinate, absorb.

engulf *(SYN.)* flood, swallow.

enhance *(SYN.)* better, uplift, improve.

enigma *(SYN.)* mystery, stumper, riddle.

enigmatic *(SYN.)* perplexing, confusing, puzzling, baffling, mystifying.

enjoy *(SYN.)* savor, like, relish.

enjoyment *(SYN.)* pleasure, delight, gratification.
(ANT.) abhorrence, displeasure.

enlarge *(SYN.)* widen, distend, amplify, broaden, extend, increase, augment, expand.
(ANT.) diminish, shrink, contract, decrease, wane, restrict.

enlighten *(SYN.)* inform, illuminate, clarify, teach, instruct.
(ANT.) confuse.

enlist *(SYN.)* enroll, prompt, join, induce, enter, register, persuade.
(ANT.) quit, leave, abandon.

enliven *(SYN.)* inspire, brighten, stimulate.

enmity *(SYN.)* antagonism, hatred, animosity, malignity, ill-will, antipathy, hostility, unfriendliness.
(ANT.) love, like, friendliness.

enormity *(SYN.)* heinousness, wickedness, barbarity, atrociousness.

enormous *(SYN.)* vast, huge, colossal, immense, gargantuan, elephantine, gigantic, stupendous, large.
(ANT.) small, slight, tiny, minute, infinitesimal, diminutive, little.

enough *(SYN.)* ample, adequate, sufficient, plenty.
(ANT.) inadequate, insufficient.

enrage *(SYN.)* anger, provoke, madden, inflame.
(ANT.) appease, soothe, calm.

enrich *(SYN.)* better, improve.

enroll *(SYN.)* record, list, recruit, register, enlist, write, induct.
(ANT.) quit, leave, abandon.

enshrine *(SYN.)* bury, entomb.

ensign *(SYN.)* banner, colors, flag, officer.

enslave *(SYN.)* keep, hold, capture.

ensue *(SYN.)* arise, succeed, follow, result.

ensure *(SYN.)* guarantee, assure, protect, defend, cover.

entangle *(SYN.)* confuse, snare, involve, ravel, snarl, tangle, trap.

enter *(SYN.)* join, go inside.

enterprise *(SYN.)* fete, deed, venture, project, adventure, undertaking, ambition, business, exploit.

enterprising *(SYN.)* energetic, resourceful.
(ANT.) lazy, indolent, sluggish, unresourceful.

entertain *(SYN.)* cheer, gladden, hold, consider, please, contemplate, divert, amuse, harbor, fascinate, interest.
(ANT.) repulse, tire, bore, disgust, annoy.

enthrall *(SYN.)* captivate, fascinate, enchant, charm, thrill.

enthusiasm *(SYN.)* fervor, fanaticism, zeal, ardor, intensity, devotion, excitement, eagerness, fervency, earnestness.
(ANT.) indifference, ennui, apathy, unconcern, detachment.

enthusiastic *(SYN.)* earnest, zealous, eager.
(ANT.) aloof, indifferent, unconcerned.

entice *(SYN.)* lure, attract, seduce.

entire *(SYN.)* complete, intact, whole, undivided.
(ANT.) divided, separated, incomplete, partial.

entirely *(SYN.)* altogether, thoroughly, wholly, solely.

entitle *(SYN.)* call, label, name, empower, allow, authorize, license, title.

entourage *(SYN.)* train, company, retinue, escort.

entrance *(SYN.)* inlet, portal, doorway, fascinate, entry, intrigue, door, thrill.
(ANT.) exit.

entreat *(SYN.)* implore, beg, plead.

entreaty *(SYN.)* plea, appeal.

entrust *(SYN.)* commit, charge, assign, delegate, consign.

enumerate *(SYN.)* count, tally, list, number.

enunciate *(SYN.)* announce, express, speak, state.

envelop *(SYN.)* embrace, cover, conceal, surround, wrap.

environment *(SYN.)* neighborhood, habitat, surroundings, setting.

envision *(SYN.)* picture, imagine, visualize.

envoy *(SYN.)* delegate, emissary, representative, agent, messenger

envy *(SYN.)* covetousness, jealousy, spitefulness, covet.

(ANT.) indifference, generosity.

epicure *(SYN.)* gourmand, gourmet, connoisseur, aesthete.

epidemic *(SYN.)* prevalent, scourge, plague, catching, pestilence, infectious.

episode *(SYN.)* happening, occurrence, event, experience.

epoch *(SYN.)* age.

equal *(SYN.)* even, uniform, like, alike, equitable, same, identical, commensurate, equivalent, regular, parallel.

(ANT.) different, unequal, irregular, uneven.

equilibrium *(SYN.)* stability, steadiness, balance, firmness.

equip *(SYN.)* fit, rig, provide, outfit, prepare, furnish.

equipment *(SYN.)* utensils, material, apparatus.

equitable *(SYN.)* square, rightful, fair, due, just, fit.

(ANT.) partial, biased, unjust, uneven.

equity *(SYN.)* impartiality, fairness, justness, justice, evenhandedness.

equivalent *(SYN.)* match, rival, equal, like, replacement.

equivocal *(SYN.)* oblique, ambiguous, vague, indeterminate, uncertain, obscure.

(ANT.) clear, precise, explicit, certain, clear-cut, definite.

equivocate *(SYN.)* temporize, evade, hedge, quibble, fudge, waffle, straddle.

era *(SYN.)* epoch, cycle, age, time, period.

eradicate *(SYN.)* remove, demolish, eliminate.

erase *(SYN.)* obliterate, remove, cancel.

(ANT.) add, include.

erect *(SYN.)* build, straight, raise, construct, vertical.

(ANT.) flat, horizontal, raze, flatten, demolish.

erection *(SYN.)* building, construction, raising, fabrication.

erode *(SYN.)* rust, consume, disintegrate.

erotic *(SYN.)* carnal, fleshy, amatory, prurient, lewd, wanton, passionate, lecherous.

err *(SYN.)* slip, misjudge.

errand *(SYN.)* chore, duty, task, exercise.

errant *(SYN.)* roving, rambling, wandering, vagrant.

erratic *(SYN.)* irregular, abnormal, uneven, occasional, sporadic, unsteady, odd, eccentric, strange, extraordinary, unconventional, bizarre, peculiar, uncertain, unusual, unstable.

(ANT.) regular, steady, normal, ordinary.

erroneous *(SYN.)* wrong, mistaken, incorrect, inaccurate, false, untrue.

(ANT.) true, right, correct, accurate.

error *(SYN.)* inaccuracy, fault, slip, oversight, fallacy, mistake, blunder.

erudite *(SYN.)* sage, wise, learned, deep, profound.

erupt *(SYN.)* vomit.

escapade *(SYN.)* caper, antic,

stunt, trick, prank.

escape (SYN.) shun, avoid, flee, decamp, elude, flight, avert, departure, abscond, fly, evade.

(ANT.) meet, confront, invite, catch.

escort (SYN.) conduct, lead, attend, accompany, protection, guard, guide, convoy, usher, squire.

especially (SYN.) unusually, principally, mainly, particularly, primarily.

essay (SYN.) test, thesis, undertake, paper, try.

essence (SYN.) substance, character, nature, principle, odor, basis, smell, perfume.

essential (SYN.) vital, intrinsic, basic, requisite, indispensable, critical, requirement, necessary, important.

(ANT.) dispensable, unimportant, inessential.

establish (SYN.) prove, fix, found, settle, institute, raise, verify, conform, form, sanction, begin, organize.

(ANT.) upset, discontinue, scatter, disperse, refute, abolish, unsettle.

esteem (SYN.) revere, deem, appreciate, honor, value, think, admire, respect, hold, prize, reverence, regard.

(ANT.) scorn, disdain, depreciate, contempt, abhor.

estimate (SYN.) calculate, gauge, judge, rate, evaluate, compute, value, figure.

estimation (SYN.) judgment, viewpoint, opinion.

etch (SYN.) stamp, engrave, impress.

eternal (SYN.) undying, immortal, ceaseless, infinite, everlasting, deathless, perpetual, endless, timeless.

(ANT.) mortal, transient, finite, brief, temporary, passing.

etiquette (SYN.) decorum, formality.

evacuate (SYN.) withdraw, depart, leave, vacate.

evade (SYN.) miss, avoid, bypass.

(ANT.) confront, meet, face.

evaluate (SYN.) value, appraise, assay.

evaporate (SYN.) disappear, vanish.

(ANT.) condense, appear.

even (SYN.) smooth, level, still, square, same, flat, balanced, equal, parallel, identical.

(ANT.) irregular, bumpy, unbalanced, unequal, divergent.

evening (SYN.) twilight, dusk, sunset.

(ANT.) sunrise, dawn.

event (SYN.) issue, end, result, circumstance, occurrence, incident, consequence, happening, episode.

even-tempered (SYN.) composed, calm, cool.

(ANT.) hotheaded.

eventual (SYN.) consequent, ultimate.

(ANT.) present, current.

eventually (SYN.) ultimately.

ever (SYN.) continuously, always, constantly.

(ANT.) never.

everlasting (SYN.) permanent, ceaseless, endless, continual.

evermore *(SYN.)* always.

everyday *(SYN.)* common, usual, ordinary, customary. *(ANT.)* rare.

evict *(SYN.)* oust, put out, expel.

evidence *(SYN.)* grounds, clue, facts, testimony, data, sign, proof.

evident *(SYN.)* apparent, clear, obvious, indubitable, plain, conspicuous, patent, manifest. *(ANT.)* hidden, unclear, uncertain, obscure, concealed.

evil *(SYN.)* immoral, harmful, badness, sinful, woe, bad, wicked. *(ANT.)* goodness, moral, useful, upright, virtuous, advantageous.

evoke *(SYN.)* summon, prompt.

evolve *(SYN.)* grow, advance, develop, result, emerge.

exact *(SYN.)* correct, faultless, errorless, detailed, accurate. *(ANT.)* inaccurate, inexact, faulty.

exaggerate *(SYN.)* stretch, expand, amplify, embroider, heighten, overstate, caricature, magnify. *(ANT.)* understate, minimize, diminish, depreciate.

exalt *(SYN.)* erect, consecrate, raise, elevate, extol, dignify. *(ANT.)* humble, degrade, humiliate.

examination *(SYN.)* investigation, inspection, test, scrutiny.

examine *(SYN.)* assess, contemplate, question, review, audit, notice, inquire, analyze, check, investigate, dissect, inspect, survey.

(ANT.) omit, disregard, overlook.

example *(SYN.)* pattern, archetype, specimen, illustration, model, instance, prototype, sample. *(ANT.)* rule, concept, principle.

exasperate *(SYN.)* aggravate, anger, madden, irritate.

excavate *(SYN.)* dig, burrow.

exceed *(SYN.)* excel, beat, surpass.

exceedingly *(SYN.)* extremely, very, especially, surprisingly.

excel *(SYN.)* better, beat, surpass.

excellence *(SYN.)* distinction, superiority. *(ANT.)* poorness, inferiority, badness.

excellent *(SYN.)* wonderful, fine, marvelous, superior. *(ANT.)* poor, terrible, bad, inferior.

except *(SYN.)* omitting, barring, reject, excluding, save, exclude.

exception *(SYN.)* affront, offense, exclusion, deviation, omission.

exceptional *(SYN.)* different, irregular, strange, unusual.

excerpt *(SYN.)* abstract, extract.

excess *(SYN.)* surplus, intemperance, extravagance, abundant, profuse. *(ANT.)* want, sparse, lack, dearth.

exchange *(SYN.)* barter, interchange, substitute, trade, change.

excite *(SYN.)* arouse, incite, agitate, stimulate, awaken.

(ANT.) lull, quiet, bore, pacify.

exclaim *(SYN.)* vociferate, cry, call out, ejaculate, shout.

exclamation *(SYN.)* shout, out-cry, clamor.

exclude *(SYN.)* omit, restrain, hinder, bar, except, prevent.
(ANT.) welcome, involve, embrace, admit, include.

exclusion *(SYN.)* exception, bar, rejection.
(ANT.) inclusion.

exclusive *(SYN.)* restricted, limited, restrictive, choice, selective, fashionable.
(ANT.) common, ordinary, unrestricted, unfashionable.

excursion *(SYN.)* voyage, tour, trip.

excuse *(SYN.)* exculpate, forgive, remit, acquit, free, pardon, condone, explanation, exempt, justify, absolve.
(ANT.) revenge, punish, convict.

execute *(SYN.)* complete, accomplish, achieve, kill, perform.

exemplify *(SYN.)* show, illustrate.

exempt *(SYN.)* excuse, free, except, release.

exercise *(SYN.)* drill, task, use, activity, lesson, training, exertion, application, gymnastics, operation, practice.
(ANT.) rest, indolence, repose.

exertion *(SYN.)* attempt, effort, strain, endeavor.

exhale *(SYN.)* blow, breathe out.

exhaust *(SYN.)* drain, tire, empty, wear out, use, finish, fatigue.

(ANT.) renew, refresh, replace.

exhaustive *(SYN.)* comprehensive, thorough, extensive, complete.
(ANT.) incomplete.

exhibit *(SYN.)* demonstrate, display, reveal, present, show, flaunt.
(ANT.) hide conceal, disguise.

exhilarate *(SYN.)* refresh, cheer, excite, stimulate.

exhort *(SYN.)* advise, coax, press, urge, prompt.

exile *(SYN.)* expulsion, proscription, deportation, expatriation, deport, extradition.
(ANT.) retrieval, welcome, recall, admittance, reinstatement.

exist *(SYN.)* stand, live, occur, be.

exit *(SYN.)* leave, depart.

exodus *(SYN.)* leaving, exit, parting, departure.

exonerate *(SYN.)* acquit, clear.

exorbitant *(SYN.)* unreasonable, outrageous, overpriced, preposterous, excessive.
(ANT.) normal, reasonable.

exotic *(SYN.)* strange, vivid, foreign, gay.
(ANT.) dull, native.

expand *(SYN.)* unfold, enlarge, broaden, inflate, swell, grow.
(ANT.) contract, shrivel, shrink.

expect *(SYN.)* await, think, hope, anticipate.

expedient *(SYN.)* helpful, desirable, rush, hasten, useful.
(ANT.) delay.

expedition *(SYN.)* trek, speed, trip, haste, voyage, journey, hurry.

expel (SYN.) exile, dislodge, discharge, oust, eject, dismiss, banish, disown.

(ANT.) favor, recall, invite, admit.

expend (SYN.) consume, waste, spend, exhaust.

(ANT.) ration, reserve, conserve.

expense (SYN.) charge, cost, payment, price.

experience (SYN.) occurrence, episode, sensation, happening, existence, background, feeling, living, encountering, knowledge.

experienced (SYN.) expert, qualified, accomplished, skilled.

(ANT.) untutored, inexperienced, naive.

experiment (SYN.) trial, test, prove, research, examine, try.

expert (SYN.) adept, handy, skillful, clever, specialist, authority, skilled, knowledgeable, ingenious.

(ANT.) untrained, unskilled, inexperienced.

expire (SYN.) terminate, die, cease, perish, end, disappear.

(ANT.) commence, continue.

explain (SYN.) illustrate, decipher, clarify, resolve, define, unravel, justify, interpret.

(ANT.) darken, baffle, obscure.

explanation (SYN.) definition, description, interpretation, account, reason, justification.

explicit (SYN.) lucid, definitive, specific, express, clear, manifest.

(ANT.) vague, implicit, ambiguous.

exploit (SYN.) feat, deed, accomplishment, adventure.

explore (SYN.) research, hunt, probe, search, investigate, look.

explosion (SYN.) bang, boom, blowup, blast, detonation, outbreak, convulsion, furor, tantrum.

explosive (SYN.) fiery, rabid, eruptive, volcanic, inflammatory.

(ANT.) stable, inert, peaceful, calm.

exponent (SYN.) explicator, supporter, expounder, interpreter.

expose (SYN.) uncover, display, bare, open, unmask, reveal.

(ANT.) hide, conceal, mask, covered.

exposition (SYN.) fair, bazaar, show, expo, exhibition.

expound (SYN.) clarify, present, explain, lecture, demonstrate.

express (SYN.) voice, tell, send, say, ship, declare, precise, specific, swift, describe.

expressive (SYN.) suggestive, meaningful, telling, significant.

(ANT.) unthinking, meaningless, nondescript.

expressly (SYN.) precisely, exactly, definitely, clearly.

(ANT.) tentatively, vaguely, ambiguously.

expulsion (SYN.) ejection, discharge, removal, elimination.

expunge (SYN.) blot out, erase, cancel, obliterate, delete, efface.

expurgate *(SYN.)* cleanse, purge, censor, edit, emasculate, abridge.

exquisite *(SYN.)* delicate, delightful, attractive, beautiful, elegant, fine, superb.

(ANT.) vulgar, dull, ugly, unattractive.

extant *(SYN.)* subsisting, remaining, surviving, present, existing.

(ANT.) lost, defunct, extinct, vanished.

extemporaneous *(SYN.)* casual, impromptu, offhand.

extemporize *(SYN.)* improvise, devise.

extend *(SYN.)* lengthen, stretch, increase, offer, give, grant, magnify, expand.

(ANT.) abbreviate, shorten, curtail.

extension *(SYN.)* expansion, increase, enlargement.

extensive *(SYN.)* vast, wide, spacious, broad.

(ANT.) narrow, cramped, confined, restricted.

extent *(SYN.)* length, degree, range, amount, measure, size, compass, reach, magnitude.

extenuating *(SYN.)* exculpating, qualifying, justifying.

exterior *(SYN.)* surface, face, outside, covering, outer, external.

(ANT.) inside, lining, interior, inner, internal.

exterminate *(SYN.)* slay, kill, destroy.

external *(SYN.)* outer, exterior, outside.

(ANT.) inner, internal, inside, interior.

externals *(SYN.)* images, effects, appearance, aspect.

extinct *(SYN.)* lost, dead, gone, vanished.

(ANT.) present, flourishing, alive, extant.

extinction *(SYN.)* eclipse, annihilation, obliteration, death.

extinguish *(SYN.)* suppress, smother, quench.

extol *(SYN.)* laud, eulogize, exalt, praise.

(ANT.) denounce, belittle, discredit, disparage.

extra *(SYN.)* surplus, spare, additional.

extract *(SYN.)* remove, withdraw, essence.

(ANT.) penetrate, introduce.

extraordinary *(SYN.)* unusual, wonderful, marvelous, peculiar, remarkable, exceptional.

(ANT.) ordinary, usual.

extravagant *(SYN.)* excessive, exaggerated, lavish, wasteful, extreme.

(ANT.) prudent, frugal, thrifty, economical, provident.

extreme *(SYN.)* excessive, overdone, outermost, limit, greatest, utmost, furthest, extravagant.

(ANT.) reasonable, moderate.

extricate *(SYN.)* rescue, free, clear, release.

exuberant *(SYN.)* buoyant, ebullient, vivacious.

(ANT.) sad, depressed.

exult *(SYN.)* rejoice, delight.

F

fable *(SYN.)* legend, parable, myth, fib, fiction, tale, story.

fabled *(SYN.)* legendary, famous, famed, historic.

fabric *(SYN.)* goods, textile, material, cloth, yard goods.

fabricate *(SYN.)* assemble, make, construct, produce, create.

(ANT.) raze, destroy, demolish.

fabrication *(SYN.)* deceit, lie, falsehood, untruth, forgery, deception.

(ANT.) verity, reality, actuality, truth, fact.

fabulous *(SYN.)* amazing, marvelous, unbelievable, fantastic, astounding, astonishing, striking.

(ANT.) ordinary, commonplace, credible, proven, factual.

facade *(SYN.)* deception, mask, front, show, pose, veneer, guise.

face *(SYN.)* cover, mug, front, assurance, audacity, visage, expression, look, features, facade, meet, surface.

(ANT.) rear, shun, avoid, evade, back, timidity.

facet *(SYN.)* perspective, view, side, phase.

facetious *(SYN.)* jocular, humorous, funny, clever, droll, witty, playful, jesting.

(ANT.) sober, serious, grave, weighty.

face to face *(SYN.)* opposing, nose to nose, confronting.

facile *(SYN.)* simple, easy, quick, clever, uncomplicated, fluent.

(ANT.) complex, difficult, com-plicated, hard, ponderous, arduous.

facilitate *(SYN.)* help, speed, ease, promote, accelerate, expedite.

facilities *(SYN.)* aid, means, resources, conveniences.

facility *(SYN.)* ability, skill, ease, skillfulness, material.

(ANT.) effort, difficulty, labor.

facsimile *(SYN.)* reproduction, likeness, replica.

fact *(SYN.)* reality, deed, certainty, incident, circumstance, event, occurrence, truth, actuality.

(ANT.) falsehood, fiction, delusion.

faction *(SYN.)* clique, party, sect.

factitious *(SYN.)* false, sham, artificial, spurious, unnatural, affected.

(ANT.) natural, real, genuine, artless.

factor *(SYN.)* part, certain, element, basis, cause.

factory *(SYN.)* installation, plant, mill, works.

factual *(SYN.)* true, correct, accurate, genuine, authentic.

(ANT.) incorrect, erroneous, fabricated, invented.

faculty *(SYN.)* power, capacity, talent, staff, gift, qualification, ability, skill.

fad *(SYN.)* fashion, vogue, rage.

faddish *(SYN.)* ephemeral, modish, temporary, passing, fleeting.

(ANT.) lasting, permanent, enduring, classic.

fade *(SYN.)* pale, bleach, weaken, dim, decline, sink, discolor.

fagged *(SYN.)* exhausted, tired, weary, pooped, worn.

fail *(SYN.)* neglect, weaken, flunk, miss, decline, disappoint, fade.
(ANT.) succeed, achieve, accomplish.

failing *(SYN.)* fault, foible, imperfection, frailty, defect, peccadillo, shortcoming.
(ANT.) steadiness, strength, integrity, firmness.

failure *(SYN.)* miscarriage, omission, decline, deficiency, fiasco, lack, dereliction, failing, unsuccessfulness, loss, default, want.
(ANT.) conquest, accomplishment, success, triumph, victory, hit, luck, achievement.

faint *(SYN.)* timid, faded, languid, halfhearted, dim, pale, wearied, feeble, indistinct, weak.
(ANT.) strong, sharp, forceful, glaring, clear, distinct, conspicuous, brave.

faint-hearted *(SYN.)* shy, cowardly, timid, bashful.
(ANT.) fearless, brave, stouthearted, courageous.

fair *(SYN.)* pale, average, light, just, sunny, mediocre, bright, clear, lovely, blond, honest, equitable, impartial, reasonable.
(ANT.) ugly, fraudulent, foul, outstanding, dishonorable, unfair.

fair-minded *(SYN.)* reasonable, fair, just, honest, unprejudiced, impartial, evenhanded.
(ANT.) bigoted, narrow-minded, unjust, closeminded, partisan.

fairness *(SYN.)* equity, justice, honesty.
(ANT.) favoritism, partiality, bias, one-sidedness.

fairy *(SYN.)* leprechaun, gnome, elf, pixie, sprite.

faith *(SYN.)* dependence, trust, reliance, creed, loyalty, doctrine, confidence, dogma, tenet, persuasion, credence, fidelity, religion.
(ANT.) mistrust, disbelief, doubt, infidelity.

faithful *(SYN.)* staunch, true, devoted, trusty, loyal, constant, credible, steadfast, strict, trustworthy, accurate.
(ANT.) untrustworthy, faithless, inaccurate, wrong, false, disloyal, treacherous.

fake *(SYN.)* falsify, distort, pretend, feign, fraud, counterfeit, cheat, artificial, phony, imitation.
(ANT.) honest, pure, real, genuine, authentic.

falderal *(SYN.)* foolery, jargon, nonsense, gibberish, blather, balderdash.

fall *(SYN.)* drop, decline, diminish, droop, topple, decrease, sink, hang, descend, subside, plunge.
(ANT.) soar, climb, steady, rise, ascend.

fallacious *(SYN.)* untrue, false, wrong, erroneous, deceptive, illusory, delusive.
(ANT.) accurate, true, exact, real, factual.

fallacy *(SYN.)* mistake, error, illusion, deception.

fall back *(SYN.)* retreat, recede, withdraw, concede.

(ANT.) progress, advance, gain, prosper, proceed.

fallow *(SYN.)* idle, unprepared, unproductive, inactive.

(ANT.) prepared, productive, cultivated.

false *(SYN.)* incorrect, wrong, deceitful, fake, imitation, counterfeit.

(ANT.) genuine, loyal, true, honest.

falsehood *(SYN.)* untruth, lie, fib, story.

(ANT.) truth.

falsify *(SYN.)* misquote, distort, mislead, adulterate.

falter *(SYN.)* stumble, tremble, hesitate, flounder.

fame *(SYN.)* distinction, glory, mane, eminence, credit, reputation, renown, acclaim, notoriety.

(ANT.) infamy, obscurity, anonymity, disrepute.

famed *(SYN.)* renowned, famous.

(ANT.) obscure, unknown, anonymous.

familiar *(SYN.)* informal, intimate, close, acquainted, amicable, knowing, cognizant, versed, unreserved, friendly, sociable, aware, known.

(ANT.) unfamiliar, distant, affected, reserved.

familiarity *(SYN.)* sociability, acquaintance, awareness, intimacy, knowledge.

(ANT.) distance, ignorance, reserve, presumption, constraint, haughtiness.

family *(SYN.)* kin, tribe, folks, group, relatives.

famine *(SYN.)* want, deficiency, starvation, need.

(ANT.) excess, plenty.

famous *(SYN.)* distinguished, noted, glorious, illustrious, famed, celebrated, well-known, eminent, renowned, prominent.

(ANT.) obscure, hidden, unknown.

fan *(SYN.)* arouse, spread, admirer, enthusiast, devotee.

fanatic *(SYN.)* bigot, enthusiast, zealot.

fancy *(SYN.)* love, dream, ornate, imagine, suppose, imagination, fantasy, ornamented, elaborate.

(ANT.) plain, undecorated, simple, unadorned.

fantastic *(SYN.)* strange, unusual, unimaginable, incredible, unbelievable, bizarre.

(ANT.) mundane, ordinary, staid, humdrum.

fantasy *(SYN.)* illusion, dream, whim, hallucination, delusion, caprice, daydream, fancy.

(ANT.) bore.

far *(SYN.)* removed, much, distant, remote, estranged, alienated.

(ANT.) close, near.

fare *(SYN.)* prosper, eat, passenger, thrive, toll, progress, succeed.

farewell *(SYN.)* good-by, valediction, departure, leaving.

(ANT.) welcome, greeting.

farm (SYN.) grow, harvest, cultivate, ranch, hire, charter, plantation.

fascinate (SYN.) charm, enchant, bewitch, enthrall.

fashion (SYN.) create, shape, style, mode, make, custom, form, method, way, vogue.

fashionable (SYN.) chic, smart, stylish, elegant, voguish.
(ANT.) dowdy, unfashionable.

fast (SYN.) fleet, firm, quick, swift, inflexible, stable, secure, expeditious, rapid, steady, constant, speedy.
(ANT.) insecure, sluggish, unstable, slow, unsteady.

fasten (SYN.) secure, bind, tie, join, connect, attach, unite.
(ANT.) open, loose, free, loosen, release, separate.

fastidious (SYN.) choosy, selective, discriminating, picky, meticulous.

fat (SYN.) stout, plump, chubby, pudgy, obese, oily, fleshy, greasy, fatty, portly, corpulent, paunchy, wide, thick, rotund.
(ANT.) slim, gaunt, emaciated, thin, slender.

fatal (SYN.) killing, lethal, doomed, disastrous, deadly, fateful, mortal.
(ANT.) nonfatal.

fate (SYN.) end, fortune, doom, issue, destiny, necessity, portion, result, lot, chance, luck, outcome, consequence, kismet.

father (SYN.) cause, sire, breed, originate, founder.

fatherly (SYN.) protective, paternal, kind, paternalistic.

fathom (SYN.) penetrate, understand, interpret, comprehend.

fatigue (SYN.) weariness, lassitude, exhaustion, enervation, languor, tiredness.
(ANT.) vivacity, rejuvenation, energy, vigor.

fault (SYN.) defect, flaw, mistake, imperfection, shortcoming, error, weakness, responsibility, omission, blemish, blame, failure.
(ANT.) perfection, completeness.

faulty (SYN.) imperfect, broken, defective, damaged, impaired.
(ANT.) flawless, perfect, whole.

favor (SYN.) rather, resemble, prefer, approval, like, support, patronize, benefit.
(ANT.) deplore, disapprove.

favorite (SYN.) prized, pet, choice, darling, treasured, preferred.

favoritism (SYN.) prejudice, bias, partiality.
(ANT.) fairness, impartiality.

fear (SYN.) horror, terror, fright, trepidation, alarm, consternation, dismay, panic, anxiety, dread, scare, apprehension.
(ANT.) fearlessness, boldness, courage, assurance.

fearless (SYN.) bold, brave, courageous, gallant, dauntless, confident.
(ANT.) timid, fearful, cowardly.

feast (SYN.) dinner, banquet, barbecue.

feat (SYN.) performance, act, operation, accomplishment, achievement, doing, transaction, deed.

(ANT.) intention, deliberation, cessation.

feature *(SYN.)* trait, quality, characteristic, attribute.

fee *(SYN.)* payment, pay, remuneration, charge, recompense.

feeble *(SYN.)* faint, puny, exhausted, impair, delicate, weak, enervated, frail, powerless, forceless, sickly, decrepit, ailing.

(ANT.) strong, forceful, powerful, vigorous, stout.

feed *(SYN.)* satisfy, nourish, food, fodder, forage.

feel *(SYN.)* sense, experience, perceive.

feeling *(SYN.)* opinion, sensibility, tenderness, affection, impression, belief, sensation, sympathy, thought, passion, sentiment, attitude, emotion.

(ANT.) fact, imperturbability, anesthesia, insensibility.

fellowship *(SYN.)* clan, society, brotherhood, fraternity, camaraderie, companionship, comradeship, association.

(ANT.) dislike, discord, distrust, enmity, strife, acrimony.

felonious *(SYN.)* murderous, criminal, larcenous.

feminine *(SYN.)* womanly, girlish, lady-like, female, maidenly, womanish.

(ANT.) masculine, male, virile.

ferocious *(SYN.)* savage, fierce, wild, blood-thirsty, brutal.

(ANT.) playful, gentle, harmless, calm.

fertile *(SYN.)* rich, fruitful, teeming, plenteous, bountiful,

prolific, luxuriant, productive, fecund.

(ANT.) unproductive, barren, sterile.

festival *(SYN.)* feast, banquet, celebration.

festive *(SYN.)* joyful, gay, joyous, merry, gala, jovial, jubilant.

(ANT.) sad, gloomy, mournful, morose.

fetching *(SYN.)* charming, attractive, pleasing, captivating, winsome.

feud *(SYN.)* dispute, quarrel, strife, argument, conflict, controversy.

(ANT.) amity, understanding, harmony, peace.

fiber *(SYN.)* line, strand, thread, string.

fickle *(SYN.)* unstable, capricious, restless, changeable, inconstant, variable.

(ANT.) stable, constant, trustworthy, steady, reliable, dependable.

fiction *(SYN.)* fabrication, romance, falsehood, tale, allegory, narrative, fable, novel, story, invention.

(ANT.) verity, reality, fact, truth.

fictitious *(SYN.)* invented, make-believe, imaginary, fabricated, unreal, counterfeit.

(ANT.) real, true, genuine, actual, proven.

fidelity *(SYN.)* fealty, devotion, precision, allegiance, exactness, constancy, accuracy, faithfulness, loyalty.

(ANT.) treachery, disloyalty.

fidget *(SYN.)* squirm, twitch,

wriggle.

fiendish *(SYN.)* devilish, demonic, diabolical, savage, satanic.

fierce *(SYN.)* furious, wild, savage, violent, ferocious, vehement.

(ANT.) calm, meek, mild, gentle, placid.

fight *(SYN.)* contend, scuffle, struggle, battle, wrangle, combat, brawl, quarrel, dispute, war, skirmish, conflict.

figure *(SYN.)* design, pattern, mold, shape, form, frame, reckon, calculate, compute, determine.

fill *(SYN.)* glut, furnish, store, stuff, occupy, gorge, pervade, content, stock, fill up, supply, replenish, satisfy.

(ANT.) void, drain, exhaust, deplete, empty.

filter *(SYN.)* screen, strainer, sieve.

filth *(SYN.)* pollution, dirt, sewage, foulness.

(ANT.) cleanliness, innocence, purity.

filthy *(SYN.)* foul, polluted, dirty, unwashed, squalid.

(ANT.) pure, clean, unspoiled.

final *(SYN.)* ultimate, decisive, concluding, ending, terminal, last, conclusive, eventual.

(ANT.) inaugural, rudimentary, beginning, initial, incipient, first, original.

finally *(SYN.)* at last, eventually, ultimately.

find *(SYN.)* observe, detect, discover, locate.

fine *(SYN.)* thin, pure, choice, small, elegant, dainty, splendid, handsome, delicate, nice, powdered, beautiful, minute, exquisite, subtle, pretty, refined.

(ANT.) thick, coarse, rough, blunt, large.

finicky *(SYN.)* fussy, meticulous, finical, fastidious, prim.

finish *(SYN.)* consummate, close, get done, terminate, accomplish, conclude, execute, perform, complete, end, achieve, fulfill, do, perfect.

(ANT.) open, begin, start, beginning.

fire *(SYN.)* vigor, glow, combustion, passion, burning, conflagration, ardor, flame, blaze, intensity, fervor.

(ANT.) apathy, cold.

firm *(SYN.)* solid, rigid, inflexible, stiff, unchanging, steadfast, dense, hard, unshakable, compact, business, company, corporation, partnership.

(ANT.) weak, limp, soft, drooping.

first *(SYN.)* chief, primary, initial, pristine, beginning, foremost, primeval, earliest, prime, primitive, original.

(ANT.) subordinate, last, least, hindmost, latest.

fishy *(SYN.)* suspicious, questionable, doubtful.

(ANT.) believable, credible.

fit *(SYN.)* adjust, suit, suitable, accommodate, conform, robust, harmonize, belong, seizure, spasm, attack, suited, appropriate, healthy, adapt.

(ANT.) misfit, disturb, improper.

fitful *(SYN.)* variable, restless, fickle, capricious, unstable, changeable.

(ANT.) trustworthy, stable, constant, steady.

fitting *(SYN.)* apt, due, suitable, proper.

(ANT.) improper, unsuitable, inappropriate.

fix *(SYN.)* mend, regulate, affix, set, tie, repair, attach, settle, link, bind, determine, establish, define, place, rectify, stick, limit, adjust, fasten.

(ANT.) damage, change, mistreat, displace, alter, disturb, mutilate.

fixation *(SYN.)* fetish, obsession, infatuation, compulsion.

flair *(SYN.)* style, dash, flamboyance, drama, gift, knack, aptitude.

flamboyant *(SYN.)* showy, flashy, ostentatious, gaudy, ostentatious.

flame *(SYN.)* blaze, fire.

flash *(SYN.)* flare, flame, wink, twinkling, instant, gleam.

flashy *(SYN.)* tawdry, tasteless, pretentious, garish, flamboyant.

flat *(SYN.)* vapid, stale, even, smooth, tasteless, horizontal, dull, level, insipid, uninteresting, boring.

(ANT.) tasty, racy, hilly, savory, stimulating, interesting, broken, sloping.

flattery *(SYN.)* compliment, praise, applause, blarney, acclaim.

flaunt *(SYN.)* exhibit, show off, display, parade.

(ANT.) conceal, hide, disguise.

flavor *(SYN.)* tang, taste, savor, essence, quality, character, season, spice.

flaw *(SYN.)* spot, imperfection, blemish, fault, deformity, blotch.

flee *(SYN.)* fly, abscond, hasten, escape, decamp, evade.

(ANT.) remain, appear, stay, arrive.

fleece *(SYN.)* filch, rob, purloin, swindle, defraud, pilfer, cheat.

fleet *(SYN.)* rapid, swift, quick, fast.

(ANT.) unhurried, sluggish, slow.

fleeting *(SYN.)* brief, swift, passing, temporary.

(ANT.) stable, fixed, lasting, permanent.

fleshy *(SYN.)* overweight, chubby, stocky, obese, stout.

(ANT.) spare, skinny.

flexible *(SYN.)* lithe, resilient, pliable, tractable, complaint, elastic, yielding, adaptable, easy, agreeable, supple, pliant, ductile.

(ANT.) hard, unbending, firm, brittle, inflexible, rigid, fixed.

flighty *(SYN.)* giddy, lightheaded, frivolous, irresponsible.

(ANT.) solid, responsible, steady.

flimsy *(SYN.)* wobbly, weak, frail, fragile, unsteady, delicate, thin.

(ANT.) durable, stable, firm, strong.

fling *(SYN.)* pitch, throw, toss,

fun, celebration, party.

flippant *(SYN.)* disrespectful, sassy, insolent, brazen, rude, impertinent.
(ANT.) courteous, polite, mannerly.

flit *(SYN.)* flutter, scurry, hasten, dart, skim.

flock *(SYN.)* gathering, group, flight, swarm, herd, school.

flog *(SYN.)* thrash, lash, switch, strike, paddle.

flood *(SYN.)* overflow, deluge, inundate, cascade.

florid *(SYN.)* gaudy, fancy, ornate, embellished.
(ANT.) spare, simple, plain, unadorned.

flourish *(SYN.)* succeed, grow, prosper, wave, thrive, bloom.
(ANT.) wither, die, decline.

flout *(SYN.)* disdain, scorn, spurn, ignore, taunt, ridicule, mock.

flow *(SYN.)* proceed, abound, spout, come, stream, run, originate, emanate, result, pour, squirt, issue, gush, spurt.

fluctuate *(SYN.)* vary, oscillate, change, hesitate, vacillate.
(ANT.) persist, stick, adhere, resolve.

fluent *(SYN.)* graceful, glib, flowing.

fluid *(SYN.)* liquid, running, liquefied.

flush *(SYN.)* abundant, flat, even, level.

fluster *(SYN.)* rattle, flurry, agitate, upset, perturb, quiver, vibrate.

fly *(SYN.)* flee, mount, shoot, decamp, hover, soar, flit, flutter, sail, escape, rush, spring, glide, abscond, dart, float.
(ANT.) sink, descend, plummet.

foam *(SYN.)* suds, froth, lather.

foe *(SYN.)* opponent, enemy, antagonist, adversary.
(ANT.) associate, ally, friend, comrade.

fog *(SYN.)* haze, mist, cloud, daze, confusion, stupor, vapor, smog.

foible *(SYN.)* frailty, weakness, failing, shortcoming, kink.

foist *(SYN.)* misrepresent, insinuate, falsify.

fold *(SYN.)* lap, double, overlap, clasp, pleat, tuck.

follow *(SYN.)* trail, observe, succeed, ensue, obey, chase, comply, accompany, copy, result, imitate, heed, adopt.
(ANT.) elude, cause, precede, avoid, flee.

follower *(SYN.)* supporter, devotee, henchman, adherent, partisan, votary, attendant, disciple, successor.
(ANT.) master, head, chief, dissenter.

following *(SYN.)* public, disciples, supporters, clientele, customers.

folly *(SYN.)* imprudence, silliness, foolishness, indiscretion, absurdity, imprudence, imbecility, stupidity, extravagance.
(ANT.) reasonableness, judgment, sense, prudence, wisdom.

fond *(SYN.)* affectionate, loving, attached, tender, devoted.
(ANT.) hostile, cool, distant, unfriendly.

fondness (SYN.) partiality, liking, affection.
(ANT.) hostility, unfriendliness.

food (SYN.) viands, edibles, feed, repast, nutriment, sustenance, diet, bread, provisions, meal, rations, victuals, fare.
(ANT.) want, hunger, drink, starvation.

fool (SYN.) oak, dunce, jester, idiot, simpleton, buffoon, harlequin, dolt, blockhead, numskull, clown, dope, trick, deceive, nincompoop.
(ANT.) scholar, genius, sage.

foolish (SYN.) senseless, irrational, crazy, silly, brainless, idiotic, simple, nonsensical, stupid, preposterous, asinine.
(ANT.) sane, sound, sensible, rational, judicious, wise, reasonable, prudent.

footing (SYN.) base, basis, foundation.

footloose (SYN.) uncommitted, free, detached, independent.
(ANT.) engaged, involved.

forbearance (SYN.) moderation, abstinence, abstention, continence.
(ANT.) greed, excess, intoxication.

forbid (SYN.) disallow, prevent, ban, prohibit, taboo, outlaw.
(ANT.) approve, let, allow, permit.

forbidding (SYN.) evil, hostile, unfriendly, sinister, scary, repulsive.
(ANT.) pleasant, beneficent, friendly.

force (SYN.) energy, might, violence, vigor, intensity, dint, power, constraint, coercion, vigor, compel, compulsion, oblige, coerce, strength.
(ANT.) weakness, frailty, persuasion, feebleness, impotence, ineffectiveness.

forceful (SYN.) dynamic, vigorous, energetic, potent, drastic, intense.

foreboding (SYN.) misgiving, suspicion, apprehension, presage, intuition.

forecast (SYN.) prophesy, predict, predetermine.

foregoing (SYN.) above, former, preceding, previous, prior.
(ANT.) later, coming, below, follow.

foreign (SYN.) alien, strange, exotic, different, unfamiliar.
(ANT.) commonplace, ordinary, familiar.

foreigner (SYN.) outsider, alien, newcomer, stranger.
(ANT.) native.

foreman (SYN.) super, boss, overseer, supervisor.

forerunner (SYN.) harbinger, proclaimer, informant.

foresee (SYN.) forecast, expect, anticipate, surmise, envisage.

forest (SYN.) grove, woodland, wood, copse, woods.

forestall (SYN.) hinder, thwart, prevent, obstruct, repel.

foretell (SYN.) soothsay, divine, predict.

forever (SYN.) evermore, always, everlasting, hereafter, endlessly.

(ANT.) fleeting, temporarily.

forfeit *(SYN.)* yield, resign, lose, sacrifice.

forgive *(SYN.)* exonerate, clear, excuse, pardon.
(ANT.) impeach, accuse, blame, censure.

forgo *(SYN.)* relinquish, release, surrender, waive, abandon.
(ANT.) keep, retain, safeguard.

forlorn *(SYN.)* pitiable, desolate, dejected, wretched.
(ANT.) optimistic, cherished, cheerful.

form *(SYN.)* frame, compose, fashion, arrange, construct, make up, devise, create, invent, mold, shape, forge, organize, produce, constitute, make.
(ANT.) wreck, dismantle, destroy, misshape.

formal *(SYN.)* exact, stiff, correct, outward, conformist, conventional, affected, regular, proper, ceremonious, decorous, methodical, precise, solemn, external, perfunctory.
(ANT.) heartfelt, unconstrained, easy, unconventional.

former *(SYN.)* earlier, onetime, previous, erstwhile, prior.

formidable *(SYN.)* alarming, frightful, imposing, terrible, terrifying, dire, fearful, forbidding.
(ANT.) unimpressive, ordinary.

forsake *(SYN.)* abandon, desert, forgo, quit, discard, neglect.

forte *(SYN.)* gift, capability, talent, specialty, aptitude, bulwark.

forth *(SYN.)* out, onward, for-ward.

forthright *(SYN.)* honest, direct, candid, outspoken, blunt sincere, plain, explicit.

forthwith *(SYN.)* instantly, promptly, immediately.
(ANT.) afterward, later, ultimately, slowly.

fortify *(SYN.)* bolster strengthen, barricade, defend.

fortuitous *(SYN.)* successful, benign, lucky, advantageous, propitious, happy, favored.
(ANT.) unlucky, condemned, persecuted.

fortunate *(SYN.)* happy, auspicious, fortuitous, successful, favored, advantageous, benign, charmed, lucky, felicitous, blessed, propitious, blissful.
(ANT.) ill-fated, cheerless, unlucky, unfortunate, cursed, condemned.

fortune *(SYN.)* chance, fate, lot, luck, riches, wealth, destiny.

fortuneteller *(SYN.)* soothsayer, clairvoyant, oracle, medium.

forward *(SYN.)* leading, front, promote, elevate, advance, first, ahead, onward, further, foremost.
(ANT.) withhold, retard, hinder, retreat, oppose.

foul *(SYN.)* base, soiled, dirty, mean, unclean, polluted, impure, vile, evil, muddy, wicked, rainy, stormy, despicable, filthy.
(ANT.) pure, neat, wholesome, clean.

found *(SYN.)* organize, establish.

foundation *(SYN.)* support, root, base, underpinning, establishment, substructure.

(ANT.) top, cover, building.

foxy *(SYN.)* cunning, sly, artful, crafty, wily, sharp, shrewd, slick.

fraction *(SYN.)* fragment, part, section, morsel, share, piece.

fracture *(SYN.)* crack, break, rupture.

fragile *(SYN.)* delicate, frail, weak, breakable, infirm, brittle, feeble.

(ANT.) tough, hardy, sturdy, strong, stout, durable.

fragment *(SYN.)* scrap, piece, bit, remnant, part, splinter, segment.

fragrance *(SYN.)* odor, smell, scent, perfume, aroma.

fragrant *(SYN.)* aromatic, scented, perfumed.

frail *(SYN.)* feeble, weak, delicate, breakable, fragile.

(ANT.) sturdy, strong, powerful.

frame *(SYN.)* support, framework, skeleton, molding, border, mount.

frank *(SYN.)* honest, candid, open, unreserved, direct, sincere.

(ANT.) tricky, dishonest.

frantic *(SYN.)* frenzied, crazed, raving, panicky.

(ANT.) composed, stoic.

fraud *(SYN.)* deception, guile, swindle, deceit, artifice, imposture, trick, cheat, imposition.

(ANT.) sincerity, fairness, integrity.

fraudulent *(SYN.)* tricky, fake, dishonest, deceitful

fray *(SYN.)* strife, fight, battle, struggle, tussle, combat, brawl.

(ANT.) truce, agreement, peace, concord

freak *(SYN.)* curiosity, abnormality, monster, oddity.

free *(SYN.)* munificent, clear, autonomous, immune, open, freed, bountiful, liberated, unfastened, immune, emancipated, unconfined, unobstructed, easy, artless, loose, familiar, bounteous, unrestricted, liberal, independent.

(ANT.) stingy, clogged, illiberal, confined, parsimonious.

freedom *(SYN.)* independence, privilege, familiarity, unrestraint, liberty, exemption, liberation.

(ANT.) servitude, constraint, bondage, slavery, necessity.

freight *(SYN.)* chipping, cargo, load, shipment.

frenzy *(SYN.)* craze, agitation, excitement.

frequent *(SYN.)* usual, habitual, common, often, customary.

(ANT.) unique, rare, solitary, uncommon, infrequent.

fresh *(SYN.)* recent, new, additional, modern, further, refreshing, natural, brisk, novel, late, current, sweet, pure, cool.

(ANT.) stagnant, decayed, musty, faded.

fret *(SYN.)* torment, worry, grieve, anguish.

fretful *(SYN.)* testy, irritable,

touchy, peevish, short-tempered.
(ANT.) calm.

friend (SYN.) crony, supporter, ally, companion, intimate, associate, advocate, comrade, mate, patron, acquaintance, chum.
(ANT.) stranger, adversary.

friendly (SYN.) sociable, kindly, affable, genial, companionable, social, neighborly, amicable.
(ANT.) hostile, antagonistic, reserved.

friendship (SYN.) knowledge, fraternity, acquaintance, intimacy, fellowship, comradeship, cognizance.
(ANT.) unfamiliarity, ignorance.

fright (SYN.) alarm, fear, panic, terror.

frighten (SYN.) scare, horrify, daunt, affright, appall, terrify, alarm, terrorize, astound, dismay, startle, panic.
(ANT.) soothe, embolden, compose, reassure.

frigid (SYN.) cold, wintry, icy, glacial, arctic, freezing.

fringe (SYN.) hem, edge, border, trimming, edging.

frisky (SYN.) animated, lively, peppy, vivacious.

frolic (SYN.) play, cavort, romp, frisk, gambol.

front (SYN.) facade, face, start, border, head.
(ANT.) rear, back.

frontier (SYN.) border, boundary.

frugal (SYN.) parsimonious, saving, stingy, provident, temperate, economical.
(ANT.) extravagant, wasteful, self-indulgent, intemperate.

fruitful (SYN.) fertile, rich, bountiful, teeming, fecund, productive, luxuriant, prolific.
(ANT.) lean, unproductive, barren, sterile.

fruitless (SYN.) barren, futile, vain, sterile, unproductive.
(ANT.) fertile, productive.

frustrate (SYN.) hinder, defeat, thwart, circumvent, outwit, foil, baffle, disappoint, discourage.
(ANT.) promote, fulfill, accomplish, further.

fugitive (SYN.) refugee, deserter, runaway.

fulfill (SYN.) do, effect, complete, accomplish, realize.

full (SYN.) baggy, crammed, entire, satiated, flowing, perfect, gorged, soaked, complete, filled, packed, extensive, plentiful, voluminous.
(ANT.) lacking, devoid, partial, empty, depleted.

full-fledged (SYN.) schooled, expert, professional, adept, qualified, senior, trained, able.
(ANT.) inexperienced, green, untried, untrained.

full-grown (SYN.) ripe, adult, mature, developed, complete.
(ANT.) green, young, unripe, adolescent.

fullness (SYN.) glut, repletion, enough, satiety, satiation, sufficiency, all, totality, satisfaction, sum, aggregate, everything.
(ANT.) need, want, hunger,

lack, insufficiency, privation, emptiness, incompleteness.

fulsome *(SYN.)* disgusting, repulsive, nauseating, revolting.

fume *(SYN.)* gas, steam, smoke, rage, rave, vapor.

fun *(SYN.)* merriment, pleasure, enjoyment, gaiety, sport, amusement.

function *(SYN.)* operation, activity, affair, ceremony, gathering, party.

fundamental *(SYN.)* basic, essential, primary, elementary.

furious *(SYN.)* angry, enraged. *(ANT.) serene, calm.*

furnish *(SYN.)* yield, give, endow, fit, produce, equip, afford, decorate, appoint. *(ANT.) divest, denude, strip.*

furor *(SYN.)* commotion, tumult, turmoil.

furthermore *(SYN.)* moreover, also, further.

furtive *(SYN.)* surreptitious, secret, hidden, clandestine. *(ANT.) honest, open.*

fury *(SYN.)* wrath, anger, frenzy, rage, violence, fierceness. *(ANT.) calmness, serenity.*

fuss *(SYN.)* commotion, bother, pester, annoy, irritate.

futile *(SYN.)* pointless, idle, useless, worthless, minor. *(ANT.) weighty, important, worthwhile, serious, valuable.*

future *(SYN.)* approaching, imminent, coming, impending. *(ANT.) former, past.*

fuzzy *(SYN.)* indistinct, blurred. *(ANT.) lucid, clear.*

G

gab *(SYN.)* jabber, babble, chatter, prattle, gossip.

gabble *(SYN.)* chatter, babble, jabber, blab, prate, gaggle, prattle.

gabby *(SYN.)* chatty, talkative, wordy, verbose.

gad *(SYN.)* wander, roam, rove, ramble, meander, cruise.

gadabout *(SYN.)* gypsy, wanderer, rambler.

gadget *(SYN.)* contrivance, device, doodad, jigger, thing, contraption.

gaffe *(SYN.)* blunder, boner, mistake, gaucherie, error, howler.

gag *(SYN.)* witticism, crack jest, joke.

gaiety *(SYN.)* joyousness, cheerfulness, lightheartedness. *(ANT.) melancholy, sadness, depression.*

gain *(SYN.)* acquire, avail, account, good, interest, attain, favor, achieve, get, secure, advantage, earn, profit, procure, service, obtain, improvement, increase, behalf, net, reach, win, benefit. *(ANT.) trouble, lose, calamity, forfeit, handicap, lose, distress.*

gainful *(SYN.)* lucrative, rewarding, profitable, beneficial, payable, productive. *(ANT.) unproductive, unprofitable, unrewarding.*

gainsay *(SYN.)* refute, contradict, controvert, deny, refuse, inpugn, contravene, disavow, differ.

(ANT.) maintain, aver, affirm, asseverate.

gait *(SYN.)* stride, walk, tread, step.

gala *(SYN.)* ball, party, carnival, fete, festival.

gale *(SYN.)* burst, surge, outburst.

gall *(SYN.)* nerve, audacity, impudence, annoy, vex, anger.

gallant *(SYN.)* bold, brave, courageous, valorous, valiant, noble, polite, fearless, heroic.

gallantry *(SYN.)* valor, daring, courage, prowess, heroism, graciousness, attentiveness, coquetry.

(ANT.) timidity, cowardice, cravenness, cloddishness.

gallery *(SYN.)* passageway, hall, aisle, hallway, passage, corridor.

galling *(SYN.)* vexing, irritating, annoying, distressful, irksome.

galore *(SYN.)* abounding, plentiful, profuse, rich, overflowing.

gamble *(SYN.)* game, wager, bet, hazard, risk, venture, chance.

gambol *(SYN.)* romp, dance, cavort, frolic.

game *(SYN.)* fun, contest, merriment, pastime, match, play, amusement, recreation, entertainment, competition, sport.

(ANT.) labor, hardship, work, business.

gamut *(SYN.)* extent, scope, sweep, horizon, range.

gang *(SYN.)* group, troop, band, company, horde, crew.

gangling *(SYN.)* rangy, lean, skinny, tall, lanky.

gangster *(SYN.)* crook, hoodlum, gunman, criminal.

gap *(SYN.)* cavity, chasm, pore, gulf, aperture, abyss, interval, space, hole, void, pore, break.

gape *(SYN.)* ogle, stare, gawk.

garb *(SYN.)* clothing, dress, vesture, array, attire, clothes, drapery, apparel, garments, costume.

(ANT.) nudity, nakedness.

garbage *(SYN.)* refuse, waste, trash, rubbish.

garbled *(SYN.)* twisted, confused, distorted.

gargantuan *(SYN.)* colossal, monumental, giant, large, enormous.

garments *(SYN.)* drapery, dress, garb, apparel, array, attire, clothes, raiment, clothing.

(ANT.) nakedness, nudity.

garnish *(SYN.)* decorate, embellish, trim, adorn, enrich, beautify.

(ANT.) expose, strip, debase, uncover, defame.

garrulous *(SYN.)* chatty, glib, verbose, talkative, communicative.

(ANT.) silent, uncommunicative, laconic, reticent, taciturn.

gash *(SYN.)* lacerate, slash, pierce, cut, hew, slice.

gasp *(SYN.)* pant, puff, wheeze.

gather *(ANT.)* assemble, collect, garner, harvest, reap, deduce, judge, amass, congregate, muster, cull, glean, accumulate, convene.

(ANT.) scatter, disperse, distribute, disband, separate.

gathering *(SYN.)* meeting, crowd, throng, company, assembly.

gaudy *(SYN.)* showy, flashy, loud, bold, ostentatious.

gaunt *(ANT.)* lank, diaphanous, flimsy, gauzy, narrow, rare, scanty, meager, gossamer, emaciated, scrawny, tenuous, thin, fine, lean, skinny, spare, slim, slight, slender, diluted.

(ANT.) wide, fat, thick, broad, bulky.

gay *(SYN.)* merry, lighthearted, joyful, cheerful, sprightly, jolly, happy, joyous, gleeful, jovial, colorful, bright, glad.

(ANT.) glum, mournful, sad, depressed, sorrowful, sullen.

gaze *(SYN.)* look, stare, view, watch, examine, observe, glance, behold, discern, seem, see, survey, witness, inspect, goggle, appear.

(ANT.) hide, overlook, avert, miss.

geld *(SYN.)* neuter, alter, castrate.

gem *(SYN.)* jewel, semiprecious stone.

general *(SYN.)* ordinary, universal, usual, common, customary, regular, miscellaneous.

(ANT.) definite, particular, exceptional, singular, particular, precise, exact, specific.

generally *(SYN.)* ordinarily, usually, customarily, normally, mainly.

(ANT.) seldom, infrequently, rare.

generate *(SYN.)* produce, bestow, impart, concede, permit, acquiesce, cede, relent, succumb, surrender, pay, supply, grant, relent, bear, afford, submit, waive, allow, breed, accord, accede, abdicate, resign, relinquish.

(ANT.) assert, refuse, struggle, resist, dissent, oppose, deny, strive.

generation *(SYN.)* age, date, era, period, seniority, senescence, senility, time, epoch.

(ANT.) infancy, youth, childhood.

generosity *(SYN.)* magnanimity, benevolence, humanity, kindness, philanthropy, altruism, liberality.

(ANT.) selfishness, malevolence, cruelty, inhumanity, unkindness.

generous *(SYN.)* giving, liberal, unselfish, magnanimous, bountiful, munificent, charitable, big, noble.

(ANT.) greedy, stingy, selfish, covetous, mean, miserly.

genesis *(SYN.)* birth, root, creation, source, origin, beginning.

genius *(SYN.)* intellect, adept, intellectual, sagacity, proficient, creativity, ability, inspiration, faculty, originality, brain, gift.

(ANT.) dullard, stupidity, dolt, moron, ineptitude, obtuseness.

genre *(SYN.)* chaste, order, set, elegance, class, excellence, kind, denomination, grade.

genteel *(SYN.)* cultured, polished, polite, refined, elegant. *(ANT.)* discourteous, churlish, common.

gentle *(SYN.)* peaceful, placid, tame, serene, relaxed, docile, benign, soothing, calm, soft, mild, friendly, kindly, cultivated. *(ANT.)* nasty, harsh, rough, fierce, mean, violent, savage.

genuine *(SYN.)* real, true, unaffected, authentic, sincere, bona fide, unadulterated, legitimate, actual, veritable, definite, proven. *(ANT.)* false, sham, artificial, fake, counterfeit, bogus, pretended, insincere, sham.

genus *(SYN.)* kind, race, species, sort, type, variety, character.

germ *(SYN.)* pest, virus, contamination, disease, pollution, taint, infection, contagion, ailment.

germinate *(SYN.)* vegetate, pullulate, sprout, develop, grow.

gesture *(SYN.)* omen, signal, symbol, emblem, indication, note, sign, token, symptom, movement.

get *(SYN.)* obtain, receive, attain, gain, achieve, acquire, procure, earn, fetch, carry, remove, prepare, take, ready, urge, induce. *(ANT.)* lose, surrender, forfeit, leave, renounce.

ghastly *(SYN.)* frightful, horrible, horrifying, frightening, grisly, hideous, dreadful.

ghost *(SYN.)* phantom, spook, apparition, specter, trace, hint, vestige, spirit.

ghoulish *(SYN.)* weird, eerie, horrifying, gruesome, sinister, scary.

giant *(SYN.)* monster, colossus, mammoth, superman, gigantic. *(ANT.)* small, tiny, dwarf, runt, midget, infinitesimal.

gibe *(SYN.)* sneer, jeer, mock, scoff, boo, hoot, hiss. *(ANT.)* approve.

giddy *(SYN.)* reeling, dizzy, flighty, silly, scatterbrained. *(ANT.)* serious.

gift *(SYN.)* endowment, favor, gratuity, bequest, talent, charity, present, largess, donation, grant, aptitude, boon, offering, faculty, genius, benefaction. *(ANT.)* purchase, loss, ineptitude, deprivation, earnings, incapacity.

gigantic *(SYN.)* huge, colossal, immense, large, vast, elephantine, gargantuan, prodigious, mammoth, monumental, enormous. *(ANT.)* small, tiny, minute, diminutive, little.

giggle *(SYN.)* chuckle, jeer, laugh, roar, snicker, titter, cackle, guffaw, mock.

gild *(SYN.)* cover, coat, paint, embellish, sweeten, retouch, camouflage.

gingerly *(SYN.)* gentle, cautiously, carefully, gently. *(ANT.)* roughly.

gird *(SYN.)* wrap, tie, bind, belt, encircle, surround, prepare. *(ANT.)* untie.

sunny.

lass, miss,

exalt,
gnify,   ns, expanse,
raise,

ase,   anation, pur-
                 ance, accepta-
                 ition, interpreta
                 g.
                 dancy.
                 bestow, contribute,
                 art, provide, donate,
                 deliver, present, fur-
                 yield, develop, offer,
                 e, hand over, award,
                 bend, sacrifice, supply.
                 withdraw, take, retain,
                 p, seize.

a (SYN.) handed over, pre-
ented, supposed, stated, disposed, assumed, inclined.

acier (SYN.) frigid, icy, ice-
berg.

glad (SYN.) happy, cheerful,
gratified, delighted, joyous,
merry, pleased, exulting,
charmed, thrilled, satisfied,
tickled, gay, bright.

(ANT.) *sad, depressed, dejected,*
melancholy, unhappy,
morose, somber, despondent.

gladness (SYN.) bliss, contentment, happiness, pleasure,
well-being, beatitude, delight,
satisfaction, blessedness.

(ANT.) *sadness, sorrow,*
despair, misery, grief.

glade (SYN.) clearing.

gladiator (SYN.) battler, fighter, competitor, combatant,
contender, contestant.

glamorous (SYN.) fascinating,
spellbinding, alluring, charm-

ing, bewitching, entrancing,
captivating, enchanting, attractive, appealing, enticing,
enthralling.

glamour (SYN.) charm, allure,
attraction, magnetism, fasci-
nation.

glance (SYN.) eye, gaze, survey,
view, examine, inspect, discern, look, see, witness, peek,
regard, skim, reflect, glimpse,
behold, observe.

(ANT.) *hide, miss, avert, over-*
look.

glare (SYN.) flash, dazzle, stare,
glower, glow, shine, glaze,
burn, brilliance, flare, blind,
scowl.

glaring (SYN.) flagrant, obvious, blatant, prominent, dazzling.

glass (SYN.) cup, tumbler, goblet, pane, crystal.

glassy (SYN.) blank, empty,
emotionless, vacant, fixed,
expressionless.

glaze (SYN.) buff, luster, cover,
wax, gloss, polish, shellac.

gleam (SYN.) flash, glimmer,
glisten, shimmer, sparkle,
twinkle, glare, beam, glow,
radiate, glimmering, shine,
burn, reflection, blaze.

glean (SYN.) reap, gather,
select, harvest, pick, separate,
cull.

glee (SYN.) mirth, joy, gladness,
enchantment, delight, bliss,
elation, merriment.

(ANT.) *depression, misery,*
dejection.

glen (SYN.) ravine, valley.

glib (SYN.) smooth, suave, flat,

plain, polished, sleek, urbane.
(ANT.) rough, rugged, blunt, harsh, bluff.

glide (SYN.) sweep, sail, fly, flow, slip, coast, cruise, move easily, skim, slide.

glimmer (SYN.) blink, shimmer, flicker, indication, hint, clue, suggestion.

glimpse (SYN.) notice, glance, peek, see, impression, look, flash.

glint (SYN.) flash, gleam, peek, glance, glimpse, sparkle, glitter.

glisten (SYN.) shimmer, shine, glimmer, twinkle, glitter, glister, sparkle.

glitch (SYN.) mishap, snag, hitch, malfunction.

glitter (SYN.) glisten, glimmer, sparkle, shine, twinkle.

gloat (SYN.) triumph, exult, glory, rejoice, revel.

global (SYN.) universal, international, worldwise.

globe (SYN.) orb, ball, world, earth, map, universe, sphere.

gloom (SYN.) bleakness, despondency, misery, sadness, woe, darkness, dejection, obscurity, blackness, shadow, shade, dimness, shadows, melancholy.
(ANT.) joy, mirth, exultation, cheerfulness, light, happiness, brightness, frivolity.

gloomy (SYN.) despondent, dismal, glum, somber, sorrowful, sad, dejected, disconsolate, dim, dark, morose, dispirited, moody, grave, pensive.
(ANT.) happy, merry, cheerful,

high-spirited, bright, joyous.

glorify (SYN.) enthrone, honor, revere, adore, di enshrine, consecrate, p worship, venerate.
(ANT.) mock, dishonor, del abuse, degrade.

glorious (SYN.) exalted, h noble, splendid, supreme, e vated, lofty, raised, majest famous, noted, stately, disti guished, celebrated, r nowned, famed, magnificen grand, proud, impressive, ele gant, sublime.
(ANT.) ridiculous, low, base, ignoble, terrible, ordinary.

glory (SYN.) esteem, praise, respect, reverence, admiration, honor, dignity, worship, eminence, homage, deference.
(ANT.) dishonor, disgrace, contempt, reproach, derision.

gloss (SYN.) luster, shine, glow, sheen.

glossary (SYN.) dictionary, thesaurus, wordbook, lexicon.

glossy (SYN.) smooth, glistening, shiny, sleek, polished.
(ANT.) matte, dull.

glow (SYN.) beam, glisten, radiate, shimmer, sparkle, glare, blaze, scintillate, shine, light, gleam, burn, flare, flame, radiate, dazzle, blush, redden, heat, warmth.

glower (SYN.) scowl, stare, frown, glare.
(ANT.) beam, grin, smile.

glowing (SYN.) fiery, intense, passionate, zealous, enthusiastic, ardent, eager, fervent, impassioned, complimentary, vehement.

(ANT.) cool, indifferent, apathetic, nonchalant.

glue (SYN.) bind, fasten, cement, paste.

glum (SYN.) morose, sulky, fretful, crabbed, sullen, dismal, dour, moody.

(ANT.) joyous, merry, amiable, gay, pleasant.

glut (SYN.) gorge, sate, content, furnish, fill, pervade, satiate, stuff, replenish, fill up, satisfy, stock.

(ANT.) empty, exhaust, deplete, void, drain.

glutton (SYN.) pig, hog, greedy eater.

gluttony (SYN.) ravenousness, piggishness, devouring, hoggishness, insatiability, swinishness, voraciousness.

(ANT.) satisfaction, fullness.

gnarled (SYN.) twisted, knotted, rugged, nodular.

gnash (SYN.) gnaw, crunch, grind.

gnaw (SYN.) chew, eat, gnash, grind, erode.

go (SYN.) proceed, depart, flee, move, vanish, exit, walk, quit, fade, progress, travel, become, fit, agree, leave, suit, harmonize, pass, travel, function, operate.

(ANT.) stay, arrive, enter, stand, come.

goad (SYN.) incite, prod, drive, urge, push, shove, jab, provoke, stimulate.

goal (SYN.) craving, destination, desire, longing, objective, finish, end, passion, aim, object, aspiration.

gobble (SYN.) devour, eat fast, gorge, gulp, stuff.

goblet (SYN.) cup, glass.

goblin (SYN.) troll, elf, dwarf, spirit.

godlike (SYN.) holy, supernatural, heavenly, celestial, divine, transcendent.

(ANT.) profane, wicked, blasphemous, diabolical, mundane.

godly (SYN.) pious, religious, holy, pure, divine, spiritual, righteous, saintly.

golden (SYN.) shining, metallic, bright, fine, superior, nice, excellent, valuable.

(ANT.) dull, inferior.

gong (SYN.) chimes, bells.

good (SYN.) honest, sound, valid, cheerful, honorable, worthy, conscientious, moral, genuine, humane, kind, fair, useful, skillful, adequate, friendly, genial, proficient, pleasant, exemplary, admirable, virtuous, reliable, precious, benevolent, excellent, pure, agreeable, gracious, safe.

(ANT.) bad, imperfect, vicious, undesirable, unkind, evil.

good-by (SYN.) so long, farewell.

good-bye (SYN.) farewell.

good-hearted (SYN.) good, kind, thoughtful, kind-hearted, considerate.

(ANT.) evil-hearted.

good-humored (SYN.) pleasant, goodnatured, cheerful, sunny, amiable.

(ANT.) petulant, cranky.

goodness *(SYN.)* good, honesty, integrity, virtue, righteousness.

(ANT.) sin, evil, dishonesty, corruption, badness.

goods *(SYN.)* property, belongings, holdings, possessions, merchandise, wares.

good will *(SYN.)* agreeability, harmony, willingness, readiness.

gore *(SYN.)* impale, penetrate, puncture, gouge.

gorge *(SYN.)* ravine, devour, stuff, gobble, valley, defile, pass, cram, fill.

gorgeous *(SYN.)* grand, ravishing, glorious, stunning, brilliant, divine, splendid, dazzling, beautiful, magnificent.

(ANT.) homely, ugly, squalid.

gory *(SYN.)* bloody.

gossamer *(SYN.)* dainty, fine, filmy, delicate, sheer, transparent.

gossip *(SYN.)* prate, rumor, prattle, hearsay, meddler, tattler, chatter, talk, chat, blabbermouth.

gouge *(SYN.)* scoop, dig, carve, burrow, excavate, chisel, notch.

gourmet *(SYN.)* gourmand, gastronome, connoisseur.

govern *(SYN.)* manage, oversee, reign, preside over, supervise, direct, command, sway, administer, control, regulate, determine, influence, guide, lead, head, rule.

(ANT.) assent, submit, acqui-

esse, obey, yield.

government *(SYN.)* control, direction, rule, command, authority.

governor *(SYN.)* controller, administrator, director, leader, manager.

gown *(SYN.)* garment, robe, frock, dress, costume, attire.

grab *(SYN.)* snatch, grip, clutch, seize, grasp, capture, pluck.

grace *(SYN.)* charm, beauty, loveliness, dignify, fairness, honor, distinguish, sympathy, attractiveness, elegance, clemency, excuse, pardon, thanks, blessing, prayer, pulchritude.

(ANT.) eyesore, homeliness, deformity, ugliness, disfigurement.

graceful *(SYN.)* elegant, fluid, natural, supple, beautiful, comely, flowing, lithe.

(ANT.) clumsy, awkward, gawky, ungainly, deformed.

gracious *(SYN.)* warm-hearted, pleasing, friendly, engaging, agreeable, kind, amiable, kindly, nice, good, courteous, polite, generous, good-natured.

(ANT.) surly, hateful, churlish, rude, disagreeable, impolite, thoughtless, discourteous, ill-natured.

grade *(SYN.)* kind, rank, elegance, denomination, sort, arrange, category, classify, rate, group, place, mark, incline, slope, excellence, caste, order.

gradual *(SYN.)* deliberate, sluggish, dawdling, laggard, slow, leisurely, moderate, easy, delaying.

(ANT.) quick, swift, fast, speedy, rapid.

graduate *(SYN.)* pass, finish, advance.

graft *(SYN.)* fraud, theft, cheating, bribery, dishonesty, transplant, corruption.

grain *(SYN.)* speck, particle, plant, bit, seed, temper, fiber, character, texture, markings, nature, tendency.

grand *(SYN.)* great, elaborate, splendid, royal, stately, noble, considerable, outstanding, distinguished, impressive, prominent, majestic, fine, dignified, large, main, principal.

(ANT.) unassuming, modest, insignificant, unimportant, humble.

grandeur *(SYN.)* resplendence, majesty, distinction, glory.

grandiose *(SYN.)* grand, lofty, magnificent, stately, noble, pompous, dignified, imposing, sublime, majestic.

(ANT.) lowly, ordinary, common, undignified, humble.

grandstand *(SYN.)* bleachers, gallery.

granite *(SYN.)* stone, rock.

grant *(SYN.)* confer, allocate, deal, divide, mete, appropriation, assign, benefaction, distribute, allowance, donate, award, mete out, deal out, consent, bestow, give, measure.

(ANT.) refuse, withhold, confiscate, keep, retain.

granular *(SYN.)* grainy, sandy, crumbly, rough, gritty.

graph *(SYN.)* design, plan, stratagem, draw up, chart, sketch, cabal, machination, outline, plot, scheme, diagram.

graphic *(SYN.)* vivid, lifelike, significant, meaningful, pictorial, descriptive, representative.

grapple *(SYN.)* grip, seize, clutch, clasp, grasp, fight, struggle.

grasp *(SYN.)* clutch, grip, seize, apprehend, capture, snare, hold, clasp, comprehend, reach, grab, understand, grapple, possession, control, domination, command, perceive.

(ANT.) release, lose, throw, liberate.

grasping *(SYN.)* possessive, greedy, selfish, acquisitive, mercenary.

(ANT.) liberal, unselfish, generous.

grate *(SYN.)* file, pulverize, grind, scrape, scratch, scrape, annoy, irritate.

grateful *(SYN.)* beholden, obliged, appreciative, thankful, indebted.

(ANT.) ungrateful, unappreciative, grudging, thankless.

gratify *(SYN.)* charm, gladden, please, satisfy.

(ANT.) frustrate.

gratifying *(SYN.)* contentment, solace, relief, comfort, ease, succor, consolation, enjoyment.

(ANT.) suffering, torment, affliction, discomfort, torture, mis-

ery.

grating *(SYN.)* harsh, rugged, severe, stringent, coarse, gruff, jarring, rigorous, strict.
(ANT.) smooth, melodious, mild, gentle, soft.

gratis *(SYN.)* complimentary, free.

gratitude *(SYN.)* gratefulness, thankfulness, appreciation.
(ANT.) ungratefulness.

gratuity *(SYN.)* tip, bonus, gift, donation.

grave *(SYN.)* sober, grim, earnest, serious, important, momentous, sedate, solemn, somber, imposing, vital, essential, staid, consequential, thoughtful.
(ANT.) light, flighty, trivial, insignificant, unimportant, trifling, merry, gay, cheery, frivolous.

gravel *(SYN.)* stones, pebbles, grain.

gravitate *(SYN.)* incline, tend, lean, approach, toward.

gravity *(SYN.)* concern, importance, pull, movement.
(ANT.) triviality.

graze *(SYN.)* scrape, feed, rub, brush, contact, skim.

grease *(SYN.)* fat, oil, lubrication.

greasy *(SYN.)* messy, buttery, waxy, fatty.

great *(SYN.)* large, numerous, eminent, illustrious, big, gigantic, enormous, immense, vast, weighty, fine, important, countless, prominent, vital, huge, momentous, serious, famed, dignified, excellent, critical, renowned, majestic, elevated, noble, grand.
(ANT.) minute, common, menial, ordinary, diminutive, small, paltry, unknown.

greed *(SYN.)* piggishness, lust, desire, greediness, avarice, covetousness.
(ANT.) unselfishness, selflessness, generosity.

greedy *(SYN.)* selfish, devouring, ravenous, avaricious, covetous, rapacious, gluttonous, insatiable, voracious.
(ANT.) full, generous, munificent, giving, satisfied.

green *(SYN.)* inexperienced, modern, novel, recent, further, naive, fresh, natural, raw, unsophisticated, undeveloped, immature, unripe, additional, brisk, artless.
(ANT.) hackneyed, musty, decayed, faded, stagnant.

greenhorn *(SYN.)* tenderfoot, beginner, apprentice, amateur, novice.

greenhouse *(SYN.)* hothouse.

greet *(SYN.)* hail, accost, meet, address, talk to, speak to, welcome, approach.
(ANT.) pass by, avoid.

gregarious *(SYN.)* outgoing, civil, affable, communicative, hospitable, sociable.
(ANT.) inhospitable, antisocial, disagreeable, hermitic.

grief *(SYN.)* misery, sadness, tribulation, affliction, heartache, woe, anguish, mourning, distress, lamentation.
(ANT.) happiness, solace, consolation, comfort, joy.

grief-stricken *(SYN.)* heartsick, ravaged, devastated, wretched, forlorn, desolate, wretched.
(ANT.) joyous, blissful, content.

grievance *(SYN.)* injury, wrong, injustice, detriment, complaint, damage, prejudice, evil, objection, protest, accusation, harm.
(ANT.) improvement, benefit, repair.

grieve *(SYN.)* lament, brood over, mourn, weep, wail, sorrow, distress, bemoan, hurt, deplore.
(ANT.) revel, carouse, celebrate, rejoice, gladden, soothe.

grieved *(SYN.)* contrite, remorseful, beggarly, mean, pitiful, shabby, vile, sorrowful, pained, hurt, sorry, contemptible, worthless.
(ANT.) splendid, delighted, cheerful, impenitent, unrepentant.

grievous *(SYN.)* gross, awful, outrageous, shameful, lamentable, regrettable.
(ANT.) agreeable, comforting, pleasurable.

grill *(SYN.)* cook, broil, question, interrogate, barbecue, grating, gridiron, cross-examine.

grim *(SYN.)* severe, harsh, strict, merciless, fierce, horrible, inflexible, adamant, ghastly, frightful, unyielding, rigid, stern.
(ANT.) pleasant, lenient, relaxed, amiable, congenial, smiling.

grimace *(SYN.)* expression, sneer, scowl, mope.

grimy *(SYN.)* unclean, grubby, soiled.

grin *(SYN.)* beam, smile, smirk.

grind *(SYN.)* mill, mash, powder, crush, crumble, pulverize, smooth, grate, sharpen, even.

grip *(SYN.)* catch, clutch, apprehend, trap, arrest, grasp, hold, bag, suitcase, lay hold of, clench, command, control, possession, domination, comprehension, seize.
(ANT.) release, liberate, lose, throw.

gripe *(SYN.)* protest, lament, complaint, grumbling.

grit *(SYN.)* rub, grind, grate, sand, gravel, pluck, courage, stamina.

groan *(SYN.)* sob, wail, howl, moan, whimper, wail, complain.

groggy *(SYN.)* dazed, dopy, stupefied, stunned, unsteady.
(ANT.) alert.

groom *(SYN.)* tend, tidy, preen, curry, spouse, consort.

groove *(SYN.)* furrow, channel, track, routine, slot, scratch.

groovy *(SYN.)* marvelous, delightful, wonderful.

grope *(SYN.)* fumble, feel around.

gross *(SYN.)* glaring, coarse, indelicate, obscene, bulky, great, total, whole, brutal, grievous, aggregate, earthy, rude, vulgar, entire, enormous, crass, rough, large.
(ANT.) appealing, delicate, refined, proper, polite, culti-

grotesque *(SYN.)* strange, weird, odd, incredible, fantastic, monstrous, absurd, freakish, bizarre, deformed, disfigured.

grotto *(SYN.)* tunnel, cave, hole, cavern.

grouch *(SYN.)* protest, remonstrate, whine, complain, grumble, murmur, mope, mutter, repine.

(ANT.) praise, applaud, rejoice, approve.

grouchy *(SYN.)* cantankerous, grumpy, surly.

(ANT.) cheerful, contented, agreeable, pleasant.

ground *(SYN.)* foundation, presumption, surface, principle, set, underpinning, premise, base, bottom, fix, basis, soil, land, earth, root, support, establish, dirt, presupposition.

(ANT.) implication, superstructure, derivative.

groundless *(SYN.)* baseless, unfounded, unwarranted, needless.

grounds *(SYN.)* garden, lawns, dregs, foundation, leftovers, reason, sediment, cause, premise, motive.

groundwork *(SYN.)* support, bottom. base, underpinning, premise, presupposition, principle, basis.

(ANT.) trimming, implication, derivative, superstructure.

group *(SYN.)* crowd, clock, party, troupe, swarm, bunch, brook, assembly, herd, band, mob, brood, class, throng, cluster, flock, lot, collection, pack, horde, gathering.

(ANT.) disassemble.

grouse *(SYN.)* mutter, grumble, gripe, scold, growl, complain.

grovel *(SYN.)* creep, crawl, cower, cringe, slouch, stoop, scramble.

groveling *(SYN.)* dishonorable, lowly, sordid, vile, mean, abject, despicable, ignoble, menial, servile, vulgar, ignominious.

(ANT.) lofty, noble, esteemed, exalted, righteous.

grow *(SYN.)* extend, swell, advance, develop, enlarge, germinate, mature, expand, flower, raise, become, cultivate, increase.

(ANT.) wane, shrink, atrophy, decay, diminish, contract.

growl *(SYN.)* complain, snarl, grumble, gnarl, clamor, bellow.

grown-up *(SYN.)* adult, of age, mature, big, senior.

(ANT.) little, childish, budding, junior, juvenile.

growth *(SYN.)* expansion, development, maturing, progress, elaboration, evolution.

(ANT.) degeneration, deterioration, curtailment, compression.

grub *(SYN.)* gouge, dig, scoop out, burrow, tunnel, excavate, plod.

grubby *(SYN.)* unkempt, grimy, slovenly, dirty.

(ANT.) tidy, spruce, neat, clean, wellgroomed.

grudge *(SYN.)* malevolence, malice, resentment, bitterness, spite, animosity, enmity, rancor, ill will.

(ANT.) kindness, love, benevolence, affection, good will, toleration.

grudgingly *(SYN.)* reluctantly, unwillingly, involuntarily.

grueling *(SYN.)* taxing, exhausting, excruciating, trying, grinding.

(ANT.) easy, light, simple.

gruesome *(SYN.)* hideous, frightful, horrible, loathsome, horrifying, grisly.

(ANT.) agreeable, soothing, delightful, charming.

gruff *(SYN.)* scratchy, crude, unpolished, stormy, brusque, rude, rough, uncivil, churlish, violent, harsh, imperfect, craggy, irregular, deep, husky, approximate, tempestuous, blunt.

(ANT.) civil, courteous, polished, calm, even, sleek, smooth, finished, gentle, placid, pleasant, tranquil.

grumble *(SYN.)* protest, mutter, complain.

grumpy *(SYN.)* cranky, grouchy, surly, crabbed, fractious, pettish.

(ANT.) winsome, amiable, pleasant, cheery.

guarantee *(SYN.)* bond, pledge, token, warrant, earnest, surety, bail, commitment, promise, secure, swear, assure, sponsor, certify, warranty, insure, endorse.

guarantor *(SYN.)* voucher, sponsor, warrantor, signatory, underwriter, surety.

guaranty *(SYN.)* warranty, token, deposit, earnest, pledge, collateral, stake.

guard *(SYN.)* protect, shield, veil, cloak, conceal, disguise, envelop, preserve, hide, defend, cover, sentry, protector, shroud, curtain.

(ANT.) unveil, expose, ignore, bare, reveal, divulge.

guardian *(SYN.)* curator, keeper, protector, custodian.

guess *(SYN.)* estimate, suppose, think, assume, reason, believe, reckon, speculate, notion, surmise, imagine.

(ANT.) know.

guest *(SYN.)* caller, client, customer, visitor, company.

(ANT.) host.

guide *(SYN.)* manage, supervise, conduct, direct, lead, steer, escort, pilot, show, usher, control, influence, regulate.

(ANT.) follower, follow.

guild *(SYN.)* association, union, society.

guile *(SYN.)* deceitfulness, fraud, wiliness, trick, deceit, chicanery, cunning, deception, craftiness, sham, sneakiness, cheat.

(ANT.) sincerity, openness, honesty, truthfulness, candor, frankness.

guileless *(SYN.)* open, innocent, naive, sincere, simple, candid.

(ANT.) treacherous, plotting.

guise *(SYN.)* aspect, pretense, mien, look, air, advent, apparition, appearance, dress, garb, coat, cover.

gulch (SYN.) gorge, valley, gully, ravine, canyon.

gulf (SYN.) ravine, cut, break, crack, chasm, canyon, abyss, cleft, separation, bay, sound, inlet.

gullible (SYN.) trustful, naive, innocent, unsuspecting, deceivable, believing.

(ANT.) skeptical, sophisticated.

gully (SYN.) ditch, gorge, ravine, valley, gulch, gulf.

gulp (SYN.) devour, swallow, gasp, repress, choke.

gun (SYN.) fire, shoot, weapon, pistol, firearm, revolver.

gush (SYN.) pour, spurt, stream, rush out, spout, flood, flush.

gust (SYN.) blast, wind, outbreak, outburst, eruption.

gymnasium (SYN.) playground, arena, court, athletic field.

gymnastics (SYN.) drill, exercise, acrobatics, calisthenics.

gyp (SYN.) swindle, cheat, defraud.

gypsy (SYN.) nomad.

H

habit (SYN.) usage, routine, compulsion, use, wont, custom, disposition, practice, addiction.

habitation (SYN.) abode, domicile, lodgings, home, dwelling.

habitual (SYN.) general, usual, common, frequent, persistent, customary, routine, often.

(ANT.) solitary, unique, exceptional, occasional, unusual, scanty, rare.

habituated (SYN.) used, accustomed, adapted, acclimated, comfortable, familiarized, addicted.

hack (SYN.) cleave, chop, slash, hew, slice, pick, sever.

hag (SYN.) beldam, crone, vixen, granny, ogress, harridan, virage.

haggard (SYN.) drawn, debilitated, spent, gaunt, worn.

(ANT.) bright, fresh, clear-eyed, animated.

haggle (SYN.) dicker, bargain.

hail (SYN.) welcome, approach, accost, speak to, address, greet.

(ANT.) pass by, avoid.

hair-raising (SYN.) horrifying, exciting, alarming, thrilling, startling, frightful, scary.

hairy (SYN.) bearded, shaggy, hirsute, bewhiskered.

hale (SYN.) robust, well, wholesome, hearty, healthy, sound, strong, salubrious.

(ANT.) noxious, frail, diseased, delicate, infirm, injurious.

half-baked (SYN.) crude, premature, makeshift, illogical, shallow.

half-hearted (SYN.) uncaring, indifferent, unenthusiastic, cool.

(ANT.) eager, enthusiastic, earnest.

half-wit (SYN.) dope, simpleton, nitwit, dunce, idiot, fool.

hall (SYN.) corridor, lobby, passage, hallway, vestibule, foyer.

hallow (SYN.) glorify, exalt,

dignify, aggrandize, consecrate, elevate, ennoble, raise, erect.

(ANT.) *dishonor, humiliate, debase, degrade.*

hallowed *(SYN.)* holy, sacred, beatified, blessed, divine.

hallucination *(SYN.)* fantasy, mirage, dream, vision, phantasm, appearance, aberration, illusion.

halt *(SYN.)* impede, obstruct, terminate, stop, hinder, desist, check, arrest, abstain, discontinue, hold, end, interrupt, bar.

(ANT.) *start, begin, proceed, speed, beginning, promote.*

halting *(SYN.)* imperfect, awkward, stuttering, faltering, hobbling, doubtful, limping, wavering.

(ANT.) *decisive, confident, smooth, graceful, facile.*

hammer *(SYN.)* beat, bang, whack, pound, batter, drive, tap, cudgel.

hamper *(SYN.)* prevent, impede, thwart, restrain, hinder, obstruct.

(ANT.) *help, assist, expedite, encourage, facilitate.*

hamstrung *(SYN.)* disabled, helpless, paralyzed.

hand *(SYN.)* assistant, helper, support, aid, laborer.

handicap *(SYN.)* retribution, penalty, disadvantage, forfeiture, hindrance, chastisement.

(ANT.) *reward, pardon, compensation, remuneration.*

handle *(SYN.)* hold, touch, finger, clutch, grip, manipulate, feel, grasp, control, oversee,

direct, treat, steer, supervise, regulate.

hand out *(SYN.)* disburse, distribute, deal, mete, circulate.

hand over *(SYN.)* release, surrender, deliver, yield, present.

handsome *(SYN.)* lovely, pretty, fair, comely, beautiful, charming, elegant, good-looking, generous.

(ANT.) *repulsive, ugly, unattractive, stingy, small, mean, petty, meager, homely, foul, hideous.*

handy *(SYN.)* suitable, adapted, favorable, fitting, near, ready, close, nearby, clever, helpful, useful, timely, accessible.

(ANT.) *inopportune, troublesome, awkward, inconvenient.*

hang *(SYN.)* drape, hover, dangle, suspend, kill, sag, execute, lynch.

hanker *(SYN.)* wish, yearn, long, desire, pine, thirst, covet.

haphazard *(SYN.)* aimless, random, purposeless, casual, indiscriminate, accidental.

(ANT.) *determined, planned, designed, deliberate.*

hapless *(SYN.)* unfortunate, ill-fated, jinxed, luckless, wretched.

happen *(SYN.)* occur, take place, bechance, betide, transpire, come to pass, chance, befall.

happening *(SYN.)* episode, event, scene, incident, affair, experience.

happiness *(SYN.)* pleasure, gladness, delight, beatitude, bliss, contentment, satisfac-

tion, joy, joyousness, blessedness, joyfulness, felicity, elation, well-being.

*(ANT.) sadness, sorrow,
despair, misery, grief.*

happy *(SYN.)* gay, joyous,
cheerful, fortunate, glad,
merry, contented, satisfied,
blessed, pleased, opportune,
delighted.

*(ANT.) gloomy, morose, sad,
miserable, depressed, blue.*

harangue *(SYN.)* oration, dia-
tribe, lecture, tirade, exhortation.

harass *(SYN.)* badger, irritate,
molest, pester, taunt, torment,
provoke, tantalize, aggravate,
annoy, nag, plague, vex.

*(ANT.) please, soothe, comfort,
delight, gratify.*

harbinger *(SYN.)* sign, messenger, proclaim, forerunner, herald.

harbor *(SYN.)* haven, port,
anchorage, cherish, entertain,
protect, shelter.

hard *(SYN.)* difficult, burdensome, arduous, rigid, puzzling, cruel, strict, unfeeling,
severe, stern, impenetrable,
compact, tough, solid, onerous, rigorous, firm, intricate,
harsh, perplexing.

*(ANT.) fluid, brittle, effortless,
gentle, tender, easy, simple,
plastic, soft, lenient, flabby,
elastic.*

hard-boiled *(SYN.)* unsympathetic, tough, harsh,
unsentimental.

harden *(SYN.)* petrify, solidify.
(ANT.) loose, soften.

hardly *(SYN.)* barely, scarcely.

hardship *(SYN.)* ordeal, test,
effort, affliction, misfortune,
trouble, experiment, proof,
essay, misery, examination,
difficulty.

(ANT.) consolation, alleviation.

hardy *(SYN.)* sturdy, strong,
tough.

*(ANT.) frail, feeble, weak, frag-
ile.*

harm *(SYN.)* hurt, mischief,
misfortune, mishap, damage,
wickedness, cripple, injury,
evil, detriment, ill, infliction,
wrong.

(ANT.) favor, kindness, benefit.

harmful *(SYN.)* damaging, injurious, mischievous, detrimental, deleterious.

*(ANT.) helpful, salutary, prof-
itable, advantageous, beneficial.*

harmless *(SYN.)* protected,
secure, snag, dependable, certain, painless, innocent, trustworthy.

*(ANT.) perilous, hazardous,
insecure, dangerous, unsafe.*

harmonious *(SYN.)* tuneful,
melodious, congenial, amicable.

*(ANT.) dissonant, discordant,
disagreeable.*

harmony *(SYN.)* unison, bargain, contract, stipulation,
pact, agreement, accordance,
concord, accord, understanding, unity.

*(ANT.) discord, dissension, dif-
ference, variance, disagreement.*

harness *(SYN.)* control, yoke.

harry *(SYN.)* vex, pester, harass, bother, plague.

harsh *(SYN.)* jarring, gruff, rugged, severe, stringent, blunt, grating, unpleasant, tough, stern, strict, unkind, rigorous, cruel, coarse.

(ANT.) smooth, soft, gentle, melodious, soothing, easy, mild.

harvest *(SYN.)* reap, gather, produce, yield, crop, gain, acquire, fruit, result, reaping, product, proceeds, glean, garner.

(ANT.) plant, squander, lose, sow.

haste *(SYN.)* speed, hurry, rush, rapidity, flurry, scramble.

(ANT.) sloth, sluggishness.

hasten *(SYN.)* hurry, sprint, quicken, rush, precipitate, accelerate, scurry, run, scamper, dispatch, press, urge, dash, expedite, speed.

(ANT.) retard, tarry, detain, linger, dawdle, delay, hinder.

hasty *(SYN.)* quick, swift, irascible, lively, nimble, brisk, active, speedy, impatient, sharp, fast, rapid.

(ANT.) slow, dull, sluggish.

hat *(SYN.)* helmet, bonnet.

hatch *(SYN.)* breed, incubate, brood.

hate *(SYN.)* loathe, detest, despise, disfavor, hatred, abhorrence, abominate, abhor, dislike.

(ANT.) love, cherish, approve, admire, like.

hateful *(SYN.)* loathsome, detestable, offensive.

(ANT.) likable, loving, admirable.

hatred *(SYN.)* detestation, dislike, malevolence, enmity, rancor, ill will, loathing, hate, hostility, abhorrence, aversion, animosity.

(ANT.) friendship, love, affection, attraction.

haughty *(SYN.)* proud, stately, vainglorious, arrogant, disdainful, overbearing, supercilious, vain.

(ANT.) meek, ashamed, lowly, humble.

haul *(SYN.)* draw, pull, drag, tow.

have *(SYN.)* own, possess, seize, hold, control, occupy, acquire, undergo, maintain, experience, receive, gain, affect, include, contain, get, take, obtain.

(ANT.) surrender, abandon, renounce, lose.

havoc *(SYN.)* devastation, ruin, destruction.

hazard *(SYN.)* peril, chance, dare, risk, offer, conjecture, jeopardy, danger.

(ANT.) safety, defense, protection, immunity.

hazardous *(SYN.)* perilous, precarious, threatening, unsafe, dangerous, critical, menacing, risky.

(ANT.) protected, secure, safe.

hazy *(SYN.)* uncertain, unclear, ambiguous, obscure, undetermined, vague, unsettled, indefinite.

(ANT.) specific, clear, lucid, precise, explicit.

head *(SYN.)* leader, summit, top, culmination, director, chief, master, commander, supervisor, start, source, crest, beginning, crisis.
(ANT.) foot, base, bottom, follower, subordinate, underling.

headstrong *(SYN.)* obstinate, stubborn, willful.
(ANT.) easygoing, amenable.

headway *(SYN.)* movement, progress.

heady *(SYN.)* thrilling, intoxicating, exciting, electrifying.

heal *(SYN.)* restore, cure.

healthy *(SYN.)* wholesome, hale, robust, sound, well, vigorous, strong, hearty, healthful, hygienic, salubrious, salutary.
(ANT.) noxious, diseased, unhealthy, delicate, frail, infirm, injurious.

heap *(SYN.)* collection, mound, increase, store, stack, pile, gather, accumulate, amass, accrue, accumulation, collect.
(ANT.) dissipate, scatter, waste, diminish, disperse.

hear *(SYN.)* heed, listen, detect, harken, perceive, regard.

heart *(SYN.)* middle, center, sympathy, nucleus, midpoint, sentiment, core, feeling, midst.
(ANT.) outskirts, periphery, border, rim, boundary.

heartache *(SYN.)* anguish, mourning, sadness, sorrow, affliction, distress, grief, lamentation, tribulation.
(ANT.) happiness, joy, solace, comfort, consolation.

heartbroken *(SYN.)* distressed, forlorn, mean, paltry, worthless, contemptible, wretched, disconsolate, downhearted, comfortless, low.
(ANT.) noble, fortunate, contented, significant.

hearten *(SYN.)* encourage, favor, impel, urge, promote, sanction, animate, cheer, exhilarate, cheer.
(ANT.) deter, dissuade, deject, discourage, dispirit.

heartless *(SYN.)* mean, cruel, ruthless, hardhearted, pitiless.
(ANT.) sympathetic, kind.

heart-rending *(SYN.)* heartbreaking, depressing, agonizing.

hearty *(SYN.)* warm, earnest, ardent, cordial, sincere, gracious, sociable.
(ANT.) taciturn, aloof, cool, reserved.

heat *(SYN.)* hotness, warmth, temperature, passion, ardor, zeal, inflame, cook, excitement, warm.
(ANT.) cool, chill, coolness, freeze, coldness, chilliness, iciness, cold.

heated *(SYN.)* vehement, fiery, intense, passionate.

heave *(SYN.)* boost, hoist, raise.

heaven *(SYN.)* empyrean, paradise.

heavenly *(SYN.)* superhuman, blissful, saintly, holy, divine, celestial, angelic, blessed.
(ANT.) wicked, mundane, profane, blasphemous, diabolical.

heavy *(SYN.)* weighty, massive,

gloomy, serious, ponderous, cumbersome, trying, burdensome, harsh, grave, intense, dull, grievous, concentrated, severe, oppressive, sluggish.

(ANT.) brisk, light, animated.

heckle (SYN.) torment, harass, tease, hector, harry.

heed (SYN.) care, alertness, circumspection, mindfulness, consider, watchfulness, reflection, study, attention, notice, regard, obey, ponder, respect, meditate, mind, observe, deliberate, examine, contemplate, weigh, esteem.

(ANT.) negligence, oversight, overlook, neglect, ignore, disregard, indifference, omission.

heedless (SYN.) sightless, headlong, rash, unmindful, deaf, unseeing, oblivious, ignorant, inattentive, disregardful, blind.

(ANT.) perceiving, sensible, aware, calculated, discerning.

height (SYN.) zenith, peak, summit, tallness, mountain, acme, apex, elevation, altitude, prominence, maximum, pinnacle, culmination.

(ANT.) base, depth, anticlimax.

heighten (SYN.) increase, magnify, annoy, chafe, intensify, amplify, aggravate, provoke, irritate, concentrate, nettle.

(ANT.) soothe, mitigate, palliate, soften, appease.

heinous (SYN.) abominable, grievous, atrocious.

hello (SYN.) greeting, good evening, good afternoon, good morning.

(ANT.) farewell, good-bye, so long.

help (SYN.) assist, support, promote, relieve, abet, succor, back, uphold, further, remedy, encourage, aid, facilitate, mitigate.

(ANT.) afflict, thwart, resist, hinder, impede.

helper (SYN.) aide, assistant, supporter.

helpful (SYN.) beneficial, serviceable, wholesome, useful, profitable, advantageous, good, salutary.

(ANT.) harmful, injurious, useless, worthless, destructive, deleterious, detrimental.

helpfulness (SYN.) assistance, cooperation, usefulness, serviceability, kindness, neighborliness, willingness, collaboration, supportiveness, readiness.

(ANT.) antagonism, hostility, opposition.

helpless (SYN.) weak, feeble, dependent, disabled, inept, incapable, incompetent.

(ANT.) resourceful, competent, enterprising.

helplessness (SYN.) impotence, feebleness, weakness, incapacity, ineptitude, shiftless, awkwardness.

(ANT.) power, strength, might, potency.

helter-skelter (SYN.) haphazardly, chaotically, irregularly.

hem (SYN.) bottom, border, edge, rim, margin, pale, verge, flounce, boundary, fringe, brim, hedge, frame.

hem in *(SYN.)* enclose, shut in, confine, restrict, limit.

hence *(SYN.)* consequently, thence, therefore, so, accordingly.

herald *(SYN.)* harbinger, crier, envoy, forerunner, precursor, augury, forecast.

herculean *(SYN.)* demanding, heroic, titanic, mighty, prodigious, laborious, arduous, overwhelming, backbreaking.

herd *(SYN.)* group, pack, drove, crowd, flock, gather.

heretic *(SYN.)* nonconformist, sectarian, unbeliever, sectary, schismatic, apostate, dissenter.

heritage *(SYN.)* birthright, legacy, patrimony, inheritance.

hermit *(SYN.)* recluse, anchorite, eremite.

hero *(SYN.)* paladin, champion, idol.

heroic *(SYN.)* bold, courageous, fearless, gallant, valiant, valorous, brave, chivalrous, adventurous, dauntless, intrepid, magnanimous.
(ANT.) fearful, weak, cringing, timid, cowardly.

heroism *(SYN.)* valor, bravery, gallant, dauntless, bold, courageous, fearless.

hesitant *(SYN.)* reluctant, unwilling, disinclined, loath, slow, averse.
(ANT.) willing, inclined, eager, ready, disposed.

hesitate *(SYN.)* falter, waver, pause, doubt, demur, delay, vacillate, wait, stammer, stutter, scruple.
(ANT.) proceed, resolve, continue, decide, persevere.

hesitation *(SYN.)* distrust, scruple, suspense, uncertainty, unbelief, ambiguity, doubt, incredulity, skepticism.
(ANT.) determination, belief, certainty, faith, conviction.

hidden *(SYN.)* undeveloped, unseen, dormant, concealed, quiescent, latent, inactive.
(ANT.) visible, explicit, conspicuous, evident.

hide *(SYN.)* disguise, mask, suppress, withhold, veil, cloak, conceal, screen, camouflage, shroud, pelt, skin, leather, cover.
(ANT.) reveal, show, expose, disclose, uncover, divulge.

hideous *(SYN.)* frightful, ugly, shocking, frightening, horrible, terrible, horrifying, terrifying, grisly, gross.
(ANT.) lovely, beautiful, beauteous.

high *(SYN.)* tall, eminent, exalted, elevated, high-pitched, sharp, lofty, proud, shrill, raised, strident, prominent, grave, important, powerful, expensive, dear, high- priced, costly, serious, extreme, towering.
(ANT.) low, mean, tiny, stunted, short, base, lowly, deep, insignificant, unimportant, inexpensive, reasonable, trivial, petty, small.

highly *(SYN.)* extremely, very, extraordinarily, exceedingly.

high-minded *(SYN.)* lofty,

noble, honorable.

(ANT.) dishonorable, base.

high-priced *(SYN.)* dear, expensive, costly.

(ANT.) economical, cheap.

high-strung *(SYN.)* nervous, tense, intense.

(ANT.) calm.

highway *(SYN.)* parkway, speedway, turnpike, superhighway, freeway.

hilarious *(SYN.)* funny, side-splitting, hysterical.

(ANT.) depressing, sad.

hinder *(SYN.)* hamper, impede, block, retard, stop, resist, thwart, obstruct, check, prevent, interrupt, delay, slow, restrain.

(ANT.) promote, further, assist, expedite, advance, facilitate.

hindrance *(SYN.)* interruption, delay, interference, obstruction, obstacle, barrier.

hinge *(SYN.)* rely, depend, pivot.

hint *(SYN.)* reminder, allusion, suggestion, clue, tip, taste, whisper, implication, intimate, suspicion, mention, insinuation.

(ANT.) declaration, affirmation, statement.

hire *(SYN.)* employ, occupy, devote, apply, enlist, lease, rent, charter, rental, busy, engage, utilize, retain, let.

(ANT.) reject, banish, discard, fire, dismiss, discharge.

history *(SYN.)* narration, relation, computation, record, account, chronicle, detail, description, narrative, annal, tale, recital.

(ANT.) confusion, misrepresentation, distortion, caricature.

hit *(SYN.)* knock, pound, strike, hurt, pummel, beat, come upon, find, discover, blow, smite.

hitch *(SYN.)* tether, fasten, harness, interruption, hindrance, interference.

hoard *(SYN.)* amass, increase, accumulate, gather, save, secret, store, cache, store, accrue, heap.

(ANT.) dissipate, scatter, waste, diminish, squander, spend, disperse.

hoarse *(SYN.)* deep, rough, husky, raucous, grating, harsh.

(ANT.) clear.

hoax *(SYN.)* ploy, ruse, wile, device, cheat, deception, antic, imposture, stratagem, stunt, guile, fraud.

(ANT.) openness, sincerity, candor, exposure, honesty.

hobbling *(SYN.)* deformed, crippled, halt, lame, unconvincing, unsatisfactory, defective, feeble, disabled maimed, weak.

(ANT.) robust, vigorous, agile, sound.

hobby *(SYN.)* diversion, pastime, avocation.

(ANT.) vocation, profession.

hobo *(SYN.)* derelict, vagrant, vagabond, tramp.

hoist *(SYN.)* heave, lift, elevate, raise, crane, elevator, derrick.

hold *(SYN.)* grasp, occupy, possess, curb, contain, stow, carry, adhere, have, clutch, keep, maintain, clasp, grip, retain, detain, accommodate, restrain, observe, conduct, check, support.

(ANT.) vacate, relinquish, surrender, abandon.

holdup *(SYN.)* heist, robbery, stickup, delay, interruption, slowdown.

hole *(SYN.)* cavity, void, pore, opening, abyss, chasm, gulf, aperture, tear, pit, burrow, lair, den, gap.

hollow *(SYN.)* unfilled, vacant, vain, meaningless, flimsy, false, hole, cavity, depression, hypocritical, depressed, empty, insincere.

(ANT.) sound, solid, genuine, sincere, full.

holocaust *(SYN.)* fire, burning, extermination, butchery, disaster, massacre.

holy *(SYN.)* devout, divine, blessed, consecrated, sacred, spiritual, pious, sainted, religious, saintly, hallowed.

(ANT.) worldly, sacrilegious, unconsecrated, evil, profane, secular.

homage *(SYN.)* reverence, honor, respect.

home *(SYN.)* dwelling, abode, residence, seat, quarters, hearth, domicile, family, house, habitat.

homely *(SYN.)* uncommonly, disagreeable, ill-natured, ugly, vicious, plain, hideous, unattractive, deformed, surly, repellent, spiteful.

(ANT.) fair, handsome, pretty, attractive, comely, beautiful.

homesick *(SYN.)* lonely, nostalgic.

honest *(SYN.)* sincere, trustworthy, truthful, fair, ingenuous, candid, conscientious, moral, upright, open, frank, forthright, honorable, straightfoward.

(ANT.) fraudulent, tricky, deceitful, dishonest, lying.

honesty *(SYN.)* frankness, openness, fairness, sincerity, trustworthiness, justice, candor, honor, integrity, responsibility, uprightness.

(ANT.) deceit, dishonesty, trickery, fraud, cheating.

honor *(SYN.)* esteem, praise, worship, admiration, homage, glory, respect, admire, heed, dignity, revere, value, deference, venerate, reverence, consider, distinction, character, principle, uprightness, honesty, adoration.

(ANT.) scorn, dishonor, despise, neglect, abuse, shame, reproach, disdain, contempt, derision, disgrace.

honorable *(SYN.)* fair, noble, creditable, proper, reputable, honest, admirable, true, trusty, eminent, respectable, esteemed, just, famed, illustrious, noble, virtuous, upright.

(ANT.) infamous, disgraceful, shameful, dishonorable, ignominious.

honorary *(SYN.)* gratuitous, complimentary.

hoodlum *(SYN.)* crook, gangster, criminal, hooligan, mobster.

hop *(SYN.)* jump, leap.

hope *(SYN.)* expectation, faith, optimism, anticipation, expectancy, confidence, desire, trust.

(ANT.) pessimism, despair, despondency.

hopeful *(SYN.)* optimistic, confident.

(ANT.) despairing, hopeless.

hopeless *(SYN.)* desperate, despairing, forlorn, fatal, incurable, disastrous.

(ANT.) promising, hopeful.

hopelessness *(SYN.)* gloom, discouragement, depression, pessimism, despondency.

(ANT.) hope, optimism, confidence, elation.

horde *(SYN.)* host, masses, press, rabble, swarm, throng, bevy, crush, mob, multitude, crowd, populace.

horizontal *(SYN.)* even, level, plane, flat, straight, sideways.

(ANT.) upright, vertical.

horrendous *(SYN.)* awful, horrifying, terrible, dreadful, horrid, ghastly.

(ANT.) splendid, wonderful.

horrible *(SYN.)* awful, dire, ghastly, horrid, terrible, repulsive, frightful, appalling, horrifying, dreadful, ghastly, fearful.

(ANT.) enjoyable, enchanting, beautiful, lovely, fascinating.

horrid *(SYN.)* repulsive, terrible, appalling, dire, awful, frightful, fearful, shocking, horrible, horrifying, horrid, ghastly, revolting, hideous.

(ANT.) fascinating, enchanting,

enjoyable, lovely, beautiful.

horror *(SYN.)* dread, awe, hatred, loathing, foreboding, alarm, apprehension, aversion, terror.

(ANT.) courage, boldness, assurance, confidence.

horseplay *(SYN.)* tomfoolery, clowning, shenanigans.

hospital *(SYN.)* infirmary, clinic, sanatorium, rest home, sanitarium.

hospitality *(SYN.)* warmth, liberality, generosity, graciousness, welcome.

hostile *(SYN.)* unfriendly, opposed, antagonistic, inimical, adverse, warlike.

(ANT.) friendly, favorable, amicable, cordial.

hostility *(SYN.)* grudge, hatred, rancor, spite, bitterness, enmity, malevolence.

(ANT.) love, friendliness, good will.

hot *(SYN.)* scorching, fervent, hot-blooded, passionate, peppery, ardent, burning, fiery, impetuous, scalding, heated, sizzling, blazing, frying, roasting, warm, intense, torrid, pungent.

(ANT.) indifferent, apathetic, impassive, passionless, bland, frigid, cold, freezing, cool, phlegmatic.

hot air *(SYN.)* bombast, blather, jabber, gabble.

hotbed *(SYN.)* sink, nest, well, den, nursery, cradle, source, incubator, seedbed.

hot-blooded *(SYN.)* passionate, ardent, excitable, wild, fer-

vent, fiery, impetuous, rash, brash, intense, impulsive.
(ANT.) stolid, impassive, cold, staid.

hotel (SYN.) hostel, motel, inn, hostelry.

hotheaded (SYN.) rash, touchy, reckless, unruly.
(ANT.) levelheaded, coolheaded, calm.

hound (SYN.) harry, pursue, pester, harass.

hourly (SYN.) frequently, steadily, constantly, unfailingly, periodically, perpetually, continually, incessantly.
(ANT.) occasionally, seldom.

house (SYN.) building, residence, abode, dwelling.

housebreaker (SYN.) robber, thief, prowler, cracksman, burglar.

household (SYN.) manage, family, home.

householder (SYN.) homeowner, occupant.

housing (SYN.) lodgings, shelter, dwelling, lodgment, case, casing, quarters, domicile, enclosure, console, bracket.

hovel (SYN.) cabin, hut, sty, shack, hole, shed.

hover (SYN.) hang, drift, poise, stand by, linger, impend, waver, hand around.

however (SYN.) notwithstanding, still, nevertheless, but, yet.

howl (SYN.) bellow, yowl, wail, yell, cry.

hub (SYN.) pivot, center, core, heart, axis, basis, focus, nucleus.

hubbub (SYN.) uproar, tumult, commotion, clamor, bustle, turmoil, racket, confusion.
(ANT.) peacefulness, stillness, silence, quiet, quiescence.

huckster (SYN.) peddler, adman, hawker, salesman, pitchman.

hue (SYN.) pigment, tint, shade, dye, complexion, paint, stain, color, tone, tincture.
(ANT.) transparency, achromatism, paleness.

huffy (SYN.) sensitive, vulnerable, testy, offended, thin-skinned, touchy, irascible, cross, offended.
(ANT.) tough, placid, stolid, impassive.

hug (SYN.) embrace, coddle, caress, kiss, pet, press, clasp, fondle, cuddle.
(ANT.) tease, vex, spurn, buffet, annoy.

huge (SYN.) great, immense, vast, ample, big, capacious, extensive, gigantic, enormous, tremendous, large, wide, colossal.
(ANT.) short, small, mean, little, tiny.

hulking (SYN.) massive, awkward, bulky, ponderous, unwieldy, overgrown, lumpish, oafish.

hullabaloo (SYN.) clamor, uproar, din, racket, tumult, hubbub, commotion, noise.
(ANT.) calm, peace, silence.

hum (SYN.) whir, buzz, whizz, purr, croon, murmur, intone.

human (SYN.) manlike, hominid, mortal, fleshly, individual, person, tellurian.

humane *(SYN.)* lenient, tender, tolerant, compassionate, forgiving, kind, forbearing, thoughtful, gentle, merciful.

(ANT.) remorseless, cruel, heartless, pitiless, unfeeling, brutal.

humanist *(SYN.)* scholar, sage, classicist, savant.

humanitarian *(SYN.)* benefactor, philanthropist.

humanitarianism *(SYN.)* good will, beneficence, philanthropy, welfarism, humanism.

humanity *(SYN.)* generosity, magnanimity, tenderness, altruism, beneficence, kindness, charity.

(ANT.) selfishness, unkindness, cruelty, inhumanity.

humble *(SYN.)* modest, crush, mortify, simple, shame, subdue, meek, abase, break, plain, submissive, compliant, unpretentious, unassuming, abash, lowly, polite, courteous, unpretending.

(ANT.) praise, arrogant, exalt, illustrious, boastful, honor, elevate.

humbly *(SYN.)* deferentially, meekly, respectfully, unassumingly, diffidently, modestly, submissively.

(ANT.) insolently, proudly, grandly, arrogantly.

humbug *(SYN.)* drivel, gammon, bosh, nonsense, rubbish, inanity.

humdrum *(SYN.)* commonplace, prosy, mundane, insipid, tedious, routine, dull, boring.

(ANT.) interesting, stimulating, arresting, striking, exciting.

humid *(SYN.)* moist, damp, misty, muggy, wet, watery, vaporous.

(ANT.) parched, dry, desiccated.

humiliate *(SYN.)* corrupt, defile, depress, pervert, abase, degrade, disgrace, adulterate, humble, shame, lower, deprave, depress.

(ANT.) restore, raise, enhance, improve, vitalize.

humiliation *(SYN.)* chagrin, dishonor, ignominy, scandal, abasement, mortification, odium, disgrace, shame.

(ANT.) honor, praise, glory, dignity, renown.

humor *(SYN.)* jocularity, wit, temperament, sarcasm, irony, amusement, facetiousness, joke, disposition, fun, clowning, satire.

(ANT.) sorrow, gravity, seriousness.

humorous *(SYN.)* funny, ludicrous, witty, curious, queer, amusing, comical, farcical, laughable, droll.

(ANT.) sober, unfunny, melancholy, serious, sad, solemn.

hunger *(SYN.)* desire, longing, inclination, stomach, zest, craving.

(ANT.) satiety, repugnance, disgust, distaste, renunciation.

hungry *(SYN.)* famished, thirsting, craving, avid, starved, ravenous.

(ANT.) gorged, satisfied, full, sated.

hunt *(SYN.)* pursuit, investigation, examination, inquiry, pursue, track, chase, search, quest, seek, probe, scour, exploration.

(ANT.) cession, resignation, abandonment.

hurl *(SYN.)* throw, cast, propel, fling, toss, pitch, thrust.

(ANT.) pull, draw, haul, hold.

hurried *(SYN.)* rushed, hasty, swift, headlong, impulsive, superficial.

(ANT.) deliberate, slow, dilatory, thorough, prolonged.

hurry *(SYN.)* quicken, speed, ado, rush, accelerate, run, hasten, race, urge, bustle, expedite.

(ANT.) retard, tarry, hinder, linger, dawdle, delay, hinder.

hurt *(SYN.)* damage, harm, grievance, detriment, pain, injustice, injure, abuse, distress, disfigured, mar, afflict, spoil, affront, insult, wound, dishonor, wrong.

(ANT.) improvement, repair, compliment, help, praise, benefit.

hurtful *(SYN.)* harmful, damaging, maleficent, injurious, baleful.

(ANT.) remedial, beneficial, good, salutary.

hurtle *(SYN.)* charge, collide, rush, crash, lunge, bump.

hush *(SYN.)* quiet, silence, still.

husk *(SYN.)* shell, hull, pod, skin, covering, crust, bark.

husky *(SYN.)* strong, brawny, strapping, muscular.

(ANT.) feeble, weak.

hustle *(SYN.)* hasten, run, race, hurry, speed.

hutch *(SYN.)* box, chest, locker, trunk, coffer, bin.

hybrid *(SYN.)* mule, mixture, crossbreed, cross, mongrel, mutt, composite.

hygiene *(SYN.)* cleanliness, sanitation, health, hygienics.

hygienic *(SYN.)* robust, strong, well, wholesome, healthy, sound.

(ANT.) frail, noxious, infirm, delicate, diseased, injurious.

hyperbole *(SYN.)* puffery, exaggeration, embellishment, overstatement, ballyhoo, amplification, magnification.

hypercritical *(SYN.)* faultfinding, captious, censorious, finicky, exacting, carping, querulous, nagging, finical, hairsplitting.

(ANT.) lax, easygoing, indulgent, lenient, tolerant.

hypnotic *(SYN.)* soothing, opiate, sedative, soporific, entrancing, arresting, charming, engaging.

hypnotize *(SYN.)* entrance, dazzle, mesmerize, fascinate, spellbind.

hypocrisy *(SYN.)* pretense, deceit, dissembling, fakery, feigning, pharisaism, cant, dissimulation.

(ANT.) openness, candor, truth, directness, honesty, frankness.

hypocrite *(SYN.)* cheat, deceiver, fake, pretender, fraud, charlatan.

hypocritical *(SYN.)* dissembling, two-faced, insincere, dishonest, duplicitous, deceitful, phony.

(ANT.) true, genuine, honest.

hypothesis (SYN.) law, theory, supposition, conjecture.

(ANT.) proof, fact, certainty.

hypothetical (SYN.) conjectural, speculative, theoretical.

(ANT.) actual.

I

idea (SYN.) conception, image, opinion, sentiment, concept, notion, thought, impression.

(ANT.) thing, matter, entity, object, substance.

ideal (SYN.) imaginary, supreme, unreal, visionary, perfect, faultless, fancied, exemplary, utopian.

(ANT.) imperfect, actual, material, real, faulty.

idealistic (SYN.) extravagant, dreamy, fantastic, fanciful, ideal, maudlin, imaginative, mawkish, sentimental, poetic, picturesque.

(ANT.) practical, literal, factual, prosaic.

identify (ANT.) recollect, apprehend, perceive, remember, confess, acknowledge, name, describe, classify.

(ANT.) ignore, forget, overlook, renounce, disown, repudiate.

identity (SYN.) uniqueness, personality, character, individuality.

ideology (SYN.) credo, principles, belief.

idiom (SYN.) language, speech, vernacular, lingo, dialect, jargon, slang, tongue.

(ANT.) babble, gibberish, drivel, nonsense.

idiot (SYN.) buffoon, harlequin, dolt, jester, dunce, blockhead, imbecile, simpleton, oaf, moron.

(ANT.) philosopher, genius, scholar, sage.

idiotic (SYN.) asinine, absurd, brainless, irrational, crazy, nonsensical, senseless, preposterous, silly, ridiculous, simple, stupid, foolish, inane, moronic, half-witted, simpleminded, dimwitted.

(ANT.) prudent, wise, sagacious, judicious, sane, intelligent, bright, brilliant, smart.

idle (SYN.) unemployed, dormant, lazy, inactive, unoccupied, indolent, slothful, inert, unused.

(ANT.) occupied, working, employed, busy, active, industrious, engaged.

idol (SYN.) unoccupied, unused, inactive, unemployed.

idolize (SYN.) revere, worship, adore.

(ANT.) despise.

ignoble (SYN.) dishonorable, ignominious, lowly, menial, vile, sordid, vulgar, abject, base, despicable, groveling, mean, vile.

(ANT.) righteous, lofty, honored, esteemed, noble, exalted.

ignominious (SYN.) contemptible, abject, despicable, groveling, dishonorable, ignoble, lowly, low, menial, mean, sordid, vulgar, vile.

(ANT.) lofty, noble, esteemed, righteous, exalted.

ignorant *(SYN.)* uneducated, untaught, uncultured, illiterate, uninformed, unlearned, untrained, unaware.

(ANT.) cultured, literate, educated, erudite, informed, cultivated, schooled, learned, lettered.

ignore *(SYN.)* omit, slight, disregard, overlook, neglect, skip.

(ANT.) notice, regard, include.

ill *(SYN.)* diseased, ailing, indisposed, morbid, infirm, unwell, unhealthy, sick, unsound.

(ANT.) robust, strong, healthy, well, sound, fit.

ill-use *(SYN.)* defame, revile, vilify, misemploy, disparage, abuse, asperse, misapply, misuse.

(ANT.) protect, cherish, respect, honor, praise.

ill-advised *(SYN.)* injudicious, illconsidered, imprudent.

illegal *(SYN.)* prohibited, unlawful, criminal, illicit, outlawed.

(ANT.) permitted, lawful, honest, legal, legitimate.

illiberal *(SYN.)* fanatical, bigoted, narrowminded, intolerant, dogmatic, prejudiced.

(ANT.) progressive, liberal radical.

illicit *(SYN.)* illegitimate, criminal, outlawed, unlawful, prohibited, illegal, unauthorized.

(ANT.) legal, honest, permitted, lawful, licit.

ill-natured *(SYN.)* crabby,

cranky, grouchy, cross, irascible.

illness *(SYN.)* complaint, infirmity, ailment, disorder, sickness.

(ANT.) healthiness, health, soundness, vigor.

illogical *(SYN.)* absurd, irrational, preposterous.

ill-tempered *(SYN.)* crabby, cranky, cross, grouchy.

illuminate *(SYN.)* enlighten, clarify, irradiate, illustrate, light, lighten, explain, interpret, elucidate, brighten, illumine.

(ANT.) obscure, confuse, darken, obfuscate, shadow, complicate.

illusion *(SYN.)* hallucination, vision, phantom, delusion, fantasy.

(ANT.) actuality, reality.

illusive *(SYN.)* fallacious, delusive, false, specious, misleading, deceptive, deceitful, delusory.

(ANT.) real, truthful, authentic, genuine, honest.

illustrate *(SYN.)* decorate, illuminate, adorn, show, picture, embellish, demonstrate.

illustration *(SYN.)* likeness, painting, picture, print, scene, sketch, view, engraving, drawing, panorama, photograph, cinema, etching, effigy, film, appearance, resemblance, image, portrait.

illustrator *(SYN.)* painter, artist.

illustrious *(SYN.)* prominent, eminent, renowned, famed, great, vital, elevated, majestic,

noble, excellent, dignified, big, gigantic, enormous, immense, huge, vast, large, countless, numerous, celebrated, critical, momentous.
(ANT.) *menial, common, minute, diminutive, small, obscure, ordinary, little.*

image (SYN.) reflection, likeness, idea, representation, notion, picture, conception.

imaginary (SYN.) fanciful, fantastic, unreal, whimsical.
(ANT.) *actual, real.*

imagination (SYN.) creation, invention, fancy, notion, conception, fantasy, idea.

imaginative (SYN.) inventive, poetical, fanciful, clever, creative, mystical, visionary.
(ANT.) *prosaic, dull, unromantic, literal.*

imagine (SYN.) assume, surmise, suppose, conceive, dream, pretend, conjecture, fancy, opine, think, envision, guess, picture.

imbecile (SYN.) idiot, simpleton, blockhead, dolt, dunce, jester, buffoon, harlequin, oaf, fool.
(ANT.) *scholar, sage, genius, philosopher.*

imbibe (SYN.) absorb, consume, assimilate, engulf, engage, occupy, engross.
(ANT.) *dispense, exude, discharge, emit.*

imitate (SYN.) duplicate, mimic, follow, reproduce, mock, ape, counterfeit, copy, impersonate.
(ANT.) *invent, distort, alter,*

diverge.

imitation (SYN.) replica, reproduction copy, duplicate, facsimile, transcript, exemplar.
(ANT.) *prototype, original.*

immaculate (SYN.) clean, spotless, unblemished.
(ANT.) *dirty.*

immature (SYN.) young, boyish, childish, youthful, childlike, puerile, girlish, juvenile, callow.
(ANT.) *old, senile, aged, elderly, mature.*

immeasurable (SYN.) unlimited, endless, eternal, immense, interminable, unbounded, boundless, illimitable, infinite.
(ANT.) *limited, confined, bounded, circumscribed.*

immediate (SYN.) present, instant, instantaneous, near, close, next, prompt, direct.
(ANT.) *distant, future.*

immediately (SYN.) now, presently, forthwith, instantly, promptly.
(ANT.) *sometime, hereafter, later, shortly, distantly.*

immense (SYN.) enormous, large, gigantic, huge, colossal, elephantine, great, gargantuan, vast.
(ANT.) *small, diminutive, little, minuscule, minute, petit, tiny.*

immensity (SYN.) hugeness, enormousness, vastness.

immerse (SYN.) plunge, dip, dunk, sink, submerge, engage, absorb, engross, douse.
(ANT.) *uplift, elevate, recover.*

immigration (SYN.) settlement,

colonization.

(ANT.) exodus, emigration.

imminent *(SYN.)* nigh, impending, overhanging, approaching, menacing, threatening.

(ANT.) retreating, afar, distant, improbable, remote.

immoderation *(SYN.)* profusion, surplus, extravagance, excess, intemperance, superabundance.

(ANT.) lack, want, deficiency, dearth, paucity.

immoral *(SYN.)* sinful, wicked, corrupt, bad, indecent, profligate, unprincipled, antisocial, dissolute.

(ANT.) pure, high-minded, chaste, virtuous, noble.

immortal *(SYN.)* infinite, eternal, timeless, undying, perpetual, endless, deathless, everlasting.

(ANT.) mortal, transient, finite, ephemeral, temporal.

immune *(SYN.)* easy, open, autonomous, unobstructed, free, emancipated, clear, independent, unrestricted, exempt, liberated, familiar, loose, unconfined, frank.

(ANT.) confined, impeded, restricted, subject.

immutable *(SYN.)* constant, faithful, invariant, persistent, unchanging, unalterable, continual, ceaseless, enduring, fixed, permanent, perpetual, unwavering.

(ANT.) mutable, vacillating, wavering, fickle.

impact *(SYN.)* striking, contact, collision.

impair *(SYN.)* harm, injure, spoil, deface, destroy, hurt, damage.

(ANT.) repair, mend, ameliorate, enhance, benefit.

impart *(SYN.)* convey, disclose, inform, tell, reveal, transmit, notify, confer, communicate, relate.

(ANT.) hide, withhold, conceal.

impartial *(SYN.)* unbiased, just, honest, reasonable, equitable.

(ANT.) fraudulent, dishonorable, partial.

impartiality *(SYN.)* indifference, unconcern, impartiality, neutrality, disinterestedness, apathy, insensibility.

(ANT.) passion, ardor, fervor, affection.

impasse *(SYN.)* standstill, deadlock, stalemate.

impede *(SYN.)* hamper, hinder, retard, thwart, check, encumber, interrupt, bar, clog, delay, obstruct, block, restrain, stop.

(ANT.) assist, promote, help, advance, further.

impel *(SYN.)* oblige, enforce, drive, coerce, force, constrain.

(ANT.) induce, prevent, convince, persuade.

impending *(SYN.)* imminent, nigh, threatening, overhanging, approaching, menacing.

(ANT.) remote, improbable, afar, distant, retreating.

impenetrable *(SYN)* rigid, tough, harsh, strict, unfeeling, rigorous, intricate, arduous, penetrable, cruel, difficult, severe, stern, firm.

(ANT.) soft, simple, gentle, ten-

der, fluid, lenient, easy, effort-less.

imperative (SYN.) critical, instant, important, necessary, serious, urgent, cogent, compelling, crucial, pressing, impelling, importunate.
(ANT.) trivial, insignificant, unimportant, petty.

imperceptible (SYN.) invisible, indiscernible, indistinguishable.
(ANT.) seen, evident, visible, perceptible.

imperfection (SYN.) flaw, shortcoming, vice, defect, blemish, failure, mistake, fault, error.
(ANT.) correctness, perfection, completeness.

imperil (SYN.) jeopardize, risk, endanger, hazard, risk.
(ANT.) guard, insure.

impersonal (SYN.) objective, detached, disinterested.
(ANT.) personal.

impersonate (SYN.) mock, simulate, imitate, ape, counterfeit, mimic, copy, duplicate.
(ANT.) alter, diverge, distort.

impertinence (SYN.) impudence, presumption, sauciness, effrontery, audacity, rudeness, assurance, boldness, insolence.
(ANT.) truckling, politeness, diffidence, subserviency.

impertinent (SYN.) rude, offensive, insolent, disrespectful, arrogant, brazen, impudent, insulting, contemptuous, abusive.
(ANT.) polite, respectful, consid-erate, courteous.

impetuous (SYN.) rash, heedless, quick, hasty, careless, passionate.
(ANT.) cautious, reasoning, careful, thoughtful, calculating.

implicate (SYN.) reproach, accuse, blame, involve, upbraid, condemn, incriminate, censure.
(ANT.) exonerate, absolve, acquit.

implore (SYN.) beg, pray, request, solicit, crave, entreat, beseech, ask, importune, supplicate, adjure, appeal, petition.
(ANT.) give, bestow, favor, grant.

imply (SYN.) mean, involve, suggest, connote, hint, mention, indicate, insinuate, signify.
(ANT.) assert, declare, express.

impolite (SYN.) rude, unpolished, impudent, boorish, blunt, discourteous, rough, saucy, surly, savage, insolent, gruff, uncivil, coarse, ignorant, crude, illiterate, raw, primitive, vulgar, untaught.
(ANT.) genteel, courteous, courtly, dignified, stately, noble, civil.

import (SYN.) influence, significance, stress, emphasis, importance, value, weight.
(ANT.) triviality, insignificance.

important (SYN.) critical, grave, influential, momentous, well-known, pressing, relevant, prominent, primary, essential, weighty, material, considerable, famous, principle, famed, sequential, notable, significant.

(ANT.) *unimportant, trifling, petty, trivial, insignificant, secondary, anonymous, irrelevant.*

impose *(SYN.)* levy, require, demand.

imposing *(SYN.)* lofty, noble, majestic, magnificent, august, dignified, grandiose, high, grand, impressive, pompous, stately.

(ANT.) *ordinary, undignified, humble, common, lowly.*

imposition *(SYN.)* load, onus, burden.

impossible *(SYN.)* preposterous.

impregnable *(SYN.)* safe, invulnerable, secure, unassailable.

(ANT.) *vulnerable.*

impress *(SYN.)* awe, emboss, affect, mark, imprint, influence.

impression *(SYN.)* influence, indentation, feeling, opinion, mark, effect, depression, guess, thought, belief, dent, sensibility.

(ANT.) *fact, insensibility.*

impressive *(SYN.)* arresting, moving, remarkable, splendid, thrilling, striking, majestic, grandiose, imposing, commanding, affecting, exciting, stirring.

(ANT.) *regular, unimpressive, commonplace.*

impromptu *(SYN.)* casual, unprepared, offhand, extemporaneous.

improper *(SYN.)* unfit, unsuitable, inappropriate, naughty, indecent, unbecoming.

(ANT.) *fitting, proper, appropriate.*

improve *(SYN.)* better, reform, refine, ameliorate, amend, help, upgrade, rectify.

(ANT.) *debase, vitiate, impair, corrupt, damage.*

improvement *(SYN.)* growth, advance, progress, development, advancement, progression.

(ANT.) *relapse, regression, decline, retrogression, delay.*

imprudent *(SYN.)* indiscreet, thoughtless, desultory, lax, neglectful, remiss, careless, inattentive, heedless, inconsiderate, reckless, ill-advised, irresponsible, unconcerned.

(ANT.) *careful, meticulous, accurate.*

impudence *(SYN.)* boldness, insolence, rudeness, sauciness, assurance, effrontery, impertinence, presumption, audacity.

(ANT.) *politeness, truckling, subserviency, diffidence.*

impudent *(SYN.)* forward, rude, abrupt, prominent, striking, bold, fresh, impertinent, insolent, pushy, insulting, brazen.

(ANT.) *bashful, flinching, polite, courteous, cowardly, retiring, timid.*

impulse *(SYN.)* hunch, whim, fancy, urge, caprice, surge, pulse.

impulsive *(SYN.)* passionate, rash, spontaneous, heedless, careless, hasty, quick, impetuous.

(ANT.) reasoning, calculating, careful, prudent, cautious.

impure *(SYN.)* dishonest, spoiled, tainted, contaminated, debased, corrupt, profligate, unsound, putrid, corrupted, crooked, depraved, vitiated, venal.

imputation *(SYN.)* diary, incrimination, arraignment, indictment.

(ANT.) exoneration, pardon, exculpation.

inability *(SYN.)* incompetence, incapacity, handicap, disability, impotence, weakness.

(ANT.) power, strength, ability, capability.

inaccurate *(SYN.)* false, incorrect, mistaken, untrue, askew, wrong, awry, erroneous, fallacious, faulty, amiss.

(ANT.) right, accurate, true, correct.

inactive *(SYN.)* lazy, unemployed, indolent, motionless, still, inert, dormant, idle, unoccupied.

(ANT.) employed, working, active, industrious, occupied.

inadequate *(SYN.)* insufficient, lacking, short, incomplete, defective, scanty.

(ANT.) satisfactory, enough, adequate, ample, sufficient.

inadvertent *(SYN.)* careless, negligent, thoughtless.

inane *(SYN.)* trite, insipid, banal, absurd, silly, common-place, vapid, foolish, stupid, hackneyed.

(ANT.) stimulating, novel, fresh, original, striking.

inanimate *(SYN.)* deceased, spiritless, lifeless, gone, dull, mineral, departed, dead, insensible, vegetable, unconscious.

(ANT.) living, stirring, alive, animate.

inattentive *(SYN.)* absent-minded, distracted, abstracted, preoccupied.

(ANT.) watchful, attending, attentive.

inaugurate *(SYN.)* commence, begin, open, originate, start, arise, launch, enter, initiate.

(ANT.) end, terminate, close, complete, finish.

incense *(SYN.)* anger, enrage, infuriate.

incentive *(SYN.)* impulse, stimulus, inducement, encouragement.

(ANT.) discouragement.

inception *(SYN.)* origin, start, source, opening, beginning, outset, commencement.

(ANT.) end, termination, close, completion, consummation.

incessant *(SYN.)* perennial, uninterrupted, continual, ceaseless, continuous, unremitting, eternal, constant, unceasing, unending, perpetual, everlasting.

(ANT.) rare, occasional, periodic, interrupted.

incident *(SYN.)* happening, situation, occurrence, circumstance, condition, event, fact.

incidental *(SYN.)* casual, contingent, trivial, undesigned, chance, fortuitous, accidental, secondary, unimportant, unintended.

(ANT.) intended, fundamental, planned, calculated, willed, decreed.

incidentally *(SYN.)* by the way.

incinerate *(SYN.)* sear, char, blaze, scald, singe, consume, scorch, burn.

(ANT.) quench, put out, extinguish.

incisive *(SYN.)* neat, succinct, terse, brief, compact, condensed, neat, summary, concise.

(ANT.) wordy, prolix, verbose, lengthy.

incite *(SYN.)* goad, provoke, urge, arouse, encourage, cause, stimulate, induce, instigate, foment.

(ANT.) quiet, bore, pacify, soothe.

inclination *(SYN.)* bent, preference, desire, slope, affection, bent, bias, disposition, bending, penchant, incline, attachment, predisposition, predication, tendency, prejudice, slant, lean, leaning.

(ANT.) nonchalance, apathy, distaste, aversion, reluctance, disinclination, uprightness, repugnance.

incline *(SYN.)* slope, nod, lean.

(ANT.) straighten.

include *(SYN.)* contain, hold, accommodate, encompass, involve, comprise, embrace.

(ANT.) omit, exclude, discharge.

income *(SYN.)* earnings, salary, wages, pay, revenue, return, receipts.

incomparable *(SYN.)* peerless, matchless, unequaled.

incompetency *(SYN.)* inability, weakness, handicap, impotence, disability, incapacity.

(ANT.) strength, ability, power, capability.

incomprehensible *(SYN.)* unintelligible, indecipherable.

inconceivable *(SYN.)* unbelievable, unimaginable, impossible.

(ANT.) possible, believable.

incongruous *(SYN.)* inconsistent, contrary, incompatible, irreconcilable, contradictory, unsteady, wavering, paradoxical, vacillating, discrepant, illogical.

(ANT.) consistent, compatible, correspondent.

inconsiderate *(SYN.)* unthinking, careless, unthoughtful, unmindful.

(ANT.) logical, consistent.

inconsistency *(SYN.)* discord, variance, contention, conflict, controversy, interference.

(ANT.) harmony, concord, amity, consonance.

inconsistent *(SYN.)* fickle, wavering, variable, changeable, contrary, unstable, illogical, contradictory, irreconcilable, discrepant, paradoxical, incompatible, self-contradictory, incongruous, unsteady, fitful, shifting.

(ANT.) unchanging, steady, logical, stable, uniform, constant.

inconspicuous *(SYN.)* retiring, unnoticed, unostentatious.

(ANT.) obvious, conspicuous.

inconstant *(SYN.)* fickle, shifting, changeable, fitful, vacillating, unstable, wavering.

(ANT.) stable, constant, steady, uniform, unchanging.

inconvenient *(SYN.)* awkward, inappropriate, untimely, troublesome.

(ANT.) handy, convenient.

incorrect *(SYN.)* mistaken, wrong, erroneous, inaccurate.

(ANT.) proper, accurate, suitable.

increase *(SYN.)* amplify, enlarge, grow, magnify, multiply, augment, enhance, expand, intensify, swell, raise, greaten, prolong, broaden, lengthen, expansion, accrue, extend, heighten.

(ANT.) diminish, reduce, atrophy, shrink, shrinkage, decrease, lessening, lessen, contract.

incredible *(SYN.)* improbable, unbelievable.

(ANT.) plausible, credible, believable.

incriminate *(SYN.)* charge, accuse, indict, arraign, censure.

(ANT.) release, exonerate, acquit, absolve, vindicate.

incrimination *(SYN.)* imputation, indictment, accusation, charge, arraignment.

(ANT.) exoneration, pardon, exculpation.

indebted *(SYN.)* obliged, grateful, beholden, thankful, appreciative.

(ANT.) unappreciative, thankless.

indecent *(SYN.)* impure, obscene, coarse, dirty, filthy, smutty, gross, disgusting.

(ANT.) modest, refined, decent, pure.

indeed *(SYN.)* truthfully, really, honestly, surely.

indefinite *(SYN.)* unsure, uncertain, vague, confused, unsettled, confusing.

(ANT.) decided, definite, equivocal.

independence *(SYN.)* liberation, privilege, freedom, immunity, familiarity, liberty, exemption, license.

(ANT.) necessity, constraint, compulsion, reliance, dependence, bondage, servitude.

independent *(SYN.)* free, unrestrained, voluntary, autonomous, self-reliant, uncontrolled, unrestricted.

(ANT.) enslaved, contingent, dependent, restricted.

indestructible *(SYN.)* enduring, lasting, permanent, unchangeable, abiding, constant, fixed, stable, changeless.

(ANT.) unstable, temporary, transitory, ephemeral.

indicate *(SYN.)* imply, denote, specify, intimate, designate, symbolize, show, manifest, disclose, mean, reveal.

(ANT.) mislead, falsify, distract, conceal, falsify.

indication *(SYN.)* proof, emblem, omen, sign, symbol, token, mark, portent, gesture, signal.

indict (SYN.) charge, accuse, incriminate, censure, arraign.

(ANT.) acquit, vindicate, absolve, exonerate.

indictment (SYN.) incrimination, arraignment, imputation, charge.

(ANT.) pardon, exoneration, exculpation.

indifference (SYN.) unconcern, apathy, impartiality, disinterestedness, insensibility, neutrality.

(ANT.) ardor, passion, affection, fervor.

indifferent (SYN.) uncaring, insensitive, unconcerned.

(ANT.) caring, concerned, earnest.

indigence (SYN.) necessity, destitution, poverty, want, need, privation, penury.

(ANT.) wealth, abundance, plenty, riches, affluence.

indigenous (SYN.) inborn, native, inherent, domestic, aboriginal, plenty, endemic, innate, natural.

indigent (SYN.) wishing, covetous, demanding, lacking, requiring, wanting, claiming, craving.

indignant (SYN.) irritated, irate, angry, aroused, exasperated.

(ANT.) calm, serene, content.

indignation (SYN.) ire, petulance, passion, choler, anger, wrath, temper, irritation, exasperation, animosity, resentment, rage.

(ANT.) self-control, peace, forbearance, patience.

indignity (SYN.) insolence, insult, abuse, affront, offense.

(ANT.) homage, apology, salutation.

indirect (SYN.) winding, crooked, devious, roundabout, cunning, tricky, tortuous, circuitous, distorted, erratic, swerving.

(ANT.) straightforward, direct, straight, honest.

indiscretion (SYN.) imprudence, folly, absurdity, extravagance.

(ANT.) prudence, sense, wisdom, reasonableness, judgment.

indispensable (SYN.) necessary, fundamental, basic, essential, important, intrinsic, vital.

(ANT.) optional, expendable, peripheral, extrinsic.

indistinct (SYN.) cloudy, dark, mysterious, vague, blurry, ambiguous, cryptic, dim, obscure, enigmatic, abstruse, hazy, blurred, unintelligible.

(ANT.) clear, lucid, bright, distinct.

indistinguishable (SYN.) identical, like, coincident, equal, same, equivalent.

(ANT.) dissimilar, opposed, contrary, disparate, distinct.

individual (SYN.) singular, unique, specific, distinctive, single, particular, undivided, human, apart, marked, person, different, special, separate.

(ANT.) universal, common, general, ordinary.

individuality (SYN.) symbol,

description, mark, kind, character, repute, class, standing, sort, nature, disposition, reputation, sign.

indolent (SYN.) slothful, lazy, idle, inactive, slow, sluggish, torpid, supine, inert.

(ANT.) diligent, active, assiduous, vigorous, zestful, alert.

indomitable (SYN.) insurmountable, unconquerable, invulnerable, impregnable, unassailable.

(ANT.) weak, puny, powerless, vulnerable.

induce (SYN.) evoke, cause, influence, persuade, effect, originate, prompt, incite, create.

inducement (SYN.) incentive, motive, purpose, stimulus, reason, impulse, cause, principle, spur, incitement.

(ANT.) result, attempt, action, effort, deed.

induct (SYN.) instate, establish, install.

(ANT.) eject, oust.

indulge (SYN.) humor, satisfy, gratify.

indulgent (SYN.) obliging, pampering, tolerant, easy.

indurate (SYN.) impenitent, unfeeling, hard, insensible, tough, obdurate, callous.

(ANT.) sensitive, soft, compassionate, tender.

industrious (SYN.) hard-working, perseverant, busy, active, diligent, assiduous, careful, patient.

(ANT.) unconcerned, indifferent, lethargic, careless, apa-

thetic, lazy, indolent, shiftless.

inebriated (SYN.) drunk, tight, drunken, intoxicated, tipsy.

(ANT.) sober, clearheaded, temperate.

ineffective (SYN.) pliant, tender, vague, wavering, defenseless, weak, inadequate, poor, irresolute, frail, decrepit, delicate, vacillating, assailable, exposed, vulnerable.

(ANT.) sturdy, robust, strong, potent, powerful.

inept (SYN.) clumsy, awkward, improper, inappropriate.

(ANT.) adroit, dexterous, adept, appropriate, proper, apt, fitting.

inequity (SYN.) wrong, injustice, unfairness, grievance, injury.

(ANT.) righteousness, lawfulness, equity, justice.

inert (SYN.) lazy, dormant, slothful, inactive, idle, indolent, motionless, unmoving, fixed, static.

(ANT.) working, active, industrious, occupied.

inertia (SYN.) indolence, torpidity, idleness, slothfulness, indolence, sluggishness, supineness.

(ANT.) assiduousness, activity, alertness, diligence.

inevitable (SYN.) definite, fixed, positive, sure, undeniable, indubitable, certain, assured, unquestionable, secure.

(ANT.) uncertain, probable, doubtful, questionable.

inexpensive *(SYN.)* low-priced, cheap, inferior, mean, beggarly, common, poor, shabby, modest, economical.

(ANT.) expensive, costly, dear.

inexperienced *(SYN.)* naive, untrained, uninformed, green.

(ANT.) experienced, skilled, sophisticated, trained, seasoned.

inexplicable *(SYN.)* hidden, mysterious, obscure, secret, dark, cryptic, enigmatical, incomprehensible, occult, recondite, inscrutable, dim.

(ANT.) plain, simple, clear, obvious, explained.

infamous *(SYN.)* shocking, shameful, scandalous.

infantile *(SYN.)* babyish, naive, immature, childish.

(ANT.) mature, grownup, adult.

infect *(SYN.)* pollute, poison, contaminate, defile, sully, taint.

(ANT.) purify, disinfect.

infection *(SYN.)* virus, poison, ailment, disease, pollution, pest, germ, taint, contamination, contagion.

infectious *(SYN.)* contagious, virulent, catching, communicable, pestilential, transferable.

(ANT.) noncommunicable, hygienic, healthful.

infer *(SYN.)* understand, deduce, extract.

inference *(SYN.)* consequence, result, conclusion, corollary, judgment, deduction.

(ANT.) preconception, foreknowledge, assumption, presupposition.

inferior *(SYN.)* secondary, lower, poorer, minor, subordinate, mediocre.

(ANT.) greater, superior, better, higher.

infinite *(SYN.)* immeasurable, interminable, unlimited, unbounded, eternal, boundless, illimitable, immense, endless, vast, innumerable, limitless.

(ANT.) confined, limited, bounded, circumscribed.

infinitesimal *(SYN.)* minute, microscopic, tiny, submicroscopic.

(ANT.) gigantic, huge, enormous.

infirm *(SYN.)* feeble, impaired, decrepit, forceless, languid, puny, powerless, enervated, weak, exhausted.

(ANT.) stout, vigorous, forceful, lusty, strong.

infirmity *(SYN.)* disease, illness, malady, ailment, sickness, disorder, complaint.

(ANT.) soundness, health, vigor, healthiness.

inflame *(SYN.)* fire, incite, excite, arouse.

(ANT.) soothe, calm.

inflammation *(SYN.)* infection, soreness, irritation.

inflammatory *(SYN.)* instigating, inciting, provocative.

inflate *(SYN.)* expand, swell, distend.

(ANT.) collapse, deflate.

inflexible *(SYN.)* firm, stubborn, headstrong, immovable, unyielding, uncompromising, dogged, contumacious, determined, obstinate, rigid, unbending, unyielding, steadfast.

(ANT.) submissive, compliant, docile, amenable, yielding, flexible, giving, elastic.

inflict *(SYN.)* deliver, deal, give, impose, apply.

influence *(SYN.)* weight, control, effect, sway.

influenced *(SYN.)* sway, affect, bias, control, actuate, impel, stir, incite.

influential *(SYN.)* important, weighty, prominent, significant, critical, decisive, momentous, grave, relevant, material, pressing, consequential.

(ANT.) petty, irrelevant, mean, trivial, insignificant.

inform *(SYN.)* apprise, instruct, tell, notify, advise, acquaint, enlighten, impart, warn, teach, advise, relate.

(ANT.) delude, mislead, distract, conceal.

informal *(SYN.)* simple, easy, natural, unofficial, familiar.

(ANT.) formal, distant, reserved, proper.

informality *(SYN.)* friendship, frankness, liberty, acquaintance, sociability, intimacy, unreserved.

(ANT.) presumption, constraint, reserve, distance, haughtiness.

information *(SYN.)* knowledge, data, intelligence, facts.

informative *(SYN.)* educational, enlightening, instructive.

informer *(SYN.)* tattler, traitor, betrayer.

infrequent *(SYN.)* unusual, rare, occasional, strange.

(ANT.) commonplace, abundant, usual, ordinary, customary, frequent, numerous.

ingenious *(SYN.)* clever, skillful, talented, adroit, dexterous, quick-witted, bright, smart, witty, sharp, apt, resourceful, imaginative, inventive, creative.

(ANT.) dull, slow, awkward, bungling, unskilled, stupid.

ingenuity *(SYN.)* cunning, inventiveness, resourcefulness, aptitude, faculty, cleverness, ingenuousness.

(ANT.) ineptitude, clumsiness, dullness, stupidity.

ingenuous *(SYN.)* open, sincere, honest, candid, straightforward, free, plain, frank, truthful, naive, innocent, unsophisticated, simple.

(ANT.) scheming, sly, contrived, wily.

ingredient *(SYN.)* component, element, constituent.

inhabit *(SYN.)* fill, possess, absorb, dwell, occupy, live.

(ANT.) relinquish, abandon, release.

inherent *(SYN.)* innate, native, congenital, inherent, intrinsic, inborn, inbred, natural, real.

(ANT.) extraneous, acquired, external, extrinsic.

inhibit *(SYN.)* curb, constrain, hold back, restrain, bridle, hinder, repress, suppress, stop, limit.

(ANT.) loosen, aid, incite, encourage.

inhuman *(SYN.)* merciless, cruel, brutal, ferocious, savage, ruthless, malignant, barbarous, barbaric, bestial.

(ANT.) kind, benevolent, forbearing, gentle, compassionate, merciful, humane, humane.

inimical *(SYN.)* hostile, warlike, adverse, antagonistic, opposed, unfriendly.

(ANT.) favorable, amicable, cordial.

iniquitous *(SYN.)* baleful, immoral, pernicious, sinful, wicked, base, bad, evil, noxious, unsound, villainous.

(ANT.) moral, good, excellent, honorable, reputable.

iniquity *(SYN.)* injustice, wrong, grievance, unfairness, injury.

(ANT.) lawful, equity, righteousness, justice.

initial *(SYN.)* original, first, prime, beginning, earliest, pristine, chief, primeval, primary, foremost, basic, elementary.

(ANT.) latest, subordinate, last, least, hindmost, final, terminal.

initiate *(SYN.)* institute, enter, arise, inaugurate, commence, originate, start, open, begin.

(ANT.) terminate, complete, end, finish, close, stop.

initiative *(SYN.)* enthusiasm, energy, vigor, enterprise.

injure *(SYN.)* harm, wound, abuse, dishonor, damage, hurt, impair, spoil, disfigure, affront, insult, mar.

(ANT.) praise, ameliorate, help, preserve, compliment, benefit.

injurious *(SYN.)* detrimental, mischievous, damaging, hurtful, deleterious, harmful, destructive.

(ANT.) profitable, helpful, advantageous, salutary, beneficial, useful.

injury *(SYN.)* harm, detriment, damage, injustice, wrong, prejudice, grievance, mischief.

(ANT.) repair, benefit, improvement.

injustice *(SYN.)* unfairness, grievance, iniquity, wrong, injury.

(ANT.) righteousness, justice, equity, lawfulness.

inmate *(SYN.)* patient, prisoner.

inn *(SYN.)* motel, lodge, hotel.

innate *(SYN.)* native, inherent, congenital, innate, real, inborn, natural, intrinsic, inbred.

(ANT.) extraneous, acquired, external, extrinsic.

innocent *(SYN.)* pure, sinless, blameless, innocuous, lawful, naive, faultless, virtuous, not guilty.

(ANT.) guilty, corrupt, sinful, culpable, sophisticated, wise, worldly.

innocuous *(SYN.)* naive, pure, innocent, blameless, virtuous, lawful, faultless, innocuous, sinless.

(ANT.) sinful, corrupt, unrighteous, culpable, guilty.

inquire *(SYN.)* ask, solicit, invite, demand, claim, entreat, interrogate, query, beg, request, question, investigate, examine.
(ANT.) dictate, insist, reply, command, order.

inquiring *(SYN.)* prying, searching, curious, inquisitive, peering, snoopy, peeping, meddling, interrogative.
(ANT.) unconcerned, indifferent, uninterested, incurious.

inquiry *(SYN.)* investigation, quest, research, examination, interrogation, exploration, query, question, scrutiny, study.
(ANT.) inattention, inactivity, disregard, negligence.

inquisitive *(SYN.)* meddling, peeping, nosy, interrogative, peering, searching, prying, snoopy, inquiring, curious.
(ANT.) unconcerned, indifferent, incurious, uninterested.

insane *(SYN.)* deranged, mad, foolish, idiotic, demented, crazy, delirious, maniacal, lunatic.
(ANT.) sane, rational, reasonable, sound, sensible, coherent.

insanity *(SYN.)* delirium, aberration, dementia, psychosis, lunacy, madness, frenzy, mania, craziness, derangement.
(ANT.) stability, rationality, sanity.

insecure *(SYN.)* uneasy, nervous, uncertain, shaky.
(ANT.) secure.

insensitive *(SYN.)* unfeeling, impenitent, callous, hard, indurate, obdurate, tough.
(ANT.) soft, compassionate, tender, sensitive.

insight *(SYN.)* intuition, acumen, penetration, discernment, perspicuity.
(ANT.) obtuseness.

insignificant *(SYN.)* trivial, paltry, petty, small, frivolous, unimportant, insignificant, trifling.
(ANT.) momentous, serious, important, weighty.

insincere *(SYN.)* false, dishonest, deceitful.
(ANT.) honest, sincere.

insinuate *(SYN.)* imply, mean, suggest, connote, signify, involve.
(ANT.) express, state, assert.

insipid *(SYN.)* tasteless, dull, stale, flat, vapid.
(ANT.) racy, tasty, savory, exciting.

insist *(SYN.)* command, demand, require.

insolence *(SYN.)* boldness, presumption, sauciness, effrontery, audacity, assurance, impertinence, rudeness.
(ANT.) politeness, truckling, diffidence, subserviency.

insolent *(SYN.)* arrogant, impertinent, insulting, rude, brazen, contemptuous, abusive, offensive, disrespectful.
(ANT.) respectful, courteous, polite, considerate.

inspect *(SYN.)* observe, discern, eye, behold, glance, scan, stare, survey, view, regard, see, watch, witness, examine, investigate.

(ANT.) overlook, miss, avert, hide.

inspection (SYN.) examination, retrospect, survey, revision, reconsideration, critique, criticism, review.

inspiration (SYN.) creativity, aptitude, gift, genius, originality, ability, faculty, sagacity, talent, proficient, master, adept, intellectual, thought, impulse, idea, notion, hunch.

(ANT.) dullard, moron, shallowness, ineptitude, stupidity, obtuseness, dolt.

install (SYN.) establish.

instance (SYN.) occasion, illustration, occurrence, example, case.

instant (SYN.) flash, moment.

instantaneous (SYN.) hasty, sudden unexpected, rapid, abrupt, immediate.

(ANT.) slowly, anticipated, gradual.

instantly (SYN.) now, presently, directly, forthwith, immediately, straight-away, at once, instantaneously.

(ANT.) sometime, distantly, hereafter, later, shortly.

instinct (SYN.) intuition, feeling.

instinctive (SYN.) offhand, voluntary, willing, spontaneous, automatic, impulsive, extemporaneous.

(ANT.) rehearsed, planned, compulsory, prepared, forced.

institute (SYN.) ordain, establish, raise, form, organize,

sanction, fix, found, launch, begin, initiate.

(ANT.) overthrow, upset, demolish, abolish, unsettle.

instruct (SYN.) teach, tutor, educate, inform, school, instill, train, inculcate, drill.

(ANT.) misinform, misguide.

instruction (SYN.) advise, warning, information, exhortation, notification, admonition, caution, recommendation, counsel, suggestion, teaching, training, education, command, order.

instrument (SYN.) channel, device, utensil, tool, agent, apparatus, means, vehicle, medium, agent, implement.

(ANT.) obstruction, hindrance, preventive, impediment.

insubordinate (SYN.) rebellious, unruly, defiant, disorderly, disobedient, undutiful, refractory, intractable, mutinous.

(ANT.) obedient, compliant, submissive, dutiful.

insufficient (SYN.) limited, lacking, deficient, short, inadequate.

(ANT.) ample, protracted, abundant, big, extended.

insulation (SYN.) quarantine, segregation, seclusion, withdrawal, isolation, loneliness, alienation, solitude.

(ANT.) union, communion, association, fellowship, connection.

insult (SYN.) insolence, offense, abuse, dishonor, affront, insult, indignity, offend, humiliate, outrage.

(ANT.) *compliment, homage, apology, salutation, flatter, praise.*

integrated (SYN.) mingled, mixed, combined, interspersed, desegregated, non-sectarian, interracial.

(ANT.) *separated, divided, segregated.*

integrity (SYN.) honesty, openness, trustworthiness, fairness, candor, justice, rectitude, sincerity, uprightness, soundness, wholeness, honor, principle, virtue.

(ANT.) *fraud, deceit, cheating, trickery, dishonesty.*

intellect (SYN.) understanding, judgment.

intellectual (SYN.) intelligent.

intelligence (SYN.) reason, sense, intellect, understanding, mind, ability, skill, aptitude.

(ANT.) *feeling, passion, emotion.*

intelligent (SYN.) clever, smart, knowledgeable, well-informed, alert, discerning, astute, quick, enlightened, smart, bright, wise.

(ANT.) *insipid, obtuse, dull, stupid, slow, foolish, unintelligent, dumb.*

intend (SYN.) plan, prepare, scheme, contrive, outline, design, sketch, plot, project, delineate.

intense (SYN.) brilliant, animated, graphic, lucid, bright, expressive, vivid, deep, profound, concentrated, serious, earnest.

(ANT.) *dull, vague, dusky, dim, dreary.*

intensify (SYN.) accrue, augment, amplify, enlarge, enhance, extend, expand, heighten, grow, magnify, raise, multiply.

(ANT.) *reduce, decrease, contract, diminish.*

intent (SYN.) purpose, design, objective, intention, aim.

(ANT.) *accidental, result, chance.*

intensity (SYN.) force, potency, power, toughness, activity, durability, fortitude, vigor, stamina.

(ANT.) *weakness, feebleness, infirmity, frailty.*

intention (SYN.) intent, purpose, objective, plan, expectation, aim, object.

(ANT.) *chance, accident.*

intentional (SYN.) deliberate, intended, studied, willful, contemplated, premeditated, designed, voluntary, purposeful, planned.

(ANT.) *fortuitous, accidental, chance.*

intentionally (SYN.) purposefully, deliberately, maliciously.

(ANT.) *accidentally.*

interest (SYN.) attention, concern, care, advantage, benefit, profit, ownership, credit, attract, engage, amuse, entertain.

(ANT.) *apathy, weary, disinterest.*

interested (SYN.) affected, concerned.

(ANT.) unconcerned, indifferent, uninterested.

interesting *(SYN.)* engaging, inviting, fascinating, attractive.

(ANT.) boring, tedious, uninteresting, wearisome.

interfere *(SYN.)* meddle, monkey, interpose, interrupt, tamper, butt in, intervene.

interference *(SYN.)* prying, intrusion, meddling, obstacle, obstruction.

interior *(SYN.)* internal, inmost, inner, inward, inside, center.

(ANT.) outer, adjacent, exterior, external, outside.

interject *(SYN.)* intrude, introduce, insert, inject, interpose.

(ANT.) overlook, avoid, disregard.

interminable *(SYN)* immense, endless, immeasurable, unlimited, vast, unbounded, boundless, eternal, infinite.

(ANT.) limited, bounded, circumscribed, confined.

internal *(SYN.)* inner, interior, inside, intimate, private.

(ANT.) outer, external, surface.

interpose *(SYN.)* arbitrate, inject, intervene, meddle, insert, interject, introduce, intercede, intrude, interfere.

(ANT.) overlook, avoid, disregard.

interpret *(SYN.)* explain, solve, translate, construe, elucidate, decode, explicate, render, unravel, define, understand.

(ANT.) misinterpret, falsify, confuse, distort, misconstrue.

interrogate *(SYN.)* quiz, analyze, inquire, audit, question, contemplate, assess, dissect, notice, scan, review, view, check, survey, scrutinize, examine.

(ANT.) overlook, omit, neglect, disregard.

interrupt *(SYN.)* suspend, delay, postpone, defer, adjourn, stay, discontinue, intrude, interfere.

(ANT.) prolong, persist, continue, maintain, proceed.

interval *(SYN.)* pause, gap.

intervene *(SYN.)* insert, intercede, meddle, inject, introduce, interpose, mediate, interfere, interrupt, intrude.

(ANT.) overlook, avoid, disregard.

intimacy *(SYN.)* fellowship, friendship, acquaintance, frankness, familiarity, unreserved, liberty.

(ANT.) presumption, distance, constraint, reserve.

intimate *(SYN.)* chummy, confidential, friendly, loving, affectionate, close, familiar, near, personal, private, secret.

(ANT.) conventional, formal, ceremonious, distant.

intimation *(SYN.)* reminder, implication, allusion, hint, insinuation.

(ANT.) declaration, statement, affirmation.

intolerant *(SYN.)* fanatical, narrow-minded, prejudiced, bigoted, illiberal, dogmatic, biased.

(ANT.) tolerant, radical, liberal,

progressive, broad-minded, fair.

intoxicated *(SYN.)* inebriated, tipsy, drunk, tight, drunken, high.

(ANT.) sober, temperate, clear-headed.

intrepid *(SYN.)* brave, fearless, insolent, abrupt, rude, pushy, adventurous, daring, courageous, prominent, striking, forward, imprudent.

(ANT.) timid, bashful, flinching, cowardly, retiring.

intricate *(SYN.)* compound, perplexing, complex, involved, complicated.

(ANT.) simple, plain, uncompounded.

intrigue *(SYN.)* design, plot, cabal, machination, stratagem, scheme, attract, charm, interest, captivate.

intrinsic *(SYN.)* natural, inherent, inbred, congenital, inborn, native.

(ANT.) extraneous, acquired, external, extrinsic.

introduce *(SYN.)* acquaint, present, submit, offer, propose.

introduction *(SYN.)* preamble, prelude, beginning, prologue, start, preface.

(ANT.) finale, conclusion, end, epilogue, completion.

intrude *(SYN.)* invade, attack, encroach, trespass, penetrate, infringe, interrupt.

(ANT.) vacate, evacuate, abandon, relinquish.

intruder *(SYN.)* trespasser, thief, prowler, robber.

intuition *(SYN.)* insight, acumen, perspicuity, penetration, discernment, instinct, clairvoyance.

invade *(SYN.)* intrude, violate, infringe, attack, penetrate, encroach, trespass.

(ANT.) vacate, abandon, evacuate, relinquish.

invalidate *(SYN.)* annul, cancel, abolish, revoke, abrogate.

(ANT.) promote, restore, sustain, establish, continue.

invaluable *(SYN.)* priceless, precious, valuable.

(ANT.) worthless.

invasion *(SYN.)* assault, onslaught, aggression, attack, intrusion.

(ANT.) surrender, opposition, resistance, defense.

invective *(SYN.)* insult, abuse, disparagement, upbraiding, reproach, defamation, aspersion.

(ANT.) laudation, plaudit, commendation.

invent *(SYN.)* devise, fabricate, design, concoct, frame, conceive, contrive, create, originate.

(ANT.) reproduce, copy, imitate.

inventive *(SYN.)* fanciful, imaginative, visionary, clever, creative.

(ANT.) unromantic, literal, dull, prosaic.

inventiveness *(SYN)* cunning, cleverness, ingenuousness, aptitude.

(ANT.) ineptitude, clumsiness, dullness, stupidity.

invert *(SYN.)* upset, turn about,

transpose, countermand, revoke, reverse, overturn, repeal.

(ANT.) stabilize, endorse.

investigate *(SYN.)* look, probe, ransack, scrutinize, ferret, examine, seek, explore, search, scour, inspect, study.

investigation *(SYN.)* exploration, interrogation, quest, question, scrutiny, inquiry, query, examination, study, research.

(ANT.) inattention, disregard, inactivity, negligence.

invigorating *(SYN.)* bracing, fortifying, vitalizing, stimulating.

invincible *(SYN.)* insurmountable, unconquerable, impregnable, indomitable, unassailable.

(ANT.) powerless, weak, vulnerable.

invisible *(SYN.)* indistinguishable, unseen, imperceptible.

(ANT.) evident, visible, seen, perceptible.

invite *(SYN.)* bid, ask, encourage, request, urge.

inviting *(SYN.)* appealing, tempting, luring, alluring, attractive.

(ANT.) unattractive, uninviting.

involuntary *(SYN.)* reflex, uncontrolled, automatic, unintentional.

(ANT.) voluntary, willful.

involve *(SYN.)* include, embrace, entangle, envelop, incriminate, embroil, implicate, contain, complicate, confuse.

(ANT.) separate, disconnect, extricate, disengage.

invulnerable *(SYN.)* indomitable, unassailable, invincible, unconquerable, impregnable.

(ANT.) powerless, vulnerable.

irate *(SYN.)* incensed, enraged, angry.

ire *(SYN.)* indignation, irritation, wrath, anger, animosity, fury, passion, temper, exasperation.

(ANT.) peace, patience, conciliation, self-control, forbearance.

irk *(SYN.)* irritate, bother, disturb, pester, trouble, vex, tease, chafe, annoy, inconvenience, provoke.

(ANT.) console, soothe, accommodate, gratify.

irrational *(SYN.)* inconsistent, preposterous, self-contradictory, unreasonable, absurd, foolish, nonsensical, ridiculous.

(ANT.) sensible, sound, rational consistent, reasonable.

irregular *(SYN.)* eccentric, unusual, aberrant, devious, abnormal, unnatural, capricious, variable, unequal, disorderly, unsettled, random, disorganized.

(ANT.) regular, methodical, fixed, usual, ordinary, even.

irrelevant *(SYN.)* foreign, unconnected, remote, alien, strange.

(ANT.) germane, relevant, akin, kindred.

irresolute *(SYN.)* frail, pliant, vacillating, ineffective, wavering, weak, yielding, fragile, pliable.

(ANT.) robust, potent, sturdy, strong, powerful.

irresponsible *(SYN.)* unreliable.

irritable *(SYN.)* hasty, hot, peevish, testy, irascible, fiery, snappish, choleric, excitable, touchy.

(ANT.) composed, agreeable, tranquil, calm.

irritate *(SYN.)* irk, molest, bother, annoy, tease, disturb, inconvenience, vex, trouble, pester.

(ANT.) console, gratify, accommodate, soothe, pacify, calm.

irritable *(SYN.)* peevish, testy, sensitive, touchy.

(ANT.) happy, cheerful.

irritation *(SYN.)* chagrin, mortification, vexation, annoyance, exasperation, pique.

(ANT.) pleasure, comfort, gratification, appeasement.

isolate *(SYN.)* detach, segregate, separate, disconnect.

(ANT.) happy, cheerful.

isolated *(SYN.)* lone, single, alone, desolate, secluded, solitary, deserted, sole.

(ANT.) surrounded, accompanied.

isolation *(SYN.)* quarantine, seclusion, separation, solitude, alienation, loneliness, segregation, detachment.

(ANT.) fellowship, union, association, communion, connection.

issue *(SYN.)* flow, proceed, result, come, emanate, originate, abound, copy, number,

edition, problem, question, concern, publish, distribute, circulate, release.

itemize *(SYN.)* register, detail, record.

J

jab *(SYN.)* thrust, poke, nudge, prod, shove, jolt, boost, tap, slap, rap, thwack, push.

jabber *(SYN.)* mumble, gossip, prattle, chatter, gab, palaver.

jacent *(SYN.)* level, flatness, plane, proneness, recline.

jacinth *(SYN.)* decoration, ornament, embellishment.

jack *(SYN.)* fellow, guy, boy, toiler, guy, man, worker.

jacket *(SYN.)* wrapper, envelope, coat, sheath, cover, casing, folder, enclosure.

jack-of-all-trades *(SYN.)* man friday, expert, proficient, amateur, adept, handyman, dab.

jade *(SYN.)* hussy, wanton, trollop, harlot, common, whore, ignoble, wench, hag, shrew.

jaded *(SYN.)* exhausted, bored, tired, fatigued, satiated, weary, hardened.

jag *(SYN.)* notch, snag, protuberance, barb, dent, cut, nick, serration, indentation, point.

jagged *(SYN.)* crooked, bent, ragged, pointy, notched, aquiline, furcated, aduncous, serrated.

(ANT.) smooth.

jail *(SYN.)* stockade, prison, reformatory, penitentiary, keep, dungeon, brig, confine, lock up, detain, imprison, hold captive, coop, cage, incarcerate.

jailbird *(SYN.)* convict, parolee, con, inmate, prisoner.

jailer *(SYN.)* guard, keeper, turnkey, warden.

jam *(SYN.)* force, pack, ram, crowd, push, wedge, squeeze, stuff, load, cram, press, crush, marmalade, jelly, conserve, preserve.

jamboree *(SYN.)* celebration, fete, spree, festival, festivity, carousal.

jangle *(SYN.)* rattle, vibrate, clank, clatter, dissonance, discord, quarrel, din, discord, dispute.

janitor *(SYN.)* custodian, doorkeeper, caretaker, superintendent, gatekeeper.

jape *(SYN.)* lampoon, banter, joke, jest, tease, ridicule.

jar *(SYN.)* rattle, shake, bounce, jolt.

jargon *(SYN.)* speech, idiom, dialect, vernacular, diction, argot, phraseology, language, parlance, slang.
(ANT.) gibberish, babble, nonsense, drivel.

jaundiced *(SYN.)* biased, prejudiced.
(ANT.) fair.

jaunt *(SYN.)* journey, trip, tour, excursion, outing, voyage, expedition.

jaunty *(SYN.)* lively, vivacious, bouyant, winsome, frisky, showy, dapper, breezy, airy.

jazzy *(SYN.)* garish, vivacious, loud, splashy, exaggerated, flashy.

jealous *(SYN.)* covetous, desirous of, envious.

jealousy *(SYN.)* suspicion, envy, resentfulness, greed, covetousness.
(ANT.) tolerance, indifference, geniality, liberality.

jeer *(SYN.)* taunt, mock, scoff, deride, make fun of, gibe, sneer.
(ANT.) flatter, praise, compliment, laud.

jell *(SYN.)* finalize, congeal, set, solidify, take form.

jeopardize *(SYN.)* risk, dare, expose, imperil, chance, venture, hazard, endanger.
(ANT.) know, guard, determine.

jerk *(SYN.)* quiver, twitch, shake, spasm, jolt, yank, fool.

jerkwater *(SYN.)* remote, hick, backwoods, unimportant, one-horse.

jest *(SYN.)* mock, joke, tease, fun, witticism, quip.

jester *(SYN.)* fool, buffoon, harlequin, clown.
(ANT.) sage, genius, scholar, philosopher.

jet *(SYN.)* squirt, spurt, gush, inky, coal-black, nozzle.

jettison *(SYN.)* heave, discharge, throw, eject, cast off, dismiss.

jetty *(SYN.)* pier, breakwater, bulwark, buttress.

jewel *(SYN.)* ornament, gemstone, gem, bauble, stone.

jib *(SYN.)* shrink, shy, dodge, retreat, balk.

jig *(SYN.)* caper, prance, jiggle, leap, skip.

jiggle *(SYN.)* shimmy, agitate,

jerk, twitch, wiggle.

jilt *(SYN.)* abandon, get rid of, reject, desert, forsake, leave.

jingle *(SYN.)* chime, ring, tinkle.

jinx *(SYN.)* hex, whammy, nemesis, curse, evil eye.

jittery *(SYN.)* jumpy, nervous, quivering, shaky, skittery.

job *(SYN.)* toil, business, occupation, post, chore, stint, career, duty, employment, profession, trade, work, situation, labor, assignment, position, undertaking, task.

jobless *(SYN.)* idle, unoccupied, inactive, unemployed.

jocularity *(SYN.)* humor, wit, joke, facetiousness, waggery.
(ANT.) sorrow, gravity.

jocund *(SYN.)* mirthful, elated, pleasant, cheerful, merry, gay, jovial, frolicsome.

jog *(SYN.)* gait, trot, sprint, run, lope.

join *(SYN.)* conjoin, attach, accompany, associate, assemble, fit, couple, combine, fasten, unite, clasp, put together, go with, adjoin, link, connect.
(ANT.) separate, disconnect, split, sunder, part, divide, detach.

joint *(SYN.)* link, union, connection, junction, coupling, common, combined, mutual, connected.
(ANT.) divided, separate.

joke *(SYN.)* game, jest, caper, prank, anecdote, quip, tease, antic, banter, laugh.

joker *(SYN.)* wisecracker, humorist, wit, comedian, trickster, comic, jester, punster.

jolly *(SYN.)* merry, joyful, gay, happy, sprightly, pleasant, jo-vial, gleeful, spirited, cheerful, glad.
(ANT.) mournful, depressed, sullen, glum.

jolt *(SYN.)* sway, waver, startle, rock, jar, totter, jerk, quake, bump, shake.

josh *(SYN.)* poke fun at, kid, tease, ridicule.

jostle *(SYN.)* shove, push, bump, thrust.

jot *(SYN.)* note, write, record.

jounce *(SYN.)* bounce, jolt, bump, jostle, jar, shake.

journal *(SYN.)* account, diary, log, chronicle, magazine, newspaper, record.

journey *(SYN.)* tour, passage, cruise, voyage, pilgrimage, jaunt, trip, outing, expedition, excursion, travel.

joust *(SYN.)* tournament, contest, skirmish, competition, fight.

jovial *(SYN.)* good-natured, kindly, merry, good humored, good-hearted, joyful, jolly, gleeful.
(ANT.) solemn, sad, serious, grim.

joy *(SYN.)* pleasure, glee, bliss, elation, delight, mirth, felicity, rapture, delight, transport, exultation, gladness, happiness, festivity, satisfaction, merriment, ecstasy.
(ANT.) grief, depression, unhappiness, sorrow, misery, gloom, sadness, affliction.

joyful *(SYN.)* gay, lucky, opportune, cheerful, happy, blissful, jovial, merry, gleeful, delighted, glad, contented, fortunate.

(ANT.) gloomy, sad, blue, solemn, serious, grim, morose, glum, depressed.

joyous *(SYN.)* jolly, gay, blithe, merry, gleeful, cheerful, jovial.

(ANT.) sad, gloomy, sorrowful, melancholy.

jubilant *(SYN.)* exulting, rejoicing, overjoyed, triumphant, gay, elated, delighted.

(ANT.) dejected.

jubilee *(SYN.)* gala, holiday, celebration, festival, fete.

judge *(SYN.)* umpire, think, estimate, decide, arbitrator, condemn, decree, critic, appreciate, adjudicator, determine, arbiter, magistrate, arbitrate, justice, consider, mediate, referee, evaluate.

judgment *(SYN.)* wisdom, perspicacity, discernment, decision, common sense, estimation, verdict, understanding, intelligence, discretion, opinion, sense.

(ANT.) thoughtlessness, senselessness, arbitrariness.

judicial *(SYN.)* legal, judicatory, forensic.

judicious *(SYN.)* sensible, wise, thoughtful.

(ANT.) ignorant.

jug *(SYN.)* bottle, jar, flask, flagon, pitcher.

juice *(SYN.)* broth, liquid, sap, distillation, serum, fluid.

jumble *(SYN.)* disarrangement,

tumult, agitation, ferment, turmoil, commotion, confuse, mix, muddle, scramble, disorder.

(ANT.) peace, arrange, compose, certainty, tranquillity.

jumbo *(SYN.)* huge, big, immense, enormous, giant, colossal, monstrous, mammoth, gigantic, tremendous.

(ANT.) mini, midget, dwarf, small, little, tiny.

jump *(SYN.)* leap, skip, bound, jerk, vault, hop, spring.

jumpy *(SYN.)* touchy, excitable, nervous, sensitive.

(ANT.) tranquil, calm, unruffled.

junction *(SYN.)* coupling, joining, union, crossroads, intersection, weld, connection, linking, meeting, seam, joint.

(ANT.) separation.

jungle *(SYN.)* woods, thicket, undergrowth, forest, bush.

junior *(SYN.)* secondary, inferior, minor, lower, younger.

junk *(SYN.)* rubbish, scraps, trash, waste, dump, discard, castoffs, debris.

jurisdiction *(SYN.)* power, commission, warrant, authority, authorization, magistracy, sovereignty.

just *(SYN.)* fair, trustworthy, precise, exact, candid, upright, honest, impartial, lawful, rightful, proper, legal, truthful, merely, only, conscientious.

(ANT.) tricky, dishonest, unjust, corrupt, lying, deceitful.

justice *(SYN.)* justness, rectitude, equity, law, impartiality, right.

(ANT.) *unfairness, inequity, wrong, partiality.*

justifiable *(SYN.)* allowable, tolerable, admissible, warranted.

(ANT.) unsuitable, inadmissible.

justify *(SYN.)* uphold, excuse, acquit, exonerate, absolve, clear, vindicate.

(ANT.) convict.

jut *(SYN.)* project, protrude, stick out.

(ANT.) indent, recess.

juvenile *(SYN.)* puerile, youthful, childish, babyish, youngster, young, child.

(ANT.) old, aged, adult, mature.

K

kaiser *(SYN.)* czar, caesar, caliph, mogul, padishah, tycoon, khan, landamman, cazique.

kavass *(SYN.)* badel, macebearer, constable.

keck *(SYN.)* vomit, belch, retch.

keen *(SYN.)* clever, cunning, acute, penetrating, exact, severe, shrewd, wily, astute, sharp, bright, intelligent, smart, sharp-witted, witty, cutting, fine, quick, energetic, lively.

(ANT.) stupid, shallow, dull, blunted, slow, bland, gentle, obtuse, blunt.

keep *(SYN.)* maintain, retain, observe, protect, confine, sustain, continue, preserve, save, guard, restrain, reserve, obey, support, honor, execute, celebrate, conserve, have, tend, detain, remain, hold on.

(ANT.) abandon, disobey, dismiss, discard, ignore, neglect, lose, relinquish.

keeper *(SYN.)* warden, jailer, ranger, guard, turnkey, watchman, escort, custodian.

keeping *(SYN.)* congeniality, uniformity, consentaneousness, conformance, congruity, union.

keepsake *(SYN.)* reminder, memorial, relic, souvenir, memento, remembrance.

keg *(SYN.)* container, drum, tub, barrel, receptacle, reservatory, cask, tank.

kelpie *(SYN.)* sprite, nixie, naiad, pixy.

kelson *(SYN.)* bottom, sole, toe, foot, root, keel.

kempt *(SYN.)* neat, trim, tidy, spruce, cleaned.

ken *(SYN.)* field, view, vision, range, scope.

kennel *(SYN.)* swarm, flock, covy, drove, herd, pound, doghouse.

kerchief *(SYN.)* neckcloth, han kerchief, scarf, headpiece, babushka.

kern *(SYN.)* peasant, carle, serf, tike, tyke, countryman.

kernel *(SYN.)* corn, seed, grain, marrow, pith, backbone, soul, heart, core, nucleus.

ketch *(SYN.)* lugger, cutter, clipper, ship, barge, sloop.

kettle *(SYN.)* pan, caldron, vat, pot, teapot, vessel, receptacle, receiver, tureen.

key *(SYN.)* opener, explanation, tone, lead, cause, source, note, answer, clue.

keynote *(SYN.)* core, model, theme, pattern, standard.

khan *(SYN.)* master, czar, kaiser, padishah, caesar.

kick *(SYN.)* punt, remonstrate, boot, excitement, pleasure, abandon, stop, hit.

kickback *(SYN.)* repercussion, backfire, rebound.

kickoff *(SYN.)* beginning, opening, start, commencement, outset.

kid *(SYN.)* joke, tease, fool, jest, tot, child.

kidnap *(SYN.)* abduct, snatch, shanghai.

kill *(SYN.)* execute, put to death, slay, butcher, assassinate, murder, cancel, destroy, slaughter, finish, end, annihilate, massacre.

(ANT.) save, protect, animate, resuscitate, vivify.

killer *(SYN.)* assassin, murderer.

killing *(SYN.)* massacre, genocide, slaughter, carnage, butchery, bloodshed.

kin *(SYN.)* relatives, family, folks, relations.

kind *(SYN.)* humane, affable, compassionate, benevolent, merciful, tender, sympathetic, breed, indulgent, forbearing, kindly, race, good, thoughtful, character, benign, family, sort, species, variety, class, type, gentle.

(ANT.) unkind, cruel, merciless, severe, mean, inhuman.

kindle *(SYN.)* fire, ignite, light, arouse, excite, set afire, stir up, trigger, move, provoke, inflame.

(ANT.) pacify, extinguish, calm.

kindred *(SYN.)* family, relations, relatives, consanguinity, kinsfolk, affinity.

(ANT.) strangers, disconnection.

kinetic *(SYN.)* vigorous, active, dynamic, energetic, mobile, forceful.

king *(SYN.)* sovereign, ruler, chief, monarch, potentate.

kingdom *(SYN.)* realm, empire, monarchy, domain.

kingly *(SYN.)* kinglike, imperial, regal, royal, majestic.

kink *(SYN.)* twist, curl, quirk, complication.

kinship *(SYN.)* lineage, blood, family, stock, relationship.

kismet *(SYN.)* fate, end, fortune, destiny.

kiss *(SYN.)* pet, caress, fondle, cuddle, osculate, embrace.

(ANT.) vex, spurn, annoy, tease, buffet.

kit *(SYN.)* outfit, collection, furnishings, equipment, rig, gear, set.

knack *(SYN.)* cleverness, readiness, deftness, ability, ingenuity, skill, talent, aptitude, talent, know-how, art, adroitness, skillfulness.

(ANT.) inability, clumsiness, awkwardness, ineptitude.

knave *(SYN.)* rogue, rascal, villain, scoundrel.

knead *(SYN.)* combine, massage, blend.

knife *(SYN.)* sword, blade.

knightly *(SYN.)* valiant, courageous, gallant, chivalrous, noble.

knit *(SYN.)* unite, join, mend, fasten, connect, combine.

knob *(SYN.)* doorknob, handle, protuberance.

knock *(SYN.)* thump, tap, rap, strike, hit, jab, punch, beat, pound, bang, hammer.

knockout *(SYN.)* stunning, overpowering, stupefying, overwhelming.

knoll *(SYN.)* hill, elevation, hump, mound, butte.

knot *(SYN.)* cluster, gathering, collection, group, crowd, twist, snarl, tangle, connection, junction, link, loop, tie.

know *(SYN.)* perceive, comprehend, apprehend, recognize, understand, discern, discriminate, ascertain, identify, be aware, distinguish.
(ANT.) doubt, suspect, dispute, ignore.

know-how *(SYN.)* skill, ability, proficiency.

knowing *(SYN.)* smart, wise, clever, sagacious, shrewd.

knowledge *(SYN.)* information, wisdom, erudition, learning, apprehension, scholarship, cognizance, acquirements, understanding, intelligence, education, experience.
(ANT.) ignorance, stupidity, illiteracy.

knowledgeable *(SYN.)* understanding, informed, aware.
(ANT.) lacking, unaware.

knurl *(SYN.)* gnarl, knot, projection, burl, node, lump, bulge, bump.

kooky *(SYN.)* odd, wild, unpredictable, weird.
(ANT.) conservative, predictable.

kosher *(SYN.)* permitted, okay, fit, proper, acceptable.

kowtow *(SYN.)* stoop, bend, kneel, genuflect, bow, flatter.

kudos *(SYN.)* acclaim, praise, approbation, approval, applause, cheer, credit, honor.

L

label *(SYN.)* mark, tag, title, name, marker, stamp, sticker, ticket, docket, identity.

labor *(SYN.)* toil, travail, effort, task, childbirth, work, parturition, striving, workers, effort, industry, workingmen, strive, exertion, employment, drudgery, endeavor.
(ANT.) recreation, indolence, idleness, leisure.

laboratory *(SYN.)* lab, workroom, workshop.

laborer *(SYN.)* wage earner, helper, worker, blue-collar worker.

laborious *(SYN.)* tiring, difficult, hard, burdensome, industrious.
(ANT.) easy, relaxing, restful.

labyrinth *(SYN.)* complex, maze, tangle.

lace *(SYN.)* openwork, fancywork, embroidery, edging.

lacerate *(SYN.)* mangle, tear roughly.

laceration *(SYN.)* cut, wound, puncture, gash, lesion, injury.

lack *(SYN.)* want, need, shortage, dearth, scarcity, require.
(ANT.) quantity, plentifulness.

lackey *(SYN.)* yesman, stooge, flatterer, flunky.

lacking *(SYN.)* insufficient, short, deficient, incomplete, defective.
(ANT.) satisfactory, enough, ample, sufficient, adequate.

lackluster *(SYN.)* dull, pallid, flat, lifeless, drab, dim.

laconic *(SYN.)* short, terse, compact, brief, curt, succinct, concise.

lacquer *(SYN.)* polish, varnish, gild.

lad *(SYN.)* youth, boy, fellow, stripling.

laden *(SYN.)* burdened, loaded, weighted.

ladle *(SYN.)* scoop, dipper.

lady *(SYN.)* matron, woman, dame, gentlewoman.

ladylike *(SYN.)* feminine, womanly, maidenly, womanish, female.
(ANT.) masculine, male, virile, mannish, manly.

lag *(SYN.)* dawdle, loiter, linger, poke, straggle, delay, tarry.

laggard *(SYN.)* dallier, idler, lingerer, slowpoke, dawdler.

lair *(SYN.)* retreat, burrow, den, nest, mew, hole.

lame *(SYN.)* feeble, maimed, disabled, crippled, deformed, hobbling, unconvincing, weak, poor, inadequate, defective, limping.
(ANT.) vigorous, convincing, plausible, athletic, robust, agile, sound.

lament *(SYN.)* deplore, wail, bemoan, bewail, regret, grieve, mourning, lamentation, moaning, wailing, weep, mourn, sorrow.
(ANT.) celebrate, rejoice.

lamentable *(SYN.)* unfortunate, deplorable.

lampoon *(SYN.)* skit, tirade, burlesque, parody, satire.

lance *(SYN.)* cut, pierce, perforate, stab, puncture, impale, knife.

land *(SYN.)* earth, continent, ground, soil, domain, estate, field.

landmark *(SYN.)* keystone, monument, point, cornerstone.

landscape *(SYN.)* scenery, panorama, countryside, scene.

landslide *(SYN.)* rockfall, glissade, avalanche.

lane *(SYN.)* alley, way, road, path, aisle, pass, avenue, passage.

language *(SYN.)* dialect, tongue, speech, lingo, jargon, cant, diction, idiom, patter, phraseology, vernacular, words, lingo, talk.
(ANT.) gibberish, nonsense, babble, drivel.

languid *(SYN.)* feeble, drooping, irresolute, debilitated, dull, lethargic, weak, faint, listless.
(ANT.) forceful, strong, vigorous.

languish *(SYN.)* decline, sink, droop, wither, waste, fail, wilt.
(ANT.) revive, rejuvenate, refresh, renew.

languor *(SYN.)* weariness, depression, torpor, inertia, apathy.

lanky *(SYN.)* skinny, gaunt, lean, scrawny, slender, thin.
(ANT.) chunky, stocky, obese, fat.

lantern *(SYN.)* torch, light, lamp, flashlight.

lap *(SYN.)* drink, lick, fold over.

lapse *(SYN.)* decline, sink, go down, slump.

larceny *(SYN.)* pillage, robbery, stealing, theft, burglary, plunder.

lard *(SYN.)* grease, fat.

large *(SYN.)* great, vast, colossal, ample, extensive, capacious, sizable, broad, massive, grand, immense, big, enormous, huge.
(ANT.) tiny, little, short, small.

largely *(SYN.)* chiefly, mainly, principally, mostly.

lariat *(SYN.)* lasso, rope.

lark *(SYN.)* fling, frolic, play, fun, spree, joke, revel.

lascivious *(SYN.)* lecherous, raunchy, lustful, wanton, lewd.

lash *(SYN.)* thong, whip, rod, cane, blow, strike, hit, beat, knout.

lass *(SYN.)* maiden, girl, damsel.
(ANT.) woman.

lasso *(SYN.)* lariat, rope, noose, snare.

last *(SYN.)* terminal, final, ultimate, remain, endure, concluding, latest, utmost, end, conclusive, hindmost, continue.

(ANT.) first, initial, beginning, opening, starting, foremost.

latch *(SYN.)* clasp, hook, fastener, lock, closing, catch.

late *(SYN.)* overdue, tardy, behind, advanced, delayed, new, slow.
(ANT.) timely, early.

lately *(SYN.)* recently, yesterday.

latent *(SYN.)* potential, undeveloped, unseen, dormant, secret, concealed, inactive, hidden, obscured, covered.
(ANT.) visible, evident, conspicuous, explicit, manifest

lather *(SYN.)* suds, foam, froth.

lateral *(SYN.)* sideways, glancing, tangential, marginal, skirting.

latitude *(SYN.)* range, scope, freedom, extent.

latter *(SYN.)* more recent, later.
(ANT.) former.

lattice *(SYN.)* grating, screen, frame, trellis, openwork, framework, grid.

laud *(SYN.)* commend, praise, extol, glorify, compliment.
(ANT.) criticize, belittle.

laudable *(SYN.)* creditable, praiseworthy, commendable, admirable.

laudation *(SYN.)* applause, compliment, flattery, praise, commendation, acclaim, glorification.
(ANT.) criticizing, condemnation, reproach, disparagement, censure.

laugh *(SYN.)* chuckle, giggle, snicker, cackle, titter, grin, smile, roar, guffaw, jeer, mock.

laughable *(SYN.)* funny, amusing, comical, humorous, ridiculous.

launch *(SYN.)* drive, fire, propel, start, begin, originate, set afloat, initiate.

(ANT.) finish, stop, terminate.

launder *(SYN.)* bathe, wash, scrub, scour.

laurels *(SYN.)* glory, distinction, recognition, award, commendation, reward, honor.

lavatory *(SYN.)* toilet, washroom, bathroom, latrine.

lavish *(SYN.)* squander, waste, dissipate, scatter, abundant, free, plentiful, liberal, extravagant, ample, wear out, prodigal.

(ANT.) economize, save, conserve, accumulate, stingy, preserve.

law *(SYN.)* decree, formula, statute, act, rule, ruling, standard, principle, ordinance, proclamation, regulation, order, edict.

lawful *(SYN.)* legal, permissible, allowable, legitimate, authorized, constitutional, rightful.

(ANT.) prohibited, criminal, illicit, illegal, illegitimate.

lawless *(SYN.)* uncivilized, uncontrolled, wild, savage, untamed.

(ANT.) obedient, law-abiding, tame.

lawn *(SYN.)* grass, meadow, turf.

lawyer *(SYN.)* counsel, attorney, counselor.

lax *(SYN.)* slack, loose, careless, vague, lenient, lazy.

(ANT.) firm, rigid.

lay *(SYN.)* mundane, worldly, temporal, place, dispose, bet, wager, hazard, risk, stake, site, earthly, profane, laic, arrange, location, put, set, ballad, deposit, position.

(ANT.) spiritual, unworldly, remove, misplace, disturb, mislay, disarrange, ecclesiastical, religious.

lay off *(SYN.)* discharge, bounce, fire, dismiss.

layout *(SYN.)* plan, arrangement, design.

lazy *(SYN.)* slothful, supine, idle, inactive, sluggish, inert, indolent.

(ANT.) alert, ambitious, forceful, diligent, active, assiduous.

lea *(SYN.)* pasture, meadow.

leach *(SYN.)* remove, extract, seep, dilute, wash out.

lead *(SYN.)* regulate, conduct, guide, escort, direct, supervise, command, steer, control.

(ANT.) follow.

leader *(SYN.)* master, ruler, captain, chief, commander, principal, director, head, chieftain.

(ANT.) follower, servant, disciple, subordinate, attendant.

leading *(SYN.)* dominant, foremost, principal, first, main, primary.

league *(SYN.)* entente, partnership, association, confederacy, coalition, society, alliance, federation.

(ANT.) separation, schism.

leak *(SYN.)* dribble, flow, drip,

opening, perforation.

lean *(SYN.)* rely, tilt, slim, slender, slope, incline, tend, trust, bend, tendency, slant, depend, spare, scant, lanky, thin, meager, inclination, narrow, sag.

(ANT.) rise, heavy, fat, erect, straighten, portly, raise.

leaning *(SYN.)* trend, proclivity, bias, tendency, bent, predisposition, proneness.

(ANT.) disinclination, aversion.

loap *(SYN.)* vault, skip, caper, dive, hurdle, jump, bound, start, hop, plunge, spring.

learn *(SYN.)* gain, find out, memorize, acquire, determine.

learned *(SYN.)* erudite, knowing, enlightened, deep, wise, discerning, scholarly, intelligent, educated, sagacious.

(ANT.) simple, uneducated, ignorant, illiterate, foolish.

learning *(SYN.)* science, education, lore, apprehension, wisdom, knowledge, scholarship.

(ANT.) misunderstanding, ignorance, stupidity.

lease *(SYN.)* charter, let, rent, engage.

leash *(SYN.)* chain, strap, shackle, collar.

least *(SYN.)* minutest, smallest, tiniest, trivial, minimum, fewest, slightest.

(ANT.) most.

leave *(SYN.)* give up, retire, desert, abandon, withdraw, relinquish, will, depart, quit, liberty, renounce, go, bequeath, consent, allowance, permission, freedom, forsake.

(ANT.) come, stay, arrive, tarry,

remain, abide.

lecherous *(SYN.)* lustful, sensual, carnal, lascivious.

lecture *(SYN.)* talk, discussion, lesson, instruct, speech, conference, sermon, report, recitation, address, oration, discourse.

(ANT.) writing, meditation, correspondence.

ledge *(SYN.)* eaves, ridge, shelf, rim, edge.

lee *(SYN.)* shelter, asylum, sanctuary, haven.

leech *(SYN.)* barnacle, bloodsucker, parasite.

leer *(SYN.)* eye, grimace, ogle, wink, squint.

leeway *(SYN.)* reserve, allowance, elbowroom, slack, clearance.

leftovers *(SYN.)* scraps, remains, residue, remainder.

legacy *(SYN.)* bequest, inheritance, heirloom.

legal *(SYN.)* legitimate, rightful, honest, allowable, allowed, permissible, lawful, permitted, authorized.

(ANT.) illicit, illegal, prohibited, illegitimate.

legalize *(SYN.)* authorize, ordain, approve, sanction.

legate *(SYN.)* envoy, agent, representative, emissary.

legend *(SYN.)* saga, fable, allegory, myth, parable, tale, story, folklore, fiction, chronicle.

(ANT.) history, facts.

legendary *(SYN.)* fictitious, traditional, mythical, imaginary, fanciful.

legible *(SYN.)* plain, readable, clear, distinct.

(ANT.) illegible.

legion *(SYN.)* outfit, unit, troop, regiment, company, battalion, force, army, team, division.

legislation *(SYN.)* resolution, ruling, lawmaking, regulation, enactment, statute, decree.

legislator *(SYN.)* statesman, congressman, senator, politician, lawmaker.

legitimate *(SYN.)* true, real, bona fide, lawful, proper, right, valid, correct, unadulterated, authentic, rightful, legal, sincere.

(ANT.) sham, counterfeit, artificial, false.

leisure *(SYN.)* respite, intermission, ease, relaxation, rest, calm, tranquillity, recreation, peace, pause.

(ANT.) motion, commotion, tumult, agitation, disturbance.

leisurely *(SYN.)* sluggish, laggard, unhurried, relaxed, casual, dawdling, slow, deliberate.

(ANT.) hurried, swift, pressed, rushed, forced, fast, speedy, quick.

lend *(SYN.)* entrust, advance, confer.

length *(SYN.)* reach, measure, extent, distance, span, longness, stretch.

lengthen *(SYN.)* stretch, prolong, draw, reach, increase, grow, protract, extend.

(ANT.) shrink, contract, shorten.

leniency *(SYN.)* grace, pity, compassion, mildness, chari-

ty, mercy, clemency.

(ANT.) vengeance, punishment, cruelty.

lenient *(SYN.)* tender, humane, clement, tolerant, compassionate, merciful, relaxed, forgiving, gentle, mild, lax, kind.

(ANT.) unfeeling, pitiless, brutal, remorseless.

leprechaun *(SYN.)* gnome, imp, goblin, fairy, elf, sprite, banshee.

lesion *(SYN.)* wound, blemish, sore, trauma, injury.

less *(SYN.)* fewer, smaller, reduced, negative, stinted.

(ANT.) more.

lessen *(SYN.)* shorten, reduce, deduct, subtract, curtail, diminish, shrink, dwindle, decline, instruction, teaching, remove, decrease.

(ANT.) swell, grow, enlarge, increase, expand, multiply, amplify.

lesson *(SYN.)* exercise, session, class, assignment, section, recitation.

let *(SYN.)* admit, hire out, contract, allow, permit, consent, leave, grant, rent.

(ANT.) deny.

letdown *(SYN.)* disillusionment, disappointment.

lethal *(SYN.)* mortal, dangerous, deadly, fatal, devastating.

lethargic *(SYN.)* sluggish, logy, slow, listless, phlegmatic, lazy.

(ANT.) vivacious, energetic.

lethargy *(SYN.)* numbness, stupor, daze, insensibility, torpor.

(ANT.) wakefulness, liveliness,

activity, readiness.

letter *(SYN.)* note, mark, message, character, symbol, sign, memorandum.

letup *(SYN.)* slowdown, slackening, lessening, abatement, reduction.

levee *(SYN.)* dike, breakwater, dam, embankment.

level *(SYN.)* smooth, even, plane, equivalent, uniform, horizontal, equal, flatten, equalize, raze, demolish, flat.
(ANT.) uneven, sloping, hilly, broken.

level-headed *(SYN.)* reasonable, sensible, calm, collected, cool.

leverage *(SYN.)* clout, power, influence, weight, rank.

levity *(SYN.)* humor, triviality, hilarity, fun, frivolity.

levy *(SYN.)* tax, duty, tribute, rate, assessment, exaction, charge, custom.
(ANT.) wages, remuneration, gift.

lewd *(SYN.)* indecent, smutty, course, gross, disgusting, impure.
(ANT.) pure, decent, refined.

liability *(SYN.)* indebtedness, answerability, obligation, vulnerability.

liable *(SYN.)* answerable, responsible, likely, exposed to, subject, amenable, probable, accountable.
(ANT.) immune, exempt, independent.

liaison *(SYN.)* union, coupling, link, connection, alliance.

liar *(SYN.)* fibber, falsifier, storyteller, fabricator, prevaricator.

libel *(SYN.)* slander, vilification, aspersion, defamation.
(ANT.) defense, praise, applause, flattery.

liberal *(SYN.)* large, generous, unselfish, open-handed, tolerant, broad, kind, unprejudiced, open-minded, lavish, plentiful, ample, abundant, extravagant, extensive.
(ANT.) restricted, conservative, stingy, confined.

liberality *(SYN.)* kindness, philanthropy, beneficence, humanity, altruism, benevolence, generosity, charity.
(ANT.) selfishness, cruelty, malevolence.

liberate *(SYN.)* emancipate, loose, release, let go, deliver, free, discharge.
(ANT.) subjugate, oppress, jail, confine, restrict, imprison.

liberated *(SYN.)* loose, frank, emancipated, careless, liberal, freed, autonomous, exempt, familiar.
(ANT.) subject, clogged, restricted, impeded.

liberty *(SYN.)* permission, independence, autonomy, license, privilege, emancipation, self-government, freedom.
(ANT.) constraint, imprisonment, bondage, captivity.

license *(SYN.)* liberty, freedom, liberation, permission, exemption, authorization, warrant, allow, consent, permit, sanction, approval.
(ANT.) servitude, constraint,

bondage, necessity.

lick *(SYN.)* taste, lap, lave.

lid *(SYN.)* top, cover, cap, plug, cork, stopper.

lie *(SYN.)* untruth, fib, illusion, delusion, falsehood, fiction, equivocation, prevarication, repose, location, perjury, misinform, site, recline, similitude.

(ANT.) variance, truth, difference.

life *(SYN.)* sparkle, being, spirit, vivacity, animation, buoyancy, vitality, existence, biography, energy, liveliness, vigor.

(ANT.) demise, lethargy, death, languor.

lift *(SYN.)* hoist, pick up, elevate, raise, heft.

light *(SYN.)* brightness, illumination, beam, gleam, lamp, knowledge, brilliance, fixture, bulb, candle, fire, ignite, burn, dawn, incandescence, flame, airy, unsubstantial, dainty, luminosity, shine, radiance, giddy, enlightenment, weightless, understanding.

(ANT.) darken, gloom, shadow, extinguish, darkness.

lighten *(SYN.)* diminish, unburden, reduce, brighten.

light-headed *(SYN.)* giddy, silly, dizzy, frivolous.

(ANT.) sober, clear-headed, rational.

lighthearted *(SYN.)* carefree, merry, gay, cheerful, happy, glad.

(ANT.) somber, sad, serious, melancholy.

like *(SYN.)* fancy, esteem, adore, love, admire, care for, prefer, cherish.

(ANT.) disapprove, loathe, hate, dislike.

likely *(SYN.)* liable, reasonable, probable, possible.

likeness *(SYN.)* similarity, resemblance, representation, image, portrait.

(ANT.) difference.

likewise *(SYN.)* besides, as well, also, too, similarly.

liking *(SYN.)* fondness, affection, partiality.

(ANT.) antipathy, dislike.

limb *(SYN.)* arm, leg, member, appendage, part, bough.

limber *(SYN.)* bending, flexible, elastic, pliable.

(ANT.) inflexible, stiff.

limbo *(SYN.)* exile, banishment, purgatory.

limelight *(SYN.)* spotlight, notice, notoriety, fame, prominence.

limerick *(SYN.)* jingle, rhyme.

limit *(SYN.)* terminus, bound, extent, confine, border, restriction, boundary, restraint, edge, frontier, check, end, limitation.

(ANT.) endlessness, vastness, boundlessness.

limn *(SYN.)* depict, portray, sketch, paint, illustrate.

limp *(SYN.)* soft, flabby, drooping, walk, limber, supple, flexible, hobble, stagger.

(ANT.) stiff.

limpid *(SYN.)* clear, open, transparent, unobstructed.

(ANT.) cloudy.

line *(SYN.)* row, file, series,

array, sequence, wire, seam, wrinkle, crease, boundary, arrangement, kind, type, division.

lineage *(SYN.)* race, family, tribe, nation, strain, folk, people, ancestry, clan.

linger *(SYN.)* wait, rest, bide, delay, dwadle, stay, loiter, remain, dilly-dally, tarry.

(ANT.) leave, expedite.

lingo *(SYN.)* vernacular, dialect, language, jargon, speech.

link *(SYN.)* unite, connector, loop, couple, attach, connective, connection, coupling, juncture, bond.

(ANT.) separate, disconnect, split.

lip *(SYN.)* edge, brim, rim.

liquid *(SYN.)* watery, fluent, fluid, flowing.

(ANT.) solid, congealed.

liquidate *(SYN.)* pay off, settle, defray.

liquor *(SYN.)* spirits, alcohol, drink, booze.

lissom *(SYN.)* nimble, quick, lively, flexible, agile.

list *(SYN.)* roll, register, slate, enumeration, series.

listen *(SYN.)* overhear, attend to, heed, hear, list, hearken.

(ANT.) ignore, scorn, disregard, reject.

listless *(SYN.)* tired, uninterested, lethargic, unconcerned, apathetic.

(ANT.) active.

literal *(SYN.)* exact, verbatim, precise, strict, faithful.

literally *(SYN.)* actually, exactly, really.

literate *(SYN.)* informed, educated, learned, versed, intelligent, knowledgeable.

(ANT.) unread, illiterate, ignorant, unlettered.

literature *(SYN.)* books, writings, publications.

lithe *(SYN.)* supple, flexible, bending, limber, pliable.

(ANT.) stiff.

litigious *(SYN.)* quarrelsome, disputatious, argumentative.

litter *(SYN.)* rubbish, trash, scatter, clutter, strew, debris, rubble, disorder.

little *(SYN.)* tiny, petty, miniature, diminutive, puny, wee, significant, small, short, brief, bit, trivial.

(ANT.) huge, large, big, long, immense.

liturgy *(SYN.)* ritual, sacrament, worship, service.

live *(SYN.)* dwell, reside, abide, survive, exist, alive, occupy, stay, active, surviving.

(ANT.) die.

livelihood *(SYN.)* keep, sustenance, support, subsistence, job, trade, profession, vocation.

lively *(SYN.)* blithe, vivaciousness, clear, vivid, active, frolicsome, brisk, fresh, animated, energetic, live, spry, vigorous, quick, nimble, bright, exciting, supple.

(ANT.) stale, dull, listless, slow, vapid.

livestock *(SYN.)* animals, cattle.

livid *(SYN.)* grayish, furious, pale, enraged.

living *(SYN.)* support, livelihood, existent, alive.

load *(SYN.)* oppress, trouble, burden, weight, freight, afflict, encumber, pack, shipment, cargo, lade, tax.

(ANT.) lighten, console, unload, mitigate, empty, ease.

loafer *(SYN.)* loiterer, bum, idler, sponger, deadbeat.

loan *(SYN.)* credit, advance, lend.

loath *(SYN.)* reluctant, unwilling, opposed.

loathe *(SYN.)* dislike, despise, hate, abhor, detest, abominate.

(ANT.) love, approve, like, admire.

loathsome *(SYN.)* foul, vile, detestable, revolting, abominable, atrocious, offensive, odious.

(ANT.) pleasant, commendable, alluring, agreeable, delightful.

lob *(SYN.)* toss, hurl, pitch, throw, heave.

lobby *(SYN.)* foyer, entry, entrance, vestibule, passageway, entryway.

local *(SYN.)* limited, regional, restricted, particular.

locality *(SYN.)* nearness, neighborhood, district, vicinity.

(ANT.) remoteness.

locate *(SYN.)* discover, find, unearth, site, situate, place.

located *(SYN.)* found, residing, positioned, situated, placed.

location *(SYN.)* spot, locale, station, locality, situation, place, area, site, vicinity, position, zone, region.

lock *(SYN.)* curl, hook, bolt, braid, ringlet, plait, close, latch, tuft, fastening, bar, hasp, fasten, tress.

(ANT.) open.

locker *(SYN.)* wardrobe, closet, cabinet, chest.

locket *(SYN.)* case, lavaliere, pendant.

locomotion *(SYN.)* movement, travel, transit, motion.

locution *(SYN.)* discourse, cadence, manner, accent.

lodge *(SYN.)* cabin, cottage, hut, club, chalet, society, room, reside, dwell, live, occupy, inhabit, abide, board, fix, settle.

lodger *(SYN.)* guest, tenant, boarder, occupant.

lofty *(SYN.)* high, stately, grandiose, towering, elevated, exalted, sublime, majestic, scornful, proud, grand, tall, pompous.

(ANT.) undignified, lowly, common, ordinary.

log *(SYN.)* lumber, wood, board, register, record, album, account, journal, timber.

logical *(SYN.)* strong, effective, telling, convincing, reasonable, sensible, rational, sane, sound, cogent.

(ANT.) crazy, illogical, irrational, unreasonable, weak.

logy *(SYN.)* tired, inactive, lethargic, sleepy, weary.

loiter *(SYN.)* idle, linger, wait, stay, tarry, dilly-dally, dawdle.

loll *(SYN.)* hang, droop, recline, repose, relax.

lone *(SYN.)* lonely, sole, unaided, single, deserted, isolated, secluded, apart, alone, solitary.

(ANT.) surrounded, accompanied.

loner *(SYN.)* recluse, maverick, outsider, hermit.

loneliness *(SYN.)* solitude, isolation, seclusion, alienation.

lonely *(SYN.)* unaided, isolated, single, solitary, lonesome, unaccompanied, deserted, alone, desolate.

(ANT.) surrounded, attended.

lonesome *(SYN.)* secluded, remote, unpopulated, barren, empty, desolate.

long *(SYN.)* lengthy, prolonged, wordy, elongated, extended, lingering, lasting, protracted, extensive, length, prolix, prolonged.

(ANT.) terse, concise, abridged, short.

long-standing *(SYN.)* persistent, established.

long-winded *(SYN.)* boring, dull, wordy.

(ANT.) curt, terse.

look *(SYN.)* gaze, witness, seem, eye, behold, see, watch, scan, view, appear, stare, discern, glance, examine, examination, peep, expression, appearance, regard, study, contemplation, survey.

(ANT.) overlook, hide, avert, miss.

loom *(SYN.)* emerge, appear, show up.

loop *(SYN.)* ringlet, noose, spiral, fastener.

loose *(SYN.)* untied, unbound, lax, vague, unrestrained, dis-

solute, limp, undone, baggy, disengaged, indefinite, slack, careless, heedless, unfastened, free, wanton.

(ANT.) restrained, steady, fastened, secure, tied, firm, fast, definite, bound, inhibited.

loosen *(SYN.)* untie, undo, loose, unchain.

(ANT.) tie, tighten, secure.

loot *(SYN.)* booty, plunder, take, steal, rob, sack, rifle, pillage, ravage, devastate.

lope *(SYN.)* run, race, bound, gallop.

lopsided *(SYN.)* unequal, twisted, uneven, askew, distorted.

loquacious *(SYN.)* garrulous, wordy, profuse, chatty, verbose.

lord *(SYN.)* peer, ruler, proprietor, boss, nobleman, master, owner, governor.

lore *(SYN.)* learning, knowledge, wisdom, stories, legends, beliefs, teachings.

lose *(SYN.)* misplace, flop, fail, sacrifice, forfeit, mislay, vanish, surrender.

(ANT.) succeed, locate, place, win, discover, find.

loss *(SYN.)* injury, damage, want, hurt, need, bereavement, trouble, death, failure, deficiency.

lost *(SYN.)* dazed, wasted, astray, forfeited, preoccupied, used, adrift, bewildered, missing, distracted, consumed, misspent, absorbed, confused, mislaid, gone, destroyed.

(ANT.) found, anchored.

lot *(SYN.)* result, destiny, bunch,

many, amount, fate, cluster, group, sum, portion, outcome, number, doom, issue.

lotion *(SYN.)* cosmetic, salve, balm, cream.

lottery *(SYN.)* wager, chance, drawing, raffle.

loud *(SYN.)* vociferous, noisy, resounding, stentorian, clamorous, sonorous, thunderous, shrill, blaring, roaring, deafening.

(ANT.) soft, inaudible, murmuring, subdued, quiet, dulcet.

lounge *(SYN.)* idle, loaf, laze, sofa, couch, davenport, relax, rest, lobby, salon, divan.

louse *(SYN.)* scoundrel, knave, cad, rat.

lousy *(SYN.)* revolting, grimy, rotten, dirty, disgusting.

lovable *(SYN.)* charming, attractive, delightful, amiable, sweet, cuddly, likable.

love *(SYN.)* attachment, endearment, affection, adoration, liking, devotion, warmth, adore, tenderness, friendliness, worship, like, cherish, fondness.

(ANT.) loathing, detest, indifference, dislike, hate, hatred.

loveliness *(SYN.)* grace, pulchritude, elegance, charm, attractiveness, comeliness, fairness, beauty.

(ANT.) ugliness, eyesore, disfigurement, deformity.

lovely *(SYN.)* handsome, fair, charming, pretty, attractive, delightful, comely, beautiful, beauteous, exquisite.

(ANT.) ugly, unsightly, homely, foul, hideous, repulsive.

lover *(SYN.)* fiance, suitor, courter, sweetheart, beau.

loving *(SYN.)* close, intimate, confidential, friendly, affectionate.

(ANT.) formal, conventional, ceremonious, distant.

low *(SYN.)* mean, vile, despicable, vulgar, abject, groveling, contemptible, lesser, menial.

(ANT.) righteous, esteemed, lofty, noble.

lower *(SYN.)* subordinate, minor, secondary, quiet, soften, disgrace, degrade, decrease, reduce, diminish, lessen, inferior.

(ANT.) greater, superior, increase, better.

low-key *(SYN.)* subdued, muted, calm, controlled, restrained, understated, gentle.

lowly *(SYN.)* lowborn, humble, base, low, mean, common, average, simple, modest.

(ANT.) royal, noble.

loyal *(SYN.)* earnest, ardent, addicted, inclined, faithful, devoted, affectionate, prone, fond, patriotic, dependable, true.

(ANT.) indisposed, detached, disloyal, traitorous, untrammeled.

loyalty *(SYN.)* devotion, steadfastness, constancy, faithfulness, fidelity, patriotism, allegiance.

(ANT.) treachery, falseness, disloyalty.

lubricate *(SYN.)* oil, grease, anoint.

lucent *(SYN.)* radiant, beaming,

vivid, illuminated, lustrous.

lucid *(SYN.)* plain, visible, clear, intelligible, unmistakable, transparent, limpid, translucent, open, shining, light, explicit, understandable, distinct.

(ANT.) unclear, vague, obscure.

luck *(SYN.)* chance, fortunate, fortune, lot, fate, fluke, destiny, karma, providence.

(ANT.) misfortune.

lucky *(SYN.)* favored, favorable, auspicious, fortunate, successful, felicitous, benign.

(ANT.) unlucky, condemned, unfortunate, persecuted.

lucrative *(SYN.)* well-paying, profitable, high-paying, productive, beneficial.

ludicrous *(SYN.)* absurd, ridiculous, preposterous.

lug *(SYN.)* pull, haul, drag, tug.

luggage *(SYN.)* bags, valises, baggage, suitcases, trunks.

lugubrious *(SYN.)* mournful, sad, gloomy, somber, melancholy.

lukewarm *(SYN.)* unenthusiastic, tepid, spiritless, detached, apathetic, mild.

lull *(SYN.)* quiet, calm, soothe, rest, hush, stillness, pause, break, intermission, recess, respite, silence.

lumber *(SYN.)* logs, timber, wood.

luminous *(SYN.)* beaming, lustrous, shining, glowing, gleaming, bright, light, alight, clear.

(ANT.) murky, dull, dark.

lummox *(SYN.)* yokel, oaf, bumpkin, clown, klutz.

lump *(SYN.)* swelling, protuberance, mass, hunk, bump.

lunacy *(SYN.)* derangement, madness, aberration, psychosis.

(ANT.) stability, rationality.

lunge *(SYN.)* charge, stab, attack, thrust, push.

lurch *(SYN.)* topple, sway, toss, roll, rock, tip, pitch.

lure *(SYN.)* draw, tug, drag, entice, attraction, haul, attract, temptation, persuade, allure.

(ANT.) drive, alienate, propel.

lurid *(SYN.)* sensational, terrible, melodramatic, startling.

lurk *(SYN.)* sneak, hide, prowl, slink, creep.

luscious *(SYN.)* savory, delightful, juicy, sweet, pleasing, delectable, palatable, delicious, tasty.

(ANT.) unsavory, acrid.

lush *(SYN.)* tender, succulent, ripe.

lust *(SYN.)* longing, desire, passion, craving, aspiration, urge.

(ANT.) hate, loathing, distaste.

luster *(SYN.)* radiance, brightness, glister, honor, fame, effulgence, gloss, sheen, shine, gleam, glow, glitter, brilliance, splendor.

(ANT.) dullness, obscurity, darkness.

lustful *(SYN.)* amorous, sexy, desirous, passionate, wanton, lubricious, want, concupiscent.

lusty *(SYN.)* healthy, strong, mighty, powerful, sturdy, strapping, hale, hardy, hefty.

(ANT.) *weak, sick, unhealthy, frail.*

luxuriant *(SYN.)* abundant, flourishing, dense, lush, rich.

luxurious *(SYN.)* rich, lavish, deluxe, splendid, magnificent. *(ANT.) simple, crude, sparse.*

luxury *(SYN.)* frills, comfort, extravagance, wealth, elegance, splendor, prosperity, swankiness, plush, well-being, grandeur, prodigality, finery, ease.

(ANT.) poverty, without, poor.

lyric *(SYN.)* musical, text, words, libretto, singing, tune.

lyrical *(SYN.)* poetic, musical.

M

macabre *(SYN.)* ghastly, grim, horrible, gruesome.

maceration *(SYN.)* dilution, washing.

machination *(SYN.)* hoax, swindle, card- sharping, cunning, plot, cabal, conspriracy.

machinator *(SYN.)* stragetist, schemer, schemist.

machine *(SYN.)* motor, mechanism, device, contrivance.

machinist *(SYN.)* engineer.

macilent *(SYN.)* gaunt, lean, lank, meager, emaciated.

mactation *(SYN.)* immolation, self-immolation, infanticide.

macula *(SYN.)* mole, patch, freckle, spot.

maculate *(SYN.)* bespot, stipple.

maculation *(SYN.)* irisation, striae, iridescence, spottiness.

mad *(SYN.)* incensed, crazy, insane, angry, furious, delirious, provoked, enraged, demented, maniacal, exasperated, wrathful, deranged, crazy, infuriated.

(ANT.) sane, calm, healthy, rational, lucid, cheerful, happy, composed, reasonable.

madam *(SYN.)* dame, woman, lady, matron, mistress.

madden *(SYN.)* anger, annoy, infuriate, enrage, provoke, convulse, asperate, outrage.

(ANT.) please, mollify, calm.

madder *(SYN.)* ruddle.

madness *(SYN.)* derangement, delirium, aberration, mania, insanity, craziness, psychosis.

(ANT.) stability, rationality.

maelstrom *(SYN.)* rapids, eddy, surge, white water, riptide.

magazine *(SYN.)* journal, periodical, arsenal, armory.

magic *(SYN.)* sorcery, wizardry, charm, legerdemain, enchantment, black art, necromancy, conjuring, bewitchery, spell.

magical *(SYN.)* mystical, marvelous, magic, miraculous, bewitching, spell-binding.

magician *(SYN.)* conjuror, sorcerer, wizard, artist, trickster.

magistrate *(SYN.)* judge, adjudicator.

magnanimous *(SYN.)* giving, bountiful, beneficent, chivalrous, generous.

(ANT.) stingy, greedy, selfish.

magnate *(SYN.)* leader, bigwig, tycoon, chief, giant.

magnet *(SYN.)* enticer, enticement, lure, temptation.

magnetic *(SYN.)* pulling, attractive, alluring, drawing, enthralling, seductive.

magnetism *(SYN.)* allure, irresistibility, attraction, appeal.

magnificence *(SYN.)* luxury, grandeur, splendor, majesty, dynamic.

magnificent *(SYN.)* rich, lavish, luxurious, splendid, wonderful, extraordinary, impressive.

(ANT.) simple, plain.

magnify *(SYN.)* heighten, exaggerate, amplify, expand, stretch, increase, enhance, intensify.

(ANT.) compress, understate, depreciate, belittle.

magnitude *(SYN.)* mass, bigness, size, area, volume, dimensions, greatness, extent, measure, importance, consequence, significance.

maid *(SYN.)* chambermaid, servant, maidservant.

maiden *(SYN.)* original, foremost, first, damsel, lass, miss.

(ANT.) accessory, secondary.

mail *(SYN.)* dispatch, send, letters, post, correspondence.

maim *(SYN.)* disable, cripple, hurt, wound, injure, mangle, mutilate, incapacitate.

main *(SYN.)* essential, chief, highest, principal, first, leading, cardinal, supreme, foremost.

(ANT.) supplemental, subordinate, auxiliary.

mainstay *(SYN.)* buttress, pillar, refuge, reinforcement, support.

maintain *(SYN.)* claim, support, uphold, defend, vindicate, sustain, continue, allege, contend, preserve, affirm, keep, justify.

(ANT.) neglect, oppose, discontinue, resist, deny.

maintenance *(SYN.)* subsistence, livelihood, living, support, preservation, upkeep.

majestic *(SYN.)* magnificent, stately, noble, august, grand, imposing, sublime, lofty, high, grandiose, dignified, royal, kingly.

(ANT.) humble, lowly, undignified, common, ordinary.

majesty *(SYN.)* grandeur, dignity, nobility, splendor, distinction.

major *(SYN.)* important, superior, larger, greater, uppermost.

(ANT.) inconsequential, minor.

make *(SYN.)* execute, cause, produce, establish, assemble, create, shape, compel, fashion, construct, build, fabricate, manufacture, form, accomplish.

(ANT.) unmake, break, undo, demolish.

make-believe *(SYN.)* pretend, imagined, simulated, false, fake.

maker *(SYN.)* inventor, creator, producer, builder, manufacturer.

makeshift *(SYN.)* proxy, deputy, understudy, expedient, agent, lieutenant, alternate, substitute.

(ANT.) sovereign, head, princi-

pal.

make-up *(SYN.)* composition, formation, structure, cosmetics.

malady *(SYN.)* disease, illness, sickness, ailment, infirmity, disorder, affliction.

(ANT.) vigor, healthiness, health.

malaise *(SYN.)* anxiety, apprehension, dissatisfaction, uneasiness, nervousness, disquiet, discontent.

male *(SYN.)* masculine, virile.

(ANT.) female, womanly, feminine.

malcontent *(SYN.)* displeased, ill-humored, querulous, discontented, quarrelsome.

malefactor *(SYN.)* perpetrator, gangster, hoodlum, wrongdoer, troublemaker, criminal, scoundrel, evildoer, lawbreaker.

malevolence *(SYN.)* spite, malice, enmity, rancor, animosity.

(ANT.) love, affection, toleration, kindness.

malfunction *(SYN.)* flaw, breakdown, snag, glitch, failure.

malice *(SYN.)* spite, grudge, enmity, ill will, malignity, animosity, rancor, resentment, viciousness, grudge, bitterness.

(ANT.) love, affection, toleration, benevolence, charity.

malicious *(SYN.)* hostile, malignant, virulent, bitter, rancorous, malevolent, spiteful.

(ANT.) kind, benevolent, affectionate.

malign *(SYN.)* misuse, defame, revile, abuse, traduce, asperse.

(ANT.) praise, protect, honor.

malignant *(SYN.)* harmful, deadly, killing, lethal, mortal, destructive.

(ANT.) benign, harmless.

malingerer *(SYN.)* quitter, idler, gold-brick.

malleable *(SYN.)* meek, tender, soft, lenient, flexible, mild, compassionate, supple.

(ANT.) tough, rigid, unyielding, hard.

malodorous *(SYN.)* reeking, fetid, noxious, vile, rancid, offensive,

malpractice *(SYN.)* wrongdoing, misdeed, abuse, malfeasance, error, mismanagement, dereliction, fault, sin, misconduct.

maltreat *(SYN.)* mistreat, ill-treatment, abuse.

maltreatment *(SYN.)* disparagement, perversion, aspersion, invective, defamation, profanation.

(ANT.) respect, approval, laudation, commendation.

mammoth *(SYN.)* enormous, immense, huge, colossal, gigantic, gargantuan, ponderous.

(ANT.) minuscule, tiny, small.

man *(SYN.)* person, human being, society, folk, soul, individual, mortal, fellow, male, gentleman.

(ANT.) woman.

manacle *(SYN.)* chain, shackle, cuff, handcuff, bond.

manage (SYN.) curb, govern, direct, bridle, command, regulate, repress, check, restrain, dominate, guide, lead, supervise, superintend, control, rule.

(ANT.) forsake, submit, abandon, mismanage, bungle.

manageable (SYN.) willing, obedient, docile, controllable, tractable, submissive, governable, wieldy, untroublesome.

(ANT.) recalcitrant, unmanageable, wild.

management (SYN.) regulation, administration, supervision, direction, control.

manager (SYN.) overseer, boss, superintendent, supervisor, executive, director, .

mandate (SYN.) order, injunction, command, referendum, dictate, writ, directive, commission.

mandatory (SYN.) compulsory, required, obligatory, imperative.

(ANT.) optional.

maneuver (SYN.) execution, effort, proceeding, enterprise, working, action, operation, agency.

(ANT.) rest, inaction, cessation.

mangle (SYN.) tear apart, cut, maim, wound, mutilate, injure.

mangy (SYN.) shoddy, frazzled, seedy, threadbare, shabby.

manhandle (SYN.) maltreat, maul, abuse, ill-treat.

manhood (SYN.) maturity, manliness.

(ANT.) youth.

mania (SYN.) insanity, enthusiasm, craze, desire, madness.

manic (SYN.) excited, hyped up, agitated.

manifest (SYN.) open, evident, lucid, clear, distinct, unobstructed, cloudless, apparent, intelligible, apparent.

(ANT.) vague, overcast, unclear, cloudy, hidden, concealed

manifesto (SYN.) pronouncement, edict, proclamation, statement.

manifold (SYN.) various, many, multiple, numerous, abundant.

(ANT.) few.

manipulate (SYN.) manage, work, operate, handle, touch.

manly (SYN.) strong, brave, masculine, courageous, stalwart.

man-made (SYN.) artificial.

(ANT.) natural.

manner (SYN.) air, demeanor, custom, style, method, deportment, mode, habit, practice, way, behavior, fashion.

mannerism (SYN.) eccentricity, quirk, habit, peculiarity, idiosyncrasy, trait.

mannerly (SYN.) well-bred, courteous, suave, polite, genteel.

manor (SYN.) land, mansion, estate, domain, villa, castle, property, palace.

manslaughter (SYN.) murder, killing, assassination, homicide, elimination.

mantle (SYN.) serape, garment, overgarment, cover, cloak, wrap.

manual (SYN.) directory, guidebook, handbook, physical, laborious, menial.

manufacture *(SYN.)* construct, make, assemble, fabricate, produce, fashion, build.

manure *(SYN.)* fertilizer, droppings, waste, compost.

manuscript *(SYN.)* copy, writing, work, paper, composition, document.

many *(SYN.)* numerous, various, divers, multitudinous, sundry, multifarious, several, manifold, abundant, plentiful.
(ANT.) infrequent, meager, few, scanty.

map *(SYN.)* sketch, plan, chart, graph, itinerary.

mar *(SYN.)* spoil, hurt, damage, impair, harm, deface, injure.
(ANT.) repair, benefit, mend.

marathon *(SYN.)* relay, race, contest.

maraud *(SYN.)* invade, plunder, loot, ransack, ravage, raid.

march *(SYN.)* promenade, parade, pace, hike, walk, tramp.

margin *(SYN.)* boundary, border, rim, edge.

marginal *(SYN.)* unnecessary, nonessential, borderline, noncritical.
(ANT.) essential.

marine *(SYN.)* naval, oceanic, nautical, ocean, maritime.

mariner *(SYN.)* seafarer, gob, seaman, sailor.

marionette *(SYN.)* doll, puppet.

maritime *(SYN.)* shore, coastal, nautical.

mark *(SYN.)* stain, badge, stigma, vestige, sign, feature,

label, characteristic, trace, brand, trait, scar, indication, impression, effect, imprint, stamp, brand.

marked *(SYN.)* plain, apparent, noticeable, evident, decided, noted, special, noteworthy.

market *(SYN.)* supermarket, store, bazaar, mart, stall, marketplace, plaza, emporium.

maroon *(SYN.)* desert, leave behind, forsake, abandon, jettison.

marriage *(SYN.)* wedding, matrimony, nuptials, espousal, union, alliance, association.
(ANT.) divorce, celibacy, separation.

marrow *(SYN.)* center, core, gist, essential, soul.

marry *(SYN.)* wed, espouse, betroth.

marsh *(SYN.)* bog, swamp, mire, everglade, estuary.

marshal *(SYN.)* adjutant, officer, order, arrange, rank.

mart *(SYN.)* shop, market, store.

martial *(SYN.)* warlike, combative, militant, belligerent.
(ANT.) peaceful.

martyr *(SYN.)* victim, sufferer, tortured, torment, plague, harass, persecute.

marvel *(SYN.)* phenomenon, wonder, miracle, astonishment, sensation.

marvelous *(SYN.)* rare, wonderful, unusual, exceptional, miraculous, wondrous, amazing, astonishing, astounding.
(ANT.) usual, common, ordinary, commonplace.

mascot *(SYN.)* pet, amulet, charm.

masculine *(SYN.)* robust, manly, virile, strong, bold, male, lusty, vigorous, hardy, mannish.

(ANT.) weak, emasculated, feminine, female, effeminate, womanish, unmasculine.

mash *(SYN.)* mix, pulverize, crush, grind, crumble, granulate.

mask *(SYN.)* veil, disguise, cloak, secrete, withhold, hide, cover, protection, protector, camouflage, conceal, screen.

(ANT.) uncover, reveal, disclose, show, expose.

masquerade *(SYN.)* pretend, disguise, pose, impersonate, costume party.

mass *(SYN.)* society, torso, body, remains, association, carcass, bulk, company, pile, heap, quantity, aggregation.

(ANT.) spirit, mind, intellect.

massacre *(SYN.)* butcher, murder, carnage, slaughter, execute, slay, genocide, killing, butchery, extermination.

(ANT.) save, protect, vivify, animate.

massage *(SYN.)* knead, rub, stroke.

masses *(SYN.)* populace, crowd, multitude, people.

massive *(SYN.)* grave, cumbersome, heavy, sluggish, ponderous, serious, burdensome, huge, immense, tremendous, gigantic.

(ANT.) light, animated, small, tiny, little.

mast *(SYN.)* pole, post.

master *(SYN.)* owner, employer, leader, ruler, chief, head, lord, teacher, manager, holder, commander, overseer, expert, maestro, genius, captain, director, boss.

(ANT.) slave, servant.

masterful *(SYN.)* commanding, bossy, domineering, dictatorial, cunning, wise, accomplished, skillful, sharp.

masterly *(SYN.)* adroit, superb, skillful, expert.

(ANT.) awkward, clumsy.

mastermind *(SYN.)* prodigy, sage, guru, mentor.

masterpiece *(SYN.)* prizewinner, classic, perfection, model.

mastery *(SYN.)* sway, sovereignty, domination, transcendence, ascendancy, influence, jurisdiction, prestige.

masticate *(SYN.)* chew.

mat *(SYN.)* cover, rug, pallet, bedding, pad.

match *(SYN.)* equivalent, equal, contest, balance, resemble, peer, mate.

matchless *(SYN.)* peerless, incomparable, unequaled, unrivaled, excellent.

(ANT.) ordinary, unimpressive.

mate *(SYN.)* friend, colleague, associate, partner, companion, comrade.

(ANT.) stranger, adversary.

material *(SYN.)* sensible, momentous, germane, palpable, important, physical, essential, corporeal, tangible, substance, matter, fabric.

(ANT.) metaphysical, spiritual, insignificant, mental, immaterial, irrelevant, intangible.

materialize *(SYN.)* take shape, finalize, embody, incarnate, emerge, appear.

maternal *(SYN.)* motherly. *(ANT.) fatherly.*

mathematics *(SYN.)* measurements, computations, numbers, add, calculation, figures.

matrimony *(SYN.)* marriage, wedding, espousal, union. *(ANT.) virginity, divorce.*

matrix *(SYN.)* template, stamp, negative, stencil, mold, form, die, cutout.

matron *(SYN.)* lady.

matted *(SYN.)* tangled, clustered, rumpled, shaggy, knotted, gnarled, tousled.

matter *(SYN.)* cause, thing, substance, occasion, material, moment, topic, stuff, concern, theme, subject, consequence, affair, business, interest. *(ANT.) spirit, immateriality.*

mature *(SYN.)* ready, matured, complete, ripe, consummate, mellow, aged, seasoned, fullgrown. *(ANT.) raw, crude, undeveloped, young, immature, innocent.*

maudlin *(SYN.)* emotional, mushy, sentimental, mawkish.

maul *(SYN.)* pummel, mistreat, manhandle, beat, batter, bruise, abuse.

mausoleum *(SYN.)* shrine, tomb, vault.

maverick *(SYN.)* nonconformist, oddball, outsider, dissenter, loner.

mawkish *(SYN.)* sentimental, emotional, nostalgic.

maxim *(SYN.)* rule, code, law, proverb, principle, saying, adage, motto.

maximum *(SYN.)* highest, largest, greatest, supremacy, climax. *(ANT.) minimum.*

may *(SYN.)* can, be able.

maybe *(SYN.)* feasibly, perchance, perhaps, possibly. *(ANT.) definitely.*

mayhem *(SYN.)* brutality, viciousness, ruthlessness.

maze *(SYN.)* complex, labyrinth, network, muddle, confusion, snarl, tangle.

meadow *(SYN.)* field, pasture, lea, range, grassland.

meager *(SYN.)* sparse, scanty, mean, frugal, deficient, slight, paltry, inadequate. *(ANT.) ample, plentiful, abundant, bountiful.*

meal *(SYN.)* refreshment, dinner, lunch, repast, breakfast.

mean *(SYN.)* sordid, base, intend, plan, propose, expect, indicate, denote, say, signify, suggest, express, average, nasty, middle, contemptible, offensive, vulgar, unkind, cruel, despicable, vile, low. *(ANT.) dignified, noble, exalted, thoughtful, gentle, openhanded, kind, generous, admirable.*

meander *(SYN.)* wind, stray, wander, twist

meaning *(SYN.)* gist, connotation, intent, purport, drift, acceptation, implication, sense, import, interpretation, denotation, signification, explanation, significance.

meaningful *(SYN.)* profound, deep, expressive, important, crucial.

meaningless *(SYN.)* nonsensical, senseless, unreasonable, preposterous.

means *(SYN.)* utensil, channel, agent, money, riches, vehicle, apparatus, device, wealth, support, medium, instrument.
(ANT.) preventive, impediment, hindrance.

measly *(SYN.)* scanty, puny, skimpy, meager, petty.

measure *(SYN.)* law, bulk, rule, criterion, size, volume, weight, standard, dimension, breadth, depth, test, touchstone, trial, length, extent, gauge.
(ANT.) guess, chance, supposition.

measureless *(SYN.)* immeasurable, immense, boundless, limitless, infinite, vast.
(ANT.) figurable, ascertainable, measurable.

meat *(SYN.)* lean, flesh, food.

mecca *(SYN.)* target, shrine, goal, sanctuary, destination.

mechanic *(SYN.)* repairman, machinist.

mechanism *(SYN.)* device, contrivance, tool, machine, machinery.

medal *(SYN.)* decoration, award, badge, medallion, reward, ribbon, prize, honor.

meddle *(SYN.)* tamper, interpose, pry, snoop, intrude,

interrupt, interfere, monkey.

meddlesome *(SYN.)* forward, bothersome, intrusive, obtrusive.

media *(SYN.)* tools, instruments, implements.

mediate *(SYN.)* settle, intercede, umpire, intervene, negotiate, arbitrate, referee.

medicinal *(SYN.)* helping, healing, remedial, therapeutic, corrective.

medicine *(SYN.)* drug, medication, remedy, cure, prescription.

mediocre *(SYN.)* medium, mean, average, moderate, fair, ordinary.
(ANT.) outstanding, exceptional.

meditate *(SYN.)* remember, muse, think, judge, mean, conceive, plan, contemplate, deem, suppose, purpose, consider, picture, reflect, believe, reckon.

medium *(SYN.)* modicum, average, middling, median.
(ANT.) extreme.

medley *(SYN.)* hodgepodge, mixture, assortment, conglomeration, mishmash, miscellany.

meek *(SYN.)* subdued, dull, tedious, flat, docile, domesticated, tame, insipid, domestic.
(ANT.) spirited, exciting, savage, wild.

meet *(SYN.)* fulfill, suffer, find, collide, gratify, engage, connect, converge, encounter, unite, join, satisfy, settle, greet, answer, undergo, meeting, contest, match, assemble, discharge, gather, convene, congregate, confront, intersect.

(ANT.) scatter, disperse, separate, cleave.

melancholy *(SYN.)* disconsolate, dejected, despondent, somber, pensive, moody, dispirited, depressed, gloomy, dismal, doleful, depression, sad, downcast, gloom, sadness, grave, downhearted, sorrowful.

(ANT.) happy, cheerful, merry.

meld *(SYN.)* unite, mix, combine, fuse, merge, blend, commingle, amalgamate.

melee *(SYN.)* battle royal, fight, brawl, free-for-all, fracas.

mellow *(SYN.)* mature, ripe, aged, cured, sweet, smooth, melodious, develop, soften.

(ANT.) unripened, immature.

melodious *(SYN.)* lilting, musical, lyric, dulcet, mellifluous, tuneful.

melodramatic *(SYN.)* dramatic, ceremonious, affected, stagy, histrionic, overwrought, sensational, stagy.

(ANT.) unemotional, subdued, modest.

melody *(SYN.)* strain, concord, music, air, song, tune, harmony.

melt *(SYN.)* dissolve, liquefy, blend, fade out, vanish, dwindle, disappear, thaw.

(ANT.) freeze, harden, solidify.

member *(SYN.)* share, part, allotment, moiety, element, concern, interest, lines, faction, role.

(ANT.) whole.

membrane *(SYN.)* layer, sheath, tissue, covering.

memento *(SYN.)* keepsake, token, reminder, trophy, sign, souvenir, remembrance.

memoirs *(SYN.)* diary, reflections, experiences, autobiography, journal, confessions.

memorable *(SYN.)* important, historic, significant, unforgettable, noteworthy, momentous, crucial.

(ANT.) passing, forgettable, transitory, commonplace.

memorandum *(SYN.)* letter, mark, token, note, indication, remark.

memorial *(SYN.)* monument, souvenir, ritual, memento, remembrance, eulogizing honoring, commemoration, reminiscent, testimonial.

memorize *(SYN.)* remember.

memory *(SYN.)* renown, remembrance, reminiscence, fame, retrospection, recollection.

(ANT.) oblivion.

menace *(SYN.)* warning, threat, intimidation, warn, threaten, imperil, forebode.

menagerie *(SYN.)* collection, zoo, kennel.

mend *(SYN.)* restore, better, refit, sew, remedy, patch, correct, repair, rectify, ameliorate, improve, reform, recover, fix.

(ANT.) hurt, deface, destroy.

mendacious *(SYN.)* dishonest, false, lying, deceitful, deceptive, tricky.

(ANT.) honest, truthful, sincere, creditable.

mendicant *(SYN.)* ragamuffin, vagabond, beggar.

menial *(SYN.)* unskilled, lowly, degrading, tedious, humble.

mental *(SYN.)* reasoning, intellectual, rational, thinking, conscious, mad, thoughtful, psychotic.

(ANT.) physical.

mentality *(SYN.)* intellect, reason, understanding, liking, disposition, judgment, brain, inclination, faculties, outlook.

(ANT.) materiality, corporeality.

mention *(SYN.)* introduce, refer to, reference, allude, enumerate, speak of.

mentor *(SYN.)* advisor, tutor, sponsor, guru, teacher, counselor, master, coach.

mercenary *(SYN.)* sordid, corrupt, venal, covetous, grasping, avaricious, greedy.

(ANT.) liberal, generous.

merchandise *(SYN.)* stock, wares, goods, sell, commodities, promote, staples, products.

merchant *(SYN.)* retailer, dealer, trader, storekeeper, salesman, businessman.

merciful *(SYN.)* humane, kindhearted, tender, clement, sympathetic, forgiving, tolerant, forbearing, lenient, compassionate, tenderhearted, kind.

(ANT.) remorseless, cruel, unjust, mean, harsh, unforgiving, vengeful, brutal, unfeeling, pitiless.

merciless *(SYN.)* carnal, ferocious, brute, barbarous, gross, ruthless, cruel, remorseless, bestial, savage, rough, pitiless, inhuman.

(ANT.) humane, courteous, merciful, openhearted, kind, civilized.

mercurial *(SYN.)* fickle, unstable, volatile, changeable, inconstant, capricious, flighty.

mercy *(SYN.)* grace, consideration, kindness, clemency, mildness, forgiveness, pity, charity, sympathy, leniency, compassion.

(ANT.) punishment, retribution, cruelty, vengeance.

mere *(SYN.)* only, simple, scant, bare.

(ANT.) substantial, considerable.

merely *(SYN.)* only, barely, simply, hardly.

meretricious *(SYN.)* gaudy, sham, bogus, tawdry, flashy, garish.

merge *(SYN.)* unify, fuse, combine, unite, amalgamate, blend, commingle.

(ANT.) separate, decompose, analyze.

merger *(SYN.)* cartel, union, conglomerate, trust, incorporation, combine, pool.

meridian *(SYN.)* climax, summit, pinnacle, zenith, peak, acme, apex, culmination.

merit *(SYN.)* worthiness, earn, effectiveness, power, value, virtue, goodness, quality, deserve, excellence, worth.

(ANT.) sin, fault, lose, consume.

merited (SYN.) proper, deserved, suitable, adequate, earned.

(ANT.) unmerited, improper.

meritorious (SYN.) laudable, excellent, commendable, good, deserving.

merry (SYN.) hilarious, lively, festive, joyous, sprightly, mirthful, blithe, gay, cheery, joyful, jolly, happy, gleeful, jovial, cheerful.

(ANT.) sorrowful, doleful, morose, gloomy, sad, melancholy.

mesh (SYN.) grid, screen, net, complex.

mesmerize (SYN.) enthrall, transfix, spellbind, bewitch, charm, fascinate, hypnotize.

mess (SYN.) dirtiness, untidiness, disorder, confusion, muddle, trouble, jumble, difficulty, predicament, confuse, dirty.

message (SYN.) letter, annotation, memo, symbol, sign, indication, note, memorandum, communication, observation, token.

messenger (SYN.) bearer, agent, runner, courier, liaison, delegate, page.

messy (SYN.) disorderly, dirty, confusing, confused, disordered, sloppy, untidy.

(ANT.) orderly, neat, tidy.

metallic (SYN.) grating, harsh, clanging, brassy, brazen.

metamorphosis (SYN.) transfiguration, change, alteration, rebirth, mutation.

mete (SYN.) deal, assign, apportion, divide, give, allocate, allot, measure.

(ANT.) withhold, keep, retain.

meteoric (SYN.) flashing, blazing, swift, brilliant, spectacular, remarkable.

meter (SYN.) record, measure, gauge.

method (SYN.) order, manner, plan, way, mode, technique, fashion, approach, design, procedure.

(ANT.) disorder.

methodical (SYN.) exact, definite, ceremonious, stiff, accurate, distinct, unequivocal.

(ANT.) easy, loose, informal, rough.

meticulous (SYN.) precise, careful, exacting, fastidious, fussy, perfectionist.

metropolitan (SYN.) civic, city, municipal.

mettle (SYN.) intrepidity, resolution, boldness, prowess, bravery, fearlessness.

(ANT.) fear, timidity, cowardice.

microscopic (SYN.) tiny, precise, fine, detailed, minute, infinitesimal, minimal.

(ANT.) general, huge, enormous.

middle (SYN.) midpoint, nucleus, center, midst, median, central, intermediate, core.

(ANT.) end, rim, outskirts, beginning, border, periphery.

middleman (SYN.) dealer, agent, distributor, broker, representative, intermediary, liaison.

midget (SYN.) gnome, shrimp, pygmy, runt, dwarf.

midst 201 miniature

(ANT.) giant.

midst *(SYN.)* center, heart, middle, thick.

midway *(SYN.)* halfway, midmost, inside, central, middle.

mien *(SYN.)* way, semblance, manner, behavior, demeanor, expression, deportment, style.

miff *(SYN.)* provoke, rile, chagrin, irk, irritate, affront, offend, annoy, exasperate.

might *(SYN.)* force, power, vigor, potency, strength.

(ANT.) frailty, vulnerability, weakness.

mighty *(SYN.)* firm, fortified, powerful, athletic, potent, muscular, robust, strong, cogent.

(ANT.) feeble, weak, brittle, insipid, frail, delicate.

migrant *(SYN.)* traveling, roaming, straying, roving, rambling, transient, meandering.

(ANT.) stationary.

migrate *(SYN.)* resettle, move, emigrate, immigrate, relocate, journey.

(ANT.) stay, remain, settle.

migratory *(SYN.)* itinerant, roving, mobile, vagabond, unsettled, nomadic, wandering.

mild *(SYN.)* soothing, moderate, gentle, tender, bland, pleasant, kind, meek, calm, amiable, compassionate, temperate, peaceful, soft.

(ANT.) severe, turbulent, stormy, excitable, violent, harsh, bitter.

milieu *(SYN.)* environment, background, locale, setting, scene, circumstances.

militant *(SYN.)* warlike, belligerent, hostile, fighting, pugnacious, aggressive, combative.

(ANT.) peaceful.

military *(SYN.)* troops, army, service, soldiers.

milksop *(SYN.)* weakling, sissy, coward.

mill *(SYN.)* foundry, shop, plant, factory, manufactory.

millstone *(SYN.)* load, impediment, burden, encumbrance, hindrance.

mimic *(SYN.)* simulate, duplicate, copy, imitate, mock, counterfeit, simulate.

(ANT.) invent, distort, alter.

mince *(SYN.)* shatter, fragment, chop, smash.

mind *(SYN.)* intelligence, psyche, disposition, intention, understanding, intellect, spirit, brain, inclination, mentality, soul, wit, liking, sense, watch, faculties, judgment, reason.

(ANT.) matter, corporeality.

mindful *(SYN.)* alert, aware, watchful, cognizant, watchful, sensible, heedful.

mine *(SYN.)* shaft, lode, pit, excavation, drill, dig, quarry, source.

mingle *(SYN.)* unite, coalesce, fuse, merge, combine, amalgamate, unify, conjoin, mix, blend, commingle.

(ANT.) separate, analyze, sort, disintegrate.

miniature *(SYN.)* small, little, tiny, midget, minute, minuscule, wee, petite, diminutive.

(ANT.) outsize.

minimize (SYN.) shorten, deduct, belittle, decrease, reduce, curtail, lessen, diminish, subtract.

(ANT.) enlarge, increase, amplify.

minimum (SYN.) lowest, least, smallest, slightest.

(ANT.) maximum.

minister (SYN.) pastor, clergyman, vicar, parson, curate, preacher, prelate, chaplain, cleric, deacon, reverend.

minor (SYN.) poorer, lesser, petty, youth, inferior, secondary, smaller, unimportant, lower.

(ANT.) higher, superior, major, greater.

minority (SYN.) youth, childhood, immaturity.

minstrel (SYN.) bard, musician.

mint (SYN.) stamp, coin, strike, punch.

minus (SYN.) lacking, missing, less, absent, without.

minute (SYN.) tiny, particular, fine, precise, jiffy, instant, moment, wee, exact, detailed, microscopic.

(ANT.) large, general, huge, enormous.

miraculous (SYN.) spiritual, supernatural, strange, wonderful, marvelous, incredible, preternatural.

(ANT.) commonplace, natural, common, plain, everyday, human.

mirage (SYN.) vision, illusion, fantasy, dream, phantom.

(ANT.) reality, actuality.

mire (SYN.) marsh, slush, slime, mud.

mirror (SYN.) glass, reflector, reflect.

mirth (SYN.) joy, glee, jollity, joyousness, gaiety, joyfulness, laughter, merriment.

(ANT.) sadness, gloom, seriousness.

misadventure (SYN.) accident, adversity, reverse, calamity, catastrophe, hardship, mischance, setback.

misappropriate (SYN.) embezzle, steal, purloin, plunder, cheat, filch, defraud.

misbehave (SYN.) trespass, act badly.

(ANT.) behave.

miscalculate (SYN.) miscount, blunder, confuse, err, mistake, misconstrue.

miscarriage (SYN.) omission, want, decay, fiasco, default, deficiency, loss, abortion, prematurity.

(ANT.) success, sufficiency, achievement.

miscarry (SYN.) flounder, fall short, falter, fail.

(ANT.) succeed.

miscellaneous (SYN.) mixed, diverse, motley, indiscriminate, assorted, sundry, heterogeneous, varied.

(ANT.) classified, selected, homogeneous, alike, ordered.

miscellany (SYN.) medley, gallimaufry, jumble, potpourri, mixture, collection.

mischief (SYN.) injury, harm, damage, evil, ill, prankishness, rascality, roguishness, playfulness, wrong, detriment, hurt.

(ANT.) kindness, boon, benefit.

mischievous *(SYN.)* roguish, prankish, naughty, playful.

(ANT.) well-behaved, good.

misconduct *(SYN.)* transgression, delinquency, wrongdoing, negligence.

miscreant *(SYN.)* rascal, wretch, rogue, sinner, criminal, villain, scoundrel.

miscue *(SYN.)* blunder, fluff, mistake, error, lapse.

misdemeanor *(SYN.)* infringement, transgression, violation, offense, wrong.

miser *(SYN.)* cheapskate, tightwad, skinflint.

(ANT.) philanthropist.

miserable *(SYN.)* abject, forlorn, comfortless, worthless, pitiable, low, distressed, heartbroken, disconsolate, despicable, wretched, uncomfortable, unhappy, poor, unlucky, paltry, contemptible, mean.

(ANT.) fortunate, happy, contented, joyful, content, wealthy, honorable, lucky, noble, significant.

miserly *(SYN.)* stingy, greedy, acquisitive, tight, tightfisted, cheap, mean, parsimonious, avaricious.

(ANT.) bountiful, generous, spendthrift, munificent, extravagant, altruistic.

misery *(SYN.)* suffering, pain, woe, evil, agony, torment, trouble, distress, anguish, grief, unhappiness, tribulation, calamity, sorrow.

(ANT.) fun, pleasure, delight, joy.

misfit *(SYN.)* crank, loner, deviate, fifth wheel, individualist.

misfortune *(SYN.)* adversity, distress, mishap, calamity, accident, catastrophe, hardship, ruin, disaster, affliction.

(ANT.) success, blessing, prosperity.

misgiving *(SYN.)* suspicion, doubt, mistrust, hesitation, uncertainty.

misguided *(SYN.)* misdirected, misled, misinformed, wrong, unwise, foolish, erroneous, unwarranted, ill-advised.

mishap *(SYN.)* misfortune, casualty, accident, disaster, adversity, reverse.

(ANT.) intention, calculation, purpose.

mishmash *(SYN.)* medley, muddle, gallimaufry, hodgepodge, hash.

misjudge *(SYN.)* err, mistake, miscalculate.

mislay *(SYN.)* misplace, lose.

(ANT.) discover, find.

mislead *(SYN.)* misdirect, deceive, misinform, deceive, delude.

misleading *(SYN.)* fallacious, delusive, deceitful, false, deceptive, illusive.

(ANT.) real, genuine, truthful, honest.

mismatched *(SYN.)* unfit, incompatible, unsuited.

misplace *(SYN.)* lose, mislay, miss.

(ANT.) find.

misrepresent *(SYN.)* misstate,

distort, falsify, twist, belie, garble, disguise.

miss *(SYN.)* lose, want, crave, yearn for, fumble, drop, error, slip, default, omit, lack, need, desire, fail.

(ANT.) suffice, have, achieve, succeed.

misshapen *(SYN.)* disfigured, deformed, grotesque, malformed, ungainly, gnarled, contorted.

missile *(SYN.)* grenade, shot, projectile.

missing *(SYN.)* wanting, lacking, absent, lost, gone, vanished.

mission *(SYN.)* business, task, job, stint, work, errand, assignment, delegation.

missionary *(SYN.)* publicist, evangelist, propagandist.

mist *(SYN.)* cloud, fog, haze, steam, haze.

mistake *(SYN.)* slip, misjudge, fault, blunder, misunderstand, confuse, inaccuracy, misinterpret, error.

(ANT.) truth, accuracy.

mistaken *(SYN.)* false, amiss, incorrect, awry, wrong, misinformed, confused, inaccurate, askew.

(ANT.) true, correct, suitable, right.

mister *(SYN.)* young man, gentleman, esquire, fellow.

mistreat *(SYN.)* wrong, pervert, oppress, harm, abuse.

mistrust *(SYN.)* suspect, doubt, distrust, dispute, question, skepticism, apprehension.

(ANT.) trust.

misunderstand *(SYN.)* misjudge, misinterpret, jumble, confuse, mistake.

(ANT.) perceive, comprehend.

misunderstanding *(SYN.)* clash, disagreement, dispute, conflict, misinterpretation.

misuse *(SYN.)* defame, malign, abuse, misapply, traduce, asperse, revile, vilify.

(ANT.) protect, honor, respect, cherish.

mite *(SYN.)* particle, mote, smidgen, trifle, iota, corpuscle.

mitigate *(SYN.)* soften, soothe, abate, assuage, relieve, allay, diminish.

(ANT.) irritate, agitate.

mix *(SYN.)* mingle, blend, consort, fuse, alloy, combine, jumble, fraternize, associate, concoct, commingle, amalgamate, join, confound, compound.

(ANT.) divide, sort, segregate, dissociate, separate.

mixture *(SYN.)* diversity, variety, strain, sort, change, kind, confusion, jumble, mess, mix, assortment, breed, hodgepodge, subspecies.

(ANT.) likeness, sameness, homogeneity, monotony.

moan *(SYN.)* wail, groan, cry, lament.

moat *(SYN.)* fortification, ditch, trench, entrenchment.

mob *(SYN.)* crowd, host, populace, swarm, riot, bevy, horde, rabble, throng, multitude.

mobile *(SYN.)* free, movable, portable.

(ANT.) stationary, immobile, fixed.

mock *(SYN.)* taunt, jeer, deride, scoff, scorn, fleer, ridicule, tease, fake, imitation, sham, gibe, sneer, fraudulent, flout.

(ANT.) praise, applaud, real, genuine, honor, authentic, compliment.

mockery *(SYN.)* gibe, ridicule, satire, derision, sham, banter, irony, sneering, scorn, travesty, jeering.

(ANT.) admiration, praise.

mode *(SYN.)* method, fashion, procedure, design, manner, technique, way, style, practice, plan.

(ANT.) disorder, confusion.

model *(SYN.)* copy, prototype, type, example, ideal, imitation, version, facsimile, design, style, archetype, pattern, standard, mold.

(ANT.) reproduction, imitation.

moderate *(SYN.)* lower, decrease, average, fair, reasonable, abate, medium, conservative, referee, umpire, suppress, judge, lessen, assuage.

(ANT.) intensify, enlarge, amplify.

moderation *(SYN.)* sobriety, forbearance, self-control, restraint, continence, temperance.

(ANT.) greed, excess, intoxication.

moderator *(SYN.)* referee, leader, arbitrator, chairman, chairperson, master of ceremonies, emcee.

modern *(SYN.)* modish, current, recent, novel, fresh, contemporary, new.

(ANT.) old, antiquated, past, bygone, ancient.

modernize *(SYN.)* refurnish, refurbish, improve, rebuild, renew, renovate.

modest *(SYN.)* unassuming, virtuous, bashful, meek, shy, humble, decent, demure, unpretentious, prudish, moderate, reserved.

(ANT.) forward, bold, ostentatious, conceited, immodest, arrogant.

modesty *(SYN.)* decency, humility, propriety, simplicity, shyness.

(ANT.) conceit, vanity, pride.

modicum *(SYN.)* particle, fragment, grain, trifle, smidgen, bit.

modification *(SYN.)* alternation, substitution, variety, change, alteration.

(ANT.) uniformity, monotony.

modify *(SYN.)* shift, vary, alter, change, convert, adjust, temper, moderate, curb, exchange, transform, veer.

(ANT.) settle, establish, retain, stabilize.

modish *(SYN.)* current, fashionable, chick, stylish, voguish.

modulate *(SYN.)* temper, align, balance, correct, regulate, adjust, modify.

module *(SYN.)* unit, measure, norm, dimension, component, gauge.

modus operandi *(SYN.)* method, technique, system, means, process, workings, procedure.

mogul *(SYN.)* bigwig, personage, figure, tycoon, magnate, potentate.

moiety *(SYN.)* part, scrap, share, allotment, piece, division, portion.

moist *(SYN.)* damp, humid, dank, muggy, clammy.

moisten *(SYN.)* wet, dampen, sponge.
(ANT.) dry.

moisture *(SYN.)* wetness, mist, dampness, condensation, evaporation, vapor, humidity.
(ANT.) aridity, dryness.

mold *(SYN.)* make, fashion, organize, produce, forge, constitute, create, combine, construct, form, pattern, format.
(ANT.) wreck, dismantle, destroy, misshape.

moldy *(SYN.)* dusty, crumbling, dank, old, deteriorating.

molest *(SYN.)* irk, disturb, trouble, annoy, pester, bother, vex, inconvenience.
(ANT.) console, accommodate.

mollify *(SYN.)* soothe, compose, quiet, humor, appease, tranquilize, pacify.

molt *(SYN.)* slough off, shed, cast off.

molten *(SYN.)* fusible, melted, smelted, redhot.

moment *(SYN.)* flash, jiffy, instant, twinkling, gravity, importance, consequence, seriousness.

momentary *(SYN.)* concise, pithy, brief, curt, terse, laconic, compendious.
(ANT.) long, extended, pro-
longed.

momentous *(SYN.)* critical, serious, essential, grave, material, weighty, consequential, decisive, important.
(ANT.) unimportant, trifling, mean, trivial, tribial, insignificant.

momentum *(SYN.)* impetus, push, thrust, force, impulse, drive, vigor, propulsion, energy.

monarch *(SYN.)* ruler, king, queen, empress, emperor, sovereign.

monastic *(SYN.)* withdrawn, dedicated, austere, unworldly, celibate, abstinent, ascetic.

monastery *(SYN.)* convent, priory, abbey, hermitage, cloister.

money *(SYN.)* cash, bills, coin, notes, currency, funds, specie, capital.

monger *(SYN.)* seller, hawker, huckster, trader, merchant, shopkeeper, retailer, vendor.

mongrel *(SYN.)* mixed-breed, hybrid, mutt.

monitor *(SYN.)* director, supervisor, advisor, observe, watch, control.

monkey *(SYN.)* tamper, interfere, interrupt, interpose.

monogram *(SYN.)* mark, stamp, signature

monograph *(SYN.)* publication, report, thesis, biography, treatise, paper, dissertation.

monologue *(SYN.)* discourse, lecture, sermon, talk, speech, address, soliloquy, oration.

monomania *(SYN.)* obsessiveness, passion, single-mindedness, extremism.

monopoly (SYN.) corner, control, possession.

monotonous (SYN.) dull, slow, tiresome, boring, humdrum, dilatory, tiring, irksome, tedious, burdensome, wearisome.

(ANT.) interesting, riveting, quick, fascinating, exciting, amusing.

monsoon (SYN.) storm, rains.

monster (SYN.) brute, beast, villain, demon, fiend, wretch.

monstrous (SYN.) tremendous, huge, gigantic, immense, enormous, revolting, repulsive, shocking, horrible, hideous, terrible.

(ANT.) diminutive, tiny, miniature, small.

monument (SYN.) remembrance, landmark, memento, commemoration, headstone, souvenir, statue, shrine.

monumental (SYN.) enormous, huge, colossal, immense, gigantic, important, significant.

mood (SYN.) joke, irony, waggery, temper, disposition, temperament, sarcasm.

(ANT.) sorrow, gravity.

moody (SYN.) morose, fretful, crabbed, changeable, sulky, dour, short-tempered, testy, temperamental, irritable, peevish, glum.

(ANT.) good-natured, even-tempered, merry, gay, pleasant, joyous.

moor (SYN.) tether, fasten, tie, dock, anchor, bind.

moorings (SYN.) marina, slip, harbor, basin, landing, dock, wharf, pier, anchorage.

moot (SYN.) unsettled, questionable, problematical, controversial, contestable.

mop (SYN.) wash, wipe, swab, scrub.

mope (SYN.) gloom, pout, whine, grumble, grieve, sulk, fret.

(ANT.) rejoice.

moral (SYN.) just, right, chaste, good, virtuous, pure, decent, honest, upright, ethical, righteous, honorable, scrupulous.

(ANT.) libertine, immoral, unethical, licentious, amoral, sinful.

morale (SYN.) confidence, spirit, assurance.

morality (SYN.) worth, virtue, strength, chastity, probity, force, merit.

(ANT.) fault, sin, corruption, vice.

morals (SYN.) conduct, scruples, guidelines, behavior, life style, standards.

morass (SYN.) fen, march, swamp, mire.

morbid (SYN.) sickly, unwholesome, awful, unhealthy, ghastly, horrible, shocking, decaying.

(ANT.) pleasant, healthy.

more (SYN.) further, greater, farther, extra, another.

(ANT.) less.

moreover (SYN.) further, in addition, also, furthermore, besides.

mores (SYN.) standards, rituals,

rules, customs, conventions, traditions.

moron (SYN.) subnormal, dunce, blockhead, imbecile, retardate, simpleton.

morose (SYN.) gloomy, moody, fretful, crabbed, sulky, glum, dour, surly, downcast, sad, unhappy.

(ANT.) merry, gay, amiable, joyous, pleasant.

morsel (SYN.) portion, fragment, bite, bit, scrap. amount, piece, taste, tidbit.

(ANT.) whole, all, sum.

mortal (SYN.) fatal, destructive, human, perishable, deadly, temporary, momentary, final.

(ANT.) superficial, divine, immortal.

mortgage (SYN.) stake, post, promise, pledge.

mortician (SYN.) funeral director, embalmer.

mortified (SYN.) embarrassed, humiliated, ashamed.

mortify (SYN.) humiliate, crush, subdue, abase, degrade, shame.

(ANT.) praise, exalt, elevate.

mortuary (SYN.) morgue, crematory, funeral parlor.

most (SYN.) extreme, highest, supreme, greatest, majority.

(ANT.) least.

mostly (SYN.) chiefly, generally, largely, mainly, principally, especially, primarily.

mother (SYN.) bring about, produce, breed, mom, mama, watch, foster, mind, nurse, originate, nurture.

(ANT.) father.

motif (SYN.) keynote, topic, subject, theme.

motion (SYN.) activity, movement, proposition, action, signal, gesture, move, proposal.

(ANT.) stability, immobility, equilibrium, stillness.

motionless (SYN.) still, undisturbed, rigid, fixed, stationary, unresponsive, immobilized.

motivate (SYN.) move, prompt, stimulate, induce, activate, propel, arouse.

motive (SYN.) inducement, purpose, cause, incentive, reason, incitement, idea, ground, principle, stimulus, impulse, spur.

(ANT.) deed, result, attempt, effort.

motley (SYN.) heterogeneous, mixed, assorted, sundry, diverse, miscellaneous.

(ANT.) ordered, classified.

motor (SYN.) engine, generator, machine.

mottled (SYN.) streaked, flecked, dappled, spotted, speckled.

motto (SYN.) proverb, saying, adage, by-word, saw, slogan, catchword, aphorism.

mound (SYN.) hillock, hill, heap, pile, stack, knoll, accumulation, dune.

mount (SYN.) scale, climb, increase, rise, prepare, ready, steed, horse, tower.

(ANT.) sink, descend.

mountain (SYN.) alp, mount, peak, ridge, height, range.

mountebank (SYN.) faker, rascal, swindler, cheat, fraud.

mounting (SYN.) backing,

pedestal, easel, support, framework, background.

mourn *(SYN.)* suffer, grieve, bemoan, sorrow, lament, weep, bewail.

(ANT.) revel, celebrate.

mournful *(SYN.)* sorrowful, sad, melancholy, gloomy, woeful, rueful, disconsolate.

(ANT.) joyful, cheerful, happy.

mourning *(SYN.)* misery, trial, distress, affliction, tribulation, sorrow, woe.

(ANT.) happiness, solace, comfort, joy.

mousy *(SYN.)* quiet, reserved, dull, colorless, withdrawn, shy, bashful.

move *(SYN.)* impel, agitate, persuade, induce, push, instigate, advance, stir, progress, propel, shift, drive, retreat, proceed, stir, transfer, budge, actuate.

(ANT.) halt, stop, deter, rest.

movement *(SYN.)* activity, effort, gesture, move, proposition, crusade, action, change, motion.

(ANT.) stillness, immobility, equilibrium.

moving *(SYN.)* poignant, stirring, touching.

mow *(SYN.)* prune, cut, shave, crop, clip.

much *(SYN.)* abundance, quantity, mass, ample, plenty, sufficient, substantial.

mucilage *(SYN.)* adhesive, glue, paste.

muck *(SYN.)* filth, mire, dirt, rot, sludge, sewage.

muddle *(SYN.)* disorder, chaos, mess.

muddled *(SYN.)* disconcerted, confused, mixed, bewildered, perplexed.

(ANT.) plain, lucid, organized.

muff *(SYN.)* blunder, bungle, spoil, mess, fumble.

muffle *(SYN.)* soften, deaden, mute, quiet, drape, shroud, veil, cover.

(ANT.) louden, amplify.

mug *(SYN.)* cup, stein, goblet, tankard.

muggy *(SYN.)* damp, warm, humid, stuffy, sticky, dank.

mulct *(SYN.)* amerce, punish, penalize.

mulish *(SYN.)* obstinate, stubborn, headstrong, rigid, tenacious, willful.

multifarious *(SYN.)* various, many, numerous, diversified, several.

(ANT.) scanty, infrequent, scarce, few.

multiply *(SYN.)* double, treble, increase, triple, propagate, spread.

(ANT.) lessen, decrease

multitude *(SYN.)* crowd, throng, mass, swarm, host, mob, army, legion.

(ANT.) scarcity, handful.

mum *(SYN.)* mute, silent, quiet, still, closemouthed, secretive.

mumble *(SYN.)* stammer, whisper, hesitate, mutter.

(ANT.) shout, yell.

mundane *(SYN.)* temporal, earthly, profane, worldly, lay, secular.

(ANT.) unworldly, religious, extraordinary, rare.

municipal *(SYN.)* urban, metropolitan.

munificent *(SYN.)* bountiful, full, generous, forthcoming, satisfied.

(ANT.) voracious, insatiable, grasping, ravenous, devouring.

murder *(SYN.)* homicide, kill, slay, slaughter, butcher, massacre, assassinate, execute.

(ANT.) save, protect, vivify, animate.

murderer *(SYN.)* slayer, killer, assassin.

murky *(SYN.)* gloomy, dark, obscure, unclear, impenetrable.

(ANT.) cheerful, light.

murmur *(SYN.)* mumble, whine, grumble, whimper, lament, mutter, complaint, remonstrate.

(ANT.) praise, applaud, rejoice.

muscle *(SYN.)* brawn, strength, power, fitness, vigor, stamina, robustness, authority, force, muscularity, might.

(ANT.) flab, weakness, frail, helpness, soft.

muse *(SYN.)* ponder, brood, think, meditate, ruminate, reflect.

museum *(SYN.)* exhibit hall, treasure house, gallery, repository.

mushroom *(SYN.)* multiply, proliferate, flourish, spread, grow, pullulate.

music *(SYN.)* symphony, harmony, consonance.

musical *(SYN.)* tuneful, melodious, dulcet, lyrical, harmonious.

muss *(SYN.)* mess, disarray, rumple, litter, clutter, disarrange.

(ANT.) fix, arrange.

must *(SYN.)* ought to, should, duty, obligation, ultimatum.

muster *(SYN.)* cull, pick, collect, harvest, accumulate, garner, reap, deduce.

(ANT.) separate, disband, scatter.

musty *(SYN.)* mildewed, rancid, airless, dank, stale, decayed, rotten, funky.

mute *(SYN.)* quiet, noiseless, dumb, taciturn, hushed, peaceful, speechless, uncommunicative.

(ANT.) raucous, clamorous, noisy, talkative, audible.

mutilate *(SYN.)* tear, cut, clip, amputate, lacerate, dismember, deform, castrate.

mutinous *(SYN.)* revolutionary, rebellious, unruly, insurgent, turbulent, riotous.

(ANT.) dutiful, obedient, complaint.

mutiny *(SYN.)* revolt, overthrow, rebellion, rebel, coup, uprising, insurrection.

mutter *(SYN.)* complain, mumble, whisper, grumble.

mutual *(SYN.)* correlative, interchangeable, shared, alternate, joint, common, reciprocal.

(ANT.) unshared, unrequited, separate, dissociated, exclusive, uncommon.

muzzle *(SYN.)* restrain, silence, bridle, bind, curb, suppress, gag, stifle, censor.

(ANT.) *loose, free, set loose, liberate, untie.*

myopia (SYN.) incomprehension, folly, shortsightedness, obtuseness, insensibility.

myriad (SYN.) considerable, many.

mysterious (SYN.) hidden, mystical, secret, cryptic, incomprehensible, occult, dim, dark, inexplicable, enigmatical, inscrutable, obscure, recondite, puzzling

(ANT.) *simple, obvious, clear, plain*

mystery (SYN.) riddle, difficulty, enigma, puzzle, strangeness.

(ANT.) *solution, key, answer, resolution.*

mystical (SYN.) secret, cryptic, hidden, dim, obscure, dark, cabalistic, transcendental, inexplicable.

(ANT.) *simple, explained, plain, clear.*

mystify (SYN.) puzzle, confound, bewilder, floor, bamboozle.

myth (SYN.) fable, parable, allegory, fiction, tradition, lie, saga.

(ANT.) *history.*

mythical (SYN.) fictitious, unreal, imaginary, story, fiction, untrue, nonexistent, false.

(ANT.) *actual, true, real.*

N

nag (SYN.) badger, harry, provoke, tease, bother, annoy, molest, taunt, vex, torment,

worry, pester, irritate, pick on, scold, plague.

(ANT.) *please, comfort, soothe.*

nail (SYN.) hold, fasten, secure, fix, catch, snare, hook, capture.

(ANT.) *release.*

naive (SYN.) frank, unsophisticated, natural, artless, ingenuous, simple, candid, open, innocent.

(ANT.) *worldly, cunning, crafty*

naked (SYN.) uncovered, unfurnished, nude, bare, open, unclad, stripped, exposed, plain, mere, simple, barren, unprotected, bald, defenseless, unclothed, undressed.

(ANT.) *covered, protected, dressed, clothed, concealed, suppressed.*

name (SYN.) title, reputation, appellation, style, fame, repute, renown, denomination, call, appoint, character, designation, surname, distinction, christen, denominate, lable, mention, specify, epithet, entitle.

(ANT.) *anonymity, hint, misname.*

nap (SYN.) nod, doze, sleep, snooze, catnap, siesta, slumber, drowse, forty winks.

narcissistic (SYN.) egotistical, egocentric, self-centered.

narcotics (SYN.) opiates, drugs, sedatives, tranquilizers, barbiturates.

narrate (SYN.) recite, relate, declaim, detail, rehearse, deliver, review, tell, describe, recount.

narrative *(SYN.)* history, relation, account, record, chronicle, detail, recital, description, story, tale.
(ANT.) distortion, caricature, misrepresentation.

narrow *(SYN.)* narrow-minded, illiberal, bigoted, fanatical, prejudiced, close, restricted, slender, cramped, confined, meager, thin.
(ANT.) progressive, wide, liberal.

nascent *(SYN.)* prime, introductory, emerging, elementary.

nasty *(SYN.)* offensive, malicious, selfish, mean, disagreeable, unpleasant, foul, dirty, filthy, loathsome, disgusting, polluted, obscene, indecent, sickening, nauseating, obnoxious, odious.
(ANT.) generous, dignified, noble, admirable, pleasant.

nation *(SYN.)* state, community, realm, nationality, commonwealth, kingdom, country, republic, land, society, tribe.

native *(SYN.)* domestic, inborn, inherent, natural, aboriginal, endemic, innate, inbred, indigenous, hereditary, original, local.
(ANT.) alien, stranger, foreigner, outsider, foreign.

natty *(SYN.)* chic, well-dressed, sharp, dapper.

natural *(SYN.)* innate, genuine, real, unaffected, characteristic, native, normal, regular, inherent, original, simple, inbred, inborn, hereditary, typical, authentic, legitimate, pure, customary.
(ANT.) irregular, false, unnatural, formal, abnormal.

nature *(SYN.)* kind, disposition, reputation, character, repute, world, quality, universe, essence, variety, features, traits.

naught *(SYN.)* nought, zero, nothing.

naughty *(SYN.)* unmanageable, insubordinate, disobedient, mischievous, unruly, bad, misbehaving, disorderly, wrong, evil, rude, improper, indecent.
(ANT.) obedient, good, well-behaved.

nausea *(SYN.)* sickness, vomiting, upset, queasiness, seasickness.

nauseated *(SYN.)* unwell, sick, queasy, squeamish.

nautical *(SYN.)* naval, oceanic, marine, ocean.

near *(SYN.)* close, nigh, dear, adjacent, familiar, at hand, neighboring, approaching, impending, proximate, imminent, bordering.
(ANT.) removed, distant, far, remote.

nearly *(SYN.)* practically, close to, approximately, almost.

neat *(SYN.)* trim, orderly, precise, clear, spruce, nice, tidy, clean, well-kept, clever, skillful, adept, apt, tidy, dapper, smart, proficient, expert, handy, well-done, shipshape, elegant.
(ANT.) unkempt, sloppy, dirty, slovenly, messy, sloppy, disor-

ganized.

nebulous *(SYN.)* fuzzy, indistinct, indefinite, clouded, hazy.

(ANT.) definite, distinct, clear.

necessary *(SYN.)* needed, expedient, unavoidable, required, essential, indispensable, urgent, imperative, inevitable, compelling, compulsory, obligatory, needed, exigent.

(ANT.) optional, nonessential, contingent, casual, accidental, unnecessary, dispensable, unneeded.

necessity *(SYN.)* requirement, fate, destiny, constraint, requisite, poverty, exigency, compulsion, want, essential, prerequisite.

(ANT.) option, luxury, freedom, choice, uncertainty.

necromancy *(SYN.)* witchcraft, charm, sorcery, conjuring, wizardry.

need *(SYN.)* crave, want, demand, claim, desire, covet, wish, lack, necessity, requirement, poverty, require, pennilessness.

needed *(SYN.)* necessary, indispensable, essential, requisite.

(ANT.) optional, contingent.

needle *(SYN.)* goad, badger, tease, nag, prod, provoke.

needless *(SYN.)* nonessential, unnecessary, superfluous, useless, purposeless.

needy *(SYN.)* poor, indigent, impoverished penniless, destitute.

(ANT.) affluent, wealthy, well-off.

nefarious *(SYN.)* detestable, vicious, wicked, atrocious, horrible, vile.

negate *(SYN.)* revoke, void, cancel, nullify.

neglect *(SYN.)* default, omission, heedlessness, carelessness, thoughtlessness, disregard, negligence, oversight, omission, ignore, slight, failure, overlook, omit, skip, pass over, be inattentive, miss.

(ANT.) diligence, do, protect, watchfulness, care, attention, careful, attend, regard, concern.

negligent *(SYN.)* imprudent, thoughtless, lax, careless, inattentive, indifferent, remiss, neglectful.

(ANT.) careful, nice, accurate, meticulous.

negligible *(SYN.)* trifling, insignificant, trivial, inconsiderable.

(ANT.) major, vital, important.

negotiate *(SYN.)* intervene, talk over, mediate, transact, umpire, referee, arbitrate, arrange, settle, bargain.

neighborhood *(SYN.)* environs, nearness, locality, district, vicinity, area, section, locality.

(ANT.) remoteness.

neighboring *(SYN.)* bordering, near, adjacent, next to, surrounding, adjoining.

neighborly *(SYN.)* friendly, sociable, amiable, affable, companionable, congenial, kind, cordial, amicable.

(ANT.) distant, reserved, cool,

unfriendly, hostile.

neophyte *(SYN.)* greenhorn, rookie, amateur, beginner, apprentice, tyro, student.

nepotism *(SYN.)* bias, prejudice, partiality, partronage, favoritism.

nerve *(SYN.)* bravery, spirit, courage, boldness, rudeness, strength, stamina, bravado, daring, impudence, mettle, impertinence.

(ANT.) frailty, cowardice, weakness.

nervous *(SYN.)* agitated, restless, excited, shy, timid, upset, disturbed, shaken, rattle, high-strung, flustered, tense, jittery, edgy, perturbed, fearful.

(ANT.) courageous, confident, calm, placid, tranquil, composed, bold.

nest *(SYN.)* den, refuge, hide-away.

nestle *(SYN.)* cuddle, snuggle.

net *(SYN.)* snare, trap, mesh, earn, gain, web, get, acquire, secure, obtain.

nettle *(SYN.)* irritate, vex, provoke, annoy, disturb, irk, needle, pester.

neurotic *(SYN.)* disturbed, psychoneurotic.

neutral *(SYN.)* nonpartisan, uninvolved, detached, impartial, cool, unprejudiced, indifferent, inactive.

(ANT.) involved, biased, partisan.

neutralize *(SYN.)* offset, counteract, nullify, negate.

nevertheless *(SYN.)* notwithstanding, however, although,

anyway, but, regardless.

new *(SYN.)* modern, original, newfangled, late, recent, novel, young, firsthand, fresh, unique, unusual.

(ANT.) antiquated, old, ancient, obsolete, outmoded.

newborn *(SYN.)* baby, infant, cub.

news *(SYN.)* report, intelligence, information, copy, message, advice, tidings, knowledge, word, story, data.

next *(SYN.)* nearest, following, closest, successive, succeeding, subsequent.

nibble *(SYN.)* munch, chew, bit.

nice *(SYN.)* pleasing, pleasant, agreeable, thoughtful, satisfactory, friendly, enjoyable, gratifying, desirable, fine, good, cordial.

(ANT.) nasty, unpleasant, disagreeable, unkind, inexact, careless, thoughtless.

niche *(SYN.)* corner, nook, alcove, cranny, recess.

nick *(SYN.)* cut, notch, indentation, dash, score, mark.

nickname *(SYN.)* byname, sobriquet.

nigh *(SYN.)* close, imminent, near, adjacent, approaching, bordering, neighboring, impending.

(ANT.) removed, distant.

nightmare *(SYN.)* calamity, horror, torment, bad dream.

nil *(SYN.)* zero, none, nought, nothing.

nimble *(SYN.)* brisk, quick, active, supple, alert, lively, spry, light, fast, speedy, swift, agile.

(ANT.) slow, heavy, sluggish, clumsy.

nincompoop *(SYN.)* nitwit, fool, moron, blockhead, ninny, idiot, simpleton.

nip *(SYN.)* bite, pinch, chill, cold, squeeze, crispness, sip, small.

nippy *(SYN.)* chilly, sharp, bitter, cold, penetrating.

nit-picker *(SYN.)* fussbudget, precise, purist, perfectionist.

nitty-gritty *(SYN.)* essentials, substance, essence.

noble *(SYN.)* illustrious, exalted, dignified, stately, eminent, lofty, grand, elevated, honorable, honest, virtuous, great, distin guished, majestic, important, prominent, magnificent, grandiose, aristocratic, upright, well-born.

(ANT.) vile, low, base, mean, dishonest, common, ignoble.

nocturnal *(SYN.)* nightly.

nod *(SYN.)* bob, bow, bend, tip, signal.

node *(SYN.)* protuberance, growth, nodule, cyst, lump, wen.

noise *(SYN.)* cry, sound, din, babel, racket, uproar, clamor, outcry, tumult, sounds, hubbub, bedlam, commotion.

(ANT.) quiet, stillness, hush, silence, peace.

noisome *(SYN.)* repulsive, disgusting, revolting, obnoxious, malodorous, rotten.

noisy *(SYN.)* resounding, loud, clamorous, vociferous, stentorian, tumultuous.

(ANT.) soft, dulcet, subdued, quiet, silent, peaceful.

nomad *(SYN.)* gypsy, rover, traveler, roamer, migrant, vagrant, wanderer.

nominate *(SYN.)* propose, choose, select.

nomination *(SYN.)* appointment, naming, choice, selection, designation.

nominee *(SYN.)* aspirant, contestant, candidate, competitor.

nonbeliever *(SYN.)* skeptic, infidel, atheist, heathen.

nonchalant *(SYN.)* unconcerned, indifferent, cool, casual, easygoing.

noncommittal *(SYN.)* neutral, tepid, undecided, cautious, uncommunicative.

nonconformist *(SYN.)* protester, rebel, radical, dissenter, renegade, dissident, eccentric.

nondescript *(SYN.)* unclassifiable, indescribable, indefinite.

nonentity *(SYN.)* nothing, menial, nullity.

nonessential *(SYN.)* needless, unnecessary.

nonpareil *(SYN.)* unsurpassed, exceptional, paramount, unrivaled.

nonplus *(SYN.)* confuse, perplex, dumfound, mystify, puzzle, baffle, bewilder.

(ANT.) illumine, clarify, solve, explain.

nonsense *(SYN.)* balderdash, rubbish, foolishness, silly, ridiculousness, stupidity, absurdity, poppycock, trash.

nonsensical *(SYN.)* silly, preposterous, absurd, unreasonable, foolish, irrational, stupid, senseless.

(ANT.) sound, consistent, reasonable.

nonstop *(SYN.)* constant, continuous, unceasing, endless.

nook *(SYN.)* niche, corner, recess, cranny, alcove.

noose *(SYN.)* snare, rope, lasso, loop.

normal *(SYN.)* ordinary, uniform, natural, unvaried, customary, regular, healthy, sound, whole, usual, typical, characteristic, standard.

(ANT.) rare, erratic, unusual, abnormal.

normally *(SYN.)* regularly, frequently, usually, customarily.

nosy *(SYN.)* inquisitive, meddling, peering, searching, prying, snooping.

(ANT.) unconcerned, incurious, uninterested.

notable *(SYN.)* noted, unusual, uncommon, noteworthy, remarkable, conspicuous, distinguished, distinctive, celebrity, starts, important, striking, special, memorable, extraordinary, rare, exceptional.

(ANT.) commonplace, ordinary, usual.

notch *(SYN.)* cut, nick, indentation, gash.

note *(SYN.)* sign, annotation, letter, indication, observation, mark, symbol, comment, remark, token, message, memorandum, record, memo, write, list, notice.

noted *(SYN.)* renowned, glorious, celebrated, famous, illustrious, well-known, distinguished, famed.

(ANT.) unknown, hidden, infamous.

noteworthy *(SYN.)* consequential, exceptional, prominent.

notice *(SYN.)* heed, perceive, hold, mark, behold, descry, recognize, observe, attend to, remark, note, regard, see, sign, announcement, poster, note, advertisement, observation, warning.

(ANT.) overlook, disregard, skip.

notify *(SYN.)* apprise, acquaint, instruct, tell, advise, warn, teach, inform, report, remind, announce, reveal.

(ANT.) mislead, delude, conceal.

notion *(SYN.)* image, conception, sentiment, abstraction, thought, idea, view, opinion.

(ANT.) thing, matter, substance, entity.

notorious *(SYN.)* celebrated, renowned, famous, well-known, popular, infamous.

nourish *(SYN.)* strengthen, nurse, feed, nurture, sustain, support.

nourishment *(SYN.)* nutriment, food, sustenance, support.

(ANT.) starvation, deprivation.

novel *(SYN.)* fiction, narrative, allegory, tale, fable, story, romance, invention, different, unusual, original, new, unique, fresh.

(ANT.) verity, history, truth, fact.

novice *(SYN.)* beginner, ama-

teur, newcomer, green-horn, learner, apprentice, freshman.
(ANT.) expert, professional, adept, master.

now *(SYN.)* today, at once, right away, immediately, present.
(ANT.) later.

noxious *(SYN.)* poisonous, harmful, damaging, toxic, detrimental.
(ANT.) harmless.

nucleus *(SYN.)* core, middle, heart, focus, hub, kernel.

nude *(SYN.)* naked, unclad, plain, open, mere, bare, exposed, stripped, uncovered.
(ANT.) dressed, concealed, protected, clothed, covered.

nudge *(SYN.)* prod, push, jab, shove, poke, prompt.

nugget *(SYN.)* clump, mass, lump, wad, chunk, hunk.

nuisance *(SYN.)* annoyance, bother, irritation, pest.

nullify *(SYN.)* abolish, cross out, delete, invalidate, obliterate, cancel, annul, revoke, rescind.
(ANT.) perpetuate, confirm, enforce.

numb *(SYN.)* unfeeling, dull, insensitive, deadened, anesthetized, stupefied.

number *(SYN.)* quantity, sum, amount, volume, aggregate, total, collection, sum, numeral, count, measure, portion, bulk, figure, multitude, digit.
(ANT.) zero, nothing, nothingness.

numeral *(SYN.)* figure, symbol, digit.

nuptials *(SYN.)* marriage, wedding, espousal, wedlock, matrimony.
(ANT.) virginity, divorce, celibacy.

nurse *(SYN.)* tend, care for, nourish, nurture, feed, foster, train, mind, attend.

nurture *(SYN.)* hold dear, foster, sustain, appreciate, prize, bring up, rear, value, treasure, cherish.
(ANT.) dislike, disregard, abandon.

nutriment *(SYN.)* food, diet, repast, meal, fare, edibles.
(ANT.) hunger, want, starvation.

nutrition *(SYN.)* nourishment, sustenance, food, nutriment.

O

oaf *(SYN.)* boor, clod, clown, lummox, fool, lout, dunce, bogtrotter.

oasis *(SYN.)* shelter, haven, retreat, refuge.

oath *(SYN.)* promise, pledge, vow, profanity, curse, agreement, commitment, swearword.

obdurate *(SYN.)* insensible, callous, hard, tough, unfeeling, insensitive, impenitent, indurate.
(ANT.) soft, compassionate, tender.

obedience *(SYN.)* docility, submission, subservience, compliance.
(ANT.) rebelliousness, disobedience.

obedient *(SYN.)* dutiful, yielding, tractable, compliant, submissive. *(ANT.)* rebellious, insubordinate, obstinate.

obese *(SYN.)* portly, fat, pudgy, chubby, plump, rotund, stout, thickset, corpulent, stocky.

(ANT.) slim, gaunt, lean, thin, slender.

obey *(SYN.)* submit, yield, mind, comply, listen to, serve, conform.

(ANT.) resist, disobey.

obfuscate *(SYN.)* bewilder, complicate, fluster, confuse.

object *(SYN.)* thing, aim, intention, design, end, objective, particular, mark, purpose, goal, target.

(ANT.) assent, agree, concur, approve, acquiesce.

objection *(SYN.)* disagreement, protest, rejection, dissent, challenge, noncompliance, difference, nonconformity, recusancy, disapproval, criticism, variance.

(ANT.) acceptance, compliance, agreement, assent.

objectionable *(SYN.)* improper, offensive, deplorable.

objective *(SYN.)* aspiration, goal, passion, desire, aim, hope, purpose, drift, design, ambition, end, object, intention, intent, longing.

(ANT.) biased, subjective.

objectivity *(SYN.)* disinterest, neutrality, impartiality.

obligate *(SYN.)* oblige, require, pledge, bind, force, compel.

obligation *(SYN.)* duty, bond, engagement, compulsion, account, contract, ability, debt.

(ANT.) freedom, choice, exemp-

tion.

oblige *(SYN.)* constrain, force, impel, enforce, coerce, drive, gratify.

(ANT.) persuade, convince, allure, free, induce, disoblige, prevent.

obliging *(SYN.)* considerate, helpful, thoughtful, accommodating.

(ANT.) discourteous.

obliterate *(SYN.)* terminate, destroy, eradicate, raze, extinguish, exterminate, annihilate, devastate, wipe out, ravage, erase.

(ANT.) make, save, construct, establish, preserve.

oblivious *(SYN.)* sightless, unmindful, headlong, rash, blind, senseless, ignorant, forgetful, undiscerning, preoccupied.

(ANT.) sensible, aware, calculated, perceiving, discerning.

oblong *SYN.)* rectangular, elliptical, elongated.

obloquy *(SYN.)* defamation, rebuke, censure.

obnoxious *(SYN.)* hateful, offensive, nasty, disagreeable, repulsive, loathsome, vile, terrible, detestable, wretched, disgusting.

obscene *(SYN.)* indecent, filthy, impure, dirty, gross, lewd, pornographic, coarse, disgusting, bawdy, offensive, smutty.

(ANT.) modest, pure, decent, refined.

obscure *(SYN.)* cloudy, enigmatic, mysterious, abstruse, cryptic, dim, dusky, ambigu-

ous, dark, indistinct, unintelligible, unclear, shadowy, fuzzy, blurred.
(ANT.) clear, famous, distinguished, noted, illumined, lucid, bright, distinct.

obsequious *(SYN.)* fawning, flattering, ingratiating.

observance *(SYN.)* protocol, ritual, ceremony, rite, parade, pomp, solemnity, formality.
(ANT.) omission.

observant *(SYN.)* aware, alert, careful, mindful, watchful, heedful, considerate, attentive, conscious, anxious, circumspect, cautious.
(ANT.) unaware, indifferent, oblivious.

observation *(SYN.)* attention, watching, comment, opinion, remark, notice, examination.

observe *(SYN.)* note, behold, discover, notice, perceive, eye, detect, inspect, keep, commemorate, mention, utter, watch, examine, mark, view, express, see.
(ANT.) neglect, overlook, disregard, ignore.

observer *(SYN.)* examiner, overseer, lookout, spectator, bystander, witness, watcher.

obsession *(SYN.)* preoccupation, mania, compulsion, passion, fetish, infatuation.

obsolete *(SYN.)* old, out-of-date, ancient, archaic, extinct, old-fashioned, discontinued, obsolescent, venerable, dated.
(ANT.) modern, stylish, current, recent, fashionable, extant.

obstacle *(SYN.)* block, hindrance, barrier, impediment, snag, check, deterrent, stoppage, hitch, bar, difficulty, obstruction.
(ANT.) help, aid, assistance, encouragement.

obstinate *(SYN.)* firm, headstrong, immovable, stubborn, determined, dogged, intractable, uncompromising, inflexible, willful, bullheaded, contumacious, obdurate, unbending, unyielding.
(ANT.) yielding, docile, amenable, submissive, pliable, flexible, compliant.

obstruct *(SYN.)* clog, barricade, impede, block, delay, hinder, stop, close, bar.
(ANT.) promote, clear, aid, help, open, further.

obstruction *(SYN.)* block, obstacle, barrier, blockage, interference.

obtain *(SYN.)* get, acquire, secure, win, procure, attain, earn, gain.
(ANT.) surrender, forfeit, lose, forego, miss.

obtrusive *(SYN.)* blatant, garish, conspicuous.

obtuse *(SYN.)* blunt, dull, slow-witted, unsharpened, stupid, dense, slow.
(ANT.) clear, interesting, lively, bright, animated, sharp.

obviate *(SYN.)* prevent, obstruct, forestall, preclude, intercept, avert, evade.

obvious *(SYN.)* plain, clear, evident, palpable, patent, self-evident, apparent, distinct, understandable, unmistakable.

(ANT.) concealed, hidden, abstruse, obscure.

obviously *(SYN.)* plainly, clearly, surely, evidently, certainly.

occasion *(SYN.)* occurrence, time, happening, excuse, opportunity.

occasional *(SYN.)* random, irregular, sporadic, infrequent, periodically, spasmodic.

(ANT.) chronic, regular, constant.

occasionally *(SYN.)* seldom, now and then, infrequently, sometimes, irregularly.

(ANT.) regularly, often.

occlude *(SYN.)* clog, obstruct, choke, throttle.

occupant *(SYN.)* tenant, lodger, boarder, dweller, resident, inhabitant.

occupation *(SYN.)* employment, business, enterprise, job, trade, vocation, work, profession, matter, interest, concern, affair, activity, commerce, engagement.

(ANT.) hobby, pastime, avocation.

occupy *(SYN.)* dwell, have, inhabit, absorb, hold, possess, fill, keep.

(ANT.) relinquish, abandon, release.

occur *(SYN.)* take place, bechance, come about, befall, chance, transpire, betide, happen.

occurrence *(SYN.)* episode, event, issue, end, result, consequence, happening, circumstance.

ocean *(SYN.)* deep, sea, main, briny.

odd *(SYN.)* strange, bizarre, eccentric, unusual, single, uneven, unique, queer, quaint, peculiar, curious, unmatched, remaining.

(ANT.) matched, common, typical, normal, even, usual, regular.

odious *(SYN.)* obscene, depraved, vulgar, despicable, mean, wicked, sordid, foul, base, loathsome, depraved, vicious, displeasing, hateful, revolting, offensive, repulsive, horrible, obnoxious, vile.

(ANT.) decent, upright, laudable, attractive, honorable.

odor *(SYN.)* fume, aroma, fragrance, redolence, smell, stink, scent, essence, stench.

odorous *(SYN.)* scented, aromatic, fragrant.

odyssey *(SYN.)* crusade, quest, journey, voyage.

offbeat *(SYN.)* uncommon, eccentric, strange, unconventional, peculiar.

off-color *(SYN.)* rude, improper, earthy, suggestive, salty.

offend *(SYN.)* annoy, anger, vex, irritate, displease, provoke, hurt, grieve, pain, disgust, wound, horrify, stricken, insult, outrage.

(ANT.) flatter, please, delight.

offender *(SYN.)* criminal, culprit, lawbreaker, miscreant.

offense *(SYN.)* indignity, injustice, transgression, affront, outrage, misdeed, sin, insult, atrocity, aggression, crime.

(ANT.) morality, gentleness,

innocence, right.

offensive *(SYN.)* attacking, aggressive, unpleasant, revolting, disagreeable, nauseous, disgusting.

(ANT.) pleasing, defending, defensive, pleasant, attractive, agreeable

offer *(SYN.)* suggestion, overture, proposal, present, suggest, propose, try, submit, tender.

(ANT.) withdrawal, denial, rejection.

offhand *(SYN.)* informal, unprepared, impromptu, spontaneous.

(ANT.) considered, planned, calculated.

office *(SYN.)* position, job, situation, studio, berth, incumbency, capacity, headquarters, duty, task, function, work, post.

officiate *(SYN.)* administer, superintend, emcee.

offset *(SYN.)* compensate, counterbalance, cushion, counteract, neutralize, soften, balance.

offshoot *(SYN.)* outgrowth, addition, supplement, appendage, accessory, branch.

offspring *(SYN.)* issue, children, progeny, descendants.

often *(SYN.)* frequently, repeatedly, commonly, generally, recurrently.

(ANT.) seldom, infrequently, rarely, occasionally, sporadically.

ogle *(SYN.)* gaze, stare, eye, leer.

ogre *(SYN.)* monster, devil, demon.

ointment *(SYN.)* balm, lotion, pomade, emollient.

old *(SYN.)* antique, senile, ancient, archaic, old-fashioned, superannuated, obsolete, venerable, antiquated, elderly, abandoned, aged.

(ANT.) new, youthful, recent, modern, young.

old-fashioned *(SYN.)* outmoded, old, dated, ancient, nostalgic.

(ANT.) modern, fashionable, current, new.

olio *(SYN.)* potpourri, variety, mixture, jumble, conglomeration.

omen *(SYN.)* sign, gesture, indication, proof, portent, symbol, token, emblem, signal.

ominous *(SYN.)* unfavorable, threatening, sinister, menacing.

omission *(SYN.)* failure, neglect, oversight, default.

(ANT.) inclusion, notice, attention, insertion.

omit *(SYN.)* exclude, delete, cancel, eliminate, ignore, neglect, skip, leave out, drop, miss, overlook.

(ANT.) insert, notice, enter, include, introduce.

omnipotent *(SYN.)* all-powerful, almighty, divine.

oncoming *(SYN.)* imminent, approaching, arriving, nearing.

onerous *(SYN.)* intricate, arduous, hard, perplexing, difficult, burdensome, puzzling.

(ANT.) simple, easy, facile, effortless.

one-sided *(SYN.)* unfair, partial, biased, prejudiced.

(ANT.) impartial, neutral.

ongoing *(SYN.)* advancing, developing, continuing, progressive.

onlooker *(SYN.)* witness, spectator, observer, bystander.

only *(SYN.)* lone, sole, solitary, single, merely, but, just.

onset *(SYN.)* commencement, beginning, opening, start, assault, attack, charge, offense, onslaught.

(ANT.) end.

onslaught *(SYN.)* invasion, aggression, attack, assault, offense, drive, criticism, onset, charge.

(ANT.) vindication, defense, surrender, opposition, resistance.

onus *(SYN.)* load, weight, burden, duty.

onward *(SYN.)* ahead, forward, frontward.

(ANT.) backward.

ooze *(SYN.)* seep, leak, drip, flow, filter.

opacity *(SYN.)* obscurity, thickness, imperviousness.

opaque *(SYN.)* murky, dull, cloudy, filmy, unilluminated, dim, obtuse, indistinct, shadowy, dark.

(ANT.) light, clear, bright.

open *(SYN.)* uncovered, overt, agape, unlocked, passable, accessible, unrestricted, candid, plain, clear, exposed, unclosed, unobstructed, free, disengaged, frank, unoccupied, honest, ajar.

open *(SYN.)* unbar, unfold, exhibit, spread, unseal, expand, unfasten.

(ANT.) close, shut, conceal, hide.

open-handed *(SYN.)* kind, generous, charitable, lavish, extravagant, bountiful.

(ANT.) mean, stingy.

openhearted *(SYN.)* frank, honest, candid, sincere, ingenuous.

(ANT.) insincere, devious.

opening *(SYN.)* cavity, hole, void, abyss, aperture, chasm, pore, gap.

openly *(SYN.)* sincerely, frankly, freely.

(ANT.) secretly.

open-minded *(SYN.)* tolerant, fair, just, liberal, impartial, reasonable, unprejudiced.

(ANT.) prejudiced, bigoted.

operate *(SYN.)* comport, avail, behave, interact, apply, manage, utilize, demean, run, manipulate, employ, act, exploit, exert, exercise, practice, conduct.

(ANT.) neglect, waste.

operation *(SYN.)* effort, enterprise, mentality, maneuver, action, instrumentality, performance, working, proceeding, agency.

(ANT.) inaction, cessation, rest, inactivity.

operative *(SYN.)* busy, active, industrious, working, effective.

(ANT.) inactive, dormant.

opiate (SYN.) hypnotic, tranquilizer, narcotic.

opinion (SYN.) decision, feeling, notion, view, idea, conviction, belief, judgment, sentiment, persuasion, impression.

(ANT.) *knowledge, fact misgiving, skepticism.*

opinionated (SYN.) domineering, overbearing, arrogant, dogmatic, positive, magisterial, obstinate.

(ANT.) *questioning, fluctuating, skeptical, open-minded, indecisive.*

opponent (SYN.) competitor, foe, adversary, contestant, enemy, rival, contender, combatant.

(ANT.) *comrade, team, ally, confederate.*

opportune (SYN.) fitting, suitable, appropriate, proper, favorable.

opportunity (SYN.) possibility, chance, occasion, time, contingency, opening.

(ANT.) *obstacle, disadvantage, hindrance.*

oppose (SYN.) defy, resist, withstand, combat, bar, counteract, confront, thwart, struggle, fight, contradict, hinder, obstruct.

(ANT.) *submit, support, agree, cooperate, succumb.*

opposed (SYN.) opposite, contrary, hostile, adverse, counteractive, unlucky, antagonistic, unfavorable, disastrous.

(ANT.) *lucky, benign, propitious, fortunate, favorable.*

opposite (SYN.) reverse, contrary, different, unlike, opposed.

(ANT.) *like, same, similar.*

opposition (SYN.) combat, struggle, discord, collision, conflict, fight, encounter, controversy, inconsistency, variance.

(ANT.) *harmony, amity, concord, consonance.*

oppress (SYN.) harass, torment, vex, afflict, annoy, harry, pester, hound, worry, persecute.

(ANT.) *encourage, support, comfort, assist, aid.*

oppression (SYN.) cruelty, tyranny, persecution, injustice, despotism, brutality, abuse.

(ANT.) *liberty, freedom.*

oppressive (SYN.) difficult, stifling, burdensome, severe, domineering, harsh, unjust, overbearing, overwhelming.

oppressor (SYN.) bully, scourge, slave-driver.

opprobrium (SYN.) disgrace, contempt, reproach, shame, discredit.

opt (SYN.) choose, prefer, pick, select.

optical (SYN.) seeing, visual.

optimism (SYN.) faith, expectation, optimism, anticipation, trust, expectancy, confidence, hope.

(ANT.) *despair, pessimism, despondency.*

optimistic (SYN.) happy, cheerful, bright, glad, pleasant, radiant, lighthearted.

(ANT.) pessimistic.

option *(SYN.)* preference, choice, selection, alternative, election, self-determination.

optional *(SYN.)* selective, elective, voluntary.

(ANT.) required.

opulence *(SYN.)* luxury, abundance, fortune, riches, wealth, plenty, affluence.

(ANT.) need, indigence, want, poverty.

opulent *(SYN.)* wealthy, rich, prosperous, well-off, affluent, well-heeled.

oracle *(SYN.)* authority, forecaster, wizard, seer, mastermind, clairvoyant.

oral *(SYN.)* voiced, sounded, vocalized, said, uttered, verbal, vocal, spoken.

(ANT.) recorded, written, documentary.

orate *(SYN.)* preach, lecture, sermonize.

oration *(SYN.)* address, lecture, speech, sermon, discourse, recital, declamation.

orb *(SYN.)* globe, sphere, ball, moon.

orbit *(SYN.)* path, lap, course, circuit, revolution, revolve, circle.

orchestra *(SYN.)* ensemble, band.

orchestrate *(SYN.)* coordinate, direct, synchronize, organize.

ordain *(SYN.)* constitute, create, order, decree, decide, dictate, command, rule, bid, sanction, appoint.

(ANT.) terminate, disband.

ordeal *(SYN.)* hardship, suffering, test, affliction, trouble, fortune, proof, examination, trial, experiment, tribulation, misery.

(ANT.) consolation, alleviation.

order *(SYN.)* plan, series, decree, instruction, command, system, method, aim, arrangement, class, injuction, mandate, instruct, requirement, dictate, bidding.

(ANT.) consent, license, confusion, disarray, irregularity, permission.

order *(SYN.)* guide, command, rule, direct, govern, manage, regulate, bid, conduct.

(ANT.) misguide, deceive, misdirect, distract.

orderly *(SYN.)* regulated, neat, well-organized, disciplined, methodical, shipshape.

(ANT.) sloppy, messy, haphazard, disorganized.

ordinarily *(SYN.)* commonly, usually, generally, mostly, customarily, normally.

ordinary *(SYN.)* common, habitual, normal, typical, usual, conventional, familiar, accustomed, customary, average, standard, everyday, inferior, mediocre, regular, vulgar, plain.

(ANT.) uncommon, marvelous, extraordinary, remarkable, strange.

ordance *(SYN.)* munitions, artillery.

organ *(SYN.)* instrument, journal, voice.

organic *(SYN.)* living, biological, animate.

organism *(SYN.)* creature, plant, microorganism.

organization *(SYN.)* order, rule, system, arrangement, method, plan, regularity, scheme, mode, process.

(ANT.) irregularity, chaos, disarrangement, chance, disorder, confusion.

organize *(SYN.)* assort, arrange, plan, regulate, systematize, devise, categorize, classify, prepare.

(ANT.) jumble, disorder, disturb, confuse, scatter.

organized *(SYN.)* planned, neat, orderly, arranged.

orient *(SYN.)* align, fit, accustom, adjust.

orifice *SYN.)* vent, slot, opening, hole.

origin *(SYN.)* birth, foundation, source, start, commencement, inception, beginning, derivation, infancy, parentage, spring, cradle.

(ANT.) product, issue, outcome, end.

original *(SYN.)* primary, fresh, new, initial, pristine, creative, first, primordial, inventive, primeval, novel, introductory.

(ANT.) banal, trite, subsequent, derivative, later, modern, terminal.

originality *(SYN.)* unconventionality, genius, novelty, creativity, imagination.

originate *(SYN.)* fashion, invent, cause, create, make, initiate, inaugurate, organize, institute, produce, engender, arise, commence, found,

establish, form, begin, generate, formulate.

(ANT.) demolish, terminate, annihilate, disband, destroy.

originator *(SYN.)* creator, inventor, discoverer.

(ANT.) follower, imitator.

ornament *(SYN.)* decoration, ornamentation, adornment, embellishment, trimming, garnish.

ornamental *(SYN.)* ornate, decorative.

ornate *SYN.)* florid, overdone, elaborate, showy, flowery, pretentious.

ornery *(SYN.)* disobedient, firm, unruly, stiff, rebellious, stubborn, headstrong, willful, contrary, rigid, mean, difficult, malicious, cross, disagreeable.

(ANT.) pleasant.

orthodox *(SYN.)* customary, usual, conventional, correct, proper, accepted.

(ANT.) different, unorthodox.

oscillate *(SYN.)* vary, change, hesitate, waver, undulate, fluctuate, vacillate.

(ANT.) persist, resolve, adhere, stick, decide.

ostentation *(SYN.)* parade, show, boasting, pageantry, vaunting, pomp, display, flourish.

(ANT.) reserve, humility, unobtrusiveness, modesty.

ostentatious *(SYN.)* flashy, showy, overdone, fancy, pretentious, garish.

ostracize *(SYN.)* hinder, omit, bar, exclude, blackball, expel, prohibit, shout out, prevent, except.

(ANT.) welcome, accept, include, admit.

other *(SYN.)* distinct, different, extra, further, new, additional, supplementary.

ought *(SYN.)* must, should, be obliged.

oust *(SYN.)* eject, banish, exclude, expatriate, ostracize, dismiss, exile, expel.

(ANT.) shelter, accept, receive, admit, harbor.

ouster *(SYN.)* expulsion, banishment, ejection, overthrow.

outbreak *(SYN.)* riot, revolt, uprising, disturbance, torrent, eruption, outburst.

outburst *(SYN.)* outbreak, eruption, torrent, ejection, discharge.

outcast *(SYN.)* friendless, homeless, deserted, abandoned, forsaken, disowned, derelict, forlorn, rejected.

outclass *(SYN.)* outshine, surpass.

outcome *(SYN.)* fate, destiny, necessity, doom, portion, consequence, result, end, fortune, effect, issue, aftermath.

outcry *(SYN.)* scream, protest, clamor, noise, uproar.

outdated *(SYN.)* old-fashioned, unfashionable, old, outmoded.

(ANT.) stylish.

outdo *(SYN.)* outshine, defeat, excel, beat, surpass.

outer *(SYN.)* remote, exterior, external.

outfit *(SYN.)* garb, kit, gear, furnish, equip, rig, clothing, provisions.

outgoing *(SYN.)* leaving, departing, friendly, congenial, amicable.

(ANT.) unfriendly, incoming.

outgrowth *(SYN.)* effect, outcome, upshot, fruit, result, consequence, product, byproduct, development.

outing *(SYN.)* journey, trip, excursion, jaunt, expedition, junket.

outlandish *(SYN.)* peculiar, odd, weird, curious, strange, queer, exotic, bazaar.

(ANT.) ordinary, common.

outlast *(SYN.)* survive, endure, outlive.

outlaw *(SYN.)* exile, bandit, outcast, badman, convict, criminal, fugitive, desperado.

outlay *(SYN.)* expense, costs, spending, disbursement, expenditure, charge.

outlet *(SYN.)* spout, opening, passage.

outline *(SYN.)* form, sketch, brief, draft, figure, profile, contour, chart, diagram, skeleton, delineation, plan, silhouette.

outlook *(SYN.)* viewpoint, view, prospect, opportunity, position, attitude, future.

outlying *(SYN.)* external, remote, outer, out-of-the-way, suburban, rural.

outmoded *(SYN.)* unfashionable, old-fashioned.

(ANT.) up-to-date, modern.

outnumber *(SYN.)* exceed.

output *(SYN.)* yield, crop, harvest, proceeds, productivity, production.

outrage *(SYN.)* aggression, transgression, vice, affront, offense, insult, indignity, atrocity, misdeed, trespass, wrong.

(ANT.) morality, right, gentleness, innocence.

outrageous *(SYN.)* shameful, shocking, disgraceful, insulting, nonsensical, absurd, foolish, crazy, excessive, ridiculous, bizarre, preposterous, offensive.

(ANT.) prudent, reasonable, sensible.

outright *(SYN.)* entirely, altogether, completely, quite, fully, thoroughly.

outset *(SYN.)* inception, origin, start, commencement, opening, source.

(ANT.) end, completion, termination, consummation, close.

outside *(SYN.)* covering, exterior, surface, facade, externals, appearance.

(ANT.) intimate, insider.

outsider *(SYN.)* immigrant, stranger, foreigner, alien, newcomer, bystander.

(ANT.) countryman, friend, acquaintance, neighbor, associate.

outsmart *(SYN.)* outmaneuver, outwit.

outspoken *(SYN.)* rude, impolite, unceremonious, brusque, unrestrained, vocal, open, straight-foward, blunt, unreserved, frank, forthright, rough.

(ANT.) suave, tactful, shy, polished, polite, subtle.

outstanding *(SYN.)* well-known, important, prominent, leading, eminent, distinguished, significant, conspicuous.

(ANT.) insignificant, unimportant.

outward *(SYN.)* apparent, outside, exterior, visible.

outweigh *(SYN.)* predominate, supersede, counteract, dwarf.

outwit *(SYN.)* baffle, trick, outsmart, bewilder, outdo, outmaneuver, confuse.

oval *(SYN.)* egg-shaped, elliptical, ovular.

ovation *(SYN.)* fanfare, homage, applause, tribute, cheers, acclamation.

overall *(SYN.)* comprehensive, complete, general, extensive, wide-spread, entire.

overbearing *(SYN.)* domineering, masterful, autocratic, dictatorial, arrogant, imperious, haughty.

(ANT.) humble.

overcast *(SYN.)* dim, shadowy, cloudy, murky, dark, mysterious, gloomy, somber, dismal, hazy.

(ANT.) sunny, bright, distinct, limpid, clear.

overcome *(SYN.)* quell, beat, crush, surmount, rout, humble, conquer, subjugate, defeat, subdue, upset.

(ANT.) retreat, surrender, capitulate, cede, lose.

overconfident *(SYN.)* egotistical, presumptuous, arrogant, conceited.

overdo *(SYN.)* stretch, exaggerate, enlarge, magnify, exhaust, overexert, strain.

overdue *(SYN.)* slow, tardy, advanced, delayed, new.
(ANT.) timely, early, beforehand.

overflow *(SYN.)* run over, flood, spill, cascade, inundate.

overflowing *(SYN.)* ample, plentiful, teeming, abundant, copious.
(ANT.) insufficient, scant, deficient, scarce.

overhang *(SYN.)* protrude, extend, projection.

overhaul *(SYN.)* recondition, rebuild, service, repair, revamp.

overhead *(SYN.)* high, above, aloft, expenses, costs.

overjoyed *(SYN.)* enchanted, delighted, ecstatic, enraptured, elated, blissful.
(ANT.) depressed.

overlap *(SYN.)* overhang, extend, superimpose.

overload *(SYN.)* burden, oppress, weight, afflict, encumber.
(ANT.) ease, lighten, console, alleviate, mitigate.

overlook *(SYN.)* miss, disregard, exclude, cancel, omit, skip, ignore, drop, delete, neglect, exclude, watch, eliminate.
(ANT.) notice, enter, include, introduce, insert.

overly *(SYN.)* exceedingly, needlessly, unreasonably.

overpass *(SYN.)* span, bridge, viaduct.

overpower *(SYN.)* overcome, conquer, defeat, surmount, vanquish, overwhelm.
(ANT.) surrender.

overrated *(SYN.)* exaggerated, misrepresented.

overrule *(SYN.)* disallow, nullify, cancel, override, repeal, revoke.

overrun *(SYN.)* spread, exceed, beset, infest, flood, abound.

oversee *(SYN.)* direct, run, operate, administer, superintend, boss, manage, supervise.

overseer *(SYN.)* leader, ruler, master, teacher, chief, commander, lord, employer, manager.
(ANT.) slave, servant.

overshadow *(SYN.)* dominate, control, outclass, surpass, domineer.

oversight *(SYN.)* omission, charge, superintendence, surveillance, inattention, error, inadvertence, neglect, mistake, inspection, control, negligence, management.
(ANT.) scrutiny, care, attention, observation.

overstep *(SYN.)* surpass, exceed, trespass, transcend, impinge, violate, intrude.

overt *(SYN.)* honest, candid, frank, plain, open, apparent.

overtake *(SYN.)* outdistance, reach, catch, pass.

overthrow *(SYN.)* defeat, demolish, upset, overcome, destroy, ruin, rout, vanquish, subvert, reverse, supplant, overturn, overpower.
(ANT.) revive, restore, con-

overture (SYN.) offer, bid, proposal, prelude, introduction, presentation, recommendation.

(ANT.) finale.

overturn (SYN.) demolish, overcome, vanquish, upset, supplant.

(ANT.) uphold, construct, build, preserve, conserve.

overweight (SYN.) pudgy, stout, heavy, obese, fat.

overwhelm (SYN.) crush, surmount, vanquish, conquer, astonish, surprise, bewilder, astound, startle, overcome.

overwrought (SYN.) distraught, hysterical.

owe (SYN.) be liable, be indebted.

own (SYN.) monopolize, possess, maintain, have.

owner (SYN.) landholder, partner, proprietor, possessor.

P

pace (SYN.) rate, gait, step.

pacific (SYN.) peaceful, calm, serene, undisturbed, composed, imperturbable, placid, still, tranquil, unruffled, peaceable, quiet.

(ANT.) turbulent, wild, excited, frantic.

pacify (SYN.) appease, lull, relieve, quell, soothe, allay, assuage, calm, satisfy, placate, alleviate.

(ANT.) incense, inflame, arouse, excite.

pack (SYN.) prepare, stow, crowd, stuff, bundle, parcel, load, crowd, gang, mob.

package (SYN.) parcel, packet, load, bundle, box, bottle, crate.

packed (SYN.) filled, complete, plentiful, crammed, full, replete, gorged, satiated, copious, entire.

(ANT.) lacking, depleted, devoid, vacant, insufficient, partial, empty.

pageant (SYN.) show, display, spectacle.

pain (SYN.) twinge, ache, pang, agony, distress, grief, anguish, paroxysm, suffering, misery.

(ANT.) happiness, pleasure, comfort, relief, ease, delight, joy.

painful (SYN.) hurting, galling, poignant, bitter, grievous, agonizing, aching.

(ANT.) sweet, pleasant, soothing.

painting (SYN.) image, picture, portrayal, scene, view, sketch, illustration, panorama.

pair (SYN.) team, couple, mate, match.

palatial (SYN.) majestic, magnificent, sumptuous, luxurious.

pale (SYN.) colorless, white, pallid, dim, faint, whiten, blanch.

(ANT.) flushed, ruddy, bright, dark.

pamphlet (SYN.) leaflet, brochure.

pang (SYN.) throb, pain, hurt.

panic (SYN.) fear, terror, fright, alarm, apprehension, trembling, horror, dread.

(ANT.) tranquillity, composure, calmness, serenity, calm, soothe.

pant *(SYN.)* wheeze, puff, gasp.

pantry *(SYN.)* cupboard, storeroom.

paper *(SYN.)* journal, newspaper, document, article, essay.

parable *(SYN.)* fable, saga, legend, myth, allegory, chronicle, fiction.

(ANT.) history, fact.

parade *(SYN.)* procession, cavalcade, succession, train, file, cortege, retinue, sequence, march, review, pageant, strut.

paradise *(SYN.)* utopia, heaven.

paradoxical *(SYN.)* unsteady, wavering, contradictory, discrepant, incompatible, inconsistent, vacillating, illogical.

(ANT.) correspondent, compatible, congruous, consistent.

parallel *(SYN.)* allied, analogous, comparable, corresponding, akin, similar, correlative, alike, like, resembling, equal, counterpart, likeness, correspondence, resemble, equal, match.

(ANT.) opposed, different, incongruous.

paralyze *(SYN.)* numb, deaden.

paraphernalia *(SYN.)* effect, gear, belonging, equipment.

parcel *(SYN.)* packet, package, bundle.

parched *(SYN.)* dry, arid, thirsty, drained, dehydrated, desiccated.

(ANT.) moist, damp.

pardon *(SYN.)* absolution, forgiveness, remission, acquittal, amnesty, excuse, exoneration, forgive, acquit.

(ANT.) sentence, penalty, conviction, punishment, condemn.

pardon *(SYN.)* condone, overlook, remit, absolve, acquit, forgive, excuse.

(ANT.) punish, chastise, accuse, condemn, convict.

pare *(SYN.)* skin, peel, reduce, trim, shave, crop.

parley *(SYN.)* interview, talk, conference, chat, dialogue, colloquy.

paroxysm *(SYN.)* twinge, pang, ache, pain.

(ANT.) ease, relief, comfort.

parsimonious *(SYN.)* avaricious, miserly, penurious, stingy, acquisitive, greedy.

(ANT.) munificent, extravagant, bountiful, altruistic, generous.

part *(SYN.)* piece, section, allotment, portion, segment, element, member, concern, side, interest, lines, role, apportionment, division, share, fragment, ingredient, organ, party, moiety, fraction, participation, divide.

(ANT.) whole, entirety.

part *(SYN.)* separate, sever, divide, sunder.

(ANT.) join, combine, unite, convene.

partake *(SYN.)* dispense, parcel, allot, assign, distribute, partition, appropriate, divide, share.

(ANT.) condense, aggregate, combine.

partial *(SYN.)* unfinished, undone, incomplete, prejudiced, unfair.

(ANT.) comprehensive, complete, entire.

partiality *(SYN.)* preconception, bias, predisposition, bigotry.

(ANT.) reason, fairness, impartiality.

participant *(SYN.)* associate, colleague, partner, shareholder.

participate *(SYN.)* join, share, partake.

participation *(SYN.)* communion, sacrament, union, intercourse, association, fellowship.

(ANT.) nonparticipation, alienation.

particle *(SYN.)* mite, crumb, scrap, atom, corpuscle, grain, iota, smidgen, grain, speck, bit, spot.

(ANT.) quantity, bulk, mass.

particular *(SYN.)* peculiar, unusual, detailed, specific, fastidious, individual, distinctive, singular, circumstantial, exact, careful, squeamish, special.

(ANT.) general, rough, universal, comprehensive, undiscriminating.

partisan *(SYN.)* follower, successor, adherent, attendant, henchman, devotee, disciple.

(ANT.) leader, chief, master, head.

partition *(SYN.)* distribution, division, separation, screen, barrier, separator, divider, wall.

(ANT.) unification, joining.

partly *(SYN.)* comparatively, partially, somewhat.

partner *(SYN.)* colleague, comrade, friend, crony, consort, associate, companion, mate, participant.

(ANT.) stranger, enemy, adversary.

party *(SYN.)* company, gathering, crowd, group.

pass *(SYN.)* proceed, continue, move, go, disregard, ignore, exceed, gap, permit, permission, toss, admission, throw.

(ANT.) note, consider, notice.

pass by *(SYN.)* dodge, avert, elude, free, ward, shun, eschew avoid, forbear.

(ANT.) meet, confront, oppose, encounter.

passable *(SYN.)* fair, average, mediocre, acceptable, adequate, satisfactory.

(ANT.) worst, excellent, first-rate, exceptional, extraordinary, superior.

passage *(SYN.)* section, passageway, corridor, section, voyage, tour, crossing.

passenger *(SYN.)* traveler, tourist, rider, voyager, commuter.

passion *(SYN.)* feeling, affection, turmoil, sentiment, perturbation, agitation, emotion, trepidation, zeal, rapture, excitement, desire, love, liking, fondness, enthusiasm.

(ANT.) tranquillity, indifference, calm, restraint, dispassion, apathy, coolness.

passionate *(SYN.)* fiery, ardent, burning, glowing, irascible, fervid, excitable hot, impetuous, emotional, impulsive, excited, zealous, enthusiastic, earnest, sincere.

(ANT.) quiet, calm, cool, apathetic, deliberate.

passive *(SYN.)* relaxed, idle, stoical, enduring, inert, inactive, patient, submissive.

(ANT.) dynamic, active, aggressive.

password *(SYN.)* watchword.

past *(SYN.)* done, finished, gone, over, former.

(ANT.) future, present, ahead.

pastime *(SYN.)* match, amusement, diversion, fun, play, sport, contest, merriment, recreation, entertainment, hobby.

(ANT.) quiescence, labor, apathy, business.

patch *(SYN.)* restore, fix, repair, ameliorate, correct, rectify, remedy, sew, mend, better.

(ANT.) rend, deface, destroy, hurt, injure.

patent *(SYN.)* conspicuous, apparent, obvious, clear, evident, unmistakable, open, overt, manifest, indubitable, protection, control, copyright, permit.

(ANT.) hidden, concealed, obscure, covert.

path *(SYN.)* avenue, street, trail, walk, course, road, route, track, lane, footpath, pathway, walkway.

pathetic *(SYN.)* piteous, sad, affecting, moving, poignant, pitiable, touching, pitiful, touching.

(ANT.) funny, comical, ludicrous.

patience *(SYN.)* perseverance, composure, endurance, fortitude, long-suffering, forbearance, calmness, passiveness, serenity, courage, persistence.

(ANT.) restlessness, nervousness, impatience, unquite, impetuosity.

patient *(SYN.)* indulgent, stoical, forbearing, composed, assiduous, passive, uncomplaining, persistent, untiring, persevering, submissive, resigned, serene, calm, quiet, unexcited, unruffled.

(ANT.) turbulent, high-strung, chafing, clamorous, hysterical.

patrol *(SYN.)* inspect, watch, guard.

patron *(SYN.)* purchaser, buyer, client, customer.

patronize *(SYN.)* support.

pattern *(SYN.)* guide, example, original, model, design, figure, decoration.

paunchy *(SYN.)* fat, pudgy, stout, plump, portly, rotund, corpulent, obese, stocky.

(ANT.) slim, slender, gaunt, lean, thin.

pause *(SYN.)* falter, hesitate, waver, demur, doubt, scruple, delay, vacillate, hesitation, rest, interruption, break, delay, intermission, recess.

(ANT.) proceed, continue, decide, resolve, persevere,

continuity, perpetuate.

pawn *(SYN.)* tool, puppet, stooge.

pay *(SYN.)* earnings, salary, allowance, stipend, wages, payment, compensation, recompense.

(ANT.) gratuity, present, gift.

payable *(SYN.)* unpaid, due, owed, owing.

peace *(SYN.)* hush, repose, serenity, tranquillity, silence, stillness, calmness, quiescence, calm, quietude, rest, quiet, peacefulness, pact.

(ANT.) noise, tumult, agitation, disturbance, excitement.

peaceable *(SYN.)* mild, calm, friendly, peaceful, amiable, gentle, pacific.

(ANT.) aggressive, hostile, warlike.

peaceful *(SYN.)* pacific, calm, undisturbed, quiet, serene, mild, placid, gentle, tranquil, peaceable.

(ANT.) noisy, violent, agitated, turbulent, disturbed, disrupted, riotous.

peak *(SYN.)* climax, culmination, summit, zenith, height, acme, consummation, apex, top, point, crest.

(ANT.) depth, floor, base, anticlimax, base, bottom.

peculiar *(SYN.)* odd, eccentric, extraordinary, unusual, individual, particular, striking, rare, exceptional, distinctive, strange, unfamiliar, uncommon, queer, curious, outlandish.

(ANT.) ordinary, common, normal, general, regular, unspecial.

peculiarity *(SYN.)* characteristic, feature, mark, trait, quality, attribute, property, distinctiveness.

pedantic *(SYN.)* formal, scholastic, erudite, academic, learned, bookish, theoretical, scholarly.

(ANT.) simple, ignorant, practical, unlearned.

peddle *(SYN.)* sell, vend, hawk.

pedestrian *(SYN.)* stroller, walker.

pedigree *(SYN.)* descent, line, parentage, lineage, ancestry, family.

peek *(SYN.)* glimpse, look, peer, peep.

peel *(SYN.)* rind, skin, peeling.

peep *(SYN.)* squeak, cheep, chirp.

peer *(SYN.)* match, rival, equal, parallel, peep, glimpse, examine, peek, scrutinize.

peeve *(SYN.)* nettle, irk, irritate, annoy, vex.

peevish *(SYN.)* ill-natured, irritable, waspish, touchy, petulant, snappish, fractious, illtempered, fretful.

(ANT.) pleasant, affable, goodtempered, genial, goodnatured.

pen *(SYN.)* coop, enclosure, cage.

penalize *(SYN.)* dock, punish.

penalty *(SYN.)* fine, retribution, handicap, punishment, chastisement, disadvantage, forfeiture, forfeit.

(ANT.) remuneration, compen-

sation, reward, pardon.

penchant *(SYN.)* disposition, propensity, tendency, partiality, inclination, bent, tendency, slant, bias.

(ANT.) justice, fairness, equity, impartiality.

penetrate *(SYN.)* bore, hole, pierce, enter.

penetrating *(SYN.)* profound, recondite, abstruse, deep, solemn, piercing, puncturing, boring, sharp, acute.

(ANT.) superficial, trivial, shallow, slight.

peninsula *(SYN.)* spit, headland, neck, point.

penitent *(SYN.)* remorseful, sorrowful, regretful, contrite, sorry, repentant.

(ANT.) remorseless, objurgate.

penniless *(SYN.)* poor, destitute, impecunious, needy, poverty-stricken, needy.

(ANT.) rich, wealthy, affluent, opulent, prosperous, well-off.

pensive *(SYN.)* dreamy, reflect, meditative, thoughtful, introspective, reflective, contemplative.

(ANT.) thoughtless, heedless, inconsiderate, precipitous, rash.

penurious *(SYN.)* avaricious, greedy, parsimonious, miserly, stingy, acquisitive, tight.

(ANT.) munificent, extravagant, bountiful, generous, altruistic.

penury *(SYN.)* poverty, want, destitution, necessity, indigence, need, privation.

(ANT.) riches, affluence, abundance, plenty, wealth.

people *(SYN.)* humans, person.

perceive *(SYN.)* note, conceive, see, comprehend, understand, discern, recognize, apprehend, notice, observe, distinguish, understand, grasp.

(ANT.) overlook, ignore, miss.

perceptible *(SYN.)* sensible, appreciable, apprehensible.

(ANT.) imperceptible, absurd, impalpable.

perception *(SYN.)* understanding, apprehension, conception, insight, comprehension, discernment.

(ANT.) misconception, ignorance, insensibility.

perceptive *(SYN.)* informed, observant, apprised, cognizant, aware, conscious, sensible, mindful, discerning, sharp, acute, observant.

(ANT.) unaware, ignorant, oblivious, insensible.

perfect *(SYN.)* ideal, whole, faultless, immaculate, complete, superlative, absolute, unqualified, utter, sinless, holy, finished, blameless, entire, excellent, pure, flawless, ideal.

(ANT.) incomplete, defective, imperfect, deficient, blemished, lacking, faulty, flawed.

perfectionist *(SYN.)* purist, pedant.

perform *(SYN.)* impersonate, pretend, act, play, do, accomplish, achieve, complete.

performance *(SYN.)* parade, entertainment, demonstration, movie, show, production, ostentation, spectacle, presentation, offering.

performer *(SYN.)* entertainer, actress, actor.

perfume *(SYN.)* cologne, scent, essence.

perfunctory *(SYN.)* decorous, exact, formal, external, correct, affected, methodical, precise, stiff, outward, proper, solemn.

(ANT.) unconventional, easy, unconstrained, natural heartfelt.

perhaps *(SYN.)* conceivable, possible, maybe.

(ANT.) absolutely, definitely.

peril *(SYN.)* jeopardy, risk, danger, hazard.

(ANT.) safety, immunity, protection, defense, security.

perilous *(SYN.)* menacing, risky, hazardous, critical, dangerous, precarious, unsafe, insecure, threatening.

(ANT.) safe, firm, protected, secure.

period *(SYN.)* era, age, interval, span, tempo, time, epoch, duration, spell, date.

periodical *(SYN.)* uniform, customary, orderly, systematic, regular, steady.

(ANT.) exceptional, unusual, abnormal, rare, erratic.

perish *(SYN.)* die, sink cease, decline, decay, depart, wane, wither, languish, expire, cease, pass away.

(ANT.) grow, survive, flourish, begin, live.

perishable *(SYN.)* decomposable, decayable.

permanent *(SYN.)* constant,

durable, enduring, abiding, fixed, changeless, unchangeable, lasting, indestructible, stable, continuing, long-lived, persistent, persisting, everlasting, unchanging, unaltered.

(ANT.) unstable, transient, ephemeral, temporary, transitory, passing, inconstant, fluctuating.

permeate *(SYN.)* penetrate, pervade, run through, diffuse, fill, saturate, infiltrate.

permissible *(SYN.)* allowable, fair, tolerable, admissible, justifiable, probable, warranted.

(ANT.) unsuitable, inadmissible, irrelevant.

permission *(SYN.)* authorization, liberty, permit, authority, consent, leave, license, freedom.

(ANT.) refusal, prohibition, denial, opposition.

permissive *(SYN.)* easy, tolerant, open-minded, unrestrictive.

(ANT.) restrictive.

permit *(SYN.)* let, tolerate, authorize, sanction, allow, grant, give.

(ANT.) refuse, resist, forbid, protest, object, prohibit, disallow.

perpendicular *(SYN.)* standing, upright, vertical.

(ANT.) horizontal.

perpetrate *(SYN.)* commit, perform, do.

(ANT.) neglect, fail, miscarry.

perpetual *(SYN.)* everlasting, immortal, ceaseless, endless, timeless, undying, infinite, eternal, unceasing, continuing, continual, continuous, permanent, constant.

(ANT.) transient, mortal, finite, temporal ephemeral, inconstant, intermittent, fluctuating.

perpetually (SYN.) continually, ever, incessantly, eternally, forever, always, constantly.

(ANT.) rarely, sometimes, never, occasionally, fitfully.

perplex (SYN.) confuse, dumbfound, mystify, puzzle, bewilder, confound, nonplus.

(ANT.) solve, explain, illumine, instruct, clarify.

perplexed (SYN.) confused, disorganized, mixed, bewildered, deranged, disordered, muddled, disconcerted.

(ANT.) plain, obvious, clear, lucid, organized.

perplexing (SYN.) intricate, complex, involved, compound, complicated.

(ANT.) uncompounded, plain, simple.

persecute (SYN.) harass, hound, torment, worry, vex, torture, harry, afflict, annoy, oppress, pester, ill-treat, victimize, maltreat.

(ANT.) support, comfort, assist, encourage, aid.

persevere (SYN.) remain, abide, endure, last, persist, continue.

(ANT.) vacillate, desist, discontinue, cease, waver, lapse.

perseverance (SYN.) persistency, constancy, pertinacity, steadfastness, tenacity, industry.

(ANT.) sloth, cessation, laziness, idleness, rest.

persist (SYN.) endure, remain, abide, persevere, continue, last.

(ANT.) vacillate, waver, desist, cease, discontinue, stop.

persistence (SYN.) persistency, constancy, perseverance, steadfastness, tenacity.

(ANT.) cessation, rest, sloth, idleness.

persistent (SYN.) lasting, steady, obstinate, stubborn, fixed, enduring, immovable, constant, indefatigable.

(ANT.) wavering, unsure, hesitant, vacillating.

person (SYN.) human, individual, somebody, someone.

personal (SYN.) secret, private.

(ANT.) general, public.

personality (SYN.) make-up, nature, disposition, character.

perspicacity (SYN.) intelligence, understanding, discernment, judgment, wisdom, sagacity.

(ANT.) thoughtlessness, stupidity, arbitrariness, senselessness.

persuade (SYN.) entice, coax, exhort, prevail upon, urge, allure, induce, influence, win over, convince.

(ANT.) restrain, deter, compel, dissuade, coerce, discourage.

persuasion (SYN.) decision, feeling, notion, view, sentiment, conviction, belief, opinion.

(ANT.) knowledge, skepticism,

fact, misgiving.

persuasive *(SYN.)* winning, alluring, compelling, convincing, stimulating, influential.
(ANT.) dubious, unconvincing.

pertain *(SYN.)* refer, relate, apply.

pertinacious *(SYN.)* firm, obstinate, contumacious, headstrong, dogged, inflexible, obdurate, uncompromising, determined, immovable, unyielding.
(ANT.) yielding, docile, amenable, submissive, compliant.

pertinent *(SYN.)* apt, material, relevant, relating, applicable, to the point, germane, apropos, apposite, appropriate.
(ANT.) unrelated, foreign, alien, extraneous.

perturbed *(SYN.)* agitated, disturbed, upset, flustered.

pervade *(SYN.)* penetrate, saturate, fill, diffuse, infiltrate, run through, permeate.

perverse *(SYN.)* obstinate, ungovernable, sinful, contrary, fractious, peevish, forward, disobedient, wicked, intractable, petulant.
(ANT.) docile, agreeable, tractable, obliging.

perversion *(SYN.)* maltreatment, outrage, desecration, abuse, profanation, misuse, reviling.
(ANT.) respect.

pervert *(SYN.)* deprave, humiliate, impair, debase, corrupt, degrade, abase, defile.
(ANT.) improve, raise, enhance.

perverted *(SYN.)* wicked, perverse, sinful.

pest *(SYN.)* annoyance, nuisance, bother, irritant, irritation.

pester *(SYN.)* disturb, annoy, irritate, tease, bother, chafe, inconvenience, molest, trouble, vex, harass, torment, worry.
(ANT.) console, soothe, accommodate, gratify.

pet *(SYN.)* darling, favorite, caress.

petition *(SYN.)* invocation, prayer, request, appeal, entreaty, supplication, suit, plea, application, solicitation, entreaty.

petty *(SYN.)* paltry, trivial, frivolous, small, unimportant, trifling, insignificant.
(ANT.) important, serious, weighty, momentous, grand, vital, significant, generous.

petulant *(SYN.)* irritable, ill-natured, fretful, snappish, peevish, ill-tempered, waspish, touchy.
(ANT.) pleasant, affable, good-tempered, genial, good-natured.

phantom *(SYN.)* apparition, ghost, specter.

phase *(SYN.)* period, stage, view, condition.

phenomenon *(SYN.)* occurrence, fact, happening, incident.

philanthropy *(SYN.)* kindness, benevolence, charity, generosity, tenderness, humanity, magnanimity, altruism.

(ANT.) unkindness, inhumanity, cruelty, malevolence, selfishness.

phlegmatic *(SYN.)* unfeeling, passionless, listless, cold, lethargic, sluggish, slow, lazy.
(ANT.) passionate, ardent, energetic.

phony *(SYN.)* counterfeit, artificial, ersatz, fake, synthetic, unreal, spurious, feigned, assumed, bogus, sham, false, forged.
(ANT.) real, genuine, natural, true.

phrase *(SYN.)* expression, term, word, name.

physical *(SYN.)* material, bodily, carnal, corporeal, natural, somatic, corporal.
(ANT.) spiritual, mental.

pick *(SYN.)* cull, opt, select, elect, choose.
(ANT.) reject, refuse.

picture *(SYN.)* etching, image, painting, portrait, print, representation, sketch, appearance, cinema, effigy, engraving, scene, view, illustration, panorama, resemblance, likeness, drawing, photograph.

piece *(SYN.)* portion, bit, fraction, morsel, scrap, fragment, amount, part, quantity, unit, section.
(ANT.) sum, whole, entirety, all, total.

piecemeal *(SYN.)* gradually, partially.
(ANT.) whole, complete, entire.

pierce *(SYN.)* puncture, perforate.

pigheaded *(SYN.)* inflexible, stubborn, obstinate.

pigment *(SYN.)* shade, tint, color, dye, hue, complexion, tincture, stain, tinge.
(ANT.) transparency, paleness.

pile *(SYN.)* accumulation, heap, collection, amass.

pilgrim *(SYN.)* wanderer, traveler.

pilgrimage *(SYN.)* trip, journey, tour, expedition.

pillar *(SYN.)* support, prop, column, shaft.

pillow *(SYN.)* bolster, cushion, pad.

pilot *(SYN.)* helmsman, aviator, steersman.

pin *(SYN.)* clip, fastening, peg, fastener.

pinch *(SYN.)* squeeze, nip.

pinnacle *(SYN.)* crown, zenith, head, summit, chief, apex, crest, top.
(ANT.) bottom, foundation, base, foot.

pioneer *(SYN.)* guide, pilgrim, pathfinder, explorer.

pious *(SYN.)* devout, religious, spiritual, consecrated, divine, hallowed, holy, saintly, sacred, reverent.
(ANT.) worldly, sacrilegious, evil, secular, profane, irreligious, impious.

pirate *(SYN.)* plunderer, buccaneer, privateer.

pistol *(SYN.)* gun, revolver, weapon, handgun.

pit *(SYN.)* well, cavity, hole, excavation.

pitch *(SYN.)* throw, cast, toss, propel, hurl, fling, thrust, establish.

(ANT.) *retain, draw, hold, pull, haul.*

pitcher *(SYN.)* jug.

piteous *(SYN.)* poignant, touching, affecting, moving, pitiable, sad, pathetic.

(ANT.) *funny, ludicrous, comical.*

pitfall *(SYN.)* lure, snare, wile, ambush, bait, intrigue, trick, trap, artifice, net, snare.

pitiable *(SYN.)* poignant, touching, moving, affecting, sad.

(ANT.) *ludicrous, funny, comical.*

pitiful *(SYN.)* distressing, pathetic, pitiable.

pitiless *(SYN.)* unmerciful, mean, unpitying, merciless, cruel.

(ANT.) *gentle, kind.*

pity *(SYN.)* sympathy, commiseration, condolence, compassion, charity, mercy.

(ANT.) *ruthlessness, hardness, cruelty, inhumanity, brutality, vindictiveness.*

pivotal *(SYN.)* crucial, critical, essential, central.

(ANT.) *peripheral, unimportant.*

place *(SYN.)* lay, arrange, dispose, put, deposit, space, region, location, plot, area, spot.

(ANT.) *mislay, remove, disarrange, disturb, misplace.*

placid *(SYN.)* pacific, serene, tranquil, calm, imperturbable, composed, peaceful, quiet, still, undisturbed, unruffled.

(ANT.) *wild, frantic, turbulent, stormy, excited.*

plagiarize *(SYN.)* recite,

adduce, cite, quote, paraphrase, repeat, extract.

(ANT.) *retort, contradict, misquote, refute.*

plague *(SYN.)* hound, pester, worry, harass, annoy, persecute, torment, vex, afflict, badger, torture, epidemic, trouble.

(ANT.) *encourage, aid, comfort, assist, support*

plain *(SYN.)* candid, simple, flat, smooth, clear, evident, sincere, unpretentious, level, distinct, absolute, visible, open, frank, palpable, undecorated, ordinary, unembellished, unadorned.

(ANT.) *embellished, abstruse, abrupt, rough, broken, insincere, adorned, fancy, elaborate, beautiful, ornamented.*

plan *(SYN.)* design, purpose, sketch, devise, invent, contrive, intend, draw, create, scheme, plot, method, procedure.

plane *(SYN.)* level, airplane.

plastic *(SYN.)* pliable, moldable, supple, flexible, synthetic.

platform *(SYN.)* stage, pulpit.

plausible *(SYN.)* likely, practical, credible, feasible, possible, probable.

(ANT.) *impracticable, impossible, visionary.*

play *(SYN.)* entertainment, amusement, pastime, sport, game, fun, diversion, recreation, show, performance, drama, theatrical.

(ANT.) *work, labor, boredom.*

toil.

playful *(SYN.)* sportive, frolicsome, frisky.

plaything *(SYN.)* game, trinket, toy, gadget.

playwright *(SYN.)* scriptwriter, dramatist.

plea *(SYN.)* invocation, request, appeal, entreaty, supplication, petition, suit.

plead *(SYN.)* beseech, defend, rejoin, supplicate, discuss, beg, appeal, ask, implore, argue, entreat.
(ANT.) deprecate, deny, refuse.

pleasant *(SYN.)* agreeable, welcome, suitable, charming, pleasing, amiable, gratifying, acceptable, pleasurable, enjoyable, nice, satisfying, satisfactory, acceptable, affable, mild, friendly.
(ANT.) offensive, disagreeable, obnoxious, unpleasant, horrid, sour, difficult, nasty.

please *(SYN.)* satisfy, suffice, fulfill, content, appease, gratify, satiate, compensate, remunerate.
(ANT.) dissatisfy, annoy, tantalize, frustrate, displease, vex.

pleasing *(SYN.)* luscious, melodious, sugary, delightful, agreeable, honeyed, mellifluous, enjoyable, welcome, pleasant, charming.
(ANT.) repulsive, sour, acrid, bitter, offensive, irritating, annoying.

pleasure *(SYN.)* felicity, delight, amusement, enjoyment gratification, happiness, joy, satisfaction, gladness,

well-being.
(ANT.) suffering, pain, vexation, trouble, affliction, discomfort, torment.

pledge *(SYN.)* promise, statement, assertion, declaration, assurance, agreement, oath, commitment, agree, vow, swear.

pledge *(SYN.)* bind, obligate, commit.
(ANT.) renounce, release, neglect, mistrust.

plentiful *(SYN.)* ample, profuse, replete, bountiful, abundant, plenteous, luxurious, fullness, fruitful, copious.
(ANT.) rare, scanty, deficient, scarce, insufficient.

plenty *(SYN.)* fruitfulness, bounty, fullness, abundance.
(ANT.) want, scarcity, need.

pliable *(SYN.)* elastic, supple, flexible, compliant, pliant, resilient, ductile.
(ANT.) rigid, unbending, hard, brittle, stiff.

plight *(SYN.)* dilemma, situation, difficulty, condition, predicament, fix, scrape, state.
(ANT.) satisfaction, ease, comfort, calmness.

plot *(SYN.)* design, plan, scheme, cabal, conspiracy, diagram, sketch, graph, chart, machination, intrigue.

plotting *(SYN.)* cunning, scheming, objective, artfulness, contrivance, purpose, intent, design.
(ANT.) accident, chance, result, candor, sincerity.

ploy *(SYN.)* ruse, guile, antic,

deception, hoax, subterfuge, wile, cheat, artifice, fraud, trick.

(ANT.) honesty, sincerity, openness, exposure, candor.

pluck *(SYN.)* yank, snatch, jerk, pull.

plug *(SYN.)* cork, stopper.

plump *(SYN.)* obese, portly, stout, thickset, rotund, chubby, fat, paunchy, stocky, corpulent, pudgy, fleshy.

(ANT.) slim, thin, gaunt, lean, slender, skinny.

plunder *(SYN.)* ravage, strip, sack, rob, pillage, raid, loot.

plunge *(SYN.)* immerse, dip, submerge.

pocketbook *(SYN.)* purse, handbag.

poem *(SYN.)* lyric, verse, poetry.

poetry *(SYN.)* rhyme, verse.

pogrom *(SYN.)* massacre, carnage, slaughter, butchery.

poignant *(SYN.)* pitiable, touching, affecting, impressive, sad, tender, moving, heart-rending.

point *(SYN.)* direct, level, train, aim, locality, position, spot, location.

(ANT.) distract, misguide, deceive, misdirect.

pointed *(SYN.)* keen, sharp, penetrating, shrewd, witty, quick, acute, cutting, piercing, astute, severe.

(ANT.) shallow, stupid, bland, blunt, gentle.

pointless *(SYN.)* vain, purposeless.

poise *(SYN.)* composure, self-

possession, equanimity, equilibrium, carriage, calmness, balance, self-control, assurance, control, dignity.

(ANT.) rage, turbulence, agitation, anger, excitement.

poison *(SYN.)* corrupt, sully, taint, infect, befoul, defile, contaminate, venom, toxin, virus.

(ANT.) purify, disinfect.

poke *(SYN.)* punch, stab, thrust, jab.

policy *(SYN.)* procedure, system, rule, approach, tactic.

polish *(SYN.)* brighten, shine, finish, brightness, gloss.

(ANT.) tarnish, dull.

polished *(SYN.)* glib, diplomatic, urbane, refined, sleek, suave, slick.

(ANT.) rough, blunt, bluff, harsh, rugged.

polite *(SYN.)* refined, well-mannered, accomplished, courteous, civil, genteel, urbane, well-bred, cultivated, considerate, thoughtful, mannerly, respectful.

(ANT.) uncouth, impertinent, rude, boorish, uncivil, discourteous.

pollute *(SYN.)* contaminate, poison, taint, sully, infect, befoul, defile, dirty.

(ANT.) purify, disinfect, clean, clarify.

pomp *(SYN.)* flourish, pageantry, vaunting, show, boasting, ostentation, parade, display.

(ANT.) reserve, humility, modesty.

pompous (SYN.) high, magnificent, stately, august, dignified, grandiose, noble, majestic, lofty, imposing, arrogant, vain, pretentious.

(ANT.) lowly, undignified, humble, common, ordinary.

ponder (SYN.) examined, study, contemplate, investigate, meditate, muse, scrutinize, cogitate, reflect, weigh, deliberate, consider.

ponderous (SYN.) burdensome, trying, gloomy, serious, sluggish, massive, heavy, cumbersome, grievous, grave, dull, weighty.

(ANT.) light, animated, brisk.

poor (SYN.) penniless, bad, deficient, destitute, inferior, shabby, wrong, scanty, pecunious, indigent, needy, poverty-stricken, unfavorable, impoverished, penniless.

(ANT.) wealthy, prosperous, rich, fortunate, good, excellent.

poppycock (SYN.) rubbish, babble, twaddle, nonsense.

popular (SYN.) favorite, general, common, familiar, prevalent, liked, prevailing, well-liked, approved, accepted, celebrated, admired, ordinary.

(ANT.) unpopular, esoteric, restricted, exclusive.

populous (SYN.) dense, thronged, crowded.

porch (SYN.) patio, veranda.

pornographic (SYN.) impure, indecent, obscene, coarse, dirty, filthy, lewd, smutty, offensive, disgusting.

(ANT.) refined, modest, pure, decent.

port (SYN.) harbor, refuge, anchorage.

portable (SYN.) transportable, movable.

portal (SYN.) entry, doorway, opening, inlet, entrance.

(ANT.) exit, departure.

portend (SYN.) foreshadow, presage, foretoken.

portentous (SYN.) significant, critical, momentous.

(ANT.) trivial.

portion (SYN.) share, bit, parcel, part, piece, section, fragment, division, quota, segment, allotment.

(ANT.) whole, bulk.

portly (SYN.) majestic, grand, impressive, dignified, stout, fat, heavy, obese.

(ANT.) slender, thin, slim.

portrait (SYN.) painting, representation, picture, likeness.

portray (SYN.) depict, picture, represent, sketch, describe, delineate, paint.

(ANT.) misrepresent, caricature, suggest.

pose (SYN.) model.

position (SYN.) caste, site, locality, situation, condition, standing, incumbency, office, bearing, posture, berth, place, job, pose, rank, attitude, location, place, spot, station, situation, occupation.

positive (SYN.) sure, definite, fixed, inevitable, undeniable, indubitable, assured, certain, unquestionable, unmistakable.

(ANT.) uncertain, doubtful,

questionable, probably, unsure, dubious, confused, negative, adverse.

positively (SYN.) unquestionably, surely, certainly, absolutely.

possess (SYN.) own, obtain, control, have, seize, hold, occupy, affect.
(ANT.) surrender, abandon, lose, renounce.

possessed (SYN.) entranced, obsessed, consumer, haunted, enchanted.

possession (SYN.) custody, ownership, occupancy.

possessions (SYN.) commodities, effects, goods, property, stock, merchandise, wares, wealth, belongings.

possible (SYN.) likely, practical, probable, feasible, plausible, credible, practicable.
(ANT.) visionary, impossible, improbable.

possibility (SYN.) opportunity, chance, contingency, occasion.
(ANT.) obstacle, disadvantage, hindrance.

possible (SYN.) feasible, practical, practicable, doable.

possibly (SYN.) perchance, perhaps, maybe.

post (SYN.) position, job, berth, incumbency, situation, shaft, pole, fort, base, station.

postpone (SYN.) delay, stay, suspend, discontinue, defer, adjourn, interrupt, put off.
(ANT.) persist, prolong, maintain, continue, proceed.

postulate (SYN.) principle,

adage, saying, proverb, truism, byword, aphorism, axiom, fundamental, maxim.

potency (SYN.) effectiveness, capability, skillfulness, efficiency, competency, ability.
(ANT.) wastefulness, inability, ineptitude.

potent (SYN.) mighty, influential, convincing, effective.
(ANT.) feeble, weak, powerless, impotent.

potential (SYN.) likely, possible, dormant, hidden, latent.

pouch (SYN.) container, bag, sack.

pound (SYN.) buffet, beat, punch, strike, thrash, defeat, subdue, pulse, smite, belabor, knock, thump, overpower, palpitate, rout, vanquish.
(ANT.) fail, surrender, stroke, defend, shield.

pour (SYN.) flow.

pout (SYN.) brood, sulk, mope.

poverty (SYN.) necessity, need, want, destitution, privation, indigence, distress.
(ANT.) plenty, abundance, wealth, riches, affluence, richness, comfort.

power (SYN.) potency, might, authority, control, predominance, capability, faculty, validity, force, vigor, command, influence, talent, ability, dominion, competency.
(ANT.) incapacity, fatigue, weakness, disablement, impotence, ineptitude.

powerful (SYN.) firm, strong, concentrated, enduring, forcible, robust, sturdy, tough, athletic, forceful, hale, impregnable, hardy, mighty, potent.

(ANT.) feeble, insipid, brittle, delicate, fragile, weak, ineffectual, powerless.

practical (SYN.) sensible, wise, prudent, reasonable, sagacious, sober, sound, workable, attainable.

(ANT.) stupid, unaware, impalpable, imperceptible, absurd, impractical.

practically (SYN.) almost, nearly.

practice (SYN.) exercise, habit, custom, manner, wont, usage, drill, tradition, performance, action, repetition.

(ANT.) inexperience, theory, disuse, idleness, speculation.

practiced (SYN.) able, expert, skilled, adept.

(ANT.) inept.

prairie (SYN.) plain, grassland.

praise (SYN.) applaud, compliment, extol, laud, glorify, commend, acclaim, eulogize, flatter, admire, celebrate, commendation, approval.

(ANT.) criticize, censure, reprove, condemn, disparage, disapprove, criticism, negation.

pray (SYN.) supplicate, importune, beseech, beg.

prayer (SYN.) plea, suit, appeal, invocation, supplication, petition, entreaty, request.

preach (SYN.) teach, urge, moralize, lecture.

preamble (SYN.) overture, prologue, beginning, introduction, prelude, start, foreword, preface.

(ANT.) end, finale, completion, conclusion, epilogue.

precarious (SYN.) dangerous, perilous, threatening, menacing, critical, risky, unsafe, hazardous.

(ANT.) secure, firm, protected, safe.

precaution (SYN.) foresight, forethought, care.

precedence (SYN.) preference, priority.

precedent (SYN.) model, example.

precept (SYN.) doctrine, tenet, belief, teaching, dogma.

(ANT.) practice, conduct, performance, deed.

precious (SYN.) dear, useful, valuable, costly, esteemed, profitable, expensive, priceless, dear.

(ANT.) poor, worthless, cheap, mean, trashy.

precipice (SYN.) bluff, cliff.

precipitate (SYN.) speedy, swift, hasty, sudden.

precipitous (SYN.) unannounced, sudden, harsh, rough, unexpected, sharp, abrupt, hasty, craggy, steep, precipitate.

(ANT.) expected, smooth, anticipated, gradual.

precise (SYN.) strict, exact, formal, rigid, definite, unequivocal, prim, ceremonious, distinct, accurate, correct.

(ANT.) loose, easy, vague, informal, careless, erroneous.

precisely (SYN.) specifically, exactly.

precision (SYN.) correction, accuracy, exactness.

preclude (SYN.) hinder, prevent, obstruct, forestall, obviate, thwart, impede.
(ANT.) permit, aid, expedite, encourage, promote.

preclusion (SYN.) omission, exception, exclusion.
(ANT.) standard, rule, inclusion.

predicament (SYN.) dilemma, plight, situation, condition, fix, difficulty, strait, scrape.
(ANT.) satisfaction, comfort, ease, calmness.

predict (SYN.) forecast, foretell.

prediction (SYN.) forecast, prophecy.

predilection (SYN.) attachment, inclination, affection, bent, desire, penchant, disposition, preference.
ANT.) repugnance, aversion, apathy, distaste, nonchalance.

predominant (SYN.) highest, paramount, cardinal, foremost, main, first, leading, supreme, principal, essential, prevalent, dominant, prevailing
(ANT.) subsidiary, auxiliary, supplemental, minor, subordinate.

predominate (SYN.) prevail, outweigh, rule.

preface (SYN.) foreword, introduction, preliminary, prelude, prologue, preamble.

prefer (SYN.) select, favor, elect, fancy.

preference (SYN.) election, choice, selection, alternative, option.

prejudice (SYN.) bias, favoritism, unfairness, partiality.

prejudiced (SYN.) fanatical, narrow-minded, dogmatic, bigoted, illiberal, intolerant.
(ANT.) radical, liberal, tolerant, progressive.

preliminary (SYN.) introductory, preparatory, prelude, preface.

premature (SYN.) early, untimely, unexpected.
(ANT.) timely.

premeditated (SYN.) intended, voluntary, contemplated, designed, intentional, willful, deliberate, studied.
(ANT.) fortuitous, accidental.

premeditation (SYN.) intention, deliberation, forethought, forecast.
(ANT.) hazard, accident, impromptu, extemporization.

premise (SYN.) basis, presupposition, assumption, postulate, principle, presumption.
(ANT.) superstructure, derivative, trimming, implication.

preoccupied (SYN.) abstracted, distracted, absorbed, meditative, inattentive, absent, absent-minded.
(ANT.) attentive, alert, conscious, present, attending, watchful.

prepare (SYN.) contrive, furnish, ready, predispose, condition, fit, arrange, plan, qualify, make ready, get ready.

preposterous (SYN.) foolish, nonsensical, silly, contradictory, unreasonable, absurd, inconsistent, irrational, self-contradictory.

(ANT.) sensible, rational, consistent, sound, reasonable.

prerequisite *(SYN.)* essential, requirement, necessity, condition, demand.

prerogative *(SYN.)* grant, right, license, authority, privilege.

(ANT.) violation, encroachment, wrong, injustice.

prescribe *(SYN.)* order, direct, designate.

presence *(SYN.)* nearness, attendance, closeness, vicinity, appearance, bearing, personality.

present *(SYN.)* donation, gift, today, now, existing, current, largess, donate, acquaint, introduce, being, give, gratuity, boon, grant.

(ANT.) reject, spurn, accept, retain, receive.

presentable *(SYN.)* polite, well-bred, respectable, well-mannered.

presently *(SYN.)* shortly, soon, directly, immediately.

preserve *(SYN.)* protect, save, conserve, maintain, secure, rescue, uphold, spare, keep, can, safeguard, defend, rescue.

(ANT.) impair, abolish, destroy, abandon, squander, injure.

preside *(SYN.)* officiate, direct, administrate.

press *SYN.)* impel, shove, urge, hasten, push, compress, squeeze, hug, crowd, propel, force, drive, embrace, smooth, iron, insist on, pressure, promote, urgency, jostle.

(ANT.) oppose, pull, falter, drag, retreat, ignore.

pressing *(SYN.)* impelling, insistent, necessary, urgent, compelling, imperative, instant, serious, important, cogent, exigent, importunate.

(ANT.) unimportant, trifling, insignificant, petty, trivial.

pressure *(SYN.)* force, influence, stress, press, compulsion, urgency, constraint, compression.

(ANT.) relaxation, leniency, ease, recreation.

prestige *(SYN.)* importance, reputation, weight, influence, renown, fame, distinction.

presume *(SYN.)* guess, speculate, surmise, imagine, conjecture, apprehend, believe, think, assume, suppose, deduce.

(ANT.) prove, ascertain, demonstrate, know, conclude.

presumption *(SYN.)* boldness, impertinence, insolence, rudeness, assurance, effrontery, impudence, assumption, audacity, supposition, sauciness.

(ANT.) politeness, truckling, diffidence.

presumptuous *(SYN.)* bold, impertinent, fresh, imprudent, rude, forward, arrogant.

presupposition *(SYN.)* basis, principle, premise, assumption, postulate.

(ANT.) superstructure, derivative, implication.

pretend *(SYN.)* feign, stimulate, act, profess, make believe,

imagine, fake, sham, affect.
(ANT.) expose, reveal, display, exhibit.

pretense *(SYN.)* mask, pretext, show, affection, disguise, garb, semblance, simulation, fabrication, lie, excuse, falsification, deceit, subterfuge.
(ANT.) sincerity, actuality, truth, fact, reality.

pretentious *(SYN.)* gaudy, ostentatious.
(ANT.) simple, humble.

pretty *(SYN.)* charming, handsome, lovely, beauteous, fair, comely, attractive, beautiful, elegant.
(ANT.) repulsive, foul, unsightly, homely, plain, hideous.

prevail *(SYN.)* win, succeed, predominate, triumph.
(ANT.) yield, lose.

prevailing *(SYN.)* common, current, general, habitual, steady, regular, universal.

prevalent *(SYN.)* ordinary, usual, common, general, familiar, popular, prevailing, wide-spread, universal, frequent.
(ANT.) odd, scarce, exceptional, extraordinary.

prevent *(SYN.)* impede, preclude, forestall, stop, block, check, halt, interrupt, deter, slow, obviate, hinder, obstruct, thwart.
(ANT.) expedite, help, allow, abet, aid, permit, encourage, promote.

previous *(SYN.)* former, anterior, preceding, prior, earlier, foregoing.

(ANT.) subsequent, following, consequent, succeeding, later.

prey *(SYN.)* raid, seize, victimize.

price *(SYN.)* worth, cost, expense, charge, value.

pride *(SYN.)* self-respect, vanity, glory, superciliousness, haughtiness, conceit, arrogance, self-importance, pretension, egotism, satisfaction, fulfillment, enjoyment, self-esteem.
(ANT.) modesty, shame, humbleness, lowliness, meekness, humility.

prim *(SYN.)* formal, puritanical, priggish, prudish.

primarily *(SYN.)* mainly, chiefly, firstly, essentially, originally.
(ANT.) secondarily.

primary *(SYN.)* first, principal, primeval, pristine, beginning, original, initial, fundamental, elementary, chief, foremost, earliest, main, prime.
(ANT.) subordinate, last, secondary, least, hindmost, latest.

prime *(SYN.)* first, primary, chief, excellent, best, superior, ready.

primeval *(SYN.)* fresh, primary, novel, inventive, creative, primordial, original, first, new, initial.
(ANT.) trite, modern, subsequent, banal, later, terminal, derivative.

primitive *(SYN.)* antiquated, early, primeval, prehistoric, uncivilized, uncultured, simple, pristine, old, aboriginal, unsophisticated, rude, rough, primary.

(ANT.) *sophisticated, modish, civilized, cultured, cultivated, late.*

primordial (SYN.) pristine, inventive, novel, creative, original, first, initial, new, primary.

(ANT.) *trite, terminal, banal, modern, derivative, subsequent, later.*

principal (SYN.) first, leading, main, supreme, predominant, chief, foremost, highest, prime, primary, leader, headmaster, paramount, essential, cardinal.

(ANT.) *supplemental, secondary, auxiliary, subsidiary, accessory, minor, subordinate.*

principle (SYN.) law, method, axiom, rule, propriety, regulation, maxim, formula, order, statute.

(ANT.) *exception, hazard, chance, deviation.*

print (SYN.) issue, reprint, publish, letter, sign, fingerprint, mark, picture, lithograph, engraving, etching.

prior (SYN.) previous, aforesaid, antecedent, sooner, earlier, preceding, former, foregoing.

(ANT.) *succeeding, following, later, consequent, subsequent.*

prison (SYN.) brig, jail, stockade, penitentiary.

pristine (SYN.) primordial, creative, first, original, fresh, inventive, novel, primary, initial.

(ANT.) *trite, terminal, derivative, modern, banal, subsequent, plagiarized, later.*

private (SYN.) concealed, hidden, secret, clandestine, unknown, personal, surreptitious, covert, individual, particular, special, latent.

(ANT.) *exposed, known, closed, general, public, conspicuous, disclosed, obvious.*

privation (SYN.) necessity, penury, destitution, need, poverty, want.

(ANT.) *wealth, affluence, abundance, plenty, riches.*

privilege (SYN.) liberty, right, advantage, immunity, freedom, license, favor, sanction.

(ANT.) *restriction, inhibition, prohibition, disallowance.*

prize (SYN.) compensation, bonus, award, premium, remuneration, rate, reward, bounty, esteem, value, recompense, requital.

(ANT.) *charge, punishment, wages, earnings, assessment.*

probable (SYN.) presumable, likely.

probe (SYN.) stretch, reach, investigate, examine, examination, scrutiny, scrutinize, inquire, explore, inquiry, investigation, extend.

(ANT.) *miss, short.*

problem (SYN.) dilemma, question, predicament, riddle, difficulty, puzzle.

procedure (SYN.) process, way, fashion, form, mode, conduct, practice, manner, habit, system, operation, management, plan.

proceed (SYN.) progress, continue, issue, result, spring, thrive, improve, advance, emanate, rise.

(ANT.) retard, withhold, withdraw, hinder, retreat, oppose.

proceeding (SYN.) occurrence, business, affair, deal, negotiation, transaction, deed.

proceedings (SYN.) account, record, document.

proceeds (SYN.) result, produce, income, reward, intake, fruit, profit, store, yield, product, return, harvest, crop.

process (SYN.) method, course, system, procedure, operation, prepare, treat.

procession (SYN.) cortege, parade, sequence, train, cavalcade, file, retinue, succession.

proclaim (SYN.) declare, assert, make known, promulgate, state, broadcast, aver, express, announce, advertise, tell, publish, profess.

proclamation (SYN.) statement, declaration, announcement, promulgation, notice, manifesto.

procrastinate (SYN.) waver, vacillate, defer, hesitate, delay, postpone.

procreate (SYN.) generate, produce, beget, engender, originate, propagate, sire, create, father.

(ANT.) murder, destroy, abort, kill, extinguish.

procure (SYN.) secure, gain, attain, obtain, acquire, earn.

(ANT.) lose.

prod (SYN.) goad, nudge, jab, push.

prodigious (SYN.) astonishing, enormous, immense, monstrous, huge, remarkable, marvelous, amazing, astounding, monumental.

(ANT.) insignificant, commonplace, small.

produce (SYN.) harvest, reaping, bear, result, originate, bring about, store, supply, make, create, crop, proceeds, bring forth, occasion, breed, generate, cause, exhibit, show, demonstrate, fabricate, hatch, display, manufacture, exhibit, give, yield.

(ANT.) conceal, reduce, destroy, consume, waste, hide.

product (SYN.) outcome, result, output, produce, goods, commodity, stock, merchandise.

productive (SYN.) fertile, luxuriant, rich, bountiful, fruitful, creative, fecund, teeming, plenteous, prolific.

(ANT.) wasteful, unproductive, barren, impotent, useless, sterile.

profanation (SYN.) dishonor, insult, outrage, aspersion, defamation, invective, misuse, abuse, reviling, maltreatment, desecration, perversion.

(ANT.) plaudit, commendation, laudation, respect, approval.

profane (SYN.) deflower, violate, desecrate, pollute, dishonor, ravish, debauch.

profess (SYN.) declare, assert, make known, state, protest, announce, aver, express, broadcast, avow, tell.

(ANT.) *suppress, conceal, repress, withhold.*

profession *(SYN.)* calling, occupation, vocation, employment.

(ANT.) *hobby, avocation, pastime.*

proffer *(SYN.)* extend, tender, volunteer, propose, advance.

(ANT.) *reject, spurn, accept, receive, retain.*

proficient *(SYN.)* competent, adept, clever, able, cunning, practiced, skilled, versed, ingenious, accomplished, skillful, expert.

(ANT.) *untrained, inexpert, bungling, awkward, clumsy.*

profit *(SYN.)* gain, service, advantage, return, earnings, emolument, improvement, benefit, better, improve, use, avail.

(ANT.) *waste, loss, detriment, debit, lose, damage, ruin.*

profitable *(SYN.)* beneficial, advantageous, helpful, wholesome, useful, gainful, favorable, serviceable, salutary, productive, good.

(ANT.) *harmful, destructive, injurious, deleterious, detrimental.*

profligate *(SYN.)* corrupt, debased, tainted, unsound, vitiated, venal, contaminated, crooked, depraved, impure.

profound *(SYN.)* deep, serious, knowing, wise, intelligent, knowledgeable, recondite, solemn, abstruse, penetrating.

(ANT.) *trivial, slight, shallow,* superficial.

profuse *(SYN.)* lavish, excessive, extravagant, improvident, luxuriant, prodigal, wasteful, exuberant, immoderate, plentiful.

(ANT.) *meager, poor, economical, sparse, skimpy.*

profusion *(SYN.)* immoderation, superabundance, surplus, extravagance, intemperance, superfluity.

(ANT.) *lack, paucity, death, want, deficiency.*

program *(SYN.)* record, schedule, plan, agenda, calendar.

progress *(SYN.)* advancement, improvement, development, betterment, advance, movement, improve, progression.

(ANT.) *delay, regression, relapse, decline.*

progression *(SYN.)* gradation, string, train, chain, arrangement, following, arrangement, order.

prohibit *(SYN.)* hinder, forbid, disallow, obstruct, prevent, stop, ban, interdict, debar.

(ANT.) *help, tolerate, allow, sanction, encourage, permit.*

prohibition *(SYN.)* prevention, ban, embargo, restriction.

(ANT.) *allowance, permission.*

prohibitive *(SYN.)* forbidding, restrictive.

project *(SYN.)* design, proposal, scheme, contrivance, outline, homework, activity, purpose, bulge, protrude, throw, cast, device, plan.

(ANT.) *production, accomplishment, performance.*

prolific (SYN.) fertile, rich, fruitful, teeming, fecund, bountiful, luxuriant, productive, plenteous.

(ANT.) unproductive, barren, sterile, impotent.

prolong (SYN.) extend, increase, protract, draw, stretch, lengthen.

(ANT.) shorten.

prominent (SYN.) distinguished, illustrious, outstanding, renowned, influential, famous, well-known, noted, notable, important, conspicuous, eminent, leading, celebrated.

(ANT.) vulgar, ordinary, common.

promise (SYN.) assurance, guarantee, pledge, undertaking, agreement, bestowal, word, contract, oath, vow.

promote (SYN.) advance, foster, encourage, assist, support, further, aid, help, elevate, raise, facilitate, forward.

(ANT.) obstruct, demote, hinder, impede.

prompt (SYN.) punctual, timely, exact, arouse, evoke, occasion, induce, urge, ineffect, cite, suggest, hint, cause, mention, propose, make, precise, originate.

(ANT.) laggardly, slow, tardy, dilatory.

promptly (SYN.) immediately, instantly, straightway, forthwith, directly, instantaneously, presently.

(ANT.) later, sometime, hereafter, distantly, shortly.

promulgate (SYN.) declare, known, protest, affirm, broadcast, profess, assert, proclaim, state, aver, tell.

(ANT.) repress, conceal, withhold.

prone (SYN.) apt, inclined, disposed, likely, predisposed.

pronounce (SYN.) proclaim, utter, announce, articulate, enunciate.

pronounced (SYN.) clear, definite.

(ANT.) minor, unnoticeable.

proof (SYN.) evidence, verification, confirmation, experiment, demonstration, testimony, trial, protected, impenetrable, corroboration, test.

(ANT.) fallacy, invalidity, failure.

propagate (SYN.) create, procreate, sire, beget, breed, father, originate, produce.

(ANT.) extinguish, kill, abort, destroy.

propel (SYN.) drive, push, transfer, actuate, induce, shift, persuade, move.

(ANT.) stay, deter, halt, rest, stop.

propensity (SYN.) leaning, proneness, trend, drift, aim, inclination, bias, proclivity, tendency, predisposition.

(ANT.) disinclination, aversion.

proper (SYN.) correct, suitable, decent, peculiar, legitimate, right, conventional, decent, just, well-mannered, seemly, fit, appropriate, fitting, respectable, special.

property (SYN.) real estate,

effects, possessions, quality, characteristic, merchandise, stock, possession, land, wealth, belongings, attribute, trait.
(ANT.) *poverty, destitution, want, deprivation.*

prophecy (SYN.) augury, prediction.

prophesy (SYN.) foretell, predict, augur.

prophet (SYN.) fortuneteller, oracle, seer, soothsayer, clairvoyant.

propitious (SYN.) lucky, opportune, advantageous, favorable, fortunate, promising, happy.

proportion (SYN.) steadiness, poise, composure, relation, balance, equilibrium, comparison, section, part, arrange, adjust, symmetry.
(ANT.) *unsteadiness, imbalance, fall.*

proposal (SYN.) plan, proposition, tender, scheme, program, offer, suggestion, overture.
(ANT.) *rejection, acceptance, denial.*

propose (SYN.) offer, proffer, recommend, plan, mean, expect, move, design, propound, present, tender.
(ANT.) *fulfill, perform, effect.*

proposition (SYN.) proposal, motion.

propound (SYN.) bring forward, offer, advance, allege, propose, assign.
(ANT.) *retreat, hinder, withhold, retard.*

proprietor (SYN.) master, owner.

(ANT.) *slave, servant*

prosaic (SYN.) commonplace, common, everyday, ordinary, routine.
(ANT.) *exciting, different, extraordinary.*

proscribe (SYN.) forbid, ban, prohibit.
(ANT.) *permit, allow.*

prospect (SYN.) anticipation, expectation, candidate, buyer, explore, search.

prospective (SYN.) planned, proposed.

prosper (SYN.) succeed, win, achieve, gain, rise, prevail, flourish, thrive.
(ANT.) *miscarry, wane, miss, fail.*

prosperous (SYN.) rich, wealthy, affluent, well-to-do, sumptuous, well-off, flourishing, thriving, opulent, luxurious.
(ANT.) *impoverished, indigent, beggarly, needy, destitute, poor.*

prostrate (SYN.) prone, supine, overcome, recumbent, crushed.

protect (SYN.) defend, preserve, save, keep, conserve, safeguard, maintain, guard, shield, secure.
(ANT.) *impair, abandon, destroy, abolish, injure.*

protection (SYN.) safeguard, shelter, security, bulwark, fence, guard, safety, assurance, defense, refuge, shield.

protest (SYN.) dissent, noncompliance, disagree, objection, disagreement, challenge, difference, complaint, nonconformity, variance, opposition, remonstrate, reject, disapprove, complain, object, rejection.

(ANT.) acquiesce, assent, compliance, concur, comply, acceptance approval.

prototype (SYN.) model, archetype, specimen, instance, illustration, example, pattern, sample.

(ANT.) rule, concept, precept, principle.

protract (SYN.) extend, strain, distend, expand, spread, stretch, elongate, distort, lengthen.

(ANT.) tighten, contract, loosen, shrink.

protuberance (SYN.) prominence, projection, bulge, protrusion, swelling.

proud (SYN.) overbearing, vain, arrogant, haughty, stately, vain, glorious, disdainful, prideful, conceited, egotistical, self-important, supercilious.

(ANT.) humble, meek, ashamed, lowly.

prove (SYN.) manifest, verify, confirm, demonstrate, establish, show, affirm, examine, corroborate, try, test.

(ANT.) contradict, refute, disprove.

proverb (SYN.) maxim, byword, saying, adage, saw, motto, apothegm

proverbial (SYN.) common, well-known.

provide (SYN.) supply, endow,

afford, produce, yield, give, fit, equip, furnish, bestow, fit out.

(ANT.) strip, denude, divest, despoil.

provident (SYN.) saving, thrifty, economical, frugal, sparing.

(ANT.) wasteful, lavish, extravagant.

provision (SYN.) supply, fund, condition, arrangement, accumulation, reserve, store, hoard.

provisions (SYN.) stock, supplies, store.

provoke (SYN.) excite, stimulate, agitate, arouse, incite, stir up, vex, bother, disquiet, excite, irritate, annoy, anger.

(ANT.) quell, allay, pacify, calm, quiet.

prowess (SYN.) fortitude, mettle, boldness, fearlessness, courage, chivalry, bravery, resolution.

(ANT.) pusillanimity, fear, cowardice, timidity.

prowl (SYN.) sneak, slink, lurk.

proximate (SYN.) nigh, imminent, adjacent, neighboring, bordering, close, impending, approaching.

(ANT.) removed, distant, far.

proximity (SYN.) vicinity, nearness.

proxy (SYN.) representative, equivalent, makeshift, alternate, deputy, substitute, expedient, lieutenant.

(ANT.) sovereign, head, principal, master.

prudence (SYN.) watchfulness,

care, heed, vigilance, wariness, carefulness, tact, judgment, wisdom, common, foresight, caution.

(ANT.) rashness, recklessness, abandon, foolishness, carelessness.

prudent *(SYN.)* reasonable, sensible, sound, discreet, practical, judicious, sagacious, sensible, provident, sage, intelligent, sober, careful, wise.

(ANT.) stupid, unaware, absurd.

pry *(SYN.)* peer, peep, meddle, peek.

prying *(SYN.)* inquisitive, meddling, curious, inquiring, nosy, peering, searching, interrogative, snoopy.

(ANT.) unconcerned, incurious, indifferent, uninterested.

psyche *(SYN.)* judgment, reason, understanding, brain, intellect, mentality, soul, mind, faculties, spirit.

(ANT.) materiality, body, matter, corporality.

psychosis *(SYN.)* derangement, insanity, madness, delirium, dementia, frenzy, lunacy, mania, aberration.

(ANT.) stability, rationality, sanity.

public *(SYN.)* common, civil, governmental, federal, unrestricted, people, society, open.

publish *(SYN.)* distribute, issue, declare, announce, reveal, proclaim, publicize, bring out.

pulchritude *(SYN.)* elegance, grace, loveliness, attractiveness, comeliness, fairness, charm, beauty.

(ANT.) ugliness, eyesore, deformity, homeliness, disfigurement.

pull *(SYN.)* attract, induce, prolong, draw, tow, drag, remove, take out, persuade, allure, entice, extract.

(ANT.) shorten, alienate, drive, propel.

pulsate *(SYN.)* beat, throb, palpitate.

pummel *(SYN.)* punish, correct, castigate, discipline, chastise, strike.

(ANT.) release, acquit, free, exonerate.

pump *(SYN.)* interrogate, question, ask, inquire, quiz, examine, query.

(ANT.) state, answer, respond, reply.

punctual *(SYN.)* timely, prompt, exact, ready, nice, precise.

(ANT.) laggardly, tardy, dilatory, late.

punish *(SYN.)* correct, pummel, chasten, reprove, strike, castigate, chastise.

(ANT.) release, exonerate, reward, pardon, acquit, free.

punishment *(SYN.)* correction, discipline.

(ANT.) turbulence, chaos, confusion.

puny *(SYN.)* feeble, impaired, exhausted, infirm, unimportant, frail, decrepit, trivial, enervated, powerless, forceless, delicate.

(ANT.) strong, forceful, lusty, vigorous.

pupil *(SYN.)* learner, student, undergraduate.

purchase *(SYN.)* get, procure, buy, shopping, acquire, obtain.

(ANT.) sell, dispose of, vend.

pure *(SYN.)* chaste, absolute, clean, immaculate, untainted, spotless, guiltless, modest, virgin, bare, unmixed, simple, undiluted, uncontaminated, innocent, chaste, undefiled, genuine, clear.

(ANT.) corrupt, mixed, defiled, foul, tainted, adulterated, polluted, tarnished.

purely *(SYN.)* entirely, completely.

purify *(SYN.)* cleanse, wash, clean, mop, sweep.

(ANT.) soil, dirty, stain, pollute.

puritanical *(SYN.)* prim, stiff.

(ANT.) permissive.

purloin *(SYN.)* loot, plagiarize, steal, pilfer, burglarize, plunder, pillage, snitch, embezzle, swipe.

(ANT.) repay, return, refund, buy.

purport *(SYN.)* import, meaning, explanation, acceptance, drift, sense, significance, intent, gist.

purpose *(SYN.)* intention, end, goal, aim, objective, application, use, drift, object, intent, design.

(ANT.) hazard, accident, fate.

pursue *(SYN.)* persist, track follow, hunt, chase, trail.

(ANT.) evade, abandon, flee, elude.

pursuit *(SYN.)* hunt, chase.

push *(SYN.)* jostle, shove, urge, press, thrust, force, drive, crowd, hasten, shove, propel, promote.

(ANT.) ignore, halt, drag, oppose.

pushy *(SYN.)* impudent, abrupt, prominent, insolent, forward, brazen, conspicuous, bold, striking.

(ANT.) retiring, timid, cowardly, bashful.

put *(SYN.)* set, place, state, express, assign, attach, establish.

putrefy *(SYN.)* disintegrate, decay, rot, waste, spoil, decompose.

(ANT.) grow, increase, luxuriate.

putrid *(SYN.)* decayed, rotten, moldy, decomposed.

puzzle *(SYN.)* mystery, mystify, confound, perplex, riddle, conundrum, confusion, question, bewilder, confuse, enigma, problem.

(ANT.) key, solution, solve, explain, answer, resolution, clue.

Q

quack *(SYN.)* faker, fake, fraud, gaggle, clack, gabble, bluffer, cackle, dissembler, charlatan, impostor.

quackery *(SYN.)* charlatanism, deceit, make- believe, fakcry, duplicity, dissimulation, pretense, fraudulence, sham, counterfeiting, show.

(ANT.) integrity, probity, verac-

ity, sincerity, honesty.

quaff *(SYN.)* swig, swill, swallow, lap up, sip, drink, ingurgitate, guzzle, imbibe.

quagmire *(SYN.)* swamp, bog, fen, ooze, morass, slough, marsh, plight, predicament, dilemma, impasse, fix, entanglement, quicksand, hole, quandary.

quail *(SYN.)* recoil, cower, flinch, blench, wince, falter, shrink, shake, hesitate, faint.

(ANT.) brave, resist, defy, withstand.

quaint *(SYN.)* odd, uncommon, old-fashioned, antique, antiquated, queer, unusual, curious, eccentric, peculiar, picturesque, singular, whimsical, droll, charming, fanciful, droll, strange.

(ANT.) usual, normal, common, novel, ordinary, modern, current, commonplace, familiar.

quake *(SYN.)* shake, tremble, shudder, quiver, pulsate, stagger, shiver, temblor, vibrate, throb, earthquake.

qualification *(SYN.)* efficiency, adaptation, restriction, aptness, skill, ability, faculty, talent, power, aptitude, competence, suitability, capability, fitness, condition, dexterity.

(ANT.) unreadiness, incapacity, disability.

qualified *(SYN.)* clever, skillful, efficient, suitable, able, capable, fit, fitted, suited, bounded, limited, contingent, eligible, delimited, adept, modified, competent.

(ANT.) deficient, inept, impotent, categorical, unlimited, unfit, incapable, unsuitable, inadequate.

qualify *(SYN.)* fit, suit, befit, ready, prepare, empower, lessen, moderate, soften, capacitate, condition, adapt, label, designate, name, call, equip, train, restrict, restrict, limit, change.

(ANT.) unfit, incapacitate, disable, disqualify, enlarge, reinforce, aggravate.

quality *(SYN.)* trait, feature, attribute, value, peculiarity, grade, caliber, character, distinction, rank, condition, status, characteristic, kind, nature, constitution, mark, type, property.

(ANT.) nature, inferiority, mediocrity, triviality, indifference, inferior, shoddy, secondrate, being, substance, essence.

qualm *(SYN.)* doubt, uneasiness, anxiety, suspicion, skepticism, question, pang, compunction, twinge, regret, uncertainty, demur, fear, remorse, misgiving.

(ANT.) security, comfort, confidence, easiness, invulnerability, firmness.

quandary *(SYN.)* predicament, perplexity, confusion, uncertainty, puzzle, plight, bewilderment, fix, difficulty, entanglement, impasse, dilemma, crisis.

(ANT.) ease, relief, certainty, assurance.

quantity *(SYN.)* sum, measure,

volume, content, aggregate, bulk, mass, portion, amount, number, multitude, extent.

(ANT.) zero, nothing.

quarantine (SYN.) segregate, separate, confine, isolate, seclude.

quarrel (SYN.) contention, argument, affray, dispute, altercation, squabble, feud, difference, disagree, bicker, differ, spar, fight, bickering, argue, disagreement, spat.

(ANT.) peace, friendliness, reconciliation, amity, agreement, sympathy, accord, concur, agree, unity, harmony.

quarrelsome (SYN.) testy, contentious, edgy, peevish, irritable, snappish, argumentative, disputatious, cranky, belligerent, combative.

(ANT.) genial, friendly, peaceful, easygoing, peaceable, tempered.

quarry (SYN.) prey, quest, game, victim, goal, aim, prize, objective.

quarter (SYN.) place, source, fount, well, origin, mainspring, ruth, mercy, pity, compassion, clemency, benevolence, forbearance.

(ANT.) ruthlessness, brutality, cruelty, barbarity, harshness, ferocity.

quarters (SYN.) residence, rooms, lodgings, dwelling, flat, billets, chambers, accommodations.

quash (SYN.) void, annul, overthrow, nullify, suppress, cancel, quench, quell, repress, invalidate.

(ANT.) incite, reinforce, sustain, authorize, sanction, validate.

quasi (SYN.) wouldbe, partial, synthetic, nominal, imitation, bogus, sham, counterfeit, mock.

(ANT.) certified, real, legitimate.

quaver (SYN.) tremble, shake, hesitate, trill, oscillate, waver, vibrate, shiver, quiver, falter, quake.

quay (SYN.) dock, wharf, pier, jetty, bank.

queasy (SYN.) sick, squeamish, nauseated, uneasy, restless, nauseous, uncomfortable.

(ANT.) untroubled, comfortable, easy, relaxed.

queen (SYN.) empress, diva, doyenne, goddess, star.

queer (SYN.) odd, quaint, curious, unusual, droll, strange, peculiar, extraordinary, singular, uncommon, eccentric, weird, funny, nutty, screwy, wacky, deviant, whimsical.

(ANT.) familiar, usual, normal, common, plain, patent, conventional, ordinary.

quell (SYN.) subdue, calm, pacify, quiet, cool, hush, appease, lull, mollify, reduce, crush, smother, suppress, stifle, extinguish, overpower, repress.

(ANT.) encourage, foment, arouse, foster, incite.

quench (SYN.) extinguish, stop, suppress, sate, allay, abate, stifle, slacken, put out, slake, satisfy, appease, refresh.

(ANT.) set, light, begin, start, kindle.

querulous *(SYN.)* faultfinding, fretful, carping, critical, complaining, censorious, captious, petulant.

(ANT.) pleased, easygoing, contented, carefree.

query *(SYN.)* inquire, interrogate, demand, investigate, probe, examine, question, inquiry, ask.

(ANT.) answer.

quest *(SYN.)* investigation, interrogation, research, examination, search, question, exploration, seek, pursue, hunt, pursuit, explore, query.

(ANT.) negligence, inactivity, disregard.

question *(SYN.)* interrogate, quiz, doubt, ask, pump, challenge, inquiry, uncertainty, interview, suspect, inquire, dispute, demand, examine, query.

(ANT.) accept, solution, reply, assurance, rejoinder, state, answer, result, response, attest, confidence, respond.

questionable *(SYN.)* uncertain, doubtful, dubious, implausible, debatable, hypothetical, unlikely.

(ANT.) obvious, assured, indubitable, proper, unimpeachable, seemly, conventional, sure, certain.

queue *(SYN.)* file, row, line, series, chain, tier, sequence, string.

quibble *(SYN.)* cavil, shift, eva-

sion, dodge, equivocation, sophism, prevaricate, quiddity, palter, objection, evade.

quick *(SYN.)* rapid, touchy, shrewd, active, hasty, testy, nimble, irascible, discerning, fast, swift, precipitate, excitable, speedy, sharp, impatient, acute, abrupt, curt, brisk, clever, keen, lively.

(ANT.) inattentive, dull, gradual, patient, slow, unaware, unhurried, backward, deliberate, sluggish.

quicken *(SYN.)* expedite, forward, rush, hurry, accelerate, push, hasten, dispatch, facilitate, speed.

(ANT.) slow, impede, hinder, hamper, delay, kill, deaden, retard, block.

quickly *(SYN.)* soon, rapidly, fast, at once, promptly, presently, swiftly, hastily, fleety, headlong, immediately, now.

(ANT.) deliberately, slowly, later, gradually.

quickness *(SYN.)* energy, vigor, intensity, action, movement, briskness, exercise, motion, rapidity, agility, enterprise.

(ANT.) sloth, idleness, inertia, dullness.

quick-witted *(SYN.)* astute, shrewd, alert, keen, penetrating, quick, knowing, intelligent, clever.

(ANT.) slow, dull, unintelligent, gradual, plodding.

quiescent *(SYN.)* latent, resting, silent, tranquil, undeveloped, still, quiet, dormant, secret,

inactive.
(ANT.) visible, aroused, evident, active, patent, astir, manifest.

quiet (SYN.) meek, passive, hushed, peaceful, calm, patient, quiescent, motionless, tranquil, gentle, undisturbed, mild, peace, silent, quiescence, hush, modest, quietude, rest, tranquillity, calmness, repose, silence, placid, serenity, soundless.
(ANT.) disturbed, agitation, excitement, loud, disturbance, restless, noisy, boisterous, anxious, perturbed, noise, agitated.

quietness (SYN.) tranquillity, repose, calm, silence, quietude, calmness, stillness, quietism, muteness, noiselessness, placidity, seclusion.
(ANT.) flurry, disturbance, fuss, turbulence, agitation, uproar, tumult.

quintessence (SYN.) heart, soul, extract, essence, distillation, core.
(ANT.) contingency, adjunct, excrescence, nonessential.

quip (SYN.) jest, sally, wisecrack, witticism, joke, jibe, pleasantry, sarcasm, retort.

quirk (SYN.) mannerism, idiosyncrasy, foible, peculiarity, oddity, quiddity, vagary, habit, trait, eccentricity.

quirky (SYN.) odd, weird, whimsical, peculiar, pixilated, erratic, kinky.
(ANT.) normal, conventional, steady.

quisling (SYN.) collaborationist, traitor, subversive, betrayer.
(ANT.) partisan, loyalist.

quit (SYN.) leave, stop, desist, depart, abandon, resign, withdraw, refrain, retreat, cease, vacate, end, relinquish, discontinue, halt, lay off, surrender, conclude, go.
(ANT.) persevere, remain, stay, endure, persist, abide, continue.

quite (SYN.) somewhat, rather, completely, truly, absolutely, really, entirely.
(ANT.) hardly, merely, barely, somewhat.

quitter (SYN.) shirker, dropout, defeatist, piker, loser, malingerer, deserter, stop, desist.

quiver (SYN.) quake, shake, shudder, tremble, vibrate, shiver.

quixotic (SYN.) unrealistic, romantic, visionary, impractical, idealistic, chimerical, lofty, fantastic, fey.
(ANT.) pragmatic, realistic, prosaic, practical.

quiz (SYN.) challenge, interrogate, inquire, pump, doubt, question, ask, dispute, test, query, examine, questioning, investigate.
(ANT.) reply, say, inform, respond, accept, answer, state.

quizzical (SYN.) teasing, coy, mocking, derisive, insolent, arch, bantering, puzzled, questioning, baffled.
(ANT.) respectful, obsequious, uninterested, normal, every-

day, usual, serious, attentive.

quota (SYN.) share, portion, apportionment, ratio, proportion, allotment.

quotation (SYN.) quote, selection, excerpt, repetition, cutting, reference.

quote (SYN.) refer to, recite, paraphrase, adduce, repeat, illustrate, cite, echo, plagiarize, excerpt, extract.

(ANT.) retort, contradict, refute.

R

rabble (SYN.) throng, mob, horde, crowd.

rabid (SYN.) frantic, frenzied, violent, raging, raving, zealous.

(ANT.) normal, sound, sober, moderate.

race (SYN.) meet, run, clan, stock, lineage, strain, match, course, stream, hasten, compete, folk, competition, dash, contest, contend, hurry, speed, tribe.

(ANT.) linger, dawdle, dwell.

rack (SYN.) frame, frame-work, bracket, scaffold, skeleton.

racket (SYN.) sound, cry, babel, noise, uproar, hubbub, clamor, fuss, disturbance, din, tumult, fracas, clatter.

(ANT.) stillness, hush, silence, quiet, tranquillity, peace.

racy (SYN.) interesting, vigorous, spirited, animated, entertaining.

radiance (SYN.) luster, brilliancy, brightness, splendor, effulgence, glowing.

(ANT.) gloom, darkness, obscurity.

radiant (SYN.) showy, superb, brilliant, illustrious, dazzling, grand, shining, bright, effulgent.

(ANT.) dark, unimpressive, dull, dim, lusterless, ordinary.

radiate (SYN.) spread, emit, diffuse, shed, irradiate, shine, gleam.

radical (SYN.) ultra, innate, essential, organic, complete, revolutionary, insurgent, natural, total, extreme, basic, original.

(ANT.) extraneous, moderate, conservative, superficial, established.

radius (SYN.) orbit, reach, extent, scope, sphere, range, sweep.

raft (SYN.) pontoon, platform, float.

rag (SYN.) dishcloth, dishrag, cloth.

rage (SYN.) passion, ire, exasperation, fashion, fad, vogue, craze, anger, temper, fury, irritation, mania, rave, rant, storm, fume.

(ANT.) peace, forbearance, conciliation, patience.

raging (SYN.) raving, severe, passionate, boisterous, violent, fierce, wild, passionate, acute.

(ANT.) feeble, soft, calm, quiet.

ragged (SYN.) tattered, torn, worn, shredded, threadbare, shabby.

raid (SYN.) assault, attack, invasion, arrest, invade,

seizure.

rail (SYN.) railing, fence, bar.

railing (SYN.) balustrade, banister, barrier, fence.

rain (SYN.) shower, drizzle, rainstorm, sprinkle, deluge.

raise (SYN.) grow, muster, elevate, heave, cultivate, awake, rouse, excite, enlarge, increase, rise, breed, hoist, bring up, rear, gather, exalt.
(ANT.) cut, destroy, decrease, lessen, depreciate, lower, abase, debase, drop, demolish, level.

rakish (SYN.) dapper, dashing, smart, debonair, natty, swanky, showy.

rally (SYN.) muster, convoke, summon, convene, convention, assemblage.

ramble (SYN.) err, amble, saunter, wander, roam, walk, meander, deviate, stroll, digress, stray.
(ANT.) stop, linger, stay, halt, settle.

rambling (SYN.) incoherent, erratic.
(ANT.) straightforward, coherent.

rambunctious (SYN.) stubborn, defiant, unruly, aggressive, contrary.

ramification (SYN.) aftermath, extension, branch, offshoot, result, consequence.

rampage (SYN.) tumult, outbreak, uproar, rage, frenzy, ebullition, storm.

rampant (SYN.) excessive, flagrant, boisterous, menacing.
(ANT.) bland, calm, mild.

ramshackle (SYN.) rickety, decrepit, flimsy, dilapidated, shaky.

rancid (SYN.) spoiled, rank, tainted, sour, musty, putrid, rotten, putrescent.
(ANT.) pure, fresh, wholesome, fragrant.

rancor (SYN.) spite, grudge, malice, animosity, malevolence, hostility.
(ANT.) kindness, toleration, affection.

random (SYN.) haphazard, chance, casual, unscheduled, unplanned.
(ANT.) intentional, specific, particular.

range (SYN.) expanse, extent, limit, area, grassland, pasture, plain, change, wander, roam, travel, rove.

rank (SYN.) estate, blood, range, grade, standing, hue, eminence, level, class, order, classify, dense, wild, rotten, degree, standing, arrange, sort, row.
(ANT.) shame, disrepute, stigma, humiliation.

ransack (SYN.) pillage, loot, rummage, plunder, despoil, ravish, search.

ransom (SYN.) release, deliverance, compensation, redeem.

rant (SYN.) declaim, rave, harangue.

rap (SYN.) thump, knock, blow, whack.

rapacious (SYN.) greedy, wolfish, avaricious, ravenous, grasping, predatory.

rapid (SYN.) speedy, quick,

swift, fast.

(ANT.) deliberate, halting, sluggish, slow.

rapidity *(SYN.)* motion, enterprise, action, vigor, liveliness, activity, quickness, exercise, energy.

(ANT.) sloth, dullness, inertia, idleness.

rapine *(SYN.)* destruction, pillage, robbery, marauding, spoiling.

rapport *(SYN.)* harmony, fellowship, agreement, mutuality, accord, empathy.

rapture *(SYN.)* joy, gladness, ecstasy, bliss, transport, exultation, delight, happiness, enchantment, ravishment.

(ANT.) woe, misery, wretch, depression.

rare *(SYN.)* unique, strange, precious, uncommon, infrequent, choice, singular, occasional, unusual, fine, matchless, incomparable, scarce.

(ANT.) worthless, common, commonplace, usual, everyday, customary.

rarely *(SYN.)* scarcely, hardly infrequently, occasionally, sparingly, barely.

(ANT.) usually, continually, often.

rascal *(SYN.)* scoundrel, villain, trickster, rogue, scamp, swindler, imp, prankster.

rash *(SYN.)* quick, careless, passionate, thoughtless, hotheaded, reckless, foolhardy, eruption, dermatitis, heedless.

(ANT.) thoughtful, considered, prudent, reasoning, calculat-

ing, careful.

raspy *(SYN.)* gruff, harsh, dissonant, grinding, hoarse, grating, strident.

rate *(SYN.)* try, adjudicate, consider, decide, condemn, decree, estimate, speed, pace, measure, judge, arbitrate, velocity, ratio, evaluate.

ratify *(SYN.)* validate, certify, confirm, establish, support, endorse, uphold.

rating *(SYN.)* assessment, position, assignment, status, classification.

ration *(SYN.)* portion, allowance, distribute, measure, allotment, share, percentage.

rational *(SYN.)* sound, wise, sane, intelligent, sensible, judicious, sober.

(ANT.) irrational, absurd, insane.

rationality *(SYN.)* cause, aim, intelligence, reason, basis, mind, understanding, ground, argument, sense.

raucous *(SYN.)* raspy, harsh, grating, hoarse, discordant, rowdy.

(ANT.) dulcet, pleasant, sweet.

ravage *(SYN.)* ruin, despoil, strip, waste, destroy, pillage, plunder, sack, havoc.

(ANT.) conserve, save, accumulate.

rave *(SYN.)* rage, storm, laud, praise.

ravenous *(SYN.)* hungry, voracious, craving, starved, gluttonous, famished.

(ANT.) replete, gorged, satiated, full.

ravine *(SYN.)* chasm, gorge, crevasse, canyon, abyss.

ravish *(SYN.)* violate, debauch.

ravishing *(SYN.)* enchanting, captivating, bewitching, fascinating, alluring.
(ANT.) loathsome, disgusting, repulsive.

raw *(SYN.)* harsh, rough, coarse, unrefined, undone, uncooked, crude, unprocessed, unpolished, natural.
(ANT.) finished, refined, processed.

ray *(SYN.)* beam.

raze *(SYN.)* ravage, wreck, destroy, flatten, annihilate, obliterate, demolish.
(ANT.) make, erect, construct, preserve establish save.

reach *(SYN.)* overtake, arrive at, extent, distance, scope, range, extend, attain, stretch.
(ANT.) fail, miss.

react *(SYN.)* result, reply, respond.
(ANT.) overlook, disregard.

reaction *(SYN.)* result, response, reception, repercussion.

readable *(SYN.)* understandable, distinct, legible, plain, clear, comprehensible.
(ANT.) obliterated, illegible, defaced.

readily *(SYN.)* quickly, promptly, easily.

ready *(SYN.)* mature, ripe, complete, seasonable, done, arrange, prompt, prepared, completed, quick, mellow.
(ANT.) undeveloped, immature, green.

real *(SYN.)* true, actual, positive, authentic, genuine, veritable.
(ANT.) counterfeit, unreal, fictitious, false, sham, supposed.

realization *(SYN.)* completion, achievement, performance, accomplishment, comprehension, insight.
(ANT.) failure.

realize *(SYN.)* discern, learn, comprehend, appreciate, perfect, actualize, understand, apprehend, know, see.
(ANT.) misunderstand, misapprehend.

really *(SYN.)* truly, actually, honestly, undoubtedly, positively, genuinely.
(ANT.) questionably, possibly, doubtfully.

realm *(SYN.)* land, domain, farm, kingdom, sphere, department, estate, world.

reap *(SYN.)* gather, harvest, gain, glean, produce, cut, pick, acquire, garner.
(ANT.) plant, seed, sow, lose, squander.

reaping *(SYN.)* proceeds, result, crop, yield, fruit, produce.

rear *(SYN.)* posterior, raise, lift, train, nurture, rump, back, elevate, construct, build, foster.

reason *(SYN.)* intelligence, objective, aim, understanding, mind, argument, cause, judgment, common sense, sanity, gather, assume, sake, motive.

reasonable *(SYN.)* prudent, rational, logical, sage, sound, moderate, intelligent, sensible, discreet.

(ANT.) unaware, imperceptible, insane, absurd, stupid, illogical, irrational.

rebel *(SYN.)* revolutionary, traitor, mutineer, mutiny, revolt, disobey.

rebellion *(SYN.)* revolt, uprising, coup, overthrow, insurrection, revolution.

(ANT.) submission, obedience, repression, peace.

rebellious *(SYN.)* unruly, forward, defiant, undutiful, disobedient.

(ANT.) obedient, compliant, submissive.

rebirth *(SYN.)* renascence, renaissance, revival.

rebuff *(SYN.)* snub, oppose, resist, reject, refuse, slight, opposition.

(ANT.) welcome, encourage, support.

rebuild *(SYN.)* restore, renew, refresh, reconstruct, renovate.

rebuke *(SYN.)* chide, scold, reproach, censure, upbraid, scolding, condemn.

(ANT.) praise, exonerate, absolve.

rebuttal *(SYN.)* contradiction, defense, answer.

(ANT.) argument, validation, corroboration.

recall *(SYN.)* recollect, remembrance, withdraw, retract, remember, recollection, reminisce, mind, memory, remind.

(ANT.) forget, overlook, ignore.

recede *(SYN.)* withdraw, ebb, retire, retreat.

receive *(SYN.)* entertain, ac-

quire, admit, accept, shelter, greet, obtain, welcome.

(ANT.) reject, offer, give, bestow, discharge, impart.

recent *(SYN.)* novel, original, late, new, newfangled, fresh, modern, current.

(ANT.) old, antiquated, ancient.

reception *(SYN.)* gathering, party.

recess *(SYN.)* hollow, opening, nook, cranny, dent, respite, rest, break, pause.

(ANT.) gather, convene.

recession *(SYN.)* slump, depression.

recipe *(SYN.)* instructions, formula, prescriptions, procedure, method.

recital *(SYN.)* history, account, relation, chronicle, narrative, detail, narration.

(ANT.) distortion, confusion, misrepresentation.

recite *(SYN.)* describe, narrate, declaim, rehearse, tell, mention, repeat, detail, recapitulate, repeat, list, relate, deliver.

reckless *(SYN.)* thoughtless, inconsiderate, careless, imprudent, rash, indiscreet, unconcerned.

(ANT.) careful, nice, accurate.

reclaim *(SYN.)* reform, rescue, reinstate, regenerate, recycle.

recline *(SYN.)* stretch, sprawl, repose, rest, lounge, loll, incline.

recluse *(SYN.)* hermit, eremite, loner, anchorite.

recognize *(SYN.)* remember, avow, own, know, admit, apprehend, recollect, recall, concede, acknowledge, confess.

(ANT.) ignore, renounce.

recollect *(SYN.)* recall, remember, memory, reflect, call to mind, reminisce.

(ANT.) forget.

recollection *(SYN.)* remembrance, retrospection, impression, recall.

(ANT.) forgetfulness, oblivion.

recommend *(SYN.)* hint, refer, advise, commend, suggest, counsel, allude, praise, approve, intimate, advocate.

(ANT.) disapprove, declare, insist.

recommendation *(SYN.)* instruction, justice, trustworthiness, counsel, admonition, caution, integrity, uprightness.

(ANT.) fraud, deceit, trickery, cheating.

reconcile *(SYN.)* meditate, unite, adapt, adjust, settle, reunite, appease.

recondition *(SYN.)* rebuild, overhaul, restore, service.

reconsider *(SYN.)* ponder, reevaluate, mull over, reflect, reassess.

record *(SYN.)* enter, write, register, chronicle, history, account, document.

recount *(SYN.)* report, convey, narrate, tell, detail, recite, describe, repeat.

recoup *(SYN.)* regain, recover, repay, retrieve.

recover *(SYN.)* regain, redeem, recapture, retrieve, salvage, better, improve, mend, heal.

(ANT.) debilitate, succumb, worsen.

recreation *(SYN.)* entertainment, amusement, enjoyment, diversion, fun.

recrimination *(SYN.)* vindication, reproach, dissension, accusation, countercharge.

recruit *(SYN.)* trainee, beginner, volunteer, draftee, select, enlist, novice.

recuperate *(SYN.)* regain, retrieve, recapture, redeem, rally, convalesce, revive, recover, repossess, restore.

(ANT.) sicken, weaken, lose, regress, forfeit.

redeem *(SYN.)* claim, recover, repossess, regain, reclaim, cash in, retrieve.

reduce *(SYN.)* lessen, decrease, lower, downgrade, degrade, suppress, abate, diminish.

(ANT.) enlarge, swell, raise, elevate, revive, increase, amplify.

reduction *(SYN.)* shortening, abridgment, abbreviation.

(ANT.) amplification, extension, enlargement.

reek *(SYN.)* odor, stench, stink, smell

refer *(SYN.)* recommend, direct, commend, regard, concern, relate, suggest, mention.

referee *(SYN.)* judge, arbitrator, umpire, arbiter, moderator, mediator, intermediary.

reference *(SYN.)* allusion, direction, mention, concern, respect, referral.

refine *(SYN.)* purify, clarify, improve, clean.

(ANT.) pollute, debase, muddy, downgrade.

refined (SYN.) purified, cultured, cultivated, courteous, courtly.

(ANT.) rude, coarse, crude, vulgar.

refinement (SYN.) culture, enlightenment, education, civilization.

(ANT.) vulgarity, ignorance, boorishness.

reflect (SYN.) muse, mirror, deliberate, cogitate, think, reproduce, ponder, consider, reason, meditate, contemplate.

reflection (SYN.) warning, conception, intelligence, appearance, likeness, image, cogitation, notification.

reform (SYN.) right, improve, correction, change, amend, improvement, better, betterment, correct, rectify.

(ANT.) spoil, damage, aggravate, vitiate.

refresh (SYN.) exhilarate, renew, invigorate.

(ANT.) exhaust, tire.

refreshing (SYN.) bracing, cool, brisk, fresh.

refreshment (SYN.) food, snack, drink, nourishment, exhilaraton, stimulation.

refuge (SYN.) safety, retreat, shelter, asylum, sanctuary, harbor.

(ANT.) peril, exposure, jeopardy, danger.

refuse (SYN.) spurn, rebuff, decline, reject, trash, rubbish, withhold, disallow, waste, garbage, deny, demur.

(ANT.) allow, accept, welcome, grant.

refute (SYN.) rebut, disprove, confute, falsify, controvert, contradict.

(ANT.) prove, confirm, accept, establish.

regain (SYN.) redeem, retrieve, recover, repossess, recapture.

(ANT.) lose.

regalement (SYN.) feast, dinner, celebration, entertainment.

regard (SYN.) estimate, value, honor, affection, notice, care, consideration, consider, relation, respect, attend, thought, reference, care, attention, esteem, concern, liking.

(ANT.) neglect, disgust, antipathy.

regards (SYN.) salutations, greetings, good wishes, respects, remembrances.

regenerate (SYN.) improve, reconstruct, remedy, reestablish, rebuild.

regime (SYN.) direction, government, administration, management, dynasty, command, leadership.

regimented (SYN.) ordered, directed controlled, orderly, rigid, disciplined.

(ANT.) loose, free, unstructured.

region (SYN.) belt, place, spot, territory, climate, area, zone, locality, station, locale.

register (SYN.) catalog, record, book, list, roll, enter, roster, chronicle.

regressive (SYN.) revisionary, retrograde.

(ANT.) progressive, civilized, advanced.

regret *(SYN.)* sorrow, qualm, lament, grief, compunction, bemoan, concern, scruple, misgiving, remorse, contrition.

(ANT.) obduracy, complacency.

regular *(SYN.)* steady, orderly, natural, normal, customary, usual, habitual, even, uniform, systematic, unvaried, methodical, symmetrical.

(ANT.) odd, exceptional, unusual, irregular, abnormal, rare.

regulate *(SYN.)* control, manage, govern, direct, legislate, set, adjust, systematize.

regulation *(SYN.)* method, rule, axiom, guide, control, standard, canon, precept, restraint, requirement.

(ANT.) chaos, deviation, hazard, turbulence, confusion.

rehabilitate *(SYN.)* renew, restore, rebuild, reestablish, repair, reconstruct.

rehearse *(SYN.)* repeat, practice, train, learn, coach, prepare, perfect, direct.

reign *(SYN.)* dominion, power, rule, sovereignty, govern, domination.

reimburse *(SYN.)* recompense, remunerate, remit, compensate.

rein *(SYN.)* restriction, bridle, check, deterrent, curb, restraint, barrier, control.

reinforce *(SYN.)* brace, strengthen, fortify, intensify, support.

reiterate *(SYN.)* reproduce, recapitulate, duplicate, repeat, rephrase.

reject *(SYN.)* spurn, rebuff, decline, renounce, expel, discard, withhold, deny, refuse.

(ANT.) endorse, grant, welcome, accept.

rejection *(SYN.)* dissent, nonconformity, variance, challenge, remonstrance, difference, noncompliance.

(ANT.) assent, acceptance, compliance.

rejoice *(SYN.)* celebrate, delight, enjoy, revel, exhilarate, elate.

rejuvenate *(SYN.)* refresh, rekindle, overhaul, revitalize, animate, invigorate.

(ANT.) deplete, weaken, exhaust, enervate.

relapse *(SYN.)* worsen, deteriorate, regress, weaken, fade, worsen, sink, fail.

(ANT.) strengthen, progress, advance, get well, rehabilitate.

relate *(SYN.)* refer, beat, report, describe, tell, correlate, narrate, recount, compare, connect.

relation *(SYN.)* entente, compact, coalition, alliance, connection, relationship, association, partnership, similarity, kinsman, treaty, marriage.

(ANT.) separation, divorce.

relationship *(SYN.)* link, tie, alliance, connection, union, bond, affinity, conjunction.

(ANT.) separation, disunion.

relative *(SYN.)* dependent, proportional, about, pertinent, regarding.

relax *(SYN.)* slacken, loosen,

repose, rest, recline, unwind.

(ANT.) increase, tighten, intensify.

relaxation *(SYN.)* comfort, ease, rest, enjoyment, lull, recess, breather, loafing.

relaxed *(SYN.)* pleasing, casual, acceptable, informal, restful, agreeable, welcome.

(ANT.) formal, planned, wretched, distressing, troubling.

release *(SYN.)* liberate, emancipate, relinquish, proclaim, publish, liberation, announce, deliver, free, discharge, set free.

(ANT.) restrict, imprison, subjugate.

relegate *(SYN.)* entrust, authorize, remand, refer, assign.

relent *(SYN.)* cede, yield, surrender, give, relax, abdicate, relinquish, waive.

(ANT.) strive, assert, struggle.

relentless *(SYN.)* eternal, stubborn, tenacious, dogged, incessant, ceaseless, persistent, determined.

relevant *(SYN.)* related, material, apt, applicable, fit, relating, germane.

(ANT.) foreign, alien, unrelated.

reliable *(SYN.)* trusty, tried, certain, secure, trustworthy, dependable.

(ANT.) unreliable, eccentric, erratic, dubious.

reliance *(SYN.)* faith, confidence, trust.

(ANT.) mistrust, doubt, skepticism.

relic *(SYN.)* remains, fossil, throwback, heirloom, sou-

venir, keepsake, heirloom.

relief *(SYN.)* help, aid, comfort, ease, backing, patronage, alms, support.

(ANT.) hostility, defiance, antagonism, resistance.

relieve *(SYN.)* diminish, soothe, calm, abate, pacify, ease, lessen, replace, spell, lighten, comfort, alleviate.

(ANT.) disturb, irritate, agitate, trouble, aggravate, worry.

religion *(SYN.)* tenet, belief, dogma, faith, creed, persuasion.

religious *(SYN.)* godly, reverent, faithful, devout, zeal, pious, divine, holy, devoted, sacred, theological.

(ANT.) profane, irreligious, skeptical, impious, lax, atheistic.

religiousness *(SYN.)* love, zeal, affection, devoutness, fidelity, ardor.

(ANT.) indifference, apathy, unfaithfulness.

relinquish *(SYN.)* capitulate, submit, yield, abandon, cede, sacrifice, disclaim.

(ANT.) overcome, conquer, rout, resist.

relish *(SYN.)* enjoyment, satisfaction, delight, gusto, appreciation, condiment, like, enjoy, enthusiasm.

(ANT.) distaste, antipathy, disfavor, dislike.

reluctance *(SYN.)* disgust, hatred, repulsion, abhorrence, distaste, repugnance, aversion.

(ANT.) enthusiasm, affection,

devotion.

reluctant *(SYN.)* slow, averse, hesitant, unwilling, loath, disinclined, balky.

(ANT.) ready, eager, willing, disposed.

rely *(SYN.)* confide, trust, lean, depend.

(ANT.) mistrust, disbelieve, question, distrust.

remain *(SYN.)* survive, rest, stay, abide, halt, endure, dwell, tarry, continue, linger.

(ANT.) finish, leave, terminate, dissipate.

remainder *(SYN.)* leftover, residue, rest, surplus, balance, excess.

remains *(SYN.)* residue, balance, rest, remnants, relics, discards, waste, junk.

remark *(SYN.)* comment, state, utterance, mention, note, observe, observation, annotation, declaration, statement.

remarkable *(SYN.)* exciting, impressive, overpowering, unusual, affecting, thrilling, splendid, special, noteworthy, extraordinary, august, touching

(ANT.) ordinary, unimpressive, commonplace, average, regular.

remedy *(SYN.)* redress, help, cure, relief, medicine, restorative, rectify, alleviate, medication, correct, reparation.

remember *(SYN.)* recollect, reminisce, recall, memorize, mind, retain, remind.

(ANT.) forget, overlook, disregard.

remembrance *(SYN.)* monument, memory, recollection, memento, recall, keepsake, souvenir, retrospection.

remiss *(SYN.)* delinquent, lax, careless, negligent, oblivious, forgetful, absentminded, sloppy, irresponsible.

remit *(SYN.)* send, pay, forward, forgive, pardon, overlook, excuse, reimburse.

remittance *(SYN.)* payment.

remnant *(SYN.)* remains, remainder, rest, residue, trace, relic.

remodel *(SYN.)* remake, reshape, rebuild, redecorate, renovate, modify, change, alter, refurbish, update.

remonstrate *(SYN.)* grouch, protest, complain, grumble, murmur, repine, dispute.

(ANT.) rejoice, applaud, praise.

remorse *(SYN.)* sorrow, qualm, contrition, regret, compunction, repentance.

(ANT.) obduracy, complacency.

remorseless *(SYN.)* savage, unrelenting, crude, barbaric, merciless, cruel, fiendish, brutal, callous.

(ANT.) kind, refined, polite, civilized.

remote *(SYN.)* inconsiderable, removed, slight, far, unlikely, distant, inaccessible, unreachable, isolated, sequestered.

(ANT.) visible, nearby, current, near, close.

remove *(SYN.)* transport, eject, move, vacate, withdraw, dislodge, transfer, doff, displace, eliminate, murder, kill, oust, extract.

(ANT.) insert, retain, leave, stay, keep.

removed *(SYN.)* aloof, distant, cool, remote.

remuneration *(SYN.)* wages, payment, pay, salary, compensation, reward.

render *(SYN.)* become, make, perform, do, offer, present, give, submit.

rendition *(SYN.)* interpretation, version, depiction, expression, characterization.

renegade *(SYN.)* defector, insurgent, dissenter, rebel, maverick, mutineer, betrayer.

renege *(SYN.)* let down, double-cross, deceive.

renew *(SYN.)* restore, renovate, overhaul, revise, modernize, reshape, redo.

renounce *(SYN.)* resign, disown, revoke, abandon, quit, retract, forgo, leave, forsake, abdicate, reject, relinquish, deny.

(ANT.) assert, uphold, recognize, maintain.

renovate *(SYN.)* restore, rehabilitate, rebuild, refresh, renew, overhaul, redesign.

renown *(SYN.)* honor, reputation, eminence, acclaim, glory, repute, luster, fame, notability.

(ANT.) obscurity, anonymity, disgrace.

renowned *(SYN.)* noted, famous, distinguished, well-known, glorious, celebrated.

(ANT.) unknown, infamous, hidden, obscure.

rent *(SYN.)* payment, rental, let, lease, hire.

repair *(SYN.)* rebuilding, mend, renew, tinker, correct, patch, restore, adjust, reconstruction, remedy, amend, rehabilitation, retrieve.

(ANT.) harm, break.

repartee *(SYN.)* badinage, banter.

repast *(SYN.)* feast, banquet, meal, refreshment, snack.

repeal *(SYN.)* end, cancel, nullify, annul, quash, abolish, cancellation, rescind, abolition, abrogate.

repeat *(SYN.)* reiterate, restate, redo, rehearse, quote, remake, relate, iterate, reproduce.

repeated *(SYN.)* continuous, frequent, recurrent, continual.

repel *(SYN.)* check, repulse, rebuff, reject, decline, discourage.

(ANT.) lure, attract.

repellent *(SYN.)* sickening, offensive, disgusting, nauseating, repugnant, obnoxious.

repent *(SYN.)* deplore, regret, rue, lament.

repentance *(SYN.)* penitence, remorse, sorrow, compunction, qualm, grief.

(ANT.) obduracy, complacency.

repentant *(SYN.)* regretful, sorrowful, contrite, sorry, penitent.

(ANT.) remorseless, obdurate.

repetitious *(SYN.)* repeated, monotonous, boring, tiresome, humdrum.

repine *(SYN.)* protest, lament, complain, whine, regret, grouch, murmur, grumble.

(ANT.) rejoice, applaud, praise.

replace *(SYN.)* alternate, return, reinstate.

replacement *(SYN.)* understudy, proxy, second, alternate, substitute, replica, surrogate.

replenish *(SYN.)* store, pervade, fill, stock, occupy, supply.

(ANT.) empty, void, deplete, exhaust, drain.

replica *(SYN.)* reproduction, copy, exemplar, imitation, duplicate, facsimile.

(ANT.) prototype.

reply *(SYN.)* retort, rejoinder, answer, retaliate, respond, confirmation.

(ANT.) summoning, inquiry.

report *(SYN.)* declare, herald, publish, announce, summary, publish, advertise.

(ANT.) suppress, conceal, withhold, bury.

reporter *(SYN.)* journalist.

repose *(SYN.)* hush, quiet, tranquillity, rest, peace, slumber, calm, stillness, sleep, calmness, dormancy.

(ANT.) tumult, excitement, agitation.

reprehensible *(SYN.)* criminal, immoral, damnable, culpable, wrong, wicked.

represent *(SYN.)* picture, draw, delineate, portray, depict, denote, symbolize.

(ANT.) misrepresent, caricature.

representation *(SYN.)* effigy, film, likeness, portrait, print, scene, appearance, drawing, scene, view, cinema.

representative *(SYN.)* delegate, agent, substitute, surrogate.

repress *(SYN.)* limit, stop, check, bridle, curb, restrain, constrain, suppress.

(ANT.) loosen, aid, incite, liberate, encourage.

reprimand *(SYN.)* rate, scold, vituperate, berate, lecture, blame, admonish, upbraid.

(ANT.) praise, approve.

reproach *(SYN.)* defamation, dishonor, insult, profanation, abuse, disparagement, misuse, reviling.

(ANT.) respect, laudation, approval, plaudit.

reproduction *(SYN.)* replica, copy, exemplar, transcript, duplicate, photocopy.

reproof *(SYN.)* rebuke, punishment, blame, censure, disapproval, scorn, disdain, admonition.

repugnance *(SYN.)* disgust, hatred, reluctance, abhorrence, aversion, loathing, antipathy, distaste, repulsion.

(ANT.) devotion, affection, enthusiasm, attachment.

repulsive *(SYN.)* repellent, ugly, homely, deformed, horrid, offensive, plain

(ANT.) fair, pretty, attractive, handsome.

reputable *(SYN.)* honest, upstanding, trustworthy, straightforward, upright, reliable.

(ANT.) notorious, corrupt, disreputable.

reputation *(SYN.)* class, nature,

standing, name, fame, kind, renown, prominence, character, distinction, disposition, repute.

repute *(SYN.)* class, nature, standing, kind, character, reputation, disposition, sort.

request *(SYN.)* sue, implore, petition, desire, appeal, question, entreaty, beseech, ask, pray, supplicate.

(ANT.) require.

require *(SYN.)* exact, need, order, command, order, lack, claim, demand, want.

requirement *(SYN.)* demand, need, necessity, condition, provision, prerequisite.

requisite *(SYN.)* vital, necessary, basic, fundamental, indispensable, essential, needed.

(ANT.) casual, nonessential, peripheral, accidental.

rescind *(SYN.)* annul, quash, revoke, abolish, invalidate, abrogate, withdraw.

rescue *(SYN.)* liberate, ransom, release, deliver, deliverance, liberation.

research *(SYN.)* exploration, quest, scrutiny, exploration, interrogation, query, examination, study, investigation.

(ANT.) inattention, disregard, negligence.

resemblance *(SYN.)* parity, similitude, analogy, likeness, correspondence.

(ANT.) distinction, difference.

resemble *(SYN.)* duplicate, mirror, look like.

resentfulness *(SYN.)* envy, jealousy, covetousness, suspicion.

(ANT.) liberality, geniality, tolerance, difference.

resentment *(SYN.)* displeasure, bitterness, indignation, rancor, outrage, hostility.

(ANT.) complacency, understanding, good will.

reservation *(SYN.)* skepticism, restriction, objection, limitation, doubt.

reserve *(SYN.)* fund, hold, keep, store, accumulation, save, stock, maintain, supply.

(ANT.) waste, squander.

reserved *(SYN.)* cautious, fearful, timorous, wary, aloof, chary, sheepish, restrained, proper, unfriendly, bashful, diffident.

(ANT.) forward, bold, wild, immodest, brazen, abandoned, friendly.

reside *(SYN.)* inhabit, dwell, abide, live, lie.

residence *(SYN.)* home, dwelling, stay, seat, abode, domicile, living quarters.

residue *(SYN.)* balance, remainder, rest, ashes, remnants, dregs, leftovers, ends.

resign *(SYN.)* vacate, withdraw, leave, surrender, quit.

resignation *(SYN.)* perseverance, endurance, fortitude, composure, forbearance.

(ANT.) unquiet, nervousness, impatience.

resigned *(SYN.)* forbearing, stoical, assiduous, passive, accepting, composed, uncomplaining.

(ANT.) turbulent, chafing.

resilience *(SYN.)* rubbery,

springy, buoyant, elasticity.
(ANT.) *unresponsive, fixed, rigid, stolid.*

resist (SYN.) defy, withstand, hinder, confront, oppose.
(ANT.) *relent, allow, yield, accede.*

resolute (SYN.) firm, resolved, set, determined, decided.
(ANT.) *irresolute, wavering, vacillating*

resolution (SYN.) resolve, courage, determination, persistence, statement, verdict, recommendation, decision, steadfastness, dedication, perseverance.
(ANT.) *indecision, inconstancy.*

resolve (SYN.) determination, resolution, courage, settle, decide, persistence, determine, confirm, decision.
(ANT.) *integrate, indecision, inconstancy.*

resort (SYN.) motel, lodge, hotel, solve.

resound (SYN.) echo, ring, reverberate.

resource (SYN.) store, source, supply, reserve.

resourceful (SYN.) inventive, ingenious, creative, clever, imaginative, skillful.

respect (SYN.) honor, approval, revere, heed, value, admire, esteem, point, detail, admiration, reverence, regard, feature, particular, consider.
(ANT.) *disrespect, neglect, abuse, disregard, despise.*

respectable (SYN.) becoming, respected, proper, seemly, tolerable, decent, acceptable,

fair, adequate, passable, suitable, honorable, valuable.
(ANT.) *unsavory, vulgar, gross, disreputable, reprehensible.*

respectful (SYN.) courteous, polite, well- behaved, well-bred, compliant, submssive.
(ANT.) *disobedient, impertinent, rude, flippant.*

respite (SYN.) deferment, adjournment, suspension.

respond (SYN.) rejoin, answer, reply, acknowledge, retort.
(ANT.) *overlook, disregard.*

response (SYN.) acknowledgment, answer, retort, reply.
(ANT.) *summoning, inquiry.*

responsibility (SYN.) duty, obligation, accountability, trust-worthiness, trust, liability, commitment.

responsible (SYN.) answerable, chargeable, liable, accountable, able, capable, upstanding, reliable, solid, indebted, creditable.
(ANT.) *careless, free, negligent.*

rest (SYN.) ease, intermission, calm, quiet, balance, surplus, repose, lounge, inactivity, motionlessness, immobility, standstill, relax, remainder, excess, surplus, relaxation, slumber, peace, tranquillity, leisure.
(ANT.) *tumult, commotion, motion, agitation.*

restful (SYN.) peaceful, quiet, tranquil, calm.
(ANT.) *tumultuous, upsetting, agitated, disturbed.*

restitution (SYN.) recompense, satisfaction, refund, amends, retrieval.

restive (SYN.) balky, disobedient, fractious, impatient, unruly, fidgety, uneasy.

restless (SYN.) sleepless, unquiet, transient, active, agitated, disturbed, jumpy, nervous, uneasy, disquieted, irresolute.
(ANT.) quiet, tranquil, calm, peaceable.

restore (SYN.) repair, recover, rebuild, reestablish, renovate, return, renew, mend, reinstall, revive, rehabilitate, replace.

restrain (SYN.) limit, curb, constraint, stop, bridle, control, reserve, constrain, repress, check, suppress, hinder.
(ANT.) incite, aid, loosen.

restraint (SYN.) order, self-control, reserve, control, regulation, limitation, confinement.
(ANT.) freedom, liberty, confusion.

restrict (SYN.) fetter, restrain, confine, limit, engage, attach, connect, link, tie, bind.
(ANT.) broaden, enlarge, untie, loose, free.

restriction (SYN.) curb, handicap, check, boundary, ban, limitation, control, deterrent.

result (SYN.) effect, issue, outcome, resolve, end, consequence, happen, determination, conclusion, reward, aftermath.
(ANT.) cause, beginning, origin.

resume (SYN.) restart, continue, recommence, reassume.

resurgence (SYN.) rebirth, comeback, recovery, revival, resuscitation, rejuvenation, renewal.

resuscitate (SYN.) restore, revive, resurrect.

retain (SYN.) keep, hold, recall, remember, employ, hire, engage.

retainer (SYN.) aide, assistant, lackey, attendant, servant.

retaliate (SYN.) repay, revenge, return, avenge.
(ANT.) condone, forgive, overlook, excuse, forget.

retard (SYN.) detain, slacken, defer, impede, hold back, delay, postpone.
(ANT.) accelerate, speed, hasten, rush.

retention (SYN.) reservation, acquisition, holding, tenacity, possession.

reticent (SYN.) reserved, subdued, quiet, shy, withdrawn, restrained, bashful, silent.
(ANT.) opinionated, outspoken, forward.

retire (SYN.) resign, quit, abdicate, depart, vacate.

retiring (SYN.) timid, bashful, withdrawn, modest, reticent, quiet, reserved.
(ANT.) gregarious, assertive, bold.

retort (SYN.) reply, answer, response, respond, rejoin, rejoinder, retaliate.
(ANT.) summoning, inquiry.

retreat (SYN.) leave, depart, retire, withdraw, retirement, withdrawal, departure, shelter, refuge.
(ANT.) advanced.

retrench (SYN.) reduce, scrape, curtail.

retribution *(SYN.)* justice, vengeance, reprisal, punishment, comeuppance, vindictiveness, revenge, retaliation.

retrieve *(SYN.)* regain, recover, recapture, repossess, reclaim, salvage, recoup.

retrograde *(SYN.)* regressive, backward, declining, deteriorating, worsening.
(ANT.) onward, progression, advanced.

return *(SYN.)* restoration, replace, revert, recur, restore, retreat.
(ANT.) keep, take, retain.

reveal *(SYN.)* discover, publish, communicate, impart, uncover, tell, betray, divulge, disclose.
(ANT.) conceal, cover, obscure, cloak, hide.

revel *(SYN.)* rejoice, wallow, bask, enjoy, delight, savor, gloat, luxuriate, relish.

revelation *(SYN.)* hallucination, dream, phantoms, apparition, ghost, mirage, specter, daydream, suprise, shocker.
(ANT.) verity, reality.

revelry *(SYN.)* merriment, merry-making, gala, carousal, feasting, festival.

revenge *(SYN.)* vindictiveness, reprisal, requital, vengeance, repayment, repay, retribution, reparation.
(ANT.) reconcile, forgive, pity.

revenue *(SYN.)* take, proceeds, income, profit, return.

revere *(SYN.)* admire, honor, worship, respect, venerate, adore.

reverence *(SYN.)* glory, worship, homage, admiration, dignity, renown, respect, esteem, veneration, adoration, honor.
(ANT.) dishonor, derision, reproach.

reverent *(SYN.)* honoring, respectful, adoring, pious, devout, humble.
(ANT.) impious, disrespectful

reverse *(SYN.)* overthrow, unmake, rescind, opposite, invert, contrary, rear, back, misfortune, defeat, catastrophe, upset, revoke.
(ANT.) stabilize, endorse, affirm.

revert *(SYN.)* revive, relapse, backslide, rebound, retreat, recur, go back.
(ANT.) keep, take, appropriate.

review *(SYN.)* reconsideration, examination, commentary, retrospection, restudy, journal, synopsis, study, reexamine, critique, inspection.

revile *(SYN.)* defame, malign, vilify, abuse, traduce, asperse, scandalize, smear.
(ANT.) honor, respect, cherish, protect.

revise *(SYN.)* change, alter, improve, correct, amend, update, rewrite, polish.

revision *(SYN.)* inspection, survey, retrospection, commentary, critique

revival *(SYN.)* renaissance, exhumation, resurgence, renewal, revitalization.

revive *(SYN.)* refresh, lessen,

decrease, renew, reduce, lower, abate, reanimate, diminish, reawaken, rejuvenate, suppress.

(ANT.) increase, amplify, intensify.

revoke *(SYN.)* nullify, cancel, abolish, quash, rescind, abrogate.

revolt *(SYN.)* mutiny, rebel, disgust, revolution, uprising, rebellion, upheaval, take over, insurgence, abolish.

revolting *(SYN.)* hateful, odious, abominable, foul, vile, detestable, loathsome, repugnant, obnoxious, sickening.

(ANT.) delightful, agreeable, pleasant.

revolution *(SYN.)* rebellion, mutiny, coup, revolt, overthrow, cycle, spin, uprising.

revolutionary *(SYN.)* insurgent, extremist, radical, subversive, mutinous.

revolve *(SYN.)* spin, wheel, rotate, circle, circle, turn, whirl, gyrate.

(ANT.) travel, proceed, wander.

revolver *(SYN.)* gun, pistol.

revulsion *(SYN.)* reversal, rebound, backlash, withdrawal, recoil.

reward *(SYN.)* bounty, premium, meed, award, compensation, prize, recompense, bonus, remuneration, accolade, wages.

(ANT.) charge, wages, punishment.

rewarding *(SYN.)* pleasing, productive, fruitful, profitable, favorable, satisfying, gratifying, fulfilling.

rhetoric *(SYN.)* style, verbosity, expressiveness, eloquence, fluency, flamboyance.

rhyme *(SYN.)* poem, verse, poetry, ballad, ditty, rhapsody, sonnet.

ribald *(SYN.)* suggestive, off-color, indecent, spicy, rude, vulgar.

rich *(SYN.)* ample, costly, wealthy, fruitful, prolific, abundant, well-off, affluent, plentiful, fertile, bountiful, luxuriant.

(ANT.) poor, unfruitful, beggarly, barren, impoverished, scarce, scanty, unproductive, destitute.

rickety *(SYN.)* unsound, unsteady, flimsy, unstable, shaky, decrepit, wobbly.

(ANT.) steady, solid, sturdy.

ricochet *(SYN.)* recoil, backfire, rebound, bounce, deviate, boomerang.

rid *(SYN.)* free, clear, shed, delivered, eliminate, disperse, unload, purge.

riddle *(SYN.)* puzzle, mystery, conundrum, problem, question, enigma.

(ANT.) key, solution, answer, resolution.

ride *(SYN.)* tour, journey, motor, manage, drive, control, guide.

ridge *(SYN.)* hillock, backbone, spine, crest, mound, hump.

ridicule *(SYN.)* gibe, banter, mock, jeering, deride, tease, taunt, satire, mockery, derision.

(ANT.) praise, respect.

ridiculous (SYN.) silly, nonsensical, absurd, inconsistent, farcical, proper, laughable, apt, preposterous, foolish.

(ANT.) sound, reasonable, consistent.

rife (SYN.) widespread, abundant, innumerable, rampant, teeming.

rifle (SYN.) plunder, pillage, rummage, ransack, rob, steal.

rift (SYN.) crevice, fault, opening, crack, flaw, fissure, split, breach, opening.

right (SYN.) correct, appropriate, suitable, ethical, fit, real, legitimate, justice, factual, just, directly, virtue, true, definite, straight, honorably, seemly.

(ANT.) immoral, unfair, wrong, bad, improper.

righteous (SYN.) ethical, chaste, honorable, good, virtuous, good, noble.

(ANT.) sinful, libertine, amoral, licentious.

rigid (SYN.) strict, unyielding, stiff, stern, austere, rigorous, inflexible, stringent, unbendable, severe, harsh, unbending.

(ANT.) supple, flexible, mild, compassionate, pliable, limp, relaxed.

rigorous (SYN.) unfeeling, rough, strict, blunt, cruel, hard, severe, grating, coarse, jarring, stern, stringent.

(ANT.) soft, mild, tender, gentle, smooth.

rile (SYN.) irritate, nettle, hector, exasperate, provoke, gripe.

rim (SYN.) verge, frontier, border, outskirts, edge, brink, lip, limit, termination, boundary, fringe, brim, margin.

(ANT.) core, mainland, center.

rind (SYN.) layer, cover, skin, hide, peel, crust, bark.

ring (SYN.) fillet, band, loop, circlet, circle, surround, encircle, peal, sound, resound, jingle, tinkle.

ringleader (SYN.) provoker, troublemaker, leader, instigator, chief, inciter, agitator.

rinse (SYN.) launder, cleanse, wash, soak, immerse, laundering, flush, rinsing, bathe, clean.

riot (SYN.) disturbance, disorder, outburst, commotion, insurgence, uproar, panic, boisterousness, lark, hoot, wow, sensation, caper, roister, frolic, eruption, confusion, tumult, revolt.

riotous (SYN.) boisterous, wild, rambunctious, roisterous, tumultuous, turbulent, noisy, loud, rowdy, rollicking.

rip (SYN.) tear, rend, wound, rive, cleave, cut, slit, slash, lacerate, shred, scramble, dart, dash, split, disunite.

(ANT.) unite, join, repair.

ripe (SYN.) ready, finished, mature, complete, full-grown, develop, mellow, seasonable, full-fledged, primed, disposed, keen, avid, consummate.

(ANT.) raw, crude, undeveloped, premature, unprepared, unripe, immature.

ripen *(SYN.)* grow, season, age, mature, mellow, develop, progress, maturate.

rip into *(SYN.)* assail, lash out at, attack, charge.

rip-off *(SYN.)* fraud, dishonesty, gyp, racket, swindle, exploitation, heist, theft, extortion, thievery, larceny, shakedown.

riposte *(SYN.)* rejoinder, comeback, quip, retort, response, reply, wise-crack.

ripple *(SYN.)* wave, ruffle, wavelet, gurgle, undulate, corrugation, rumple, crumple, spurtle, dribble, bubble.

rise *(SYN.)* thrive, awaken, ascend, climb, mount, tower, arise, wake, scale, flourish, prosper, advance, proceed, soar.

(ANT.) fall, drop, plunge, fade, slump, decline, sinking, depression, waning, comedown, setback, retrogression, descend.

risk *(SYN.)* hazard, peril, danger, endanger, chance, jeopardy, threat, vulnerability, contingency, precariousness, shakiness.

(ANT.) protection, safety, immunity, defense.

risky *(SYN.)* menacing, chancy, threatening, critical, perilous, insecure, unsafe, dicey, unsound, dangerous.

(ANT.) guarded, safe, certain, firm, secure.

rite *(SYN.)* pomp, solemnity, ceremony, observance, ceremonial, formality.

ritual *(SYN.)* pomp, solemnity, ceremony, parade, rite, ritualism, routine, custom, tradition.

rival *(SYN.)* enemy, opponent, contestant, compete, foe, adversary, oppose, competitor, contest, antagonist.

(ANT.) colleague, confederate, allay, collaborator, helpmate, teammate.

rivalry *(SYN.)* contest, struggle, duel, race, vying, opposition, contention, competition.

(ANT.) collaboration, partnership, coalition, alliance, teamwork, cooperation.

river *(SYN.)* brook, stream, headstream, watercourse, tributary, creek.

rivet *(SYN.)* weld, bolt, fasten, attach, secure, bind, join, staple, nail, couple.

road *(SYN.)* street, way, highway, pike, drive, highway, expressway.

roam *(SYN.)* err, saunter, deviate, rove, range, wander, digress, ramble, stroll.

(ANT.) stop, linger, stay, halt, settle.

roar *(SYN.)* cry, bellow, yell, shout, yowl, howl, bawl, hoot, bang, boom, blast, blare, scream, whoop, holler, yelp.

roast *(SYN.)* deride, ridicule, kid, ride, mock, tease, twit, parody, burlesque.

rob *(SYN.)* fleece, steal, despoil, pilfer, pillage, sack, loot, plunder, burglarize, ransack, hold up, rip off, thieve.

robbery *(SYN.)* larceny, plundering, thievery, stealing, theft, pillage, swiping, caper, snatching, burglary, plunder.

robe *(SYN.)* housecoat, bathrobe, dressing gown, caftan, muumuu, smock, cape.

robot *(SYN.)* computer, android, automaton, pawn, workhorse, drudge, laborer.

robust *(SYN.)* well, hearty, hale, sound, healthy, strong, able-bodied, stalwart.
(ANT.) fragile, feeble, debilitated, reserved, refined, puny, frail, delicate, infirm.

rock *(SYN.)* pebble, boulder, stone, gravel, granite, roll, sway, swagger, limestone.

rocky *(SYN.)* unstable, faint, rocklike, stony, pebbly, gravelly, trembly, rough, bumpy, formidable, quavering, challenging, unsteady, dizzy.
(ANT.) effortless, easy, slight, simple, sound, rugged, stout, hardy, strong, robust.

rod *(SYN.)* bar, pole, wand, stick, pike, staff, billy, baton.

rogue *(SYN.)* criminal, rascal, outlaw, scoundrel, scamp, good-for-nothing, villain.

roguish *(SYN.)* prankish, playful, mischievous, elfish, waggish, devilish, tricky.
(ANT.) grave, humorless, solemn, staid, lawabiding.

roil *(SYN.)* churn, muddy, rile, mire, disturb.

roister *(SYN.)* bluster, swagger, swashbuckle, vaunt, bluff,

flourish, rollick.

role *(SYN.)* task, part, function, portrayal, face, character.

roll *(SYN.)* revolve, rotate, whirl, swing, rock, waver, reel, lumber, swagger, stagger, progress, proceed, turn, spin.

rollicking *(SYN.)* spirited, animated, frolicsome, exuberant, lighthearted, carefree.

roll up *(SYN.)* amass, collect, accumulate, gather.

romance *(SYN.)* affair, enchantment, novel, tale, adventure, enterprise, daring, story.

romantic *(SYN.)* poetic, mental, dreamy, fanciful, imaginative, extravagant, impractical, exaggerated, wild, idealistic, mawkish, ideal, maudlin.
(ANT.) homely, familiar, unromantic, pessimistic, unemotional, cynical, prosaic, factual.

romp *(SYN.)* caper, gambol, frolic, play, conquer, triumph, horseplay, frisk.
(ANT.) defeat, rout.

room *(SYN.)* enclosure, cell, chamber, space, stay, lodge, cubicle, reside.

roomy *(SYN.)* broad, large, wide, sizable, generous, capacious, ample, spacious, extensive, commodious, vast.
(ANT.) tight, limited, crowded, confined, narrow.

roost *(SYN.)* coop, henhouse, perch, hearth, hutch, residence, abode, lodgings.

root *(SYN.)* reason, bottom, base, groundwork, cause, support, underpinning, beginning,

mainspring, source, basis.
(ANT.) cover, top, building.

rooted *(SYN.)* fixed, fast, firm, steadfast, immovable, stationary.

root for *(SYN.)* back, support, boost, sponsor, promote, bolster, encourage, hail, cheer.

rope *(SYN.)* string, wire, cord, cable, line, strand, rigging, ropework, cordage.

ropy *(SYN.)* wiry, stringy, viscous, threadlike, viscoid.

roster *(SYN.)* list, census, muster, enrollment, listing, register.

rosy *(SYN.)* reddish, pink, healthy, happy, fresh, cheerful, bright, glowing, promising, favorable.
(ANT.) pale, pallid, gray, wan, disheartening, ashen, unfavorable, gloomy.

rot *(SYN.)* putrefy, waste, decay, mold, decompose, dwindle, spoil, decline, decomposition, wane, rotting, ebb.
(ANT.) increase, grow, luxuriate.

rotary *(SYN.)* axial, rotating, turning, gyral, revolving, rolling, whirling, rotational.

rotate *(SYN.)* spin, twirl, wheel, circle, twist, orbit, invert, swivel, gyrate, wind, alternate, recur.
(ANT.) stop, arrest, stand.

rotation *(SYN.)* turning, rolling, succession, gyration, revolution, return, rhythm, swirling, spinning.

rote *(SYN.)* repetition, system, convention, routine, mecha-

nization, habitude, habit, custom, perfunctoriness.

rotten *(SYN.)* decayed, decomposed, spoiled, putrid, contaminated, tainted.
(ANT.) unspoiled, pure, sweet, fresh.

rough *(SYN.)* jagged, scratchy, crude, incomplete, severe, craggy, stormy, rugged, unpolished, approximate, uneven, irregular, bumpy, coarse, rude.
(ANT.) calm, polished, civil, mild, refined, placid, gentle, smooth, sleek, sophisticated, suave.

roughly *(SYN.)* nearly, about, approximately.

round *(SYN.)* rotund, chubby, curved, bulbous, entire, complete, spherical, circular, bowed.
(ANT.) slender, trim, slim, thin, lean.

roundness *(SYN.)* sphericalness, globularity, rotundity, globularness, sphericity.

rouse *(SYN.)* waken, awaken, stimulate, arise, excite, summon, stir.
(ANT.) rest, calm, sleep, restrain, sedate.

rousing *(SYN.)* exciting, galvanic, stimulating, electric, moving, exhilarating, stirring, inciting.
(ANT.) flat, uninteresting, drab, monotonous, boring, tiresome, slow, dull.

rout *(SYN.)* defeat, beat, quell, vanquish, conquer, humble, subdue, scatter.

(ANT.) cede, retreat, surrender.

route *(SYN.)* street, course, trail, way, avenue, passage, thoroughfare, track, road, path.

routine *(SYN.)* way, habit, use, custom, practice, fashion, method, system, channel, circuit.

(ANT.) unusual, rate, uncommon.

rover *(SYN.)* traveler, adventurer, wanderer, voyager.

row *(SYN.)* file, order, series, rank, progression, sequence, arrangement.

rowdy *(SYN.)* disorderly, unruly, brawling, scrapper.

royal *(SYN.)* lordly, regal, noble, courtly, ruling, stately, dignified, supreme, majestic, sovereign.

(ANT.) servile, common, low, humble, vulgar.

rub *(SYN.)* shine, polish, scour, scrape.

rubbish *(SYN.)* debris, garbage, trash, waste, junk, clutter.

ruddy *(SYN.)* rosy, reddish, healthy, robust, blushing, sanguine.

rude *(SYN.)* gruff, impudent, blunt, impolite, boorish, insolent, saucy, rough, crude, coarse, impertinent.

(ANT.) courtly, civil, stately, genteel, calm, dignified, polished, courteous, cultivated, polite.

rudimentary *(SYN.)* essential, primary, fundamental, original.

rue *(SYN.)* lament, repine, sorrow, deplore, regret, bemoan.

ruffian *(SYN.)* crook, hoodlum, thug.

ruffle *(SYN.)* rumple, disarrange, disorder, disturb, trimming, frill.

rug *(SYN.)* carpet.

rugged *(SYN.)* jagged, craggy, scratchy, irregular, uneven, harsh, severe, tough.

(ANT.) smooth, level, even.

ruin *(SYN.)* wreck, exterminate, devastate, annihilate, raze, demolish, spoil, wreck, destroy, destruction, devastation, disintegration, decay.

(ANT.) save, establish, preserve.

ruination *(SYN.)* obliteration, annihilation, havoc, catastrophe.

rule *(SYN.)* law, guide, order, regulation, sovereignty, control.

ruler *(SYN.)* commander, chief, leader, governor, yardstick.

ruling *(SYN.)* judgment, decision.

ruminate *(SYN.)* brood, reflect, meditate, ponder, consider, speculate, mull, think about.

rummage *(SYN.)* root, scour, ransack.

rumor *(SYN.)* gossip, innuendo, hearsay.

rumple *(SYN.)* tousle, furrow, crease, wrinkle, dishevel.

run *(SYN.)* race, hurry, speed, hasten, sprint, dart, scamper, dash.

runaway *(SYN.)* fugitive, deserter, refugee.

run-down *(SYN.)* ramshackle, dilapidated, weakened, unhealthy, summary, outline, draft.

rupture *(SYN.)* fracture, fissure, cleft, severance.

rural *(SYN.)* country, farm, rustic, backwoods.
(ANT.) citified, urban.

rush *(SYN.)* dash, speed, hurry, hasten, run, scoot, hustle, scurry, acceleration, demand, movement.
(ANT.) tarry, linger, stop, stay, halt.

rut *(SYN.)* road, trench, walkway, ditch, passageway, trail, path.

ruthless *(SYN.)* cruel, heartless, savage, brutal, barbaric.

S

sabotage *(SYN.)* subversion, treason, treachery, damage.

sack *(SYN.)* pouch, bag.

sacrament *(SYN.)* communion, fellowship, intercourse, participation, union.
(ANT.) nonparticipation, alienation.

sacred *(SYN.)* consecrated, blessed, devout, divine, holy, hallowed, pious, religious, spiritual.
(ANT.) profane, evil, sacrilegious, worldly, secular, blasphemous.

sad *(SYN.)* dejected, cheerless, despondent, depressed, disconsolate, doleful, glum, saddening.
(ANT.) cheerful, glad, merry.

safe *(SYN.)* dependable, certain, harmless, secure, trust-

worthy.
(ANT.) hazardous, dangerous, unsafe, insecure, perilous.

safeguard *(SYN.)* fence, bulwark, protection, shelter, refuge, shield, guard, defense, security.

sag *(SYN.)* incline, bend, lean, slant, tend, depend, rely, trust.
(ANT.) raise, erect, straighten, rise.

sagacity *(SYN.)* erudition, discretion, foresight, insight, information, judgment, intelligence, knowledge, learning, reason.
(ANT.) foolishness, imprudence, stupidity, nonsense.

sage *(SYN.)* intellectual, disciple, learner, savant, scholar, pupil, student, wise, judicious, sagacious, rational, logical, expert.
(ANT.) dunce, fool, dolt, idiot.

saintly *(SYN.)* virtuous, moral, holy, devout, righteous, good.

sake *(SYN.)* motive, reason, purpose, benefit, advantage.

salary *(SYN.)* compensation, allowance, earnings, pay, fee, payment, recompense, wages.
(ANT.) gratuity, present, gift.

salient *(SYN.)* distinguished, clear, manifest, noticeable, prominent.
(ANT.) hidden, obscure.

salubrious *(SYN.)* healthy, hale, sound, robust, strong, well, hygienic, salutary.
(ANT.) diseased, delicate, frail, infirm, noxious.

saloon *(SYN.)* pub, bar.

salutary *(SYN.)* beneficial, advantageous, profitable, useful.

(ANT.) destructive, deleterious, detrimental, harmful.

salute *(SYN.)* receive, greet.

salvage *(SYN.)* retrieve, rescue, recover.

salvation *(SYN.)* release, rescue, deliverance.

same *(SYN.)* equal, coincident, equivalent, like, indistinguishable.

(ANT.) disparate, contrary, dissimilar, opposed, distinct.

sample *(SYN.)* example, case, illustration, model, instance, pattern, prototype, specimen, token.

sanction *(SYN.)* approval, approbation, authorization, authority, let, permit.

(ANT.) reproach, reprimand, stricture, censure, forbid, refuse, resist.

sanctuary *(SYN.)* harbor, haven, asylum, refuge, retreat, shelter.

(ANT.) danger, hazard, exposure, jeopardy, peril.

sane *(SYN.)* balanced, rational, normal, reasonable.

(ANT.) crazy, insane, irrational.

sanguinary *(SYN.)* bloody, sanguineous, gory.

sanguine *(SYN.)* confident, optimistic.

sanitary *(SYN.)* purified, clean, hygienic, disinfected.

(ANT.) soiled, fouled, unclean, dirty.

sap *(SYN.)* undermine, exhausted, drain, weaken.

sarcastic *(SYN.)* biting, acri-

monious, cutting, caustic, derisive, sardonic, satirical, ironic, sneering.

(ANT.) agreeable, affable, pleasant.

sardonic *(SYN.)* bitter, caustic, acrimonious, harsh.

(ANT.) mellow, pleasant, sweet.

satanic *(SYN.)* demonic, fiendish, diabolic, diabolical.

sate *(SYN.)* fill, occupy, furnish, stuff, pervade, stock, replenish, store, supply, content, satiate.

(ANT.) empty, drain, deplete, void.

satiate *(SYN.)* compensate, appease, content, please, gratify.

(ANT.) displease, dissatisfy, annoy, frustrate, tantalize.

satire *(SYN.)* cleverness, fun, banter, humor, irony, raillery.

(ANT.) platitude, sobriety, commonplace, solemnity.

satirical *(SYN.)* biting, caustic, acrimonious, cutting, ironic, derisive, sarcastic, sneering.

(ANT.) agreeable, affable, pleasant.

satisfaction *(SYN.)* blessedness, beatitude, bliss, delight, contentment, felicity, pleasure.

(ANT.) grief, misery, sadness, despair.

satisfactory *(SYN.)* ample, capable, adequate, commensurate, enough, sufficient, fitting.

(ANT.) scant, lacking, deficient, unsatisfactory, poor.

satisfy *(SYN.)* compensate,

appease, content, gratify, ful-fill.

(ANT.) displease, dissatisfy, annoy, frustrate, tantalize.

saturate *(SYN.)* fill, diffuse, infiltrate, penetrate, permeate.

saucy *(SYN.)* insolent, bold, impudent, impertinent.

(ANT.) shy, demure.

savage *(SYN.)* brutal, cruel, barbarous, ferocious, inhuman, merciless, malignant, ruthless, wild, uncivilized, uncultivated, rough.

(ANT.) compassionate, forbearing, kind, benevolent, gentle, humane, merciful, tame, cultivated.

save *(SYN.)* defend, conserve, keep, maintain, guard, preserve, protect, safeguard, rescue, secure, uphold, spare, free, liberate.

(ANT.) abolish, destroy, abandon, impair, injure.

savory *(SYN.)* delectable, delightful, delicious, palatable, luscious.

(ANT.) distasteful, nauseous, acrid, unpalatable, unsavory.

say *(SYN.)* converse, articulate, declare, express, discourse, harangue, talk, speak, tell, utter.

(ANT.) hush, refrain, be silent.

saying *(SYN.)* aphorism, adage, byword, maxim, proverb, motto.

scalding *(SYN.)* hot, scorching, burning, torrid, warm, fervent, ardent, fiery, impetuous, pungent.

(ANT.) cool, cold, freezing, pas-

sionless, frigid, bland.

scale *(SYN.)* balance, proportion, ration, range, climb, mount.

scamp *(SYN.)* troublemaker, rascal.

scan *(SYN.)* examine, study.

scandal *(SYN.)* chagrin, humiliation, abashment, dishonor, disgrace, disrepute, odium.

(ANT.) glory, honor, dignity, praise.

scandalize *(SYN.)* asperse, defame, abuse, disparage, revile, vilify.

(ANT.) honor, respect, cherish.

scandalous *(SYN.)* disgraceful, discreditable, dishonorable, ignominious, disreputable.

(ANT.) renowned, honorable, esteemed.

scant *(SYN.)* succinct, summary, concise, terse, inadequate, deficient, insufficient, limited.

(ANT.) ample, big, extended, abundant, protracted.

scanty *(SYN.)* inadequate, scarce, sparse, insufficient, meager.

(ANT.) abundant, plentiful.

scarce *(SYN.)* occasional, choice, infrequent, exceptional, incomparable, precious, singular, rare, uncommon, unique, sparse.

(ANT.) usual, frequent, ordinary, abundant, numerous, worthless.

scarcely *(SYN.)* barely, hardly.

scarcity *(SYN.)* want, insufficiency, lack, need, dearth.

(ANT.) abundance.

scare *(SYN.)* alarm, papal,

affright, astound, dismay, daunt, frighten, intimidate, horrify.

(ANT.) compose, reassure, soothe.

scared *(SYN.)* apprehensive, afraid, frightened, fearful.

(ANT.) bold, assured, courageous, composed, sanguine.

scarf *(SYN.)* kerchief.

scatter *(SYN.)* dispel, disperse, diffuse, disseminate, separate, dissipate, spread.

(ANT.) assemble, accumulate, amass, gather, collect.

scene *(SYN.)* exhibition, view, display.

scent *(SYN.)* fragrance, fume, aroma, incense, perfume, odor, redolence, stench, stink, smell.

schedule *(SYN.)* program, timetable.

scheme *(SYN.)* plot, conspiracy, cabal, design, machination, intrigue, plan, chart, stratage, diagram, graph, sketch, program, devise.

scheming *(SYN.)* create, design, intend, mean, draw, sketch.

scholar *(SYN.)* intellectual, pupil, learner, disciple, sage, student, teacher, professor.

(ANT.) dunce, idiot, fool, ignoramus.

scholarly *(SYN.)* bookish, erudite, formal, academic, learned, pedantic, theoretical, scholastic.

(ANT.) practical, simple, ignorant.

scholarship *(SYN.)* cognizance, erudition, apprehension, in-

formation, learning, science, wisdom.

(ANT.) illiteracy, stupidity, ignorance, misunderstanding.

science *(SYN.)* enlightenment, discipline, knowledge, scholarship.

(ANT.) superstition, ignorance.

scoff *(SYN.)* ridicule, belittle, mock.

scold *(SYN.)* berate, blame, lecture, rate, rebuke, censure, admonish, reprehend, reprimand.

(ANT.) commend, praise, approve.

scope *(SYN.)* area, compass, expanse, amount, extent, magnitude, degree, measure, reach.

scorch *(SYN.)* burn, char, consume, blaze, incinerate, sear, singe.

(ANT.) put out, quench, extinguish.

score *(SYN.)* reckoning, tally, record, mark, rating.

scorn *(SYN.)* contumely, derision, contempt, detestation, hatred, disdain, despise, hate, spurn.

(ANT.) esteem, respect, awe.

scornful *(SYN.)* disdainful, contemptuous.

scoundrel *(SYN.)* rogue, villain, cad.

scour *(SYN.)* wash, clean, scrub.

scourge *(SYN.)* affliction, lash, whip.

scowl *(SYN.)* glower, frown, glare.

scramble *(SYN.)* combine,

mix, blend, hasten, clamber, climb.

scrap *(SYN.)* fragment, rag, apportionment, part, portion, piece, section, share, segment, crumb.

(ANT.) whole, entirety.

scrape *(SYN.)* difficulty, dilemma, condition, fix, predicament, plight, situation, strait, scour.

(ANT.) comfort, ease, calmness.

scratch *(SYN.)* scrape, scar.

scrawny *(SYN.)* gaunt, skinny, spindly.

(ANT.) husky, burly.

scream *(SYN.)* screech, shriek, yell.

screen *(SYN.)* partition, cover, separation, protection.

scrimp *(SYN.)* skimp, save, economize, conserve.

script *(SYN.)* penmanship, hand, handwriting, text, lines.

scrounge *(SYN.)* sponge, borrow.

scrub *(SYN.)* cleanse, mop, purify, clean, sweep, wash, scour.

(ANT.) pollute, dirty, stain, sully.

scrupulous *(SYN.)* conscientious, candid, honest, honorable, fair, just, sincere, truthful, critical.

(ANT.) dishonest, fraudulent, lying, deceitful, tricky, careless.

scrutinize *(SYN.)* criticize, appraise, evaluate, examine, inspect.

(ANT.) neglect, overlook, approve.

scurrilous *(SYN.)* insulting, outrageous.

scurry *(SYN.)* scamper, scramble, hasten, hustle, hurry.

scuttle *(SYN.)* swamp, ditch, sink.

seal *(SYN.)* emblem, stamp, symbol, crest, signet.

search *(SYN.)* exploration, examination, investigation, inquiry, pursuit, quest, explore, scrutinize, investigate, hunt, probe, rummage, ransack, seek, scour.

(ANT.) resignation, abandonment.

searching *(SYN.)* inquiring, inquisitive, nosy, interrogative, curious, peering, prying.

(ANT.) unconcerned, incurious, uninterested, indifferent.

season *(SYN.)* mature, perfect, ripen, develop, age.

seasoned *(SYN.)* veteran, skilled.

secede *(SYN.)* quit, withdraw, resign.

secluded *(SYN.)* deserted, desolate, isolated, alone, lonely, lone, unaided, only, sole, solitary, single, separate, isolated, sheltered.

(ANT.) attended, surrounded, accompanied.

seclusion *(SYN.)* insulation, isolation, loneliness, alienation, quarantine, segregation, separation, retirement.

(ANT.) fellowship, union, connection, association, communion.

secondary *(SYN.)* minor, poorer, inferior, lower, subordinate.

(ANT.) greater, higher, superior.

secret *(SYN.)* concealed, hidden, latent, covert, private, surreptitious, unknown.

(ANT.) disclosed, exposed, known, open, public.

secrete *(SYN.)* clothe, conceal, cover, cloak, curtain, envelop, disguise, hide, mask, guard, protect.

(ANT.) divulge, reveal, expose, unveil.

sect *(SYN.)* segment, denomination, faction, group.

section *(SYN.)* district, country, domain, dominion, division, place, province, territory.

secular *(SYN.)* lay earthly, laic, mundane, temporal, profane, worldly, temporal.

(ANT.) religious, spiritual, unworldly, ecclesiastical.

secure *(SYN.)* certain, definite, fixed, assured, indubitable, positive, inevitable, undeniable, sure.

(ANT.) probable, questionable, doubtful, loose, endangered, free.

security *(SYN.)* bond, earnest, pawn, bail, guaranty, pledge.

sedate *(SYN.)* calm, controlled, serene, composed.

sediment *(SYN.)* residue, lees, dregs, grounds.

see *(SYN.)* contemplate, descry, behold, discern, espy, distinguish, glimpse, inspect, look at, observe, perceive, scan, watch, view, witness, regard, examine, study.

seek *(SYN.)* explore, hunt, examine, look, investigate, probe, ransack, search, scour, rummage.

seem *(SYN.)* look, appeal.

(ANT.) exist, be, disappear, withdraw, vanish.

segment *(SYN.)* apportionment, division, fragment, moiety, allotment, part, portion, piece, scrap, share, section, element, faction.

(ANT.) whole, entirety.

segregate *(SYN.)* exclude, separate.

(ANT.) include, combine.

seize *(SYN.)* check, detain, hinder, apprehend, arrest, obstruct, stop, restrain, grab, grasp, clutch.

(ANT.) free, liberate, release, activate, discharge, loosen.

seldom *(SYN.)* infrequently, rarely.

select *(SYN.)* cull, opt, pick, choose, elect, prefer.

(ANT.) reject, refuse.

selection *(SYN.)* election, choice, alternative, option, preference.

self-denial *(SYN.)* abstinence, continence, abstention, forbearance, fasting, sobriety, temperance.

(ANT.) gluttony, excess, greed, intoxication, self-indulgence.

self-important *(SYN.)* egotistical, proud, conceited, egocentric.

self-indulgence *(SYN.)* egotism, narrowness, self-seeking, stinginess, ungenerousness.

(ANT.) charity, magnanimity, altruism, liberality.

selfish *(SYN.)* illiberal, narrow, self-centered, stingy, ungenerous, greedy, mean, miserly.

(ANT.) charitable.

sell *(SYN.)* market, retail, merchandise, vend, trade, barter.

send *(SYN.)* discharge, emit, dispatch, cast, propel, impel, throw, transmit, forward, ship, mail.

(ANT.) get, hold, retain, receive, bring.

senescence *(SYN.)* dotage, senility, age, seniority.

(ANT.) infancy, youth, childhood.

senile *(SYN.)* antiquated, antique, aged, ancient, archaic, obsolete, old, elderly, venerable.

(ANT.) new, youthful, young, modern.

senior *(SYN.)* superior, older, elder.

(ANT.) minor, junior.

sensation *(SYN.)* feeling, image, impression, apprehension, sense, sensibility, perception.

(ANT.) insensibility, torpor, stupor, apathy.

sensational *(SYN.)* exciting, marvelous, superb, thrilling, startling.

sense *(SYN.)* drift, connotation, acceptation, explanation, gist, implication, intent, import, interpretation, purport, meaning, purpose, signification, significance.

sense *(SYN.)* perception, sensation, feeling, awareness, insight, consciousness, appreciate.

sensibility *(SYN.)* sensation, emotion, feeling, passion, tenderness.

(ANT.) coldness, imperturbability, anesthesia, insensibility, fact.

sensible *(SYN.)* apprehensible, perceptible, alive, aware, awake, cognizant, comprehending, perceiving, conscious, sentient, intelligent, discreet, practical, judicious, prudent, reasonable, sober, wise.

(ANT.) impalpable, imperceptible, absurd, stupid, unaware, foolish.

sensitive *(SYN.)* perceptive, prone, impressionable, responsive, susceptible, sentient, tender, sore, delicate, tender, tense, touchy.

(ANT.) dull, hard, callous, insensitive.

sensual *(SYN.)* lascivious, earthy, lecherous, carnal, sensory, voluptuous, wanton, erotic, sexual.

(ANT.) chaste, ascetic, virtuous, continent.

sentence *(SYN.)* convict, condemn.

(ANT.) pardon, absolve acquit.

sentiment *(SYN.)* affection, emotion, sensation, feeling, passion, tenderness, impression, opinion.

(ANT.) coldness, imperturbability, anesthesia, insensibility, fact.

sentimental *(SYN.)* extravagant, fanciful, fantastic, dreamy, fictitious, idealistic, ideal, maudlin, imaginative, mawkish, poetic.

(ANT.) literal, practical, prosaic.

separate *(SYN.)* part, sever, sunder, divide, allot, dispense, share, distribute, disconnect, split, isolate, segregate, different.

(ANT.) convene, join, combine.

separation *(SYN.)* insulation, isolation, loneliness, alienation, quarantine, seclusion, retirement.

(ANT.) communion, fellowship, union, association, connection.

sequence *(SYN.)* chain, graduation, order, progression, arrangement, following, series, succession.

serene *(SYN.)* composed, imperturbable, calm, dispassionate, pacific, placid, peaceful, quiet, tranquil, still, undisturbed.

(ANT.) frantic, turbulent, wild, excited, stormy, agitated, turbulent.

serenity *(SYN.)* calmness, hush, calm, quiet, peace, quiescence, quietude, rest, repose, stillness, silence, tranquillity.

(ANT.) tumult, excitement, noise, agitation, disturbance.

series *(ANT.)* following, chain, arrangement, graduation, progression, order, sequence, train.

serious *(SYN.)* important, mo-

mentous, great, earnest, grave, sedate, sober, staid, alarming, solemn, critical, dangerous, risky, solemn.

(ANT.) trivial, informal, relaxed, small.

servant *(SYN.)* attendant, butler, domestic, valet, manservant.

serve *(SYN.)* assist, attend, help, succor, advance, benefit, answer, promote, content, satisfy, suffice, supply, distribute, wait on, aid.

(ANT.) command, direct, dictate, rule.

service *(SYN.)* advantage, account, avail, benefit, behalf, good, gain.

(ANT.) distress, calamity, trouble, handicap.

serviceable *(SYN.)* beneficial, good, helpful, advantageous, profitable, salutary, wholesome.

(ANT.) destructive, deleterious, detrimental, injurious, harmful.

servile *(SYN.)* base, contemptible, despicable, abject, groveling, dishonorable, ignoble, lowly, low, menial, mean, sordid, vulgar, vile.

(ANT.) honored, exalted, lofty, esteemed, righteous, noble.

servitude *(SYN.)* confinement, captivity, bondage, slavery.

(ANT.) liberation, freedom.

set *(SYN.)* deposit, dispose, lay, arrange, place, put, position, pose, station, appoint, fix, assign, settle.

(ANT.) mislay, misplace, dis-

turb, remove, disarrange.

settle *(SYN.)* close, conclude, adjudicate, decide, end, resolve, agree upon, establish, satisfy, pay, lodge, locate, reside, determine.

(ANT.) suspend, hesitate, doubt, vacillate, waver.

settlement *(SYN.)* completion, close, end, finale, issue, conclusion, termination, deduction, decision, inference.

(ANT.) commencement, prelude, start, inception, beginning.

sever *(SYN.)* part, divide, sunder, split, cut, separate.

(ANT.) convene, connect, gather, join, unite, combine.

several *(SYN.)* some, few, a handful.

severe *(SYN.)* arduous, distressing, acute, exacting, hard, harsh, intense, relentless, rigorous, sharp, stern, rigid, stringent, strict, cruel, firm, unyielding, unmitigated, difficult, unpleasant, dangerous, violent.

(ANT.) merciful, genial, indulgent, lenient, considerate.

sew *(SYN.)* mend, patch, fix, stitch, refit, restore, repair.

(ANT.) destroy, hurt, deface, injure.

shabby *(SYN.)* indigent, impecunious, needy, penniless, worn, ragged, destitute, poor, threadbare, deficient, inferior, scanty.

(ANT.) rich, wealthy, ample, affluent, opulent, right, sufficient, good.

shack *(SYN.)* hovel, hut, shanty,

shed.

shackle *(SYN.)* chain, fetter, handcuff.

shade *(SYN.)* complexion, dye, hue, paint, color, stain, pigment, darkness, shadow, tincture, dusk, gloom, darken, conceal, screen, tint.

(ANT.) transparency, paleness.

shadowy *(SYN.)* dark, dim, gloomy, murky, black, obscure, dusky, unilluminated, dismal, evil, gloomy, sinister, indistinct, hidden, vague, wicked, indefinite, mystic, secret, occult.

(ANT.) bright, clear, light, pleasant, lucid.

shady *(SYN.)* shifty, shaded, questionable, devious.

shaggy *(SYN.)* hairy, unkempt, uncombed, woolly.

shake *(SYN.)* flutter, jar, jolt, quake, agitate, quiver, shiver, shudder, rock, totter, tremble, vibrate, waver.

shaky *(SYN.)* questionable, uncertain, iffy, faltering, unsteady.

(ANT.) sure, definite, positive, certain.

shallow *(SYN.)* exterior, cursory, flimsy, frivolous, slight, imperfect, superficial.

(ANT.) complete, deep, abstruse, profound, thorough.

sham *(SYN.)* affect, act, feign, assume, pretend, simulate, profess.

(ANT.) exhibit, display, reveal, expose.

shame *(SYN.)* chagrin, humiliation, abashment, disgrace,

dishonor, ignominy, embarrassment, disrepute, odium mortify, humiliate, abash, humble, opprobrium, scandal.
(ANT.) pride, glory, praise, honor.

shape (SYN.) create, construct, forge, fashion, form, make, produce, mold, constitute, compose, arrange, combine, organize, frame, outline, figure, invent, appearance, pattern, cast, model, devise.
(ANT.) disfigure, misshape, dismantle, wreck.

shapeless (SYN.) rough, amorphous, vague.

shapely (SYN.) attractive, well-formed, curvy, alluring.
(ANT.) shapeless.

share (SYN.) parcel, bit, part, division, portion, ration, piece, fragment, allotment, partake, apportion, participate, divide, section
(ANT.) whole.

shared (SYN.) joint, common, reciprocal, correlative, mutual.
(ANT.) unrequited, dissociated.

sharp (SYN.) biting, pointed, cunning, acute, keen, barbed rough, fine, cutting, shrill, pungent, witty, acrid, blunt, steep, shrewd.
(ANT.) gentle, bland, shallow, smooth, blunt.

sharpen (SYN.) whet, hone, strop.

shatter (SYN.) crack, rend, break, pound, smash, burst, demolish, shiver, infringe.
(ANT.) renovate, join, repair,

mend.

shattered (SYN.) fractured, destroyed, reduced, separated, broken, smashed, flattened, rent, wrecked.
(ANT.) united, integral, whole.

shawl (SYN.) stole, scarf.

sheepish (SYN.) coy, embarrassed, shy, humble, abashed, timid, modest, timorous.
(ANT.) daring, outgoing, adventurous, gregarious.

sheer (SYN.) thin, transparent, clear, simple, utter, absolute, abrupt, steep.

sheet (SYN.) leaf, layer, coating, film.

shelter (SYN.) retreat, safety, cover, asylum, protection, sanctuary, harbor, guard, haven, security.
(ANT.) unveil, expose, bare, reveal.

shield (SYN.) envelop, cover, clothe, curtain, protect, protection, cloak, guard, conceal, defense, shelter, hide, screen, veil, shroud.
(ANT.) unveil, divulge, reveal, bare.

shift (SYN.) move, modify, transfer, substitute, vary, change, alter, spell, turn, transfigure.
(ANT.) settle, establish, stabilize.

shifting (SYN.) wavering, inconstant, changeable, fitful, variable, fickle.
(ANT.) unchanging, stable, uniform.

shiftless (SYN.) idle, lazy, slothful.

(ANT.) energetic.

shifty *(SYN.)* shrewd, crafty, tricky.

shine *(SYN.)* flicker, glisten, glow, blaze, glare, flash, beam, shimmer, glimmer, radiate, brush, polish, twinkle, buff, luster, gloss, scintillate, radiance, gleam.

shining *(SYN.)* dazzling, illustrious, showy, superb, brilliant, effulgent, magnificent, splendid, bright.

(ANT.) ordinary, dull, unimpressive.

shiny *(SYN.)* bright, glossy, polished, glistening.

(ANT.) lusterless, dull.

shipshape *(SYN.)* clean, neat.

(ANT.) sloppy, messy.

shiver *(SYN.)* quiver, quake, quaver, tremble, shudder, shake, break, shatter.

shock *(SYN.)* disconcert, astonish, surprise, astound, amaze, clash, disturbance, bewilder, outrage, horrify, revolt, agitation, stagger, blow, impact, collision, surprise, startle, upset, stun.

(ANT.) prepare, caution, admonish.

shocking *(SYN.)* hideous, frightful, severe, appalling, horrible, awful, terrible, dire, fearful.

(ANT.) safe, happy, secure, joyous.

shore *(SYN.)* seaside, beach, coast.

(ANT.) inland.

short *(SYN.)* abrupt, squat, con-

cise, brief, low, curtailed, dumpy, terse, inadequate, succinct, dwarfed, small, abbreviated, lacking, abridge, undersized, slight, little.

(ANT.) extended, ample, protracted.

shortage *(SYN.)* deficiency, deficit, shortfall.

(ANT.) surplus, enough.

shorten *(SYN.)* curtail, limit, cut, abbreviate, reduce, abridge, lessen, restrict.

(ANT.) lengthen, elongate.

shortening *(SYN.)* reduction, abridgment, abbreviation.

(ANT.) enlargement, amplification.

shortly *(SYN.)* soon, directly, presently.

shortsighted *(SYN.)* myopic, nearsighted, unimaginative, unthinking, thoughtless.

shout *(SYN.)* cry, yell, roar, vociferate, bellow.

(ANT.) whisper, intimate.

shove *(SYN.)* propel, drive, urge, crowd, jostle, force, push, promote.

(ANT.) retreat, falter, oppose, drag, halt.

shovel *(SYN.)* spade.

show *(SYN.)* flourish, parade, point, reveal, explain, array, movie, production, display, exhibit, note, spectacle, demonstrate, entertainment, tell, usher, guide, prove, indicate, present, lead.

showy *(SYN.)* ceremonious, stagy, affected, theatrical, artificial.

(ANT.) unaffected, modest,

unemotional, subdued.

shred (SYN.) particle, speck, iota, mite, bit, smidgen, tear, slit, cleave, rip, disunite, rend, mince, tatter, lacerate.

(ANT.) bulk, unite, quantity, mend, aggregate, repair.

shrewd (SYN.) cunning, covert, artful, stealthy, foxy, astute, ingenious, guileful, crafty, sly, surreptitious, wily, tricky, clever, intelligent, clandestine.

(ANT.) frank, sincere, candid, open.

shriek (SYN.) screech, scream, howl, yell.

shrill (SYN.) keen, penetrating, sharp, acute, piercing, severe.

(ANT.) gentle, bland, shallow.

shrink (SYN.) diminish, shrivel, dwindle.

shrivel (SYN.) wizen, waste, droop, decline, sink, dry, languish, wither.

(ANT.) renew, refresh, revive, rejuvenate.

shun (SYN.) escape, avert, forestall, avoid, forbear, evade, ward, elude, dodge.

(ANT.) encounter, confront, meet.

shut (SYN.) seal, finish, stop, close, terminate, conclude, clog, end, obstruct.

(ANT.) begin, open, start, unbar, inaugurate, unlock, commence.

shy (SYN.) reserved, fearful, bashful, retiring, cautious, demure, timid, shrinking, wary, chary.

(ANT.) brazen, bold, immodest,

self confident, audacious.

sick (SYN.) ill, morbid, ailing, unhealthy, diseased, infirm.

(ANT.) sound, well, robust, strong.

sickness (SYN.) illness, ailment, disease, complaint, disorder, vigor.

(ANT.) soundness, healthiness, vigor.

side (SYN.) surface, face, foe, opponent, rival, indirect, secondary, unimportant.

siege (SYN.) blockade.

sieve (SYN.) screen, strainer, colander.

sight (SYN.) eyesight, vision, scene, view, display, spectacle, eyesore.

sightless (SYN.) unmindful, oblivious, blind, unseeing, heedless, ignorant.

(ANT.) sensible, discerning, aware, perceiving.

sign (SYN.) omen, mark, emblem, token, suggestion, indication, clue, hint, approve, authorize, signal, gesture, symbol, portent.

signal (SYN.) beacon, sign, alarm.

significance (SYN.) connotation, drift, acceptation, explanation, implication, gist, importance, interpretation, intent, weight, meaning, purpose, signification.

significant (SYN.) grave, important, critical, material, indicative, meaningful, crucial, momentous, telling, vital, weighty.

(ANT.) irrelevant, insignificant, meaningless, unimportant,

negligible.

signify (SYN.) designate, imply, denote, intimate, reveal, indicate, mean, communicate, show, specify.

(ANT.) distract, divert, mislead, conceal, hide.

silence (SYN.) motionless, peaceful, placid, hushed, stillness, quiescent, still, soundlessness, quiet, tranquil, noiselessness, hush, muteness, undisturbed.

(ANT.) strident, loud, racket, disturbed, clamor, agitated, perturbed.

silent (SYN.) dumb, hushed, mute, calm, noiseless, quiet, peaceful, still, soundless, speechless, tranquil, uncommunicative, taciturn.

(ANT.) communicative, loud, noisy, raucous, talkative, clamorous.

silhouette (SYN.) contour, delineation, brief, draft, form, figure, outline, profile, plan, sketch.

silly (SYN.) asinine, brainless, crazy, absurd, foolish, irrational, witless, nonsensical, ridiculous, stupid.

(ANT.) sane, wise, judicious, prudent.

similar (SYN.) alike, akin, allied, comparable, analogous, correlative, corresponding, correspondent, parallel, resembling, like.

(ANT.) dissimilar, divergent, opposed, different, incongruous.

similarity (SYN.) likeness, parity, analogy, correspondence, resemblance.

(ANT.) distinction, variance, difference.

simple (SYN.) effortless, elementary, pure, easy, facile, mere, single, uncompounded, homely, humble, unmixed, plain, artless, naive, frank, natural, unsophisticated, open, asinine, foolish, credulous, silly.

(ANT.) artful, complex, intricate, adorned, wise.

simpleton (SYN.) idiot, fool, ignoramus.

simulate (SYN.) copy, counterfeit, duplicate, imitate, impersonate, mock, mimic.

(ANT.) distort, diverge, alter, invent.

sin (SYN.) evil, crime, iniquity, transgress, guilt, offense, ungodliness, trespass, vice, wickedness, wrong.

(ANT.) purity, goodness, purity, virtue, righteousness.

sincere (SYN.) earnest, frank, heartfelt, genuine, candid, honest, true, straightforward, faithful, truthful, up-right, trustworthy.

(ANT.) hypocritical, insincere, affected, dishonest, untruthful.

sincerity (SYN.) fairness, frankness, honesty, justice, candor, integrity, openness, responsibility, rectitude.

(ANT.) deceit, dishonesty, cheating.

sinful (SYN.) bad, corrupt, dissolute, antisocial, immoral, licentious, profligate, evil, indecent, vicious.

(ANT.) pure, noble, virtuous.

sing *(SYN.)* chant, croon, hum, carol, lilt, warble.

singe *(SYN.)* burn, char, consume, blaze, incinerate, scorch, sear, scald.

(ANT.) put out, quench, extinguish.

single *(SYN.)* individual, marked, particular, distinctive, separate, special, specific, lone, one, solitary, sole, unwed, unmarried, singular, unique.

(ANT.) ordinary, universal, general.

singular *(SYN.)* exceptional, eccentric, odd, peculiar, rate, extraordinary, strange, unusual, striking, characteristic, remarkable, rare, individual, distinctive, uncommon, special.

(ANT.) general, normal, ordinary.

sink *(SYN.)* diminish, droop, subside, hang, decline, fall, extend, drop, descend

(ANT.) mount, climb, soar, steady, arise.

sip *(SYN.)* drink, taste, swallow.

sire *(SYN.)* breed, create, father, engender, beget, generate, procreate, originate, produce, propagate.

(ANT.) destroy, ill, extinguish, murder, abort.

site *(SYN.)* place, position, location, station, locality.

situation *(SYN.)* circumstance, plight, state, site, location, locale, predicament, position, condition.

size *(SYN.)* bigness, bulk, dimensions, area, expanse, amplitude, measurement, extent, largeness, magnitude, mass, volume.

skeptic *(SYN.)* doubter, infidel, agnostic, deist, questioner, unbeliever.

(ANT.) believer, worshiper, adorer.

skepticism *(SYN.)* hesitation, questioning, wavering, distrust, mistrust, suspicion.

(ANT.) confidence, reliance, trust.

sketch *(SYN.)* draft, figure, form, outline, contour, delineation, drawing, picture, represent, silhouette, draw, profile.

sketchy *(SYN.)* indefinite, vague, incomplete, indistinct.

(ANT.) definite, detailed, complete.

skill *(SYN.)* cunning, deftness, dexterity, ability, adroitness, cleverness, talent, readiness, skillfulness.

(ANT.) ineptitude, inability.

skillful *(SYN.)* adept, clever, able, accomplished, competent, expert, ingenious, cunning, proficient, practiced, versed, skilled.

(ANT.) untrained, inept, clumsy, bungling, awkward.

skimpy *(SYN.)* cheap, scanty, meager.

(ANT.) abundant, generous.

skin *(SYN.)* outside, covering, peel, rind, shell, pare.

skinny *(SYN.)* gaunt, thin, rawboned.

(ANT.) fat, hefty, heavy.

skip *(SYN.)* drop, eliminate, ignore, exclude, cancel, delete, disregard, omit, overlook neglect, miss.

(ANT.) notice, introduce, include, insert.

skirmish *(SYN.)* brawl, battle, conflict, combat, dispute, encounter, contend, quarrel, squabble, scuffle, wrangle, struggle.

slack *(SYN.)* lax, limp, indefinite, free, disengaged, unbound, untied, unfastened, vague, dissolute, heedless, careless, unrestrained, limp, lazy, loose, inactive, sluggish.

(ANT.) restrained, tied, right, stiff, taunt, rigid, fast, inhibited.

slander *(SYN.)* libel, calumny, backbiting, aspersion, scandal, vilification.

(ANT.) praise, flattery, commendation, defense.

slang *(SYN.)* jargon, dialect.

slant *(SYN.)* disposition, inclination, bias, bent, partiality, slope, tilt, pitch, penchant, prejudice, proneness, proclivity, turn, incline, lean, tendency.

(ANT.) justice, fairness, impartiality, equity.

slash *(SYN.)* gash, cut, slit, lower, reduce.

slaughter *(SYN.)* butcher, kill, massacre, slay, butchering, killing.

slave *(SYN.)* bondservant, serf.

slavery *(SYN.)* captivity, imprisonment, serfdom, confinement, bondage, thralldom, servitude.

(ANT.) freedom, liberation.

slay *(SYN.)* assassinate, kill, murder.

sleek *(SYN.)* smooth, polished, slick.

(ANT.) blunt, harsh, rough, rugged.

sleep *(SYN.)* drowse, nap, nod, catnap, repose, doze, rest, slumber, snooze.

sleepy *(SYN.)* tired, drowsy, nodding.

slender *(SYN.)* lank, lean, meager, emaciated, gaunt, scanty, rare, skinny, scrawny, slight, spare, trim, slim, tenuous, thin.

(ANT.) fat, broad, overweight, thick, wide, bulky.

slide *(SYN.)* glide, slip, skim, skid.

slight *(SYN.)* lank, lean, meager, emaciated, gaunt, fine, narrow, scanty, scrawny, skinny, sparse, small, rare, slender, spare, insignificant, tenuous, unimportant, slim, thin.

(ANT.) regard, notice, enormous, large, major, huge, include.

slim *(SYN.)* thin, slender, lank, slight, weak, insignificant, unimportant.

slip *(SYN.)* error, fault, inaccuracy, shift, err, slide, mistake, glide, blunder.

(ANT.) precision, truth, accuracy.

slit *(SYN.)* slash, cut, tear, slot.

slogan *(SYN.)* catchword, motto.

slope *(SYN.)* incline, leaning, inclination, bending, slant.

sloth *(SYN.)* indolence, idleness, inactivity, inertia, supineness, sluggishness, torpidity.

(ANT.) alertness, assiduousness, diligence, activity.

slothful *(SYN.)* indolent, idle, inactive, lazy, inert, supine, sluggish, torpid.

(ANT.) alert, diligent, active, assiduous.

slovenly *(SYN.)* sloppy, bedraggled, unkempt, messy.

(ANT.) meticulous, neat.

slow *(SYN.)* deliberate, dull, delaying, dawdling, gradual, leisurely, tired, sluggish, unhurried, late, delayed.

(ANT.) rapid, quick, swift, speedy, fast.

sluggish *(SYN.)* dull, deliberate, dawdling, delaying, laggard, gradual, leisurely, tired, slow, lethargic.

(ANT.) swift, rapid, speedy, energetic, fast, quick, vivacious.

slumber *(SYN.)* drowse, catnap, nod, doze, repose, sleep, rest, snooze.

slump *(SYN.)* drop, decline, descent.

sly *(SYN.)* covert, artful, astute, crafty, clandestine, foxy, furtive, cunning, insidious, guileful, stealthy, subtle, shrewd, tricky, surreptitious, wily, secretive.

(ANT.) sincere, ingenuous, open, candid.

small *(SYN.)* little, minute, petty, diminutive, puny, wee, tiny, trivial, slight, miniature.

(ANT.) immense, enormous, large, huge.

smart *(SYN.)* dexterous, quick, skillful, adroit, apt, clever, bright, witty, ingenious, sharp, intelligent.

(ANT.) foolish, stupid, unskilled, awkward, clumsy, bungling, slow, dumb.

smash *(SYN.)* burst, crush, demolish, destroy, break, crack, fracture, pound, fringe, rack, rupture, shatter, rend.

(ANT.) mend, renovate, restore, repair.

smear *(SYN.)* wipe, rub, spread.

smell *(SYN.)* fragrance, fume, odor, perfume, incense, aroma, fetidness, stench, stink, scent, sniff, detect, bouquet.

smidgen *(SYN.)* crumb, mite, small, bit, particle, shred, speck, scrap.

(ANT.) bulk, mass, quantity, aggregate.

smile grin.

(ANT.) frown.

smite *(SYN.)* knock, hit, dash, beat, belabor, buffet, pound, punch, pummel, thrash, thump, defeat, overthrow, overpower, subdue, vanquish, rout.

(ANT.) surrender, fail, defend, shield, stroke.

smooth *(SYN.)* polished, sleek, slick, glib, diplomatic, flat, level, plain, suave, urbane, even, unwrinkled.

smother *(ANT.)* rugged, harsh, rough, blunt, bluff, uneven.

smother *(SYN.)* suffocate, asphyxiate, stifle.

smutty *(SYN.)* disgusting, filthy, impure, coarse, dirty, lewd, offensive, obscene, pornographic.
(ANT.) modest, refined, decent, pure.

snappy *(SYN.)* quick, stylish, chic.

snare *(SYN.)* capture, catch, arrest, clutch, grasp, grip, apprehend, seize, trap, net.
(ANT.) throw, release, lose, liberate.

snarl *(SYN.)* growl.

snatch *(SYN.)* grasp, seize, grab.

sneak *(SYN.)* steal, skulk, slink.

sneer *(SYN.)* fleer, flout, jeer, mock, gibe, deride, taunt, scoff, scorn.
(ANT.) laud, flatter, praise, compliment.

sneering *(SYN.)* derision, gibe, banter, jeering, mockery, sarcasm, ridicule, satire.

snoopy *(SYN.)* inquisitive, interrogative, curious, inquiring, meddling, peeping, prying, peering.
(ANT.) uninterested, incurious, unconcerned, indifferent.

snub *(SYN.)* rebuke, insult, slight.

snug *(SYN.)* constricted, close, contracted, compact, firm, narrow, taut, tense, stretched, tight, comfortable, sheltered.
(ANT.) loose, lax, slack, relaxed, open.

soak *(SYN.)* saturate, drench, steep, wet.

soar *(SYN.)* flutter, fly, flit, float, glide, sail, hover, mount.
(ANT.) plummet, sink, fall, descend.

sob *(SYN.)* weep, cry, lament.

sober *(SYN.)* sedate, serious, staid, earnest, grave, solemn, moderate.
(ANT.) ordinary, joyful, informal, boisterous, drunk, fuddled, inebriated.

sobriety *(SYN.)* forbearance, abstinence, abstention, self-denial, moderation, temperance.
(ANT.) self-indulgence, excess, intoxication.

social *(SYN.)* friendly, civil, gregarious, affable, communicative, hospitable, sociable, group, genial, polite.
(ANT.) inhospitable, hermitic, antisocial, disagreeable.

society *(SYN.)* nation, community, civilization, organization, club, association, fraternity, circle, association, company, companionship.

soft *(SYN.)* gentle, lenient, flexible, compassionate, malleable, meek, mellow, subdued, mild, tender, supple, pliable, elastic, pliant.
(ANT.) unyielding, rough, hard, tough, rigid.

soften *(SYN.)* assuage, diminish, abate, allay, alleviate, mitigate, relieve, soothe, solace.
(ANT.) irritate, increase, aggravate, agitate.

soil *(SYN.)* defile, discolor, spot,

befoul, blemish, blight, stain, earth, dirt, loam, dirty.

(ANT.) purify, honor, cleanse, bleach, decorate.

solace (SYN.) contentment, ease, enjoyment, comfort, consolation, relief, succor.

(ANT.) torture, torment, misery, affliction, discomfort.

sole (SYN.) isolated, desolate, deserted, secluded, unaided, lone, alone, only, single, solitary.

(ANT.) surrounded, accompanied, attended.

solemn(SYN.) ceremonious, imposing, formal, impressive, reverential, ritualistic, grave, sedate, earnest, sober, staid, serious, dignified.

(ANT.) ordinary, joyful, informal, boisterous, cheerful, gay, happy.

solicit (SYN.) beg, beseech, request, seek, pray.

solicitous (SYN.) anxious, concerned.

solicitude (SYN.) concern, worry, anxiety, care, attention, regard, vigilance, caution, wariness.

(ANT.) indifference, disregard, neglect, negligence.

solid (SYN.) hard, dense, compact, firm.

(ANT.) loose.

solitary (SYN.) isolated, alone, lonely, deserted, unaided, secluded, single, lone, sole.

(ANT.) surrounded, attended, accompanied

solitude (SYN.) loneliness, privacy, refuge, retirement,

seclusion, retreat, alienation, asylum, concealment.

(ANT.) publicity, exposure, notoriety.

solution (SYN.) explanation, answer.

solve (SYN.) explain, answer, unravel.

somatic (SYN.) corporeal, corporal, natural, material, bodily, physical.

(ANT.) spiritual, mental.

somber (SYN.) dismal, dark, bleak, doleful, cheerless, natural, physical, serious, sober, gloomy, grave.

(ANT.) lively, joyous, cheerful, happy.

sometimes (SYN.) occasionally.

(ANT.) invariably, always.

soon (SYN.) shortly, early.

(ANT.) tardy, late, overdue, belated.

soothe (SYN.) encourage, console, solace, comfort, cheer, gladden, sympathize, calm, pacify.

(ANT.) dishearten, depress, antagonize, aggravate, disquiet, upset, unnerve.

soothing (SYN.) gentle, benign, docile, calm, mild, placid, peaceful, serene, relaxed, tractable, tame.

(ANT.) violent, savage, fierce, harsh.

sophisticated (SYN.) cultured, worldly, blase, cultivated, urbane, cosmopolitan, suave, intricate, complex, advanced.

(ANT.) uncouth, ingenuous, simple, naive, crude.

sorcery *(SYN.)* enchantment, charm, black, magic, voodoo, witchcraft, wizardry.

sordid *(SYN.)* vicious, odious, revolting, obscene, foul, loathsome, base, depraved, debased, vile, vulgar, abject, wicked, ignoble, despicable, mean, worthless, wretched, dirty, unclean.
(ANT.) upright, decent, honorable.

sore *(SYN.)* tender, sensitive, aching, hurting, painful.

sorrow *(SYN.)* grief, distress, heartache, anguish, misery, sadness, mourning, tribulation, gloom, depression.
(ANT.) consolation, solace, joy, happiness, comfort.

sorrowful *(SYN.)* dismal, doleful, dejected, despondent, depressed, gloomy, melancholy, glum, moody, somber, sad, grave, aggrieved.
(ANT.) merry, happy, cheerful, joyous.

sorry *(SYN.)* hurt, pained, sorrowful, afflicted, grieved, contrite, repentant, paltry, poor, wretched, remorseful, mean, shabby, contemptible, vile, regretful, apologetic.
(ANT.) delighted, impenitent, cheerful, unrepentant, splendid.

sort *(SYN.)* class, stamp, category, description, nature, kind, type, variety.
(ANT.) peculiarity, deviation.

sound *(SYN.)* effective, logical, telling, binding, powerful, weighty, legal, strong, conclusive, valid.
(ANT.) weak, null, counterfeit.

sour *(SYN.)* glum, sullen, bitter, peevish, acid, rancid, tart, acrimonious, sharp, bad-tempered, cranky.
(ANT.) wholesome, kindly, genial, benevolent, sweet.

source *(SYN.)* birth, foundation, agent, determinant, reason, origin, cause, start, incentive, motive, spring, principle, beginning.
(ANT.) product, harvest, outcome, consequence, end.

souvenir *(SYN.)* memento, monument, commemoration, remembrance.

sovereign *(SYN.)* monarch, king, emperor, queen, empress.

sovereignty *(SYN.)* command, influence, authority, predominance, control.
(ANT.) debility, incapacity, disablement, ineptitude, impotence.

space *(SYN.)* room, area, location.

spacious *(SYN.)* capacious, large, vast, ample, extensive, wide, roomy.
(ANT.) limited, confined, narrow, small, cramped.

span *(SYN.)* spread, extent.

spare *(SYN.)* preserve, safeguard, uphold, conserve, protect, defend, rescue, reserve, additional, unoccupied.
(ANT.) impair, abolish, injure, abandon.

sparing *(SYN.)* economical, thrifty, frugal.

(ANT.) lavish.

sparkle *(SYN.)* gleam, glitter, twinkle, beam, glisten, radiate, shine, blaze.

spat *(SYN.)* quarrel, dispute, affray, wrangle, altercation.

(ANT.) friendliness, agreement, reconciliation, peace.

spawn *(SYN.)* yield, bear.

speak *(SYN.)* declare, express, say, articulate, harangue, converse, talk, utter.

(ANT.) refrain, hush, quiet.

special *(SYN.)* individual, uncommon, distinctive, peculiar, exceptional, unusual, extraordinary, different.

(ANT.) general, wide-spread, broad, prevailing, average, ordinary.

specialist *(SYN.)* authority, expert.

species *(SYN.)* variety, type, kind, class, sort.

specific *(SYN.)* limited, characteristic, definite, peculiar, explicit, categorical, particular, distinct, precise.

(ANT.) generic, general, nonspecific.

specify *(SYN.)* name, call, mention, appoint, denominate, designate, define.

(ANT.) miscall, hint.

specimen *(SYN.)* prototype, example, sample, model, pattern, type.

speck *(SYN.)* scrap, jot, bit, mite, smidgen, crumb, iota, particle, spot.

(ANT.) quantity, bulk, aggregate.

spectacle *(SYN.)* demonstration, ostentation, movie, array, exhibition, show, display, performance, parade, splurge.

spectator *(SYN.)* viewer, observer.

speculate *(SYN.)* assume, deduce, surmise, imagine, consider, view, think, guess, suppose, conjecture.

(ANT.) prove, demonstrate, conclude.

speech *(SYN.)* gossip, discourse, talk, chatter, lecture, conference, discussion, address, dialogue, articulation, accent.

(ANT.) silence, correspondence, writing, meditation.

speed *(SYN.)* forward, push, accelerate, hasten, rapidity, dispatch, swiftness.

(ANT.) impede, slow, block, retard.

spellbound *(SYN.)* fascinated, entranced, hypnotized, mesmerized, rapt.

spend *(SYN.)* pay, disburse, consume.

(ANT.) hoard, save.

spendthrift *(SYN.)* squanderer, profligate.

sphere *(SYN.)* globe, orb, ball, environment, area, domain.

spherical *(SYN.)* round, curved, globular.

spicy *(SYN.)* indecent, off-color, suggestive, indelicate.

spin *(SYN.)* revolve, turn, rotate, whirl, twirl, tell, narrate, relate.

spine *(SYN.)* vertebrae, backbone.

spirit *(SYN.)* courage, phantom,

verve, fortitude, apparition, mood, soul, ghost.

(ANT.) listlessness, substance, languor.

spirited *(SYN.)* excited, animated, lively, active, vigorous, energetic.

(ANT.) indolent, lazy, sleepy.

spiritless *(SYN.)* gone, lifeless, departed, dead, insensible, deceased, unconscious.

(ANT.) stirring, alive, living.

spiritual *(SYN.)* sacred, unearthly, holy, divine, immaterial, supernatural.

(ANT.) material, physical, corporeal.

spite *(SYN.)* grudge, rancor, malice, animosity, malevolence, malignity.

(ANT.) kindness, toleration, affection.

spiteful *(SYN.)* vicious, disagreeable, surly, ill-natured.

(ANT.) pretty, beautiful, attractive, fair.

splendid *(SYN.)* glorious, illustrious, radiant, brilliant, showy, superb, bright.

(ANT.) ordinary, mediocre, dull.

splendor *(SYN.)* effulgence, radiance, brightness, luster, magnificence, display.

(ANT.) darkness, obscurity, dullness.

splinter *(SYN.)* fragment, piece, sliver, chip, shiver.

split *(SYN.)* rend, shred, cleave, disunite, sever, break, divide, opening, lacerate.

(ANT.) repair, unite, join, sew.

spoil *(SYN.)* rot, disintegrate, waste, decay, ruin, damage, mold, destroy.

(ANT.) luxuriate, grow, flourish.

spoken *(SYN.)* verbal, pronounced, articulated, vocal, uttered, oral.

(ANT.) written, documentary.

spokesman *(SYN.)* agent, representative.

spontaneous *(SYN.)* impulsive, voluntary, automatic, instinctive, willing, extemporaneous, natural, unconscious.

(ANT.) studied, forced, planned, rehearsed, prepared.

sport *(SYN.)* match, play, amusement, fun, pastime, entertainment, athletics.

sporting *(SYN.)* considerate, fair, sportsmanlike.

spot *(SYN.)* blemish, mark, stain, flaw, blot, location, place, site, splatter.

spotty *(SYN.)* erratic, uneven, irregular, inconsistent.

(ANT.) regular, even.

spout *(SYN.)* spurt, squirt, tube, nozzle.

spray *(SYN.)* splash, spatter, sprinkle.

spread *(SYN.)* unfold, distribute, open, disperse, unroll, unfurl, scatter, jelly.

(ANT.) shut, close, hide, conceal.

sprightly *(SYN.)* blithe, hopeful, vivacious, buoyant, lively, light, nimble.

(ANT.) hopeless, depressed, sullen, dejected, despondent.

spring *(SYN.)* commencement, foundation, start, beginning, inception, jump, cradle, begin, birth, bound, originate.

(ANT.) issue, product, end.

sprinkle *(SYN.)* strew, spread, scatter, rain.

spruce *(SYN.)* orderly, neat, trim, clear, nice.

(ANT.) unkempt, sloppy, dirty.

spry *(SYN.)* brisk, quick, agile, nimble, energetic, supple, alert, active, lively.

(ANT.) heavy, sluggish, inert, clumsy.

spur *(SYN.)* inducement, purpose, cause, motive, impulse, reason, incitement.

(ANT.) effort, action, result, attempt.

squabble *(SYN.)* bicker, debate, altercate, contend, discuss, argue, quarrel.

(ANT.) concede, agree, assent.

squalid *(SYN.)* base, indecent, grimy, dirty, pitiful, filthy, muddy, nasty.

(ANT.) wholesome, clean, pure.

squander *(SYN.)* scatter, lavish, consume, dissipate, misuse.

(ANT.) preserve, conserve, save, accumulate.

squeamish *(SYN.)* particular, careful.

stab *(SYN.)* stick, gore, pierce, knife, spear, bayonet.

stability *(SYN.)* steadiness, balance, proportion, composure, symmetry.

(ANT.) imbalance, unsteadiness.

stable *(SYN.)* firm, enduring, constant, fixed, unwavering, steadfast, steady.

(ANT.) variable, irresolute, changeable.

stack *(SYN.)* mass, pile, mound, heap, accumulate.

staff *(SYN.)* pole, stick, club, personnel, crew, employees.

stage *(SYN.)* frame, platform, boards, theater, scaffold, period, phase, step, direct, produce, present.

stagger *(SYN.)* totter, sway, reel, vary, falter, alternate.

staid *(SYN.)* solemn, sedate, earnest, sober, grave.

(ANT.) joyful, informal, ordinary.

stain *(SYN.)* blight, dye, tint, befoul, spot, defile, mark, dishonor, disgrace, smirch, blot, blemish, discolor, color, tinge.

(ANT.) honor, bleach, decorate, purify.

stair *(SYN.)* staircase, stairway, steps.

stake *(SYN.)* rod, pole, picket, post, pale, bet, wager, concern, interest.

stale *(SYN.)* tasteless, spoiled, old, inedible, dry, uninteresting, trite, flat, dull, vapid, insipid.

(ANT.) new, fresh, tasty.

stalk *(SYN.)* dog, follow, track, shadow, hunt.

stall *(SYN.)* hesitate, stop, delay, postpone.

stammer *(SYN.)* falter, stutter.

stamp *(SYN.)* crush, trample, imprint, mark, brand, block, seal, die.

stand *(SYN.)* tolerate, suffer, stay, stand up, endure, bear, abide, halt, arise, rise, remain, sustain, rest.

(ANT.) run, yield, advance.

standard *(SYN.)* law, proof,

pennant, emblem, measure, example, gauge, model, banner, symbol, test.

(ANT.) guess, chance, irregular, unusual, supposition.

standing *(SYN.)* rank, position, station.

staple *(SYN.)* main, principal, chief, essential, necessary.

stare *(SYN.)* gaze.

start *(SYN.)* opening, source, commence, onset, surprise, shock, beginning, origin, begin, initiate, jerk, jump, advantage, lead, commencement, outset.

(ANT.) end, completion, termination, close.

startle *(SYN.)* astonish, disconcert, aback, alarm, shock, agitate, surprise, astound, amaze, stun.

(ANT.) caution, prepare, admonish, forewarn.

starved *(SYN.)* longing, voracious, hungry, craving, avid, famished.

(ANT.) satisfied, sated, gorged, full.

state *(SYN.)* circumstance, predicament, case, situation, condition, affirm, declare, express, nation, country, status, recite, tell, recount.

(ANT.) imply, conceal, retract.

stately *(SYN.)* lordly, elegant, regal, sovereign, impressive, magnificent, courtly, grand, imposing, majestic, noble, supreme, dignified.

(ANT.) low, common, mean, servile, humble, vulgar.

statement *(SYN.)* announce-

ment, mention, allegation, declaration, thesis, assertion, report.

station *(SYN.)* post, depot, terminal, position, place.

statuesque *(SYN.)* imposing, stately, regal, majestic, dignified.

status *(SYN.)* place, caste, standing, condition, state, rank, position.

statute *(SYN.)* law, ruling, decree, rule.

(ANT.) intention, deliberation.

staunch *(SYN.)* faithful, true, reliable, loyal, devoted.

(ANT.) treacherous, untrustworthy.

stay *(SYN.)* delay, continue, hinder, check, hold, hindrance, support, brace, line, rope, linger, sojourn, abide, halt, stand, rest, remain, tarry, arrest, wait.

(ANT.) hasten, progress, go, depart, advance, leave.

stead *(SYN.)* place.

steadfast *(SYN.)* solid, inflexible, constant, stable, unyielding, secure.

(ANT.) unstable, insecure, unsteady.

steady *(SYN.)* regular, even, unremitting, stable, steadfast, firm, reliable, solid.

steal *(SYN.)* loot, rob, swipe, burglarize, pilfer, shoplift, embezzle, snitch.

(ANT.) restore, buy, return, refund.

stealthy *(SYN.)* sly, secret, furtive.

(ANT.) direct, open, obvious.

steep *(SYN.)* sharp, hilly, sheer, abrupt, perpendicular, precipitous.

(ANT.) gradual, level, flat.

steer *(SYN.)* manage, guide, conduct, lead, supervise, escort, navigate, drive, control, direct.

stem *(SYN.)* stalk, trunk, arise, check, stop, orginate, hinder.

stench *(SYN.)* odor, fetor, fetidness, stink, aroma, smell, fume, scent.

step *(SYN.)* stride, pace, stage, move, action, measure, come, go, walk.

stern *(SYN.)* harsh, rigid, exacting, rigorous, sharp, severe, strict, hard, unyielding, unmitigated, stringent.

(ANT.) indulgent, forgiving, yielding, lenient, considerate.

stick *(SYN.)* stalk, twig, rod, staff, pole, pierce, spear, stab, puncture, gore, cling, adhere, hold, catch, abide, remain, persist.

stickler *(SYN.)* nitpicker, perfectionist, disciplinarian.

sticky *(SYN.)* tricky, delicate, awkward.

stiff *(SYN.)* severe, unbendable, unyielding, harsh, inflexible, unbending, rigid, firm, hard, solid, rigorous.

(ANT.) supple, yielding, compassionate, mild, lenient, resilient.

stifle *(SYN.)* choke, strangle, suffocate.

stigma *(SYN.)* trace, scar, blot, stain, mark, vestige.

still *(SYN.)* peaceful, undisturbed, but, mild, hushed, calm, patient, modest, nevertheless, motionless, meek, quiescent, stationary, besides, however, quiet, tranquil, serene, placid.

(ANT.) agitated, perturbed, loud.

stimulate *(SYN.)* irritate, excite, arouse, disquiet, rouse, activate, urge, invigorate, animate, provoke.

(ANT.) quell, calm, quiet, allay.

stimulus *(SYN.)* motive, goad, arousal, provocation, encouragement.

(ANT.) discouragement, depressant.

stingy *(SYN.)* greedy, penurious, avaricious, mean, cheap, selfish, miserly, tight, tightfisted.

(ANT.) munificent, generous, giving, extravagant, openhanded, bountiful.

stipend *(SYN.)* payment, earnings, salary, allowance, pay, compensation, wages.

(ANT.) gratuity, gift.

stipulate *(SYN.)* require, demand.

stir *(SYN.)* instigate, impel, push, agitate, induce, mix, rouse, move, propel.

(ANT.) halt, stop, deter.

stock *(SYN.)* hoard, store, strain, accumulation, supply, carry, keep, provision, fund, breed, sort.

(ANT.) sameness, likeness, homogeneity, uniformity.

stoical *(SYN.)* passive, forbearing, uncomplaining, composed, patient.

(ANT.) turbulent, chafing, hysterical.

stolid *(SYN.)* obtuse, unsharpened, dull, blunt, edgeless.

(ANT.) suave, tactful, polished, subtle.

stone *(SYN.)* pebble, gravel, rock.

stony *(SYN.)* insensitive, unsentimental, cold.

stoop *(SYN.)* bow, bend, lean, crouch.

stop *(SYN.)* terminate, check, abstain, hinder, arrest, close, bar, cork, halt, end, conclude, obstruct, finish, quit, pause, discontinue, stay, impede, cease.

(ANT.) start, proceed, speed, begin.

store *(SYN.)* amass, hoard, collect, market, shop, reserve, supply, deposit, bank, save, accrue, increase, stock.

(ANT.) dissipate, waste, disperse.

storm *(SYN.)* gale, tempest, tornado, thunderstorm, hurricane, rage, assault, besiege.

story *(SYN.)* yarn, novel, history, tale, falsehood, account, fable, anecdote, narrative, fabrication, lie, level, floor, fiction, report.

stout *(SYN.)* plump, obese, chubby, fat, paunchy, overweight, portly, heavy, sturdy, strong, pudgy, thickset.

(ANT.) thin, slender, flimsy, gaunt, slim.

straight *(SYN.)* erect, honorable, square, just, direct,

undeviating, unbent, **right**, upright, honest, uncurving, directly, moral, correct, orderly, vertical.

(ANT.) dishonest, bent, circuitous, twisted, crooked.

straightforward *(SYN.)* forthright, direct, open, candid, aboveboard.

(ANT.) devious.

strain *(SYN.)* stock, kind, variety, stretch, breed, tighten, harm, injure, screen, filter, sprain, sort.

strainer *(SYN.)* colander, sieve, filter.

strait *(SYN.)* fix, situation, passage, dilemma, channel, trouble, predicament, difficulty, distress, crisis.

(ANT.) ease, calmness, satisfaction, comfort.

strange *(SYN.)* bizarre, peculiar, odd, abnormal, irregular, unusual, curious, uncommon, singular, extraordinary, foreign, eccentric, unfamiliar.

(ANT.) regular, common, familiar, conventional.

stranger *(SYN.)* foreigner, outsider, newcomer, alien, outlander, immigrant.

(ANT.) friend, associate, acquaintance.

strap *(SYN.)* strip, belt, thong, band.

stratagem *(SYN.)* design, ruse, cabal, plot, machination, subterfuge, trick, wile, conspiracy.

strategy *(SYN.)* technique, management, tactics.

stray *(SYN.)* ramble, rove, deviate, lost, strayed, wander, digress, roam, stroll.

(ANT.) linger, stop, halt, settle.

stream *(SYN.)* issue, proceed, brook, flow, come, abound, spout, run.

street *(SYN.)* way, road, boulevard, avenue.

strength *(SYN.)* power, might, toughness, durability, lustiness, soundness, vigor, potency.

(ANT.) weakness, frailty, feebleness.

strengthen *(SYN.)* verify, assure, confirm, fix, sanction, ratify, substantiate.

strenuous *(SYN.)* forceful, energetic, active, vigorous, determined.

stress *(SYN.)* urgency, press, emphasize, accentuate, accent, weight, strain, importance, compulsion, pressure.

(ANT.) relaxation, lenience, ease.

stretch *(SYN.)* strain, expand, elongate, extend, lengthen, spread, distend, protract, distort.

(ANT.) tighten, loosen, slacken, contract.

strict *(SYN.)* rough, stiff, stringent, harsh, unbending, severe, rigorous.

(ANT.) easygoing, lenient, mild.

strife *(SYN.)* disagreement, conflict, discord, quarrel, difference, unrest.

(ANT.) tranquillity, peace, concord.

strike *(SYN.)* pound, hit, smite, beat, assault, attack, affect,

impress, overwhelm, sitdown, walkout, slowdown.

striking *(SYN.)* arresting, imposing, splendid, august, impressive, thrilling, stirring, awesome, aweinspiring.

(ANT.) ordinary, unimpressive, commonplace, regular.

stringent *(SYN.)* harsh, rugged, grating, severe, gruff.

strip *(SYN.)* disrobe, undress, remove, uncover, peel, ribbon, band, piece.

strive *(SYN.)* aim, struggle, attempt, undertake, design, endeavor, try.

(ANT.) omit, abandon, neglect, decline.

stroke *(SYN.)* rap, blow, tap, knock, feat, achievement, accomplishment, caress.

stroll *(SYN.)* amble, walk, ramble.

strong *(SYN.)* potent, hale, athletic, mighty, sturdy, impregnable, resistant.

(ANT.) feeble, insipid, brittle, weak, bland, fragile.

structure *(SYN.)* construction, arrangement.

struggle *(SYN.)* fray, strive, fight, contest, battle, skirmish, oppose, clash.

(ANT.) peace, agreement, truce.

stubborn *(SYN.)* firm, obstinate, determined, inflexible, obdurate, uncompromising, contumacious, rigid, unbending, intractable.

(ANT.) docile, yielding, amenable, submissive.

student *(SYN.)* pupil, observer, disciple, scholar, learner.

studio *(SYN.)* workroom, workshop.

study *(SYN.)* weigh, muse, master, contemplate, reflect, examination, examine.

stuff *(SYN.)* thing, subject, material, theme, matter, substance, fill, ram, cram, pack, textile, cloth, topic.

(ANT.) spirit, immateriality.

stumble *(SYN.)* sink, collapse, tumble, drop, topple, lurch, trip, fall.

(ANT.) steady, climb, soar, arise.

stun *(SYN.)* shock, knock out, dumbfound, take, amaze, alarm.

(ANT.) forewarn, caution, prepare.

stunning *(SYN.)* brilliant, dazzling, exquisite, ravishing.

(ANT.) drab, ugly.

stunt *(SYN.)* check, restrict, hinder.

stupid *(SYN.)* dull, obtuse, half-witted, brainless, foolish, dumb, witless, idiotic.

(ANT.) smart, intelligent, clever, quick, bright, alert, discerning.

stupor *(SYN.)* lethargy, torpor, daze, languor, drowsiness, numbness.

(ANT.) wakefulness, liveliness, activity.

sturdy *(SYN.)* hale, strong, rugged, stout, mighty, enduring, hardy, well-built.

(ANT.) fragile, brittle, delicate.

style *(SYN.)* sort, type, kind, chic, smartness, elegance.

subdue *(SYN.)* crush, overcome, rout, beat, reduce, lower, defeat, vanquish.

(ANT.) retreat, cede, surrender.

subject *(SYN.)* subordinate, theme, case, topic, dependent, citizen, matter.

sublime *(SYN.)* lofty, raised, elevated, supreme, exalted, splendid, grand.

(ANT.) ordinary, vase, low, ridiculous.

submerge *(SYN.)* submerse, dunk, sink, dip, immerse, engage, douse.

(ANT.) surface, rise, uplift, elevate.

submissive *(SYN.)* deferential, yielding, dutiful, compliant.

(ANT.) rebellious, intractable, insubordinate.

submit *(SYN.)* quit, resign, waive, yield, tender, offer, abdicate, cede, surrender.

(ANT.) fight, oppose, resist, struggle, deny, refuse.

subordinate *(SYN.)* demean, reduce, inferior, assistant, citizen, liegeman.

(ANT.) superior.

subsequent *(SYN.)* later, following.

(ANT.) preceding, previous.

subside *(SYN.)* decrease, lower, sink, droop, hang, collapse.

(ANT.) mount, steady, arise, climb.

subsidy *(SYN.)* support, aid, grant.

substance *(SYN.)* stuff, essence, importance, material, matter.

(ANT.) spirit, immaterial.

substantial *(SYN.)* large, considerable, sizable, actual, real, tangible, influential.

(ANT.) *unimportant, trivial.*

substantiate *(SYN.)* strengthen, corroborate, confirm.

substitute *(SYN.)* proxy, expedient, deputy, makeshift, replacement, alternate, representative, surrogate, exchange, equivalent.

(ANT.) *sovereign, master, head.*

substitution *(SYN.)* change, mutation, vicissitude, alteration, modification.

(ANT.) *uniformity, monotony.*

subterfuge *(SYN.)* pretext, excuse, cloak, simulation, disguise, garb, pretension.

(ANT.) *reality, truth, actuality, sincerity.*

subtle *(SYN.)* suggestive, indirect.

(ANT.) *overt, obvious.*

subtract *(SYN.)* decrease, reduce, curtail, deduct, diminish, remove.

(ANT.) *expand, increase, add, enlarge, grow.*

succeed *(SYN.)* thrive, follow, replace, achieve, win, flourish.

(ANT.) *flop, miscarry, anticipate, fail, precede.*

success *(SYN.)* advance, prosperity, luck.

(ANT.) *failure.*

successful *(SYN.)* fortunate, favorable, lucky, triumphant.

succession *(SYN.)* chain, course, series, order, string, arrangement, progression, train, following.

successive *(SYN.)* serial, sequential.

succinct *(SYN.)* pithy, curt, brief, short, compendious, terse.

(ANT.) *prolonged, extended, long, protracted.*

succor *(SYN.)* ease, solace, comfort, enjoyment, consolation.

(ANT.) *suffering, discomfort, torture, affliction, torment.*

sudden *(SYN.)* rapid, swift, immediate, abrupt, unexpected, unforeseen, hasty.

(ANT.) *slowly, anticipated.*

suffer *(SYN.)* stand, experience, endure, bear, feel, allow, let, permit, sustain.

(ANT.) *exclude, banish, overcome.*

suffering *(SYN.)* distress, ache, anguish, pain, woe, misery, torment.

(ANT.) *ease, relief, comfort.*

sufficient *(SYN.)* fitting, enough, adequate, commensurate.

(ANT.) *scant, deficient.*

suffix *(SYN.)* ending.

(ANT.) *prefix.*

suggest *(SYN.)* propose, offer, refer, advise, hint, insinuate, recommend, allude.

(ANT.) *dictate, declare, insist.*

suggestion *(SYN.)* exhortation, recommendation, intelligence, caution, admonition, advice.

suit *(SYN.)* conform, accommodate, fit.

(ANT.) *misapply, disturb.*

suitable *(SYN.)* welcome, agreeable, acceptable, gratifying.

(ANT.) *offensive, disagreeable.*

sullen *(SYN.)* fretful, morose, crabbed, dismal, silent, sulky, bitter, sad, somber, glum, gloomy.

(ANT.) pleasant, joyous, merry.

sultry *(SYN.)* close, hot, stifling.

sum *(SYN.)* amount, total, aggregate, whole, increase, add.

(ANT.) fraction, reduce, deduct.

summary *(SYN.)* digest, outline, abstract, synopsis, concise, brief.

summit *(SYN.)* peak, top, head, crest, zenith, crown, pinnacle.

(ANT.) bottom, foundation, base.

summon *(SYN.)* invoke, call, invite.

(ANT.) dismiss.

sundry *(SYN.)* miscellaneous, several, different, various, divers.

(ANT.) similar, identical, alike, same, congruous.

superannuated *(SYN.)* old, archaic, aged, senile, ancient, venerable, elderly.

(ANT.) youthful, modern, young.

superb *(SYN.)* splendid, wonderful, extraordinary, marvelous.

supercilious *(SYN.)* contemptuous, snobbish, overbearing, vainglorious, arrogant, haughty, stately.

(ANT.) meek, ashamed, lowly.

superficial *(SYN.)* flimsy, shallow, cursory, slight, exterior.

(ANT.) thorough, deep, abstruse, profound.

superintend *(SYN.)* rule, control, govern, command, manage.

(ANT.) ignore, follow, submit, abandon.

superintendent *(SYN.)* manager, supervisor, overseer, director, administrator.

superior *(SYN.)* greater, finer, better, employer, boss.

(ANT.) inferior.

superlative *(SYN.)* pure, consummate, sinless, blameless, holy, perfect, faultless, ideal, unqualified, immaculate.

(ANT.) defective, imperfect, deficient, blemished.

supervise *(SYN.)* rule, oversee, govern, command, direct, superintend, manage, control.

(ANT.) forsake, abandon.

supervision *(SYN.)* oversight, inspection, charge, management.

supervisor *(SYN.)* manager, boss, foreman, director.

supplant *(SYN.)* overturn.

(ANT.) uphold, conserve.

supple *(SYN.)* lithe, pliant, flexible, limber, elastic, pliable.

(ANT.) stiff, brittle, unbending.

supplement *(SYN.)* add, extension, complement, addition, extend.

supplicate *(SYN.)* beg, petition, solicit, adjure, beseech, entreat.

(ANT.) cede, give, bestow, grant.

supplication *(SYN.)* invocation, plea, appeal, request, entreaty.

supply *(SYN.)* provide, inventory, hoard, reserve, store, accumulation, stock, furnish, endow, give.

support (SYN.) groundwork, aid, favor, base, prop, assistance, comfort, basis, succor, living, subsistence, encouragement, backing, livelihood, help, maintain.

(ANT.) discourage, abandon, oppose, opposition, attack.

supporter (SYN.) follower, devotee, adherent, henchman, attendant, disciple, votary.

(ANT.) muster, head, chief.

suppose (SYN.) believe, presume, deduce, apprehend, think, assume, imagine, speculate, guess.

(ANT.) prove, demonstrate, ascertain.

supposition (SYN.) theory, conjecture.

(ANT.) proof, fact.

suppress (SYN.) diminish, reduce, overpower, lessen, decrease, subdue, lower.

(ANT.) revive, amplify, intensify, enlarge.

supremacy (SYN.) domination, predominance, ascendancy.

supreme (SYN.) greatest, best, highest, main, principal, cardinal, first, chief, foremost, paramount.

(ANT.) supplemental, minor, subsidiary, auxiliary.

sure (SYN.) confident, fixed, inevitable, certain, positive, trustworthy, reliable, unquestionable, convinced, steady, assured, unfailing, stable, firm, safe, destined, fated.

(ANT.) probable, uncertain, doubtful.

surface (SYN.) outside, exterior, cover, covering.

surge (SYN.) heave, swell, grow.

(ANT.) wane, ebb, diminish.

surly (SYN.) disagreeable, hostile, unfriendly, ugly, antagonistic.

surmise (SYN.) judge, think, believe, assume, suppose, presume, guess, thought, suspect.

surname (SYN.) denomination, epithet, title, name, appellation.

surpass (SYN.) pass, exceed, excel, outstrip, outdo.

surplus (SYN.) extravagance, intemperance, superabundance, excess, immoderation, remainder, extra, profusion, superfluity.

(ANT.) want, lack, dearth, paucity.

surprise (SYN.) miracle, prodigy, wonder, awe, phenomenon, marvel, bewilderment, wonderment.

(ANT.) expectation, triviality, indifference, familiarity.

surrender (SYN.) relinquish, resign, yield, abandon, sacrifice.

(ANT.) overcome, rout, conquer.

surreptitious (SYN.) sneaky, sneaking, underhead, sly, furtive.

(ANT.) openhanded, open, straight-forward.

surround (SYN.) confine, encompass, circle, encircle, girdle, fence, circumscribe, limit, envelop.

(ANT.) open, distend, expose,

enlarge.

surveillance *(SYN.)* inspection, oversight, supervision, management, control.

survey *(SYN.)* scan, inspect, view, examine, inspection, examination.

survive *(SYN.)* live, remain, continue, persist.
(ANT.) die, fail, succumb.

suspect *(SYN.)* waver, disbelieve, presume, suppose, mistrust, distrust, question, suspected, assume, defendant, questionable.
(ANT.) decide, believe, trust.

suspend *(SYN.)* delay, hang, withhold, interrupt, postpone, dangle, adjourn, poise, defer.
(ANT.) persist, proceed, maintain.

suspicious *(SYN.)* suspecting, distrustful, doubtful, doubting, questioning, suspect, skeptical.

suspicion *(SYN.)* unbelief, distrust, suspense, uncertainty, doubt.
(ANT.) determination, conviction, faith, belief.

sustain *(SYN.)* bear, carry, undergo, foster, keep, prop, help, advocate, back, encourage, maintain, assist, suffer, approve.
(ANT.) discourage, betray, oppose, destroy.

sustenance *(SYN.)* fare, food, diet, rations, nutriment, edibles, victuals, repast, feed.
(ANT.) hunger, want, drink.

swallow *(SYN.)* gorge, gulp, eat, mouthful.

swamp *(SYN.)* fen, bog, marsh, quagmire, morass, flood, overcome, deluge.

swarm *(SYN.)* throng, horde, crowd.

swarthy *(SYN.)* sable, dark.
(ANT.) bright, light.

sway *(SYN.)* control, affect, stir, actuate, impel, impress, bend, wave, swing, persuade, influence.

swear *(SYN.)* declare, state, affirm, vouchsafe, curse, maintain.
(ANT.) demur, oppose, deny, contradict.

sweat *(SYN.)* perspiration, perspire.

sweeping *(SYN.)* extensive, wide, general, broad, tolerant, comprehensive, vast.
(ANT.) restricted, confined.

sweet *(SYN.)* engaging, luscious, pure, clean, fresh, melodious, winning, unsalted, pleasant.
(ANT.) bitter, harsh, nasty, irascible, discordant, irritable, acrid.

swell *(SYN.)* increase, grow, expand, enlarge.
(ANT.) diminish, shrink.

swift *(SYN.)* quick, fast, fleet, speedy, rapid, expeditious.

swindle *(SYN.)* bilk, defraud, con, deceive, cheat, guile, imposture, deception, artifice, deceit, trick.
(ANT.) sincerity, honesty, fairness.

swing *(SYN.)* rock, sway, wave.

switch *(SYN.)* shift, change, turn.

swoon *(SYN.)* faint.

symbol *(SYN.)* sign, character.

sympathetic *(SYN.)* considerate, compassionate, gentle, benevolent, tender, affable.

(ANT.) unkind, merciless, indifferent, intolerant, cruel.

sympathize *(SYN.)* gladden, sheer, solace, comfort, encourage.

(ANT.) depress, antagonize.

sympathy *(SYN.)* compassion, agreement, tenderness, commiseration, pity.

(ANT.) indifference, unconcern, antipathy, malevolence.

symptom *(SYN.)* indication, sign.

synopsis *(SYN.)* outline, digest.

synthetic *(SYN.)* counterfeit, artificial, phony, unreal, bogus, sham.

(ANT.) natural, true, genuine.

system *(SYN.)* organization, procedure, regularity, arrangement.

(ANT.) confusion, chance, disorder.

systematic *(SYN.)* orderly, organized, grouped, classified, measured, constant, methodical.

(ANT.) irregular, random, disorganized, erratic.

T

table *(SYN.)* catalog, list, schedule, postpone, chart, index, shelve, delay, put off.

tablet *(SYN.)* pad, notebook, capsule, pill, sketchpad, pill, paper,

tacit *(SYN.)* understood, assumed, implied, unspoken, acknowledged, expected.

(ANT.) said, spoken.

taciturn *(SYN.)* quiet, reserved, silent.

(ANT.) talkative.

tack *(SYN.)* add, join, attach, clasp, fasten.

tackle *(SYN.)* rigging, gear, apparatus, equipment, grab, seize, down, try, undertake.

(ANT.) evade, avoid.

tacky *(SYN.)* gummy, sticky, gooey.

tact *(SYN.)* dexterity, poise, diplomacy, judgment, savoir-faire, skill, finesse, sense, prudence.

(ANT.) incompetence, vulgarity, blunder, rudeness, awkwardness, insensitivity, grossness.

tactful *(SYN.)* discreet, considerate, judicious, adroit, sensitive, diplomatic, skillful, discriminating, politic.

(ANT.) coarse, gruff, tactless, boorish, unfeeling, churlish, rude.

tactical *(SYN.)* foxy, cunning, proficient, adroit, clever, expert.

(ANT.) blundering, gauche, clumsy, inept.

tactics *(SYN.)* plan, strategy, approach, maneuver, course.

tag *(SYN.)* sticker, label, mark, identification, marker, name.

tail *(SYN.)* rear, back, follow, end, shadow, pursue, trail, heel.

tailor *(SYN.)* modiste, couturier, modify, redo, shape, fashion.

taint *(SYN.)* spot, stain, tarnish, soil, mark, discolor.
(ANT.) cleanse, disinfect, clean.

tainted *(SYN.)* crooked, impure, vitiated, profligate, debased, spoiled, corrupted, depraved, dishonest, contaminated.

take *(SYN.)* accept, grasp, catch, confiscate, adopt, assume, receive, attract, claim, necessitate, steal, ensnare, capture, demand, select, appropriate, obtain, captivate, hold, seize, win, escort, note, get, remove, gain, choose.

taking *(SYN.)* charming, captivating, winning, attractive.

takeover *(SYN.)* revolution, merger, usurpation, confiscation.

tale *(SYN.)* falsehood, history, yarn, chronicle, account, fable, fiction, narration, story, narrative.

talent *(SYN.)* capability, knack, skill, endowment, gift, cleverness, aptitude, ability, genius.
(ANT.) ineptitude, incompetence, stupidity.

talented *(SYN.)* skillful, smart, adroit, dexterous, clever, apt, witty, ingenious.
(ANT.) dull, clumsy, awkward, unskilled, stupid, slow.

talk *(SYN.)* conversation, gossip, report, speech, communicate, discuss, confer, chatter, conference, preach, dialogue, reason, jabber, discourse, lecture, communication, consul, plead, argue, converse, rant, chat, mutter, speak, rangue, rumor, deliberate, discussion.

(ANT.) silence, correspondence, meditation, writing.

talkative *(SYN.)* glib, communicative, chattering, loquacious, voluble, garrulous.
(ANT.) uncommunicative, laconic, reticent, silent.

tall *(SYN.)* elevated, high, towering, big, lofty, imposing, gigantic.
(ANT.) tiny, low, short, small, stunted.

tally *(SYN.)* score, count, compute, reckon, calculate, estimate, list, figure, correspond, agree, match.

tame *(SYN.)* domesticated, dull, insipid, docile, broken, uninteresting, gentle, subdued, insipid, flat, unexciting, boring, empty, break, domesticate, mild, tedious.
(ANT.) spirited, savage, wild, exciting, animated, undomesticated.

tamper *(SYN.)* mix in, interrupt, interfere, meddle, interpose.

tang *(SYN.)* zest, sharpness, tartness, taste.

tangible *(SYN.)* material, sensible, palpable, corporeal, bodily.
(ANT.) metaphysical, mental, spiritual.

tangle *(SYN.)* confuse, knot, snarl, twist, ensnare, embroil, implicate.

tangy *(SYN.)* pungent, peppery, seasoned, sharp, tart.

tantalize *(SYN.)* tease, tempt, entice, titillate, stimulate, frustrate.

tantrum *(SYN.)* outburst, fit, fury, flare-up, conniption, rampage.

tap *(SYN.)* pat, rap, hit, strike, blow, faucet, spout, spigot.

tape *(SYN.)* ribbon, strip, fasten, bandage, bind, record, tie.

taper *(SYN.)* narrow, candle, decrease, lessen.

tardy *(SYN.)* slow, delayed, overdue, late, belated.
(ANT.) prompt, timely, punctual, early.

target *(SYN.)* aim, goal, object, objective.

tariff *(SYN.)* duty, tax, levy, rate.

tarnish *(SYN.)* discolor, blight, defile, sully, spot, befoul, disgrace, stain.
(ANT.) honor, purify, cleanse, bleach, decorate, gleam, sparkle.

tarry *(SYN.)* dawdle, loiter, linger, remain, delay, procrastinate.

tart *(SYN.)* sour, acrid, pungent, acid, sharp, distasteful, bitter.
(ANT.) mellow, sweet, delicious, pleasant.

task *(SYN.)* work, job, undertaking, labor, chore, duty, stint.

taste *(SYN.)* tang, inclination, liking, sensibility, flavor, savor, try, sip, sample, zest, experience, undergo, appreciation, relish, discernment, judgment.
(ANT.) indelicacy, disinclination, antipathy, insipidity.

tasty *(SYN.)* delectable, delicious, luscious, palatable, tempting.

tattered *(SYN.)* ragged, torn, shoddy, shabby, frazzled, frayed.

tattle *(SYN.)* inform, divulge, disclose, blab, reveal.

taunt *(SYN.)* tease, deride, flout, scoff, sneer, mock, annoy, pester, bother, ridicule, jeer.
(ANT.) praise, compliment, laud, flatter.

taunting *(SYN.)* ironic, caustic, cutting, sardonic, derisive, biting, acrimonious, sarcastic, satirical.
(ANT.) pleasant, agreeable, affable, amiable.

taut *(SYN.)* tight, constricted, firm, stretched, snug, tense, extended.
(ANT.) slack, loose, relaxed, open, lax.

tavern *(SYN.)* pub, bar, cocktail lounge.

tawdry *(SYN.)* pretentious, showy, vulgar, tasteless, sordid, garish.

tax *(SYN.)* duty, assessment, excise, levy, toll, burden, strain, tribute, tariff, assess, encumber, overload, custom, exaction, rate.
(ANT.) reward, gift, remuneration, wages.

taxi *(SYN.)* cab, taxicab.

teach *(SYN.)* inform, school, educate, train, inculcate, instruct.
(ANT.) misinform, misguide.

teacher *(SYN.)* tutor, instructor, professor, lecturer.

team *(SYN.)* company, band,

party, crew, gang, group.

teamwork *(SYN.)* cooperation.

tear *(SYN.)* rend, shred, sunder, cleave, rip, lacerate, teardrop, disunite, rend, divide, drop, wound, split, slit, sever.

(ANT.) mend, join, unite, sew.

tease *(SYN.)* badger, harry, bother, irritate, nag, pester, taunt, vex, annoy, disturb, harass, worry, tantalize, plague, aggravate, provoke.

(ANT.) please, delight, soothe, comfort, gratify.

technical *(SYN.)* industrial, technological, specialized, mechanical.

technique *(SYN.)* system, method, routine, approach, procedure.

tedious *(SYN.)* boring, dilatory, humdrum, sluggish, monotonous, dull, irksome, dreary, tiring, burdensome, tiresome, wearisome.

(ANT.) interesting, entertaining, engaging, exciting, amusing, quick.

teem *(SYN.)* abound, swarm.

teeming *(SYN.)* overflowing, bountiful, abundant, ample, profuse, plenteous, rich, copious.

(ANT.) scant, scarce, deficient, insufficient.

teeter *(SYN.)* sway, hesitate, hem and haw, waver.

telecast *(SYN.)* broadcast.

televise *(SYN.)* telecast.

tell *(SYN.)* report, mention, state, betray, announce, recount, relate, narrate, rehearse, mention, utter, confess, disclose, direct, request, acquaint, instruct, notify, inform, determine, reveal, divulge.

telling *(SYN.)* persuasive, convincing, forceful, effective.

temerity *(SYN.)* rashness, foolhardiness, audacity, boldness, recklessness, precipitancy.

(ANT.) prudence, wariness, caution, hesitation, timidity.

temper *(SYN.)* fury, choler, exasperation, anger, passion, petulance, disposition, nature, rage, soothe, soften, wrath, indignation, irritation, pacify, animosity, mood, resentment.

(ANT.) peace, self-control, forbearance, conciliation.

temperament *(SYN.)* humor, mood, temper, nature, disposition.

temperamental *(SYN.)* testy, moody, touchy, sensitive, irritable.

(ANT.) calm, unruffled, serene.

temperance *(SYN.)* abstinence, sobriety, forbearance, abstention.

(ANT.) intoxication, excess, self-indulgence, gluttony, wantonness.

temperate *(SYN.)* controlled, moderate, calm, restrained.

(ANT.) excessive, extreme, prodigal.

tempest *(SYN.)* draft, squall, wind, blast, gust, storm, hurricane, commotion, tumult, zephyr.

(ANT.) calm, tranquillity, peace.

tempo *(SYN.)* measure, beat, cadence, rhythm.

temporal *(SYN.)* mundane, earthly, lay, profane, worldly, laic.

(ANT.) spiritual, ecclesiastical, religious, heavenly.

temporary *(SYN.)* brief, momentary, shortlived, fleeting, ephemeral, passing, short.

(ANT.) lasting, permanent, immortal, everlasting, abiding.

tempt *(SYN.)* entice, allure, lure, attract, seduce, invite, magnetize.

tenacious *(SYN.)* persistent, determined, unchanging, unyielding.

tenable *(SYN.)* correct, practical, rational, reasonable, sensible.

tenacity *(SYN.)* perseverance, steadfastness, industry, constancy, persistence, pertinacity.

(ANT.) laziness, rest, idleness, sloth.

tenant *(SYN.)* renter, lessee, lodger, leaseholder, dweller, resident.

tend *(SYN.)* escort, follow, care for, lackey, watch, protect, take care of, attend, guard, serve.

tendency *(SYN.)* drift, inclination, proneness, leaning, bias, aim, leaning, disposition, predisposition, propensity, trend, impulse.

(ANT.) disinclination, aversion, deviation.

tender *(SYN.)* sympathetic, sore, sensitive, painful, gentle, meek, delicate, fragile, prof-

fer, bland, mild, loving, offer, affectionate, soothing, propose, soft.

(ANT.) rough, severe, fierce, chewy, tough, cruel, unfeeling, harsh.

tenderfoot *(SYN.)* novice, apprentice, beginner, amateur.

tenderhearted *(SYN.)* kind, sympathetic, merciful, softhearted, understanding, sentimental, affectionate, gentle, sensitive.

tenet *(SYN.)* dogma, belief, precept, doctrine, creed, opinion.

(ANT.) deed, conduct, practice, performance.

tense *(SYN.)* strained, stretched, excited, tight, nervous.

(ANT.) loose, placid, lax, relaxed.

tension *(SYN.)* stress, strain, pressure, anxiety, apprehension, distress.

tentative *(SYN.)* hypothetical, indefinite, probationary, conditional.

tenure *(SYN.)* administration, time, regime, term.

tepid *(SYN.)* temperate, mild, lukewarm.

(ANT.) boiling, scalding, passionate, hot.

term *(SYN.)* period, limit, time, boundary, duration, name, phrase, interval, session, semester, expression, word.

terminal *(SYN.)* eventual, final, concluding, decisive, ending, fatal, latest, last, ultimate, conclusive.

(ANT.) original, first, rudimen-

tary, incipient, inaugural.

terminate *(SYN.)* close, end, finish, abolish, complete, cease, stop, conclude, expire, culminate.

(ANT.) establish, begin, initiate, start, commence.

terminology *(SYN.)* vocabulary, nomenclature, terms, phraseology.

terms *(SYN.)* conditions, provisions, agreement, stipulations.

terrible *(SYN.)* frightful, dire, awful, gruesome, horrible shocking, horrifying, terrifying, horrid, hideous, appalling, shocking.

(ANT.) secure, happy, joyous, pleasing, safe.

terrific *(SYN.)* superb, wonderful, glorious, great, magnificent, divine, colossal, sensational, marvelous.

terrify *(SYN.)* dismay, intimidate, startle, terrorize, appall, frighten, petrify, astound, alarm, affright, horrify, scare.

(ANT.) soothe, allay, reassure, compose, embolden.

territory *(SYN.)* dominion, province, quarter, section, country, division, region, domain, area, place, district.

terror *(SYN.)* fear, alarm, dismay, horror, dread, consternation, fright, panic.

(ANT.) calm, security, assurance, peace.

terse *(SYN.)* concise, incisive, succinct, summary, condensed, compact, neat, pithy, summary.

(ANT.) verbose, wordy, lengthy, prolix.

test *(SYN.)* exam, examination, trial, quiz, analyze, verify, validate.

testify *(SYN.)* depose, warrant, witness, state, attest, swear.

testimony *(SYN.)* evidence, attestation, declaration, proof, witness, confirmation.

(ANT.) refutation, argument, disproof, contradiction.

testy *(SYN.)* ill-natured, irritable, snappish, waspish, fractious, fretful, touchy, peevish, petulant.

(ANT.) pleasant, affable, good-tempered, genial, good-natured.

tether *(SYN.)* tie, hamper, restraint, bridle.

text *(SYN.)* textbook, book, manual.

textile *(SYN.)* material, cloth, goods, fabric.

texture *(SYN.)* construction, structure, composition, grain, finish.

thankful *(SYN.)* obliged, grateful, appreciative.

(ANT.) ungrateful, resenting.

thaw *(SYN.)* liquefy, melt, dissolve.

(ANT.) solidify, freeze.

theater *(SYN.)* arena, playhouse, battlefield, stadium, hall.

theatrical *(SYN.)* ceremonious, melodramatic, stagy, artificial, affected, dramatic, showy, dramatic.

(ANT.) unemotional, subdued, modest, unaffected.

theft *(SYN.)* larceny, robbery, stealing, plunder, burglary, pillage, thievery, depredation.

theme *(SYN.)* motive, topic, argument, subject, thesis, text, point, paper, essay, composition.

theoretical *(SYN.)* bookish, learned, scholarly, pedantic, academic, formal, erudite.
(ANT.) practical, ignorant, common sense, simple.

theory *(SYN.)* doctrine, guess, presupposition, postulate, assumption, speculation.
(ANT.) practice, verity, fact, proof.

therefore *(SYN.)* consequently, thence so, accordingly, hence, then.

thick *(SYN.)* compressed, heavy, compact, viscous, close, concentrated, crowded, dense.
(ANT.) watery, slim, thin, sparse, dispersed, dissipated.

thief *(SYN.)* burglar, robber, criminal.

thin *(SYN.)* diluted, flimsy, lean, narrow, slender, spare, emaciated, lank, diaphanous, gauzy, meager, slender, tenuous, slim, rare, sparse, scanty, gossamer, scanty, slight.
(ANT.) fat, wide, broad, thick, bulky.

think *(SYN.)* picture, contemplate, ponder, esteem, intend, mean, imagine, deliberate, contemplate, recall, speculate, recollect, deem, apprehend, consider, devise, plan, judge, purpose, reflect, suppose,
assume, meditate, muse.
(ANT.) forget, conjecture, guess.

thirst *(SYN.)* appetite, desire, craving, longing.

thirsty *(SYN.)* craving, arid, dry, dehydrated, parched, desirous.
(ANT.) satisfied.

thorn *(SYN.)* spine, barb, prickle, nettle, bramble.

thorough *(SYN.)* entire, complete, perfect, total, finished, unbroken, careful, consummate, undivided.
(ANT.) unfinished, careless, slapdash, imperfect, haphazard, lacking.

thoroughfare *(SYN.)* avenue, street, parkway, highway, boulevard.
(ANT.) byway.

though *(SYN.)* in any case, notwithstanding, however, nevertheless.

thought *(SYN.)* consideration, pensive, attentive, heedful, prudent, dreamy, reflective, introspective, meditation, notion, view, deliberation, sentiment, fancy, idea, impression, reasoning, contemplation, judgment, regard.
(ANT.) thoughtlessness.

thoughtful *(SYN.)* considerate, attentive, dreamy, pensive, provident, introspective, meditative, cautious, heedful, kind, courteous, friendly, pensive.
(ANT.) thoughtless, heedless, inconsiderate, rash, precipitous, selfish.

thoughtless *(SYN.)* inattentive, unconcerned, negligent, lax,

desultory, inconsiderate, careless, imprudent, inaccurate, neglectful, indiscreet, remiss.
(ANT.) meticulous, accurate, nice, careful.

thrash *(SYN.)* whip, beat, defeat, flog, punish, flog, strap, thresh.

thread *(SYN.)* yarn, strand, filament, fiber, string, cord.

threadbare *(SYN.)* shabby, tacky, worn, ragged, frayed.

threat *(SYN.)* menace, warning, danger, hazard, jeopardy, omen.

threaten *(SYN.)* caution, warning, forewarn, menace, intimidate, loom.

threatening *(SYN.)* imminent, nigh, approaching, impending, overhanging, sinister, foreboding.
(ANT.) improbable, retreating, afar, distant, remote.

threshold *(SYN.)* edge, verge, start, beginning, doorsill, commencement.

thrift *(SYN.)* prudence, conservation, saving, economy.

thrifty *(SYN.)* saving, economical, sparing, frugal, provident, stingy, saving, parsimonious.
(ANT.) wasteful, spendthrift, intemperate, self-indulgent, extravagant.

thrill *(SYN.)* arouse, rouse, excite, stimulation, excitement, tingle.
(ANT.) bore.

thrive *(SYN.)* succeed, flourish, grow, prosper.
(ANT.) expire, fade, shrivel, die, fail, languish.

throb *(SYN.)* pound, pulsate, palpitate, beat, pulse.

throe *(SYN.)* pang, twinge, distress, suffering, pain, ache, grief, agony.
(ANT.) pleasure, relief, ease, solace, comfort.

throng *(SYN.)* masses, press, crowd, bevy, populace, rabble, horde, host, mass, teem, mob, multitude.

throttle *(SYN.)* smother, choke, strangle.

through *(SYN.)* completed, done, finished, over.

throughout *(SYN.)* all over, everywhere, during.

throw *(SYN.)* propel, cast, pitch, toss, hurl, send, thrust, fling.
(ANT.) retain, pull, draw, haul, hold

thrust *(SYN.)* jostle, push, promote, crowd, force, drive, hasten, push, press, shove, urge.
(ANT.) ignore, falter, retreat, drag, oppose, halt.

thug *(SYN.)* mobster, hoodlum, mugger, gangster, assassin, gunman.

thump *(SYN.)* blow, strike, knock, jab, poke, pound, beat, clout, bat, rap, bang.

thunderstruck *(SYN.)* amazed, astounded, astonished, flabbergasted, awed, surprised, dumbfounded, spellbound bewildered.

thus *(SYN.)* hence, therefore, accordingly, so, consequently.

thwart *(SYN.)* defeat, frustrate, prevent, foil, stop, baffle, circumvent, hinder, obstruct, disappoint, balk, outwit.

(ANT.) promote, accomplish, fulfill, help, further.

ticket (SYN.) stamp, label, tag, seal, token, pass, summons, certificate, ballot, sticker, slate, citation.

tickle (SYN.) delight, entertain, thrill, amuse, titillate, excite.

ticklish (SYN.) fragile, delicate, rough, difficult.

tidings (SYN.) message, report, information, word, intelligence, news.

tidy (SYN.) trim, clear, neat, precise, spruce, orderly, shipshape.

(ANT.) disheveled, unkempt, sloppy, dirty, slovenly.

tie (SYN.) bond, join, relationship, bind, restrict, fetter, connect, conjunction, association, alliance, union, fasten, engage, attach, restrain, oblige, link, affinity.

(ANT.) separation, disunion, unfasten, open, loose, untie, free, isolation.

tier (SYN.) line, row, level, deck, layer.

tiff (SYN.) bicker, squabble, argue, row, clash, dispute, altercation.

tight (SYN.) firm, taut, pennypinching, constricted, snug, taut, parsimonious, secure, fast, strong, sealed, fastened, watertight, locked, close, compact, stingy.

(ANT.) slack, lax, open, relaxed, loose.

till (SYN.) plow, work, money-box, depository, cultivate, vault.

tilt (SYN.) slant, slope, incline, tip, lean.

timber (SYN.) lumber, wood, logs.

time (SYN.) epoch, span, term, age, duration, interim, period, tempo, interval, space, spell, season.

timeless (SYN.) unending, lasting, perpetual, endless, immemorial.

(ANT.) temporary, mortal, temporal.

timely (SYN.) prompt, exact, punctual, ready, precise.

(ANT.) slow, dilatory, tardy, late.

timepiece (SYN.) clock, watch.

timetable (SYN.) list, schedule.

timid (SYN.) coy, humble, sheepish, abashed, embarrassed, modest, bashful, diffident, shamefaced, retiring, fearful, faint-hearted, shy, timorous.

(ANT.) gregarious, bold, daring, adventurous, fearless, outgoing.

tinge (SYN.) color, tint, dye, stain, flavor, imbue, season, impregnate.

tingle (SYN.) shiver, chime, prickle.

tinker (SYN.) potter, putter, fiddle with, dawdle, dally, dabble.

tinkle (SYN.) sound, peal, ring, jingle, chime, toll.

tint (SYN.) color, tinge, dye, stain, hue, tone, shade.

tiny (SYN.) minute, little, petty,

wee, slight, diminutive, miniature, small, insignificant, trivial, puny.

(ANT.) huge, large, immense, big, enormous.

tip (SYN.) point, end, top, peak, upset, tilt, reward, gift, gratuity, clue, hint, suggestion, inkling.

tirade (SYN.) outburst, harangue, scolding.

tired (SYN.) weary, exhausted, fatigued, rundown, sleepy, faint, spent, wearied, worn, jaded.

(ANT.) rested, fresh, hearty, invigorated, energetic, tireless, eager.

tireless (SYN.) active, enthusiastic, energetic, strenuous.

(ANT.) exhausted, wearied, fatigued.

tiresome (SYN.) dull, boring, monotonous, tedious.

(ANT.) interesting.

titan (SYN.) colossus, powerhouse, mammoth.

title (SYN.) epithet, privilege, name, appellation, claim, denomination, due, heading, ownership, right, deed, designation.

toddle (SYN.) stumble, wobble, shuffle.

toil (SYN.) labor, drudgery, work, travail, performance, business, achievement, employment, occupation, slave, sweat, effort.

(ANT.) recreation, ease, vacation, relax, loll, play, leisure, repose.

token (SYN.) mark, sign, sample, indication, evidence, symbol.

tolerant (SYN.) extensive, vast, considerate, broad, patient, large, sweeping, liberal, wide.

(ANT.) intolerant, bigoted, biased, restricted, narrow, confined.

tolerate (SYN.) endure, allow, bear, authorize, permit, brook, stand, abide.

(ANT.) forbid, protest, prohibit, discriminating, unreasonable.

toll (SYN.) impost, burden, rate, assessment, duty, custom, excise, tribute, levy, burden, strain.

(ANT.) reward, wages, gift, remuneration.

tomb (SYN.) vault, monument, catacomb, grave, mausoleum.

tone (SYN.) noise, sound, mood, manner, expression, cadence.

tongs (SYN.) tweezers, hook, grapnel, forceps.

tongue (SYN.) diction, lingo, cant, jargon, vernacular, dialect, idiom, speech, phraseology.

(ANT.) nonsense, drivel, babble, gibberish.

too (SYN.) furthermore, moreover, similarly, also, in addition, besides, likewise.

tool (SYN.) devise, medium, apparatus, agent, implement, utensil, agent, vehicle, instrument.

(ANT.) preventive, hindrance, impediment, obstruction.

top (SYN.) crown, pinnacle, peak, tip, cover, cap, zenith, apex, crest, chief, head, summit.

(ANT.) bottom, foundation, base, foot.

topic (SYN.) subject, thesis, issue, argument, matter, theme, point.

topple (SYN.) collapse, sink, fall, tumble.

torment (SYN.) pain, woe, pester, ache, distress, misery, harass, throe, annoy, vex, torture, anguish, suffering, misery.

(ANT.) relief, comfort, ease, gratify, delight.

torpid (SYN.) sluggish, idle, lazy, inert, inactive, supine, slothful, indolent, motionless, lethargic.

(ANT.) alert, assiduous, diligent, active.

torpor (SYN.) lethargy, daze, numbness, stupor, drowsiness, insensibility, languor.

(ANT.) wakefulness, liveliness, activity, alertness, readiness.

torrent (SYN.) flood, downpour, deluge.

torrid (SYN.) scorching, ardent, impetuous, passionate, scalding, warm, fiery, hot- blooded, sultry, tropical, intense, sweltering, burning, hot.

(ANT.) passionless, impassive, cold, frigid, apathetic, freezing, phlegmatic, indifferent, temperate.

torso (SYN.) form, frame, body.

(ANT.) soul, mind, spirit, intellect.

torture (SYN.) anguish, badger, plague, distress, ache, torment, pester, pain, hound,

agony, woe, worry, vex, persecute, suffering, throe, afflict, misery.

(ANT.) aid, relief, comfort, ease, support, encourage, mitigation.

toss (SYN.) throw, cast, hurl, pitch, tumble, thrust, pitch, fling, propel.

(ANT.) retain, pull, draw, haul, hold.

total (SYN.) entire, complete, concluded, full, finished, thorough, whole, entirely, collection, aggregate, conglomeration, unbroken, perfect, undivided, consummate.

(ANT.) part, element, imperfect, unfinished, ingredient, particular, lacking.

tote (SYN.) move, transfer, convey, drag, carry.

totter (SYN.) falter, stagger, reel, sway, waver, stumble, wobble.

touch (SYN.) finger, feel, handle, move, affect, concern, mention, hint, trace, suggestion, knack, skill, ability, talent.

touching (SYN.) pitiable, affecting, moving, sad, adjunct, bordering, tangent, poignant, tender, effective, impressive, adjacent.

(ANT.) removed, enlivening, animated, exhilarating.

touchy (SYN.) snappish, irritable, fiery, choleric, testy, hot, irascible, nervous, excitable, petulant, sensitive, jumpy, peevish.

(ANT.) composed, agreeable,

tranquil, calm, serene, stolid, cool.

tough *(SYN.)* sturdy, difficult, trying, vicious, incorrigible, troublesome, hard, stout, leathery, strong, laborious, inedible, sinewy, cohesive, firm, callous, obdurate, vicious.

(ANT.) vulnerable, submissive, easy, brittle, facile, weak, fragile, tender, frail.

toughness *(SYN.)* stamina, sturdiness, fortitude, durability, intensity, force, might, stoutness, power, sturdiness, vigor.

(ANT.) weakness, feebleness, infirmity, frailty.

tour *(SYN.)* rove, travel, go, visit, excursion, ramble, journey, roam.

(ANT.) stop, stay.

tourist *(SYN.)* traveler, sightseer, vagabond, voyager.

tournament *(SYN.)* tourney, match, contest, competition.

tout *(SYN.)* vend, importune, peddle, solicit, sell, hawk.

tow *(SYN.)* tug, take out, unsheathe, haul, draw, remove, extract, pull, drag.

(ANT.) propel, drive.

towering *(SYN.)* elevated, exalted, high, lofty, tall, proud, eminent.

(ANT.) base, mean, stunted, small, tiny, low.

town *(SYN.)* hamlet, village, community, municipality.

toxic (SYN.) deadly, poisonous, fatal, lethal, harmful.

(ANT.) beneficial.

toy *(SYN.)* play, romp, frolic,

gamble, stake, caper, plaything, wager, revel.

trace *(SYN.)* stigma, feature, indication, trait, mark, stain, scar, sign, trial, trace, suggestion, characteristic, vestige, symptoms.

track *(SYN.)* persist, pursue, follow, sign, mark, spoor, trace, path, route, road, carry, hunt, chase.

(ANT.) escape, evade, abandon, flee, elude.

tract *(SYN.)* area, region, territory, district, expanse, domain.

tractable *(SYN.)* yielding, deferential, submissive, dutiful, compliant, obedient.

(ANT.) rebellious, intractable, insubordinate, obstinate.

trade *(SYN.)* business, traffic, commerce, dealing, craft, occupation, profession, livelihood, swap, barter, exchange.

trademark *(SYN.)* logo, brand name, identification, emblem, insignia, monogram.

tradition *(SYN.)* custom, legend, folklore, belief, rite, practice.

traduce *(SYN.)* defame, malign, vilify, revile, abuse, asperse, scandalize, disparage.

(ANT.) protect, honor, cherish, praise, respect, support, extol.

tragedy *(SYN.)* unhappiness, misfortune, misery, adversity, catastrophe.

tragic *(SYN.)* miserable, unfortunate, depressing, melancholy, mournful.

(ANT.) happy, cheerful, comic.

trail *(SYN.)* persist, pursue, chase, follow, drag, draw, hunt, track.
(ANT.) evade, flee, abandon, elude, escape.

train *(SYN.)* direct, prepare, aim, point, level, teach, drill, tutor, bid, instruct, order, command.
(ANT.) distract, deceive, misguide, misdirect.

traipse *(SYN.)* roam, wander, saunter, meander.

trait *(SYN.)* characteristic, feature, attribute, peculiarity, mark, quality, property.

traitor *(SYN.)* turncoat, betrayer, spy, double-dealer, conspirator.

traitorous *(SYN.)* disloyal, faithless, apostate, false, recreant, perfidious, treasonable, treacherous.
(ANT.) devoted, true, loyal, constant.

tramp *(SYN.)* bum, beggar, rover, hobo, march, stamp, stomp, vagabond, wanderer, vagrant.
(ANT.) laborer, worker, gentleman.

trample *(SYN.)* crush, stomp, squash.

tranquil *(SYN.)* composed, calm, dispassionate, imperturbable, peaceful, pacific, placid, quiet, still, serene, undisturbed, unruffled.
(ANT.) frantic, stormy, excited, disturbed, upset, turbulent, wild.

tranquillity *(SYN.)* calmness, calm, hush, peace, quiet, quiescence, quietude, repose, serenity, rest, stillness, silence, placid.
(ANT.) disturbance, agitation, excitement, tumult, noise.

transact *(SYN.)* conduct, manage, execute, treat, perform.

transaction *(SYN.)* business, deal, affair, deed, settlement, occurrence, negotiation, proceeding.

transcend *(SYN.)* overstep, overshadow, exceed.

transcribe *(SYN.)* write, copy, rewrite, record.

transfer *(SYN.)* dispatch, send, transmit, remove, transport, transplant, consign, move, shift, reasign, assign, relegate.

transform *(SYN.)* change, convert, alter, modify, transfigure, shift, vary, veer.
(ANT.) establish, continue, settle, preserve, stabilize.

transgression *(SYN.)* atrocity, indignity, offense, insult, outrage, aggression, injustice, crime, misdeed, trespass, sin, wrong, vice.
(ANT.) innocence, morality, gentleness, right.

transient *(SYN.)* ephemeral, evanescent, brief, fleeting, momentary, temporary.
(ANT.) immortal, abiding, permanent, lasting, timeless, established.

transition *(SYN.)* change, variation, modification.

translate *(SYN.)* decipher, construe, decode, elucidate, explicate, explain, interpret, solve, render, unravel.

(ANT.) distort, falsify, misinterpret, confuse, misconstrue.

transmit *(SYN.)* confer, convey, communicate, divulge, disclose, impart, send, inform, relate, notify, reveal, dispatch, tell.

(ANT.) withhold, hide, conceal.

transparent *(SYN.)* crystalline, clear, limpid, lucid, translucent, thin, evident, manifest, plain, explicit, obvious, open.

(ANT.) opaque, muddy, turbid, thick, questionable, ambiguous.

transpire *(SYN.)* befall, bechance, betide, happen, chance, occur.

transport *(SYN.)* carry, bear, convey, remove, move, shift, enrapture, transfer, lift, entrance, ravish, stimulate.

transpose *(SYN.)* change, switch, reverse.

trap *(SYN.)* artifice, bait, ambush, intrigue, net, lure, pitfall, ensnare, deadfall, snare, ruse, entrap, bag, trick, stratagem, wile.

trash *(SYN.)* refuse, garbage, rubbish, waste.

trashy *(SYN.)* insignificant, worthless, slight.

trauma *(SYN.)* ordeal, upheaval, jolt, shock, disturbance.

travail *(SYN.)* suffering, torment, anxiety, distress, anguish, misery, ordeal.

travel *(SYN.)* journey, go, touring, ramble, rove, voyage, cruise, tour, roam.

(ANT.) stop, stay, remain, hiber-
nate.

travesty *(SYN.)* farce, joke, misrepresentation, counterfeit, mimicry.

treachery *(SYN.)* collusion, cabal, combination, intrigue, conspiracy, disloyalty, betrayal, treason, plot.

(ANT.) allegiance, steadfastness, loyalty.

treason *(SYN.)* cabal, combination, betrayal, sedition, collusion, intrigue, conspiracy, machination, plot, disloyalty, treachery,

treasure *(SYN.)* cherish, hold dear, abundance, guard, prize, appreciate, value, riches, wealth, foster, sustain, nurture.

(ANT.) disregard, neglect, dislike, abandon, reject.

treat *(SYN.)* employ, avail, manipulate, exploit, operate, utilize, exert, act, exercise, practice, handle, manage, deal, entertain, indulge, host, negotiate, tend, attend, heal, use.

(ANT.) waste, neglect, overlook, ignore.

treaty *(SYN.)* compact, agreement, pact, bargain, covenant, alliance, marriage.

(ANT.) schism, separation, divorce.

trek *(SYN.)* tramp, hike, plod, trudge.

tremble *(SYN.)* flutter, jolt, jar, agitate, quake, quiver, quaver, rock, shake shudder, shiver, sway, vibrate, waver.

trembling *(SYN.)* apprehension,

alarm, dread, fright, fear, horror, terror, panic.

(ANT.) composure, calmness, tranquillity, serenity.

tremendous *(SYN.)* enormous, huge, colossal, gigantic, great, large.

tremor *(SYN.)* flutter, vibration, palpitation.

trench *(SYN.)* gully, gorge, ditch, gulch, moat, dugout, trough.

trenchant *(SYN.)* clear, emphatic, forceful, impressive, meaningful.

trend *(SYN.)* inclination, tendency, drift, course, tendency, direction.

trendy *(SYN.)* modish, faddish, stylish, voguish, popular, current.

trepidation *(SYN.)* apprehension, alarm, dread, fright, fear, horror, panic, terror.

(ANT.) boldness, bravery, fearlessness, courage, assurance.

trespass *(SYN.)* atrocity, indignity, affront, insult, outrage, offense, aggression, crime, misdeed, injustice, vice, wrong, sin.

(ANT.) evacuate, vacate, relinquish, abandon.

trespasser *(SYN.)* invader, intruder, encroacher.

trial *(SYN.)* experiment, ordeal, proof, test, examination, attempt, effort, endeavor, essay, affliction, misery, hardship, suffering, difficulty, misfortune, tribulation, trouble.

(ANT.) consolation, alleviation.

tribe *(SYN.)* group, race, clan,

bunch.

tribulation *(SYN.)* anguish, distress, agony, grief, misery, sorrow, torment, suffering, woe, disaster, calamity, evil, trouble, misfortune.

(ANT.) elation, delight, joy, fun, pleasure.

tribunal *(SYN.)* judges, arbitrators, decision makers, judiciary.

trick *(SYN.)* artifice, antic, deception, device, cheat, fraud, hoax, guile, imposture, ruse, ploy, stratagem, trickery, deceit, jest, joke, prank, defraud, subterfuge, wile, stunt.

(ANT.) exposure, candor, openness, honesty, sincerity.

trickle *(SYN.)* drip, drop, dribble, leak, seep.

tricky *(SYN.)* artifice, antic, covert, cunning, foxy, crafty, furtive, guileful, insidious, sly, shrews, stealthy, surreptitious, subtle, underhand.

(ANT.) frank, candid, ingenuous, sincere, open.

trifling *(SYN.)* insignificant, frivolous, paltry, petty, trivial, small, unimportant.

(ANT.) momentous, serious, important, weighty.

trigger *(SYN.)* generate, provoke, prompt, motivate, activate.

trim *(SYN.)* nice, clear, orderly, precise, tidy, spruce, adorn, bedeck, clip, shave, prune, cut, shear, compact, neat, decorate, embellish, garnish.

(ANT.) deface, deform, spoil,

mar, important, serious, momentous, weighty.

trio *(SYN.)* threesome, triad, triple.

trip *(SYN.)* expedition, cruise, stumble, err, journey, jaunt, passage, blunder, bungle, slip, excursion, tour, pilgrimage, voyage, travel.

trite *(SYN.)* common, banal, hackneyed, ordinary, stereotyped, stale.

(ANT.) modern, fresh, momentous, stimulating, novel, new.

triumph *(SYN.)* conquest, achievement, success, prevail, win, jubilation, victory.

(ANT.) succumb, failure, defeat.

triumphant *(SYN.)* celebrating, exultant, joyful, exhilarated, smug.

trivial *(SYN.)* insignificant, frivolous, paltry, petty, trifling, small, unimportant.

(ANT.) momentous, important weighty, serious.

troops *(SYN.)* militia, troopers, recruits, soldiers, enlisted men.

trophy *(SYN.)* award, memento, honor, testimonial, prize.

tropical *(SYN.)* sultry, sweltering, humid, torrid.

trouble *(SYN.)* anxiety, affliction, calamity, distress, hardship, grief, pain, misery, sorrow, woe, bother, annoyance, care, embarrassment, irritation, torment, pains, worry, disorder, problem, disturbance, care, effort, exertion, toil, inconvenience, misfortune, labor.

(ANT.) console, accommodate, gratify, soothe, joy, peace.

troublemaker *(SYN.)* rebel, scamp, agitator, demon, devil, ruffian.

troublesome *(SYN.)* bothersome, annoying, distressing, irksome, disturbing, trying, arduous, vexatious, difficult, burdensome, laborious.

(ANT.) amusing, accommodating, gratifying, easy, pleasant.

trounce *(SYN.)* lash, flog, switch, whack, punish, whip, stomp.

truant *(SYN.)* delinquent, absentee, vagrant, malingerer.

truce *(SYN.)* armistice, ceasefire, interval, break, intermission, respite.

trudge *(SYN.)* march, trek, lumber, hike.

true *(SYN.)* actual, authentic, accurate, correct, exact, genuine, real, veracious, veritable, constant, honest, faithful, loyal, reliable, valid, legitimate, steadfast, sincere, trustworthy.

(ANT.) erroneous, counterfeit, false, spurious, fictitious, faithless, inconstant, fickle.

truly *(SYN.)* indeed, actually, precisely, literally, really, factually.

truncate *(SYN.)* prune, clip, pare, shorten.

truss *(SYN.)* girder, brace, framework, shoring.

trust *(SYN.)* credence, confidence, faith, dependence, reliance, trust, depend on, rely on, reckon on, believe, hope, credit, commit, entrust, confide.

(ANT.) incredulity, doubt, skepticism, mistrust.

trusted *(SYN.)* trustworthy, reliable, true, loyal, staunch, devoted.

trustworthy *(SYN.)* dependable, certain, reliable, secure, safe.

(ANT.) fallible, dubious, questionable, unreliable, uncertain

truth *(SYN.)* actuality, authenticity, accuracy, correctness, exactness, honesty, fact, rightness, truthfulness, veracity, verity.

(ANT.) falsity, falsehood, fiction, lie, untruth.

truthful *(SYN.)* frank, candid, honest, sincere, open, veracious, accurate, correct, exact, reliable.

(ANT.) misleading, sly, deceitful.

try *(SYN.)* endeavor, attempt, strive, struggle, undertake, afflict, test, prove, torment, trouble, essay, examine, analyze, investigate, effort, aim, design, aspire, intend.

(ANT.) decline, ignore, abandon, omit, neglect, comfort, console.

trying *(SYN.)* bothersome, annoying, distressing, irksome, disturbing, troublesome, arduous, vexatious, difficult, tedious

(ANT.) amusing, easy, accommodating, pleasant, gratifying.

tryout *(SYN.)* audition, trial, chance, test.

tryst *(SYN.)* rendezvous, meeting, appointment.

tub *(SYN.)* basin, vessel, sink, bowl.

tube *(SYN.)* hose, pipe, reed.

tubular *(SYN.)* hollow, cylindrical.

tuck *(SYN.)* crease, fold, gather, bend.

tuft *(SYN.)* bunch, group, cluster.

tug *(SYN.)* pull, wrench, tow, haul, draw, yank, jerk.

tuition *(SYN.)* instruction, schooling, teaching, education.

tumble *(SYN.)* toss, trip, fall, sprawl, wallow, lurch, flounder, plunge, topple, stumble.

tumult *(SYN.)* chaos, agitation, commotion, confusion, disarray, disarrangement, disorder, noise, hubbub, ferment, stir, to do, ado, disturbance, uproar, turmoil.

(ANT.) peacefulness, order, peace, certainty, tranquillity.

tune *(SYN.)* song, concord, harmony, air, melody, strain.

(ANT.) antipathy, aversion, discord.

tunnel *(SYN.)* passage, grotto, cave.

turbid *(SYN.)* dark, cloudy, thick, muddy, murky.

turbulent *(SYN.)* gusty, blustery, inclement, rough, roaring, stormy, tempestuous, disorderly, violent, tumultuous, unruly, windy.

(ANT.) clear, calm, quiet, peace-

ful, tranquil.

turf *(SYN.)* lawn, grassland, sod, grass.

turmoil *(SYN.)* chaos, agitation, commotion, confusion, disarray, disarrangement, disorder, jumble, uproar, ferment, pandemonium.

(ANT.) order, peace, certainty, quiet, tranquillity.

turn *(SYN.)* circulate, circle, invert, rotate, revolve, spin, twist, twirl, whirl, wheel, avert, reverse, become, sour, spoil, ferment, deviate, deflect, divert, swerve, change, alter, transmute.

(ANT.) fix, stand, arrest, stop, continue, endure, proceed, perpetuate.

turncoat *(SYN.)* renegade, defector, deserter, betrayer, traitor.

(ANT.) loyalist.

turret *(SYN.)* watchtower, belfry, steeple, tower, cupola, lookout.

tussle *(SYN.)* wrestle, struggle, contend, battle, fight, scuffle.

tutor *(SYN.)* instruct, prime, school, teach, train, prepare, drill.

tweak *(SYN.)* squeeze, pinch, nip.

twig *(SYN.)* sprig, branch, shoot, stem.

twilight *(SYN.)* sunset, sundown, nightfall, eventide, dusk.

twin *(SYN.)* lookalike, imitation, copy, double, replica.

twine *(SYN.)* string, cordage, rope, cord.

twinge *(SYN.)* smart, pang, pain.

twinkle *(SYN.)* shine, gleam, glisten, sparkle, glitter, shimmer, scintillate.

twirl *(SYN.)* rotate, spin, wind, turn, pivot, wheel, swivel, whirl.

twist *(SYN.)* bow, bend, crook, intertwine, curve, incline, deflect, lean, braid, distort, contort, warp, interweave, stoop, turn.

(ANT.) resist, break, straighten, stiffen.

twitch *(SYN.)* fidget, shudder, jerk.

tycoon *(SYN.)* millionaire, industrialist, businessman.

tyke *(SYN.)* rascal, urchin, brat, ragamuffin, imp.

type *(SYN.)* mark, emblem, sign, category, symbol, character, class, description, nature, kind, variety, example, sample, sort, stamp, model, exemplar, pattern.

(ANT.) deviation, monstrosity, eccentricity, peculiarity.

typhoon *(SYN.)* hurricane, cyclone, storm, tornado, whirlwind, twister.

typical *(SYN.)* common, accustomed, conventional, familiar, customary, habitual ordinary, characteristic, normal, plain, representative, regular, usual.

(ANT.) marvelous, extraordinary, remarkable, odd, atypical, uncommon, strange.

typify *(SYN.)* symbolize, illustrate, signify, represent, incarnate.

tyrannize *(SYN.)* oppress, victimize, threaten, brutalize, coerce.

tyrant *(SYN.)* dictator, autocrat, despot, oppressor, slave driver, disciplinarian, persecutor.

tyro *(SYN.)* amateur, beginner, novice, freshman, rookie, student, apprentice.

(ANT.) professional, veteran.

U

ugly *(SYN.)* hideous, homely, plain, deformed, repellent, uncomely, repulsive, ill-natured, unsightly, nasty, unpleasant, wicked, disagreeable, spiteful, surly, vicious.

(ANT.) beautiful, fair, pretty, attractive, handsome, comely, good, harmless, pleasant.

ultimate *(SYN.)* extreme, latest, final, concluding, decisive, hindmost, last, terminal, utmost, greatest, maximum.

(ANT.) foremost, opening, first, beginning, initial.

umbrage *(SYN.)* anger, displeasure, resentment, better.

(ANT.) happy, harmony.

umbrella *(SYN.)* cover, shade, parasol, shield.

unable *(SYN.)* ineffective, ineffectual, inept.

(ANT.) effective.

umpire *(SYN.)* judge, referee, arbitrator.

unadulterated *(SYN.)* genuine, clear, clean, immaculate, spotless, pure, absolute, untainted, sheer, bare.

(ANT.) foul, sullied, corrupt, tainted, polluted, tarnished, defiled.

unalterable *(SYN.)* fixed, unchangeable, steadfast, inflexible.

unanimity *(SYN.)* accord, unity, agreement.

unannounced *(SYN.)* hasty, precipitate, abrupt, unexpected.

(ANT.) courteous, expected, anticipated.

unassuming *(SYN.)* humble, lowly, compliant, modest, plain, meek, simple, unostentatious, retiring, submissive, unpretentious.

(ANT.) haughty, showy, pompous, proud, vain, presumptuous, arrogant, boastful, pretentious.

unattached *(SYN.)* apart, separate, unmarried, single, free, independent.

(ANT.) committed, involved, entangled.

unavoidable *(SYN.)* inescapable, certain, inevitable, unpreventable.

unawares *(SYN.)* abruptly, suddenly, unexpectedly, off guard.

unbalanced *(SYN.)* crazy, mad, insane, deranged.

unbearable *(SYN.)* insufferable, intolerable, unacceptable, oppressive.

(ANT.) tolerable, acceptable, bearable.

unbeliever *(SYN.)* dissenter, apostate, heretic, schismatic, nonconformist, sectary, sectarian.

unbending *(SYN.)* firm, inflexible, decided, determined, obstinate.
(ANT.) flexible.

unbiased *(SYN.)* honest, equitable, fair, impartial, reasonable, unprejudiced, just.
(ANT.) partial, fraudulent, dishonorable.

unbroken *(SYN.)* complete, uninterrupted, continuous, whole.

unburden *(SYN.)* clear, disentangle, divest, free.

uncanny *(SYN.)* amazing, remarkable, extraordinary, strange.

uncertain *(SYN.)* dim, hazy, indefinite, obscure, indistinct, unclear, undetermined, unsettled, ambiguous, unsure, doubtful, questionable, dubious, vague.
(ANT.) explicit, lucid, specific, certain, unmistakable, precise, clear.

uncertainty *(SYN.)* distrust, doubt, hesitation, incredulity, scruple, ambiguity, skepticism, uncertainty, suspense, suspicion, unbelief.
(ANT.) faith, belief, certainty, conviction, determination.

uncivil *(SYN.)* impolite, rude, discourteous.
(ANT.) polite.

uncivilized *(SYN.)* barbaric, barbarous, barbarian, brutal, crude, inhuman, cruel, merciless, rude, remorseless, uncultured, savage, unrelenting.
(ANT.) humane, kind, polite, civilized, refined.

unclad *(SYN.)* exposed, nude, naked, bare, stripped, defenseless, uncovered, open, unprotected.
(ANT.) concealed, protected, clothed, covered, dressed.

uncommon *(SYN.)* unusual, rare, odd, scarce, strange, peculiar, queer, exceptional, remarkable.
(ANT.) ordinary, usual.

uncompromising *(SYN.)* determined, dogged, firm, immovable, contumacious, headstrong, inflexible, obdurate, intractable, obstinate, pertinacious, stubborn, unyielding.
(ANT.) docile, compliant, amenable, yielding, submissive, pliable.

unconcern *(SYN.)* disinterestedness, impartiality, indifference, apathy, insensibility, neutrality.
(ANT.) affection, fervor, passion, ardor.

unconditional *(SYN.)* unqualified, unrestricted, arbitrary, absolute, pure, complete, actual, authoritative, perfect, entire, ultimate, tyrannous.
(ANT.) conditional, contingent, accountable, dependent, qualified.

unconscious *(SYN.)* lethargic, numb, comatose.

uncouth *(SYN.)* green, harsh, crude, coarse, ill-prepared, rough, raw, unfinished, unrefined, vulgar, rude, impolite, discourteous, unpolished, ill-mannered, crass.
(ANT.) well-prepared, cultivat-

ed, refined, civilized, finished.

uncover (SYN.) disclose, discover, betray, divulge, expose, reveal, impart, show.
(ANT.) conceal, hide, cover, obscure, cloak.

undependable (SYN.) changeable, unstable, uncertain, shifty, irresponsible.
(ANT.) stable, dependable, trustworthy.

under (SYN.) beneath, underneath, following, below, lower, downward.
(ANT.) over, above, up, higher.

undercover (SYN.) hidden, secret.

undergo (SYN.) endure, feel, stand, bear, indulge, suffer, sustain, experience, let, allow, permit, feel, tolerate.
(ANT.) overcome, discard, exclude, banish.

underhand (SYN.) sly, secret, sneaky, secretive, stealthy, crafty.
(ANT.) honest, open, direct, frank.

undermine (SYN.) demoralize, thwart, erode, weaken, subvert, sabotage.

underscore (SYN.) emphasize, stress.

understand (SYN.) apprehend, comprehend, appreciate, conceive, discern, know, grasp, hear, learn, realize, see, perceive.
(ANT.) misunderstand, mistake, misapprehend, ignore.

understanding (SYN.) agreement, coincidence, concord, accordance, concurrence, harmony, unison, compact, contract, arrangement, bargain, covenant, stipulation.
(ANT.) variance, difference, discord, dissension, disagreement.

understudy (SYN.) deputy, agent, proxy, representative, agent, alternate, lieutenant, substitute.
(ANT.) head, principal, sovereign, master.

undertake (SYN.) venture, attempt.

undertaking (SYN.) effort, endeavor, attempt, experiment, trial, essay.
(ANT.) laziness, neglect, inaction.

undersigned (SYN.) casual, chance, contingent, accidental, fortuitous, incidental, unintended.
(ANT.) decreed, planned, willed, calculated.

undesirable (SYN.) obnoxious, distasteful, repugnant.
(ANT.) appealing, inviting, attractive.

undivided (SYN.) complete, intact, entire, integral, total, perfect, unimpaired, whole.
(ANT.) partial, incomplete.

undoing (SYN.) ruin, downfall, destruction, failure, disgrace.

undying (SYN.) endless, deathless, eternal, everlasting, ceaseless, immortal, infinite, perpetual, timeless.
(ANT.) transient, mortal, temporal, ephemeral, finite, impermanent.

unearthly (SYN.) metaphysical,

ghostly, miraculous, marvelous, preternatural, superhuman, spiritual, foreign, strange, weird, supernatural.
(ANT.) physical, plain, human, natural, common, mundane.

uneducated *(SYN.)* uncultured, ignorant, illiterate, uninformed, unlearned, untaught, unlettered.
(ANT.) erudite, cultured, educated, literate, formed.

unemployed *(SYN.)* inert, inactive, idle, jobless, unoccupied.
(ANT.) working, occupied, active, industrious, employed.

uneven *(SYN.)* remaining, single, odd, unmatched, rugged, gnarled, irregular.
(ANT.) matched, even, flat, smooth.

unexceptional *(SYN.)* commonplace, trivial, customary.

unexpected *(SYN.)* immediate, hasty, surprising, instantaneous, unforeseen, abrupt, rapid, startling, sudden.
(ANT.) slowly, expected, gradual, predicted, anticipated, planned.

unfaithful *(SYN.)* treacherous, disloyal, deceitful, capricious.
(ANT.) true, loyal, steadfast, faithful.

unfasten *(SYN.)* open, expand, spread, exhibit, unbar, unlock, unfold, unseal.
(ANT.) shut, hide, conceal, close.

unfavorable *(SYN.)* antagonistic, contrary, adverse, opposed, opposite, disastrous, counteractive, unlucky.

(ANT.) benign, fortunate, lucky, propitious.

unfeeling *(SYN.)* hard, rigorous, cruel, stern, callous, numb, hard, strict, unsympathetic, severe.
(ANT.) tender, gentle, lenient, humane.

unfold *(SYN.)* develop, create, elaborate, amplify, evolve, mature, expand.
(ANT.) wither, restrict, contract, stunt, compress.

unfurnished *(SYN.)* naked, mere, bare, exposed, stripped, plain, open, simple.
(ANT.) concealed, protected, covered.

ungainly *(SYN.)* clumsy, awkward, bungling, clownish, gawky.
(ANT.) dexterous, graceful, elegant.

unhappy *(SYN.)* sad, miserable, distressed, depressed.
(ANT.) joyful, happy, joyous, cheerful.

unhealthy *(SYN.)* infirm, sick, diseased, sickly.
(ANT.) vigorous, well, healthy, hale.

uniform *(SYN.)* methodical, natural, customary, orderly, normal, consistent, ordinary, regular, unvarying, unchanging, systematic, steady, unvaried.
(ANT.) rare, unusual, erratic, exceptional, changeable.

unimportant *(SYN.)* petty, trivial, paltry, trifling, insignificant, indifferent, minor, petty.

uninformed *(SYN.)* illiterate,

uncultured, uneducated, ignorant, unlearned, untaught, unlettered.

(ANT.) informed, literate, erudite, cultured, educated.

uninhibited (SYN.) loose, open, liberated, free.

(ANT.) constrained, tense, suppressed.

unintelligible (SYN.) ambiguous, cryptic, dark, cloudy, abstruse, dusky, mysterious, indistinct, obscure, vague.

(ANT.) lucid, distinct, bright, clear.

uninteresting (SYN.) burdensome, dilatory, dreary, dull, boring, slow humdrum, monotonous, tardy, sluggish, tedious, wearisome, tiresome.

(ANT.) entertaining, exciting, quick, amusing.

union (SYN.) fusion, incorporation, combination, joining, concurrence, solidarity, agreement, unification, concord, harmony, alliance, unanimity, coalition, confederacy, amalgamation, league, marriage.

(ANT.) schism, disagreement, separation, discord.

unique (SYN.) exceptional, matchless, distinctive, choice, peculiar, singular, rare, sole, single, incomparable, uncommon, solitary, unequaled.

(ANT.) typical, ordinary, commonplace, frequent, common.

unison (SYN.) harmony, concurrence, understanding, accordance, concord, agreeable, coincidence.

(ANT.) disagreement, difference, discord, variance.

unite (SYN.) attach, blend, amalgamate, combine, conjoin, associate, connect, embody, consolidate, join, link, fuse, unify, merge.

(ANT.) sever, divide, separate, sever, disrupt, disconnect.

universal (SYN.) frequent, general, popular, common, familiar, prevailing, prevalent, usual.

(ANT.) scarce, odd, regional, local, extraordinary, exceptional.

unkempt (SYN.) sloppy, rumpled, untidy, messy, bedraggled.

(ANT.) presentable, wellgroomed, tidy, neat.

unkind (SYN.) unfeeling, unsympathetic, unpleasant, cruel, harsh.

(ANT.) considerate, sympathetic, amiable, kind.

unlawful (SYN.) illegitimate, illicit, illegal, outlawed, criminal, prohibited.

(ANT.) permitted, law, honest, legal, legitimate, authorized.

unlike (SYN.) dissimilar, different, distinct, contrary, diverse, divergent, opposite.

(ANT.) conditional, accountable, qualified, dependent.

unlucky (SYN.) cursed, inauspicious, unfortunate.

(ANT.) prosperous, fortunate, blessed.

unmerciful (SYN.) cruel, merciless, heartless, brutal.

unmistakable (SYN.) clear,

patent, plain, visible, obvious.

unnecessary *(SYN.)* pointless, needless, superfluous, purposeless.

unoccupied *(SYN.)* empty, vacant, uninhabited.

unparalleled *(SYN.)* peerless, unequaled, rare, unique, unmatched.

unpleasant *(SYN.)* offensive, disagreeable, repulsive, obnoxious, unpleasing.

unqualified *(SYN.)* inept, unfit, incapable, incompetent, unquestioned, absolute, utter.

unreasonable *(SYN.)* foolish, absurd, irrational, inconsistent, nonsensical, ridiculous, silly.

(ANT.) reasonable, sensible, sound, consistent, rational.

unruly *(SYN.)* unmanageable, disorganized, disorderly, disobedient.

(ANT.) orderly.

unsafe *(SYN.)* hazardous, insecure, critical, dangerous, perilous, menacing, risky, precarious, threatening.

(ANT.) protected, secure, firm, safe.

unselfish *(SYN.)* bountiful, generous, liberal, giving, beneficent, magnanimous, openhanded, munificent.

(ANT.) miserly, stingy, greedy, selfish, covetous.

unsightly *(SYN.)* ugly, unattractive, hideous.

unsophisticated *(SYN.)* frank, candid, artless, ingenuous, naive, open, simple, natural.

(ANT.) sophisticated, worldly,

cunning, crafty.

unsound *(SYN.)* feeble, flimsy, weak, fragile, sick, unhealthy, diseased, invalid, faulty, false.

unstable *(SYN.)* fickle, fitful, inconstant, capricious, restless, variable.

(ANT.) steady, stable, trustworthy, constant.

unswerving *(SYN.)* fast, firm, inflexible, constant, secure, stable, solid, steady, steadfast, unyielding.

(ANT.) loose, sluggish, insecure, flexible, unsteady, unstable, slow.

untainted *(SYN.)* genuine, pure, spotless, clean, clear, unadulterated, guiltless, innocent, chaste, modest, undefiled, sincere, virgin.

(ANT.) polluted, tainted, sullied, tarnished, defiled, corrupt, foul.

untamed *(SYN.)* fierce, savage, uncivilized, barbarous, outlandish, rude, undomesticated, frenzied, mad, turbulent, impetuous, wanton, boisterous, wayward, stormy, extravagant, wild, tempestuous, foolish, rash, giddy, reckless.

(ANT.) quiet, gentle, calm, civilized, placid.

untidy *(SYN.)* messy, sloppy, disorderly, slovenly.

unusual *(SYN.)* capricious, abnormal, devious, eccentric, aberrant, irregular, variable, extraordinary, odd, peculiar, uncommon, strange, exceptional, unnatural.

(ANT.) methodical, regular, us-

ual, fixed, ordinary.

unyielding (SYN.) fast, firm, inflexible, constant, solid, secure, stable, steadfast, unswerving, steady.
(ANT.) sluggish, slow, insecure, loose, unsteady, unstable.

uphold (SYN.) justify, espouse, assert, defend, maintain, vindicate.
(ANT.) oppose, submit, assault, deny, attack.

upright (SYN.) undeviating, right, unswerving, direct, erect, unbent, straight, fair, vertical.
(ANT.) bent, dishonest, crooked, circuitous, winding.

uprising (SYN.) revolution, mutiny, revolt, rebellion.

uproar (SYN.) noise, disorder, commotion, tumult, disturbance.

upset (SYN.) disturb, harass, bother, annoy, haunt, molest, inconvenience, pester, perplex, tease, plague, trouble, worry, overturned, toppled, capsize, fluster, agitate.
(ANT.) soothe, relieve, please, gratify.

upshot (SYN.) conclusion, result, outcome.

urbane (SYN.) civil, considerate, cultivated, courteous, genteel, polite, accomplished, refined.
(ANT.) rude, uncouth, boorish, uncivil.

urge (SYN.) craving, desire, longing, lust, appetite, aspiration, yearning, incite, coax, entice, force, drive, prod,

press, plead, persuade, recommend, advise.
(ANT.) loathing, hate, distaste, aversion, coerce, deter, restrain, compel, dissuade, discourage.

urgency (SYN.) emergency, exigency, pass, pinch, strait, crisis.

urgent (SYN.) critical, crucial, exigent, imperative, impelling, insistent, necessary, instant, serious, pressing, cogent, important, importunate, immediate.
(ANT.) trivial, unimportant, petty, insignificant.

usage (SYN.) use, treatment, custom, practice, tradition.

use (SYN.) custom, practice, habit, training, usage, manner, apply, avail employ, operate, utilize, exert, exhaust, handle, manage, accustom, inure, train, exploit, manipulate, spend, expend, consume, exercise, work.
(ANT.) disuse, neglect, waste, ignore, overlook, idleness.

useful (SYN.) beneficial, helpful, good, serviceable, wholesome, advantageous.
(ANT.) harmful, injurious, deleterious, destructive, detrimental.

useless (SYN.) bootless, empty, idle, pointless, vain, valueless, worthless, abortive, fruitless, unavailing, ineffectual, vapid.
(ANT.) profitable, potent, effective.

usher (SYN.) guide, lead.

usual *(SYN.)* customary, common, familiar, general, normal, habitual, accustomed, everyday, ordinary, regular.

(ANT.) irregular, exceptional, rare, extraordinary, abnormal.

utilize *(SYN.)* use, apply, devote, busy, employ, occupy, avail.

(ANT.) reject, banish, discharge, discard.

utopian *(SYN.)* perfect, ideal, faultless, exemplary, supreme, visionary, unreal.

(ANT.) real, material, imperfect, actual, faulty.

utter *(SYN.)* full, perfect, whole, finished, entire, speak, say, complete, superlative, supreme, total, absolute, pronounce, unqual- ified, downright, express, voice, declare.

(ANT.) imperfect, deficient, lacking, faulty, incomplete.

utterance *(SYN.)* expression, speech, articulation, communication, remark.

V

vacancy *(SYN.)* void, emptiness, vacuum, hollowness, blankness, vacuity, depletion, nothingness.

(ANT.) plenitude, fullness, profusion, completeness.

vacant *(SYN.)* barren, empty, blank, bare, unoccupied, void.

(ANT.) filled, packed, employed, full, replete, busy, engaged.

vacate *(SYN.)* abjure, relinquish, abdicate, renounce, abandon, resign, surrender, desert, waive.

(ANT.) stay, uphold, maintain.

vacation *(SYN.)* rest, holiday, break.

(ANT.) labor, work, routine.

vacillate *(SYN.)* hesitate, oscillate, undulate, change, fluctuate, vary.

(ANT.) persist, stick, decide.

vacillating *(SYN.)* contrary, illogical, contradictory, contrary, inconsistent, incongrous, incompatible, paradoxical, irreconcilable, unsteady, wavering.

(ANT.) correspondent, congruous, consistent, compatible.

vacuity *(SYN.)* space, emptiness, vacuum, void, blank, nothingness, ignorance, unawareness, senselessness, mindlessness, chatter, nonsense, froth, absurdity.

(ANT.) matter, fullness, content, substance, knowledge, intelligence.

vacuous *(SYN.)* dull, blank, uncomprehending, foolish, thoughtless, absentminded.

(ANT.) responsive, alert, attentive, intelligent, aware.

vacuum *(SYN.)* void, gap, emptiness, hole, chasm, nothingness.

vagabond *(SYN.)* pauper, ragamuffin, scrub, beggar, mendicant, hobo, starveling, tramp.

(ANT.) responsible, established, rooted, installed, reliable.

vagary *(SYN.)* notion, whim, fantasy, fancy, daydream, caprice, conceit, quirk, whimsy, impulse.

vagrant *(SYN.)* hobo, rover, tramp, beggar, wanderer, vagabond.

(ANT.) settled, worker, laborer, rooted, ambitious, gentleman.

vague *(SYN.)* indefinite, hazy, dim, indistinct, ambiguous, obscure, unclear, unsure.

(ANT.) certain, spelled out, specific, lucid, clear, definite, distinct, precise, unequivocal.

vain *(SYN.)* fruitless, empty, bootless, futile, idle, abortive, ineffectual, unavailing, vapid, pointless, valueless, useless, trivial, unfruitful, unsuccessful, conceited.

(ANT.) meek, modest, potent, rewarding, self-effacing, diffident, profitable, effective, humble.

vainglory *(SYN.)* conceit, pride, self-esteem, arrogance, superciliousness, vanity.

(ANT.) shame, modesty, meekness, humility, lowliness.

valet *(SYN.)* groom, dresser, attendant, manservant.

valiant *(SYN.)* bold, brave, courageous, adventurous, audacious, chivalrous, daring, fearless, dauntless, heroic, brave, gallant, magnanimous, intrepid, unafraid.

(ANT.) weak, cowardly, timid.

valid *(SYN.)* cogent, conclusive, effective, convincing, binding, efficacious, logical, powerful, legal, sound, weighty, well-founded, real, genuine, actual, true, trustworthy, authentic, strong, telling, logical, satisfactory.

(ANT.) weak, unconvincing, void, unproved, spurious, counterfeit.

validate *(SYN.)* corroborate, substantiate, support, confirm, prove, uphold, sustain, authenticate.

(ANT.) contradict, cancel.

valise *(SYN.)* satchel, bag, baggage.

valley *(SYN.)* dale, dell, lowland, basin, gully, vale, ravine.

(ANT.) hill, upland, headland.

valor *(SYN.)* courage, heroism, bravery, boldness, intrepidity.

valuable *(SYN.)* profitable, useful, costly, precious, dear, expensive, worthy, important, esteemed.

(ANT.) poor, cheap, worthless.

value *(SYN.)* price, merit, usefulness, value, virtue, utility, appreciate, prize, hold dear, treasure, excellence, benefit, cost, rate, evaluate, appraise, esteem, importance, worthiness.

(ANT.) uselessness, cheapness.

vanish *(SYN.)* evaporate, disappear.

(ANT.) appear.

vanity *(SYN.)* complacency, egotism, pride, self-esteem, conceit, caprice, fancy, idea, conception, notion, haughtiness, self-respect, whim, smugness, vainglory, arrogance, imagination.

(ANT.) humility, diffidence.

vanquish *(SYN.)* defeat, crush, humble, surmount, master, beat, conquer, overcome, rout, quell.

(ANT.) surrender, cede, lose, retreat, capitulate.

vapid *(SYN.)* hackneyed, inane, insipid, trite, banal, commonplace.

(ANT.) striking, novel, fresh, original, stimulating.

vapor *(SYN.)* steam, fog, mist, smog, haze, steam.

variable *(SYN.)* fickle, fitful, inconstant, unstable, shifting, changeable, unsteady, vacillating.

(ANT.) unchanging, uniform, stable, steady, constant.

variant *(SYN.)* dissimilar, different, distinct, contrary, diverse, divergent, opposite, unlike, incongruous, divers, various.

(ANT.) similar, same, congruous, identical, alike.

variation *(SYN.)* change, alternation, alteration, substitution, variety, substitute, exchange.

(ANT.) uniformity, stability, monotony.

variety *(SYN.)* dissimilarity, diversity, heterogeneity, assortment, change, difference, medley, mixture, miscellany, variousness, form, type, class, breed, sort, kind, strain, stock.

(ANT.) likeness, monotony, uniformity, sameness, homogeneity.

various *(SYN.)* miscellaneous, sundry, divers, several, contrary, distinct, dissimilar, divergent, opposite, different.

(ANT.) identical, similar, same, alike, congruous.

vary *(SYN.)* exchange, substi-

tute, alter, change, modify, shift, convert, transform, transfigure, diversify.

(ANT.) settle, stabilize, continue, establish, preserve.

vassalage *(SYN.)* confinement, captivity, imprisonment, slavery, thralldom.

(ANT.) liberation, freedom.

vast *(SYN.)* big, capacious, extensive, huge, great, ample, immense, wide, unlimited, enormous, measureless, large.

(ANT.) tiny, small, short, little.

vault *(SYN.)* caper, jerk, jump, leap, bound, crypt, sepulcher, hop, spring, safe, start, tomb, grave, catacomb, skip.

vaunt *(SYN.)* crow, flaunt, glory, boast.

(ANT.) minimize, humble, deprecate, apologize.

vaunting *(SYN.)* flourish, display, ostentation, parade, show, pomp.

(ANT.) modesty, reserve, humility.

vehement *(SYN.)* excitable, fervent, ardent, burning, fiery, glowing, impetuous, hot, irascible, passionate.

(ANT.) calm, quiet, cool, apathetic, deliberate.

veil *(SYN.)* clothe, conceal, cover, cloak, web, hide, curtain, disguise, gauze, film, envelop, screen, mask, shield.

(ANT.) reveal, unveil, bare, divulge.

velocity *(SYN.)* quickness, rapidity, speed, swiftness.

venal *(SYN.)* greedy, mercenary, sordid, corrupt.

(ANT.) *liberal, honorable, generous.*

venerable *(SYN.)* antiquated, aged, antique, ancient, elderly, old, superannuated, old-fashion.

(ANT.) *young, new, youthful, modern.*

venerate *(SYN.)* approve, esteem, admire, appreciate, wonder, respect.

(ANT.) *dislike, despise.*

vengeance *(SYN.)* requital, reprisal, reparation, retribution, revenge.

(ANT.) *forgiveness, remission, pardon, mercy.*

venom *(SYN.)* toxin, poison, bitterness, spite, hate.

vent *(SYN.)* eject, emit, expel, shoot, spurt, emanate, hurl, shed, discharge, breathe.

venture *(SYN.)* speculate, attempt, test, dare, hazard, gamble, chance, risk.

(ANT.) *insure, secure, protect.*

verbal *(SYN.)* oral, spoken, literal, unwritten, vocal.

(ANT.) *printed, written, recorded.*

verbose *(SYN.)* communicative, glib, chattering, chatty, garrulous, loquacious, talkative.

(ANT.) *uncommunicative, silent.*

verbosity *(SYN.)* long-windedness, verboseness, redundancy, wordiness.

(ANT.) *terseness, laconic, conciseness.*

verdict *(SYN.)* judgment, finding, opinion, decision.

verge *(SYN.)* lip, rim, edge, margin, brink, brim.

verification *(SYN.)* confirmation, demonstration, evidence, proof, test, experiment, testimony, trial.

(ANT.) *terseness, laconic, conciseness.*

verify *(SYN.)* confirm, substantiate, acknowledge, determine, assure, establish, approve, settle, ratify, strengthen, corroborate, affirm, sanction.

veritable *(SYN.)* authentic, correct, genuine, real, true, accurate, actual.

(ANT.) *false, fictitious, spurious, erroneous, counterfeit.*

versed *(SYN.)* conversant, familiar, intimate, knowing, acquainted, aware.

(ANT.) *inclined, level, prone, oblique.*

version *(SYN.)* interpretation, rendition.

vertical *(SYN.)* erect, perpendicular, upright.

(ANT.) *horizontal.*

very *(SYN.)* exceedingly, extremely, greatly, considerably.

vessel *(SYN.)* craft, boat, ship.

vestige *(SYN.)* stain, scar, mark, brand, stigma, characteristic, trace, feature, trait, symptoms, hint, token, suggestion, indication.

veto *(SYN.)* refusal, denial, refuse, deny, negate, forbid, prohibit.

(ANT.) *approve, approval.*

vex *(SYN.)* embitter, exasperate, aggravate, annoy, chafe, bother, provoke, pester, plague, nettle, anger.

(ANT.) soften soothe, palliate, mitigate.

vexation *(SYN.)* chagrin, irritation, annoyance, mortification, irritation, pique.

(ANT.) comfort, pleasure, appeasement, gratification.

vibrate *(SYN.)* flutter, jar, quake, jolt, quaver, agitate, transgression, wickedness, ungodliness, tremble, wrong.

vice *(SYN.)* iniquity, crime, offense, evil, guilt, sin, ungodliness, wickedness, depravity, corruption, wrong.

(ANT.) righteousness, virtue, goodness, innocence, purity.

vicinity *(SYN.)* district, area, locality, neighborhood, environs, proximity, nearness, adjacency.

(ANT.) remoteness, distance.

vicious *(SYN.)* bad, evil, wicked, sinful, corrupt, cruel, savage, dangerous.

victimize *(SYN.)* cheat, dupe, swindle, deceive, take advantage of.

victor *(SYN.)* champion, winner.

(ANT.) loser.

victory *(SYN.)* conquest, jubilation, triumph, success, achievement, ovation.

(ANT.) defeat, failure.

view *(SYN.)* discern, gaze, glance, behold, eye, discern, stare, watch, examine, witness, prospect, vision, vista, sight, look, panorama, opinion, judgment, belief, impression, perspective, range, regard, thought, observation, survey, scene, conception, outlook, inspect, observe.

(ANT.) miss, overlook, avert, hide, be neutral, thoughtless.

viewpoint *(SYN.)* attitude, standpoint, aspect, pose, disposition, position, stand, posture.

vigilant *(SYN.)* anxious, attentive, careful, alert, circumspect, cautious, observant, wary, watchful, wakeful.

(ANT.) inattentive, neglectful, careless.

vigor *(SYN.)* spirit, verve, energy, zeal, fortitude, vitality, strength, liveliness.

(ANT.) listlessness.

vigorous *(SYN.)* brisk, energetic, active, blithe, animated, frolicsome, strong, spirited, lively, forceful, sprightly, vivacious, powerful, supple.

(ANT.) vapid, dull, listless, insipid.

vile *(SYN.)* base, foul, loathsome, depraved, debased, sordid, vulgar, wicked, abject, ignoble, mean, worthless, sinful, bad, low, wretched, evil, offensive, disgusting.

(ANT.) decent, honorable, upright, laudable, attractive.

vilify *(SYN.)* asperse, defame, disparage, abuse, malign, revile, scandalize.

(ANT.) protect, honor, praise, cherish.

village *(SYN.)* hamlet, town.

(ANT.) metropolis, city.

villain *(SYN.)* rascal, rogue, cad, brute, scoundrel, devil, scamp.

vindicate *(SYN.)* clear, assert, defend, absolve, excuse, acquit, support.

(ANT.) accuse, convict, abandon.

violate *(SYN.)* disobey, invade, defile, break, infringe, desecrate, pollute, dishonor, debauch, profane, ravish.

(ANT.) obey, protect, respect, honor.

violence *(SYN.)* constraint, force, compulsion, coercion.

(ANT.) weakness, persuasion, feebleness, impotence, frailty.

violent *(SYN.)* strong, forceful, powerful, forcible, angry, fierce, savage, passionate, furious.

(ANT.) gentle.

virile (SYN.) hardy, male, mannish, lusty, bold, masculine, strong.

(ANT.) feminine, weak, effeminate, emasculated.

virtue *(SYN.)* integrity, probity, purity, chastity, goodness, rectitude, effectiveness, force, honor, power, efficacy, quality, strength, merit, righteousness, advantage.

(ANT.) fault, vice, corruption.

virtuous *(SYN.)* good, ethical, chaste, honorable, moral, just, pure, righteous, upright.

(ANT.) licentious, unethical, amoral, libertine, immoral.

virulent *(SYN.)* hostile, malevolent, malignant, bitter, spiteful, wicked.

(ANT.) affectionate, benevolent.

vision *(SYN.)* dream, hallucination, mirage, eyesight, sight,

fantasy, illusion, specter, revelation, phantom, spook, ghost, imagination, foresight, apparition.

(ANT.) verity, reality.

visionary *(SYN.)* faultless, ideal, perfect, supreme.

(ANT.) real, actual, faulty.

visit *(SYN.)* attend, see, call on, appointment.

visitor *(SYN.)* caller, guest.

vista *(SYN.)* view, scene, aspect.

vital *(SYN.)* cardinal, living, paramount, alive, essential, critical, indispensable, urgent.

(ANT.) lifeless, unimportant, inanimate, nonessential.

vitality *(SYN.)* buoyancy, being, life, liveliness, existence, spirit.

(ANT.) death, dullness, demise.

vitiate *(SYN.)* allay, abase, corrupt, adulterate, debase, defile, depress, deprave, degrade, impair, humiliate, pervert, improve, restore, vitalize, restore.

vivacious *(SYN.)* lively, spirited.

vivid *(SYN.)* brilliant, striking, clear, bright, intense, lively.

(ANT.) dim, vague, dull, dreary.

vocal *(SYN.)* said, uttered, oral, spoken, definite, outspoken.

vocation *(SYN.)* commerce, employment, business, art, job, profession, trade, occupation, career, calling, work, trading.

(ANT.) pastime, hobby, avocation.

void *(SYN.)* barren, emptiness, space, annul, cancel, empty,

bare, unoccupied, meaningless, invalid, useless, invalidate, vacant, vacuous.
(ANT.) employed, replete, engaged.

volatile *(SYN.)* effervescent, resilient, buoyant, animated, cheerful, hopeful, lively, spirited.
(ANT.) depressed, sullen, hopeless, dejected, despondent.

volition *(SYN.)* desire, intention, pleasure, preference, choice, decision, resolution, testament, wish.
(ANT.) disinterest, compulsion, indifference.

voluble *(SYN.)* glib, communicative, verbose, loquacious, chatty.
(ANT.) silent, uncommunicative, laconic, taciturn.

volume *(SYN.)* capacity, skill, power, talent, faculty, magnitude, mass, book, dimensions, quantity.
(ANT.) stupidity, inability, impotence, incapacity.

voluntary *(SYN.)* extemporaneous, free, automatic, spontaneous.
(ANT.) forced, planned, required, rehearsed, compulsory, prepared.

volunteer *(SYN.)* extend, offer, advance, propose, tender, sacrifice.
(ANT.) receive, spurn, reject, accept, retain.

vow *(SYN.)* oath, pledge, promise.

voyage *(SYN.)* journey, excursion.

vulgar *(SYN.)* ordinary, popular, common, general, crude, coarse, low, rude, obscene, unrefined.
(ANT.) polite, refined, select, aristocratic.

vulnerable *(SYN.)* unguarded, defenseless, unprotected.

W

wacky *(SYN.)* strange, crazy, peculiar.

wad *(SYN.)* hunk, clump, chunk.

wafer *(SYN.)* cracker, lozenge.

waft *(SYN.)* convey, glide, sail, float.

wage *(SYN.)* payment, salary, earnings, compensation, income, conduct, pursue, make.

wagon *(SYN.)* carriage, buggy, cart, surrey, stagecoach.

waif *(SYN.)* guttersnipe, ragamuffin, tramp, vagrant, urchin.

wail *(SYN.)* mourn, moan, cry, bewail, lament, bemoan, sorrow, weep, sob.

wait *(SYN.)* linger, tarry, attend, bide, watch, delay, await, abide, stay, serve, pause, remain, postponement, rest, expect.
(ANT.) hasten, act, leave, commence, start, expedite.

waive *(SYN.)* renounce, abandon, surrender, relinquish, forgo, yield, drop.
(ANT.) uphold, maintain.

wake *(SYN.)* awaken, rouse, waken, arouse, stimulate, activate.

(ANT.) doze, sleep.

waken *(SYN.)* wake, arouse, rouse, awaken, stimulate, activate.

(ANT.) doze, sleep.

walk *(SYN.)* step, stroll, march, amble, saunter, hike, lane, path, passage, traverse.

wall *(SYN.)* barricade, divider, partition, panel, stockade, screen, fence, obstruction.

wallow *(SYN.)* plunge, roll, flounder, grovel.

wan *(SYN.)* colorless, haggard, gaunt, pale, pallid, pasty.

wander *(SYN.)* rove, stroll, deviate, ramble, digress, range, err, meander, saunter.

(ANT.) linger, stop, conform, settle.

wane *(SYN.)* abate, weaken, fade, ebb, decrease, wither, subside, decline, dwindle.

(ANT.) expand, increase.

want *(SYN.)* penury, destitution, crave, desire, requirement, poverty, wish, require, need.

(ANT.) wealth, plenty, satisfy, abundance, comfortable.

wanton *(SYN.)* lecherous, immoral, loose, lewd, salacious, lustful, wayward, impulsive.

war *(SYN.)* battle, hostilities, combat, fight, strife, contention.

warble *(SYN.)* sing, trill, chirp.

ward *(SYN.)* annex, wing, section, precinct, zone.

warden *(SYN.)* custodian, guard, guardian, keeper, turnkey, jailer, curator, gamekeeper.

ward off *(SYN.)* repel, thwart, deflect, foil, deter, forestall, repulse.

wardrobe *(SYN.)* chiffonier, bureau, closet, armoire.

warehouse *(SYN.)* arsenal, storehouse, depository, stockroom, storeroom, depot.

wares *(SYN.)* merchandise, staples, inventory, commodities, goods, products, stock.

wariness *(SYN.)* heed, care, watchfulness, caution, vigilance.

(ANT.) carelessness, abandon.

warlike *(SYN.)* hostile, unfriendly, combative, belligerent, antagonistic, pugnacious, bellicose, opposed, aggressive.

(ANT.) cordial, amicable.

warm *(SYN.)* sincere, cordial, hearty, earnest, sympathetic, ardent, heated, gracious, temperate, enthusiastic, lukewarm, tepid, eager, sociable.

(ANT.) cool, aloof, taciturn, brisk, indifferent.

warmhearted *(SYN.)* loving, kind, kindhearted, friendly, generous, compassionate.

warmth *(SYN.)* friendliness, cordiality, geniality, understanding, compassion.

(ANT.) chilly, coolness.

warn *(SYN.)* apprise, notify, admonish, caution, advise, inform.

warning *(SYN.)* advice, information, caution, portent, admonition, indication, notice, sign, notification.

warp *(SYN.)* turn, bend, twist, distort, deprave.

warrant *(SYN.)* pledge, assurance, warranty, guarantee, authorize, approve, mandate, sanction.

warrior *(SYN.)* combatant, fighter, soldier, mercenary, guerrilla.

wary *(SYN.)* careful, awake, watchful, heedful, attentive, alive, mindful, cautious, thoughtful.

(ANT.) unaware, indifferent, careless, apathetic.

wash *(SYN.)* launder, cleanse, rub, touch, reach, border, wet, clean, scrub, bathe.

(ANT.) soil, dirty, stain.

waspish *(SYN.)* irritable, petulant, fractious, ill-tempered, testy, snappish, touchy.

(ANT.) pleasant, genial.

waste *(SYN.)* forlorn, bleak, wild, solitary, dissipate, abandoned, spend, deserted, bare, consume, dwindle, decay, misspend, decrease, wither, wear, effluent, useless, unused, garbage, rubbish, refuse, trash, squander, uninhabited.

(ANT.) cultivated, attended.

wasteful *(SYN.)* wanton, costly, lavish, extravagant.

watch *(SYN.)* inspect, descry, behold, distinguish, guard, attend, observe, contemplate, espy, perceive, look at, protect, chronometer, timepiece, patrol, vigil, duty, shift, regard, note, view, scan, sentinel, watchman, sentry, discern.

watchful *(SYN.)* alert, careful, attentive, vigilant, wary, cautious.

watertight *(SYN.)* impregnable, firm, solid.

wave *(SYN.)* ripple, whitecap, undulation, breaker, surf, swell, sea, surge, tide, flow, stream.

wavering *(SYN.)* fickle, shifting, variable, changeable, vacillating, fitful.

(ANT.) unchanging, constant, uniform.

wavy *(SYN.)* rippling, serpentine, curly.

wax *(SYN.)* raise, heighten, expand, accrue, enhance, extend, multiply, enlarge, augment, amplify.

(ANT.) contract, reduce, atrophy, diminish.

way *(SYN.)* habit, road, course, avenue, route, mode, system, channel, method, track, fashion, walk, approach, manner, technique, means, procedure, trail, proceed, progress, path, style.

waylay *(SYN.)* surprise, accost, ambush, attack, pounce, intercept.

wayward *(SYN.)* stubborn, headstrong, contrary, obstinate, naughty, disobedient, rebellious, refractory.

weak *(SYN.)* frail, debilitated, delicate, poor, wavering, infirm, bending, lame, defenseless, vulnerable, fragile, pliant, feeble, watery, diluted, undecided, assailable, irresolute, yielding, tender.

(ANT.) strong, potent, sturdy, powerful.

weaken *(SYN.)* exhaust, sap, disable, devitalize.

weakness *(SYN.)* incompetence, inability, impotence, handicap, fondness, liking, affection, disability, incapacity, feebleness.

(ANT.) strength, ability, dislike, power.

wealth *(SYN.)* fortune, money, riches, possessions, means, abundance, opulence, affluence, property, quantity, profession, luxury.

(ANT.) want, need.

wear *(SYN.)* erode, fray, grind, apparel, clothes, garb, attire.

wearied *(SYN.)* weak, languid, faint, irresolute, feeble, timid.

(ANT.) brave, vigorous.

weary *(SYN.)* faint, spent, worn, tired, fatigued, exhausted, tiresome, bored, wearied, tedious, jaded.

(ANT.) rested, hearty, fresh.

weasel *(SYN.)* cheat, traitor, betrayer.

weave *(SYN.)* lace, interlace, plait, intertwine, braid, knit.

web *(SYN.)* netting, network, net, cobweb, trap, entanglement.

wed *(SYN.)* espouse, marry.

wedlock *(SYN.)* marriage, union, espousal, wedding, matrimony.

weep *(SYN.)* mourn, sob, bemoan, cry, lament, whimper, wail.

weigh *(SYN.)* heed, deliberate, consider, study, ponder, contemplate, reflect, evaluate.

(ANT.) neglect, ignore.

weight *(SYN.)* emphasis, load, burden, import, stress, influence, pressure, value, gravity, significance.

(ANT.) triviality, levity, insignificance, lightness, buoyancy.

weird *(SYN.)* odd, eerie, strange, unnatural, peculiar, spooky.

welcome *(SYN.)* take, entertain, greet, accept, receive, reception, gain, greeting, shelter.

(ANT.) reject, bestow, impart, discharge.

weld *(SYN.)* bond, solder, connect, fuse.

well *(SYN.)* hearty, happy, sound, hale, beneficial, good, convenient, healthy, favorably, fully, thoroughly, surely, adequately, competently, certainly, completely, trim, undoubtedly, fit, profitable.

(ANT.) infirm, depressed, weak.

well-being *(SYN.)* delight, happiness, satisfaction, contentment, gladness.

(ANT.) sorrow, grief, sadness, despair.

well-bred *(SYN.)* cultured, polite, genteel, courtly, refined, cultivated.

(ANT.) crude, vulgar, boorish, rude.

well-known *(SYN.)* famous, illustrious, celebrated, noted, eminent, renowned.

(ANT.) unknown, ignominious, obscure, hidden.

wet *(SYN.)* moist, dank, soaked, damp, drenched, dampen, moisten.

(ANT.) arid, dry, parched.

wharf (SYN.) pier, dock.

wheedle (SYN.) coax, cajole, persuade.

whim (SYN.) fancy, notion, humor, quirk, caprice, whimsy, inclination, vagary.

whimsical (SYN.) quaint, strange, curious, odd, unusual, droll, eccentric, peculiar.

(ANT.) normal, common, usual, familiar.

whine (SYN.) whimper, cry, moan, complain.

whip (SYN.) scourge, thrash, beat, lash.

whirl (SYN.) rotate, twirl, spin, revolve, reel.

whole (SYN.) total, sound, all, intact, complete, well, integral, unimpaired, healed, entire, uncut, undivided, unbroken, undamaged, intact, perfect.

(ANT.) partial, defective, imperfect, deficient.

wholesome (SYN.) robust, well, hale, sound, salubrious, good, hygienic, salutary, nourishing, healthful, strong, nutritious, hearty.

(ANT.) frail, noxious, infirm, delicate, injurious, diseased.

wicked (SYN.) deleterious, iniquitous, immoral, bad, evil, base, ungodly, unsound, sinful, bitter, blasphemous, malicious, evil-minded, profane, baleful, hostile, rancorous, unwholesome.

(ANT.) moral, good, reputable, honorable.

wide (SYN.) large, broad, sweeping, extensive, vast, expanded.

(ANT.) restricted, narrow.

width (SYN.) wideness, extensiveness, breadth.

wield (SYN.) handle, brandish, employ, flourish.

wild (SYN.) outlandish, uncivilized, untamed, irregular, wanton, foolish, mad, barbarous, rough, waste, desert, uncultivated, boisterous, unruly, savage, primitive, giddy, unrestrained, silly, wayward, uncontrolled, crazy, ferocious, undomesticated, desolate.

(ANT.) quiet, gentle, placid, tame, restrained, civilized.

will (SYN.) intention, desire, volition, decision, resolution, wish, resoluteness, choice, determination, pleasure.

(ANT.) disinterest, coercion, indifference.

willing (SYN.) agreeing, energetic, enthusiastic, consenting, agreeable, eager.

wilt (SYN.) sag, droop, weaken.

wily (SYN.) cunning, foxy, sly, crafty.

win (SYN.) gain, succeed, prevail, achieve, thrive, obtain, get, acquire, earn, flourish.

(ANT.) lose, miss, forfeit, fail.

wind (SYN.) gale, breeze, storm, gust, blast, air, breath, flurry, puff, blow, hurricane, typhoon, cyclone, tornado, suggestion, hint, clue, zephyr, squall, coil, crank, screw, meander, wander, twist, weave, draft.

wisdom (SYN.) insight, judgment, learning, sense, discretion, reason, prudence, erudition, foresight, intelligence, sageness, knowledge, information, sagacity.

(ANT.) nonsense, foolishness, stupidity, ignorance.

wise *(SYN.)* informed, sagacious, learned, penetrating, enlightened, advisable, prudent, profound, deep, erudite, scholarly, knowing, sound, intelligent, expedient, discerning.

(ANT.) simple, shallow, foolish.

wish *(SYN.)* crave, hanker, long, hunger, yearning, lust, craving, yearn, want, appetite, covet, longing, desire, urge.

(ANT.) hate, aversion, loathing, distaste.

wit *(SYN.)* sense, humor, pleasantry, satire, intelligence, comprehension, understanding, banter, mind, wisdom, intellect, fun, drollery, humorist, wag, comedian, raillery, irony, witticism.

(ANT.) solemnity, commonplace, sobriety.

witch *(SYN.)* magician, sorcerer, enchanter, sorceress, enchantress, warlock.

witchcraft *(SYN.)* magician, sorcerer, enchanter, sorceress.

withdraw *(SYN.)* renounce, leave, abandon, recall, retreat, go, secede, desert, quit, retire, depart, retract, remove, forsake.

(ANT.) enter, tarry, abide, place, stay.

wither *(SYN.)* wilt, languish, dry, shrivel, decline, fade,

decay, waste, wizen, weaken, droop, sink, fail, shrink.

(ANT.) renew, refresh, revive.

withhold *(SYN.)* forbear, abstain, repress, check, refrain.

(ANT.) persist, continue.

withstand *(SYN.)* defy, contradict, bar, thwart, oppose, hinder, combat, resist, counteract.

(ANT.) succumb, cooperate, support.

witness *(SYN.)* perceive, proof, spectator, confirmation, see, attestation, watch, observe, eyewitness, declaration, notice, testimony.

(ANT.) refutation, contradiction, argument.

witty *(SYN.)* funny, talented, apt, bright, sharp, clever.

(ANT.) foolish, slow, dull, clumsy, awkward.

wizard *(SYN.)* magician, conjuror, sorcerer.

wizardry *(SYN.)* voodoo, legerdemain, conjuring, witchcraft, charm.

woe *(SYN.)* sorrow, disaster, trouble, evil, agony, suffering, anguish, sadness, grief, distress, misery, torment, misfortune.

womanly *(SYN.)* girlish, womanish, female, ladylike.

(ANT.) mannish, virile, male, masculine.

(ANT.) pleasure, delight, fun.

wonder *(SYN.)* awe, curiosity, miracle, admiration, surprise, wonderment, marvel, conjecture, amazement, question, astonishment.

(ANT.) expectation, familiarity,

indifference, apathy, triviality.

wonderful *(SYN.)* extraordinary, marvelous, astonishing, remarkable, astounding.

wont *(SYN.)* practice, use, custom, training, habit, usage, manner.

(ANT.) inexperience, disuse.

word *(SYN.)* phrase, term, utterance, expression, articulate.

wordy *(SYN.)* talkative, verbose, garrulous.

work *(SYN.)* opus, employment, achievement, performance, toil, business, exertion, occupation, labor, job, product, accomplishment, travail, effort.

(ANT.) recreation, leisure, vacation, ease.

working *(SYN.)* busy, active, industrious.

(ANT.) lazy, dormant, passive, inactive.

world *(SYN.)* globe, earth, universe.

wordly *(SYN.)* bodily, flesh, animal, carnal, corporeal, gross, voluptuous, base.

(ANT.) refined, temperate, exalted, spiritual.

worn *(SYN.)* tired, jaded, exhausted, wearied, faint, weary.

(ANT.) invigorated, fresh, rested.

worry *(SYN.)* concern, trouble, disquiet, anxiety, fear, pain, harry, gall, grieve, persecute, annoy, disturb, fidget, chafe, agonize, bother, haze, pester.

(ANT.) console, comfort, contentment, satisfaction, peace.

worship *(SYN.)* honor, revere, adore, idolize, reverence, glorify, respect, deify, venerate.

(ANT.) curse, scorn, blaspheme, despise.

worth *(SYN.)* value, price, deserving, excellence, usefulness, utility, merit.

(ANT.) uselessness, valuelessness, cheapness.

worthless *(SYN.)* empty, idle, abortive, ineffectual, bootless, pointless, vain, unavailing.

(ANT.) meek, effective, modest, potent.

wound *(SYN.)* mar, harm, damage, hurt, dishonor, injure, injury, spoil, wrong, disfigure.

(ANT.) compliment, benefit, preserve, help.

wrangle *(SYN.)* spat, bickering, affray, argument, dispute, quarrel, altercation, contention, disagreement.

(ANT.) peace, friendliness, reconciliation, harmony.

wrap *(SYN.)* cover, protect, shield, cloak, mask, clothe, curtain, guard, conceal.

(ANT.) reveal, bare, unveil, expose.

wrath *(SYN.)* fury, anger, irritation, rage, animosity, passion, temper, petulance, choler, resentment.

(ANT.) patience, conciliation, peace.

wreck *(SYN.)* ravage, devastation, extinguish, destroy, annihilate, damage, raze, demolish, destruction, ruin, devastate.

(ANT.) make, construct, preserve, establish.

wrench *(SYN.)* tug, jerk, twist.

wrestle *(SYN.)* fight, tussle, grapple.

wretch *(SYN.)* cad, knave, scoundrel, rogue.

wretched *(SYN.)* forlorn, miserable, comfortless, despicable, paltry, low, worthless, disconsolate, sorry, heart-broken.

(ANT.) noble, contented, happy, significant.

wring *(SYN.)* twist, extract.

writer *(SYN.)* creator, maker, author, father, composer.

writhe *(SYN.)* twist, squirm.

wrong *(SYN.)* awry, incorrect, improper, amiss, naughty, inappropriate, criminal, faulty, erroneous, bad, evil, imprecise, inaccurate, askew, sin, incorrectness, false, unsuitable, impropriety, wickedness, immoral.

(ANT.) proper, true, correct, suitable, perfect, appropriate, accurate.

wry *(SYN.)* amusing, witty, dry, droll, quizzical, sarcastic, displaced, awry.

Y

yacht *(SYN.)* sailboat, boat, cruiser.

yank *(SYN.)* pull, wrest, draw, haul, tug, jerk, wrench, heave, extract, pluck, grab.

yap *(SYN.)* howl, bark.

yard *(SYN.)* pen, confine, court, enclosure, compound, garden, backyard, patio, grounds.

yarn *(SYN.)* wool, tale, narrative, thread, story, fiber, anecdote, spiel.

yaw *(SYN.)* tack, pitch, toss, roll, rse,

yawn *(SYN.)* ope

yearly *(SYN.)* ann

yearn *(SYN.)* pine, crave, hope, wish

yearning *(SYN.)* sire, longing, ap urge, aspiration, w

(ANT.) distaste, loat ination, hate

yell *(SYN.)* call, scre whoop, howl, ro wail, bawl, bellow yelp.

yelp *(SYN.)* screech, howl, bark.

yen *(SYN.)* longing, cr fancy, appetite, desire, hunger, longing, conc cence, want.

yet *(SYN.)* moreover, also, ad tionally, although, but, fin ther, besides.

yield *(SYN.)* produce, afford, breed, grant, accord, cede, relent, succumb, bestow, allow, permit, give way, submit, bear, surrender, supply, fruits, give up, abdicate, return, impart, harvest, permit, accede, acquiesce, crop, capitulate, pay, concede, defer, generate, resign, waive, cede, relinquish.

(ANT.) assert, deny, refuse, resist, overpower, struggle, master, oppose, forbid, prevent, overcome, strive.

yielding *(SYN.)* dutiful, submissive, compliant, obedient, tractable, succumb, relent.

ebellious, intractable, ...rdinate.

...*YN.)* tether, leash, bri-
...rness, bond, collar, bur-
...weight.

...*YN.)* hick, peasant, hay-
..., innocent, ignoramus,

...) *sophisticate, refined, cul-
...ed, worldly.*

...g *(SYN.)* immature, unde-
...loped, youthful, underde-
...eloped, juvenile, junior,
...nderage, growing, adoles-
...cent, untested, vigorous,
...dynamic, spirited, inexperi-
...enced, minor.

...*NT.)* old, mature, elderly,
adult, experienced, aged.

youngster *(SYN.)* kid, lad,
stripling, minor, youth, child,
fledgling, kid.

(ANT.) adult, elder.

youthful *(SYN.)* childish, immature, young, boyish, childlike, girlish, puerile.

(ANT.) elderly, aged, mature.

yowl *(SYN.)* yell, shriek, cry,
wail, whoop, howl, scream.

yummy *(SYN.)* good, great,
delicious, appetizing, pleasing, joyable, tasty, savory,

*(ANT.) unappetizing, tastless,
unsavory.*

Z

zany *(SYN.)* clownish, comical, foolish, silly, scatterbrained.

zap *(SYN.)* drive, vim, pep,
determination.

zeal *(SYN.)* fervor, eagerness,
passion, feverency, vehe-
mence, devotion, intensity,
excitement, ardor, fanaticism,
enthusiasm.

*(ANT.) unconcern, ennui, apa-
thy, indifference.*

zealot *(SYN.)* champion, crank,
fanatic, bigot.

zealous *(SYN.)* enthusiastic,
fiery, keen, eager, fervid,
ardent, intense, vehement, fervent, glowing, hot, impassioned, passionate.

*(ANT.) cool, nonchalant, ap-
athetic.*

zenith *(SYN.)* culmination,
apex, height, acme, consummation, top, summit, pinnacle,
climax, peak.

*(ANT.) floor, nadir, depth, base,
anticlimax.*

zero *(SYN.)* nonexistent, nil,
nothing, none.

zest *(SYN.)* enjoyment, savor,
eagerness, relish, satisfaction,
gusto, spice, tang, pleasure,
thrill, delight, exhilaration.

zestful *(SYN.)* delightful,
thrilling, exciting, stimulating,
enjoyable, gusto, zeal, passion, spirit.

zip *(SYN.)* vigor, vim, energy,
vitality, spirited, animation,
provocative.

zone *(SYN.)* region, climate,
tract, belt, sector, section, district, area, circuit, commune
band, locality, precinct, territory, location, neighborhood,
site, ward, terrain.

zoo *(SYN.)* menagerie.

zoom *(SYN.)* zip, fly, speed,
whiz, roar, race.